R0006473267

D1468794

BIG
in Asia

Also by the authors:

By Michael Backman

*Inside Knowledge: Streetwise in Asia**

*The Asian Insider: Unconventional Wisdom for Asian Business**

Big in Asia: 25 Strategies for Business Success (with Charlotte Butler)*

Asian Eclipse: Exposing the Dark Side of Business in Asia

By Charlotte Butler

Dare to Do: The Story of William Soeyradjaja and PT Astra International

Big in Asia: 25 Strategies for Business Success (with Michael Backman)*

Managers & Mantras: One Company's Struggle for Simplicity (with John Keary)

* Published by Palgrave Macmillan

MICHAEL BACKMAN AND CHARLOTTE BUTLER

BIG
in Asia

30 STRATEGIES FOR BUSINESS SUCCESS

Expanded and fully updated NEW EDITION

palgrave
macmillan

© Michael Backman and Charlotte Butler 2007

All rights reserved. No reproduction, copy or transmission of this publication may be made without written permission.

No paragraph of this publication may be reproduced, copied or transmitted save with written permission or in accordance with the provisions of the Copyright, Designs and Patents Act 1988, or under the terms of any licence permitting limited copying issued by the Copyright Licensing Agency, 90 Tottenham Court Road, London W1T 4LP.

Any person who does any unauthorised act in relation to this publication may be liable to criminal prosecution and civil claims for damages.

The authors have asserted their right to be identified as the authors of this work in accordance with the Copyright, Designs and Patents Act 1988.

First published 2007 by
PALGRAVE MACMILLAN
Houndmills, Basingstoke, Hampshire RG21 6XS and
175 Fifth Avenue, New York, N.Y. 10010
Companies and representatives throughout the world

PALGRAVE MACMILLAN is the global academic imprint of the Palgrave Macmillan division of St. Martin's Press, LLC and of Palgrave Macmillan Ltd. Macmillan® is a registered trademark in the United States, United Kingdom and other countries. Palgrave is a registered trademark in the European Union and other countries.

ISBN-13: 978–0–230–00027–8
ISBN 10: 0–230–00027–4

This book is printed on paper suitable for recycling and made from fully managed and sustained forest sources.

A catalogue record for this book is available from the British Library.

A catalog record for this book is available from the Library of Congress.

10 9 8 7 6 5 4 3 2 1
16 15 14 13 12 11 10 09 08 07

Printed in China

The Chinese character that appears on the cover and is used throughout the book is that for "Big."

Contents

List of Figures and Tables		vii
Preface		viii

Part I   Hit the Ground Running

Strategy 1	▷ Ignorance is not Bliss	1
Strategy 2	▷ Know the Firm, Know the Family: Dealing with Asian Family Firms	15
Strategy 3	▷ Women in Asia: Beyond the Stereotype	25
Strategy 4	▷ Understand Asia's Overseas Chinese	40
Strategy 5	▷ Understand Asia's Overseas Indians	52
Strategy 6	▷ Dealing with Information Ambiguity, Local Consultants and Accounting Firms	69

Part II   On the Ground

Strategy 7	▷ Network like a Local, Negotiate like a Westerner	80
Strategy 8	▷ Taking the M&A Route?	94
Strategy 9	▷ Managing Partnerships with Southeast Asian Firms	108
Strategy 10	▷ Managing Partnerships with Japanese and South Korean Firms	122
Strategy 11	▷ China or India?	143
Strategy 12	▷ Avoid Post-acquisition Trauma	160

Part III		Building Up	
Strategy 13	▷	Send the Right People	173
Strategy 14	▷	Cross the Cultural Divide	186
Strategy 15	▷	Localizing the Labor Force	196
Strategy 16	▷	Managing Change	211
Strategy 17	▷	Outsourcing: Where and Why?	225
Strategy 18	▷	Selling Consulting Services in Asia	238

Part IV		Staying Up	
Strategy 19	▷	Tilt the Playing Field	250
Strategy 20	▷	Think Global, Act Local – But How Far?	265
Strategy 21	▷	Building a Profile in Asia	279
Strategy 22	▷	Caveat Emptor: Beware the Banks of Asia	293
Strategy 23	▷	Avoid Blood Loss as a Minority Shareholder	303
Strategy 24	▷	China! The Frenzy Continues	315

Part V		Staying Clean	
Strategy 25	▷	Negotiate the Law in Asia: Bankruptcy, Contracts and Defamation	339
Strategy 26	▷	Intellectual Property Abuse: Contain the Risks	348
Strategy 27	▷	Ethical Traps on the Road to Being Big in Asia	363
Strategy 28	▷	Corruption: The Business Practice that Dare Not Speak its Name	376
Strategy 29	▷	Dancing with the Devil: Doing Business with Asia's Politicians and their Families	390
Strategy 30	▷	When Things Go Wrong	396

	Acknowledgements	411
	Abbreviations	413
	Index	415

List of Figures and Tables

Figures

▷ 3.1   Changes in female literacy and education in China, 1990–2000   34

▷ 11.1   China and India: mobile phone market penetration 2004–10   150

Tables

▷ 0.1   Comparing Asia: who ranks where   x

▷ 4.1   Southeast Asia's Chinese   41

▷ 5.1   Recent Indian heads of worldwide multinational corporations   65

▷ 11.1   India and China compared   144

▷ 14.1   Comparison between local employees and Western expatriates   187

▷ 21.1   Not going it alone: Starbucks' initial partners in Asia   281

▷ 22.1   Local banks in Asia (the top three in selected Asian countries, ranked by assets)   294

Preface

Big in Asia is now in its third edition. It is our publisher's bestselling book on corporate Asia. Many readers have found it to be extremely helpful when investing or trading in Asia, be they from Asia or outside, so we decided on a comprehensive update. And we have expanded it. Five new strategies have been added, bringing the total to 30. So this edition of *Big in Asia* is very up to date and even bigger.

The revisions are based on changes in Asia since the last edition was published, but also on feedback from our readers. We have added more information and strategic ideas on China and India, not just in stand-alone strategies on these two important economies but throughout the book.

There's discussion on staffing problems in Asia, especially how to localize your workforce and particularly your managers. There's a strategy on outsourcing business processes. India is looked at, of course, but there's ample reminder that India is not the only and may not even be the best choice for your company when it comes to remote area outsourcing. A strategy has been added on women in the workplace in Asia. We have found that many ideas about women in Asia are out of date or were simply never in date, and that underemphasizing Asian women as managers will cost you and your business money, opportunity and knowledge. Women, it turns out, might offer a solution, at least in part, to Asia's corporate governance problems.

A strategy about building brands in Asia has been added. Is it always a good idea to "go native?" Or if your brand is foreign, should it retain vestiges of its foreignness? As always, real examples and case studies are provided. No brand "X" and brand "Y" from us. If it's Palmolive or Ford, we will say so.

And one final thing. We call it like it is. If something is a non-starter, then we say so. If we are dubious about something that's all the rage, again we say so. It's the contrarians who shall inherit the earth. The faddists will burst with their bubbles.

MICHAEL BACKMAN AND CHARLOTTE BUTLER
London and Paris

Preface

Table 0.1 Comparing Asia: who ranks where

Country or territory	Disposable income (GDP per capita: purchasing power parity basis, US$)	Population (millions)	Corruption (perceived corruption: rank out of 158 countries; the higher the rank, the more corrupt)	Adult literacy (%)	Aging population (median age of population, years)
Hong Kong	36,800	6.9	15	93.5	39.4
Japan	30,400	127.4	equal 21	99.0	42.6
Singapore	29,700	4.4	5	92.5	36.8
Taiwan	26,700	22.9	equal 32	86.0	34.1
Brunei	23,600	0.37	n.a.	93.9	27.0
South Korea	20,300	48.4	equal 40	97.9	34.5
Malaysia	10,400	24.0	39	88.7	23.9
Thailand	8,300	65.4	equal 59	92.6	30.9
China	6,200	1,306.0	equal 78	90.9	32.3
Philippines	5,100	87.9	equal 117	92.6	22.3
Sri Lanka	4,300	20.1	equal 78	92.3	29.4
Indonesia	3,700	242.0	equal 137	87.9	26.5
India	3,400	1,080.3	equal 88	59.5	24.7
Vietnam	3,000	83.5	equal 107	90.3	25.5
Pakistan	2,400	162.4	equal 144	48.7	19.6
Mongolia	2,200	2.8	n.a.	97.8	24.3
Bangladesh	2,100	144.3	equal 158	43.1	21.9
Cambodia	2,100	13.6	equal 130	73.6	19.9
Laos	1,900	6.2	77	66.4	18.7
Burma	1,800	42.9	equal 155	85.3	26.1
North Korea	1,800	22.9	n.a.	99.0	31.7
Nepal	1,500	27.7	equal 117	45.2	20.1
Bhutan	1,400	2.2	n.a.	42.2	20.3
East Timor	400	1.0	n.a.	58.6	20.4
***	***	***	***	***	***
US	41,800	295.7	17	97.0	36.3
Australia	32,000	20.1	9	100.0	36.0
UK	30,900	60.4	equal 11	99.0	39.0
Germany	30,400	84.2	16	99.0	42.6
France	29,900	60.9	18	99.0	39.1
Spain	25,500	40.4	23	97.9	39.9

Sources: CIA Factbook, 2006; Transparency International, www.transparency.org.

Strategy

Ignorance is not Bliss

WHAT'S IN THIS CHAPTER?

▷ Becoming Powerful
▷ Ignorance is not Bliss
▷ The Costs of Ignorance
▷ A SWOT Analysis of Asia
▷ The External Environment
▷ Political Risks
▷ Legislation
▷ The Competitive Arena
▷ Information Sources
▷ Hitting the Ground Running is Preferable to Simply Hitting the Ground
▷ Points to Remember

Becoming Powerful

Information is power – it reduces risk. Most Western managers know this, and can quote Sun Tzu's maxim about the need to "know your enemy" by heart. Yet many investors and multinationals entering the Asian business arena economize on this most essential of business inputs, and sow the seeds of failure from the start. Dazzled by the market statistics – a billion consumers in China, another billion in India, 200 million in Indonesia – too often they have walked blindly into a joint venture or strategic alliance with only a minimum knowledge of the prevailing operating and cultural norms, handicapping themselves from the start.

Even companies with a long presence in the region, or who have moved in and out of Asia during recent decades, have failed to use the information available to them effectively, so have not always performed as well as they should have done.

For this, Western firms have not been entirely to blame. In Asia, information is a highly prized asset, and its businesspeople are past masters at collecting, controlling and using it. Before the 1997–98 economic crisis, gathering certain types of data about a company was virtually impossible. For example, an investment decision could rarely, if ever, be taken on the basis of a hard analysis of the local company's balance sheet. Any books offered for inspection would almost certainly be neither the true nor the only set. The key facts and figures would be safely locked in the head of the company owner and so, short of hypnosis, difficult to extract. Consequently, Western companies were often forced to take decisions on less than perfect financial information.

However, their failure to gather other, more easily accessible information about the country, the business environment or the background of the local partner before signing on the dotted line is less excusable. It also cost them dear. For this neglect both weakened their ability to make a deal that would safeguard their investment against some of the most common dangers of operating in the region and, even more crucially, gave the upper hand in the relationship to their Asian partner from the start. From there on, the only way for many Western companies was down.

Why this kamikaze approach to a region of such major importance? Why have companies adopted an almost "what the hell, let's get in at any price" attitude and entered countries in the region in unseemly haste, only to repent at leisure as they searched for a market that never met the glowing forecasts, tried vainly to find and then – even more difficult – keep good local managers or train an unskilled workforce they could not sack, struggled with abysmal infrastructure to get their goods to market and, finally, realized that even if there were any profits, they couldn't necessarily repatriate them? The most basic research effort could have given them enough information to avoid such pitfalls. Fed into their strategic planning, it would have given them a much stronger hand at every stage of their entry, whether via a joint venture or, even more critically, via an acquisition. Western managers would never dream of acting like this in their home markets – at least not if they wished to stay in business. So why this flagrant neglect of basic business practice when it comes to Asia?

Ignorance is not Bliss

The speedy withdrawal of many new investors from Asia during the region's 1997–98 economic crisis and its aftermath was due largely to ignorance. Other markets in the US and Europe might be volatile and go through periods of recession, but Western managers are well informed about these markets and their business cycles, and this knowledge gives them the faith to ride out the bad periods. Lacking the same experience or knowledge of Asia, the majority failed to balance the underlying strengths of the region against this serious but transitory period of crisis. Just as their view of Asia's potential had been exaggerated, so their view of the economic crisis and its implications was equally extreme. An economist at the Economist Intelligence Unit (EIU) in Hong Kong observed that where once, during the boom years, expatriate managers had often asked him to give a talk to visitors that would temper their unrealistically high business expectations, "they were now trying to convince head office to stay in the region." Both positions were based on a fundamental lack of knowledge.[1]

The Costs of Ignorance

In Asia, information can make the difference between success and failure, control and impotence. This is because information:

■ Changes the Balance of Power

In the boom years and the bad, Asian companies had the upper hand over their Western partners. In the good times, since demand vastly outnumbered supply, they were able to cherry-pick those foreign firms that they knew matched their need for technological and financial resources. Siam Cement, for example, was so deluged by companies desperate to enter Thailand that, as a senior executive remarked: "Our financial manager is a guy who sits back and waits for them to make an offer." Within a few years it had joint ventures with French, US, German, Italian and Mexican companies, and had diversified into auto parts, ceramics, steel, electrical machinery and building materials.

Western companies, by contrast, often failed to appreciate the reasons for their relative impotence or to draw the lesson that any failure was mainly their own fault, since, from start to finish, they had locked themselves into a vicious cycle of ignorance. Their lack of knowledge of the region and the companies in which they invested meant that when they took an equity stake, usually in a family-run business owned by an ethnic Chinese entrepreneur, they negotiated from a position of weakness. Once the partnership was up and running, their further lack of knowledge about how their partners ran their businesses, about how the systems worked, about the markets and consumers they were serving and local financial practices handicapped them at every turn. Naturally, their Asian partners were ready to take advantage of such willing victims.

Many Western companies that retired licking their wounds after the failure of their Asian investment in effect scored a spectacular own goal. Out of ignorance, they wasted both their investment and a potential fund of goodwill: Asian companies have long memories for those who stay during the good times, but "take away the umbrella when it rains." For example, the US auto company Ford stayed in Thailand despite the currency crash and fulfilled plans for a new car plant. It also helped to establish other satellite supply companies and a dealership, enhancing its reputation in the country as a long-term "friend."

■ Closes Options

Those companies that had not taken advantage of their time in the region to build up a fund of business knowledge and experience were left with only one option when the downturn came: withdrawal.

By contrast, those companies that had taken a more systematic approach to investing in Asia found themselves with not just the option of staying, but of reaping a great reward. For those Western companies with faith in the long-term future of operations in Asia, based on their knowledge and experience, the currency crash was a window of opportunity to expand. Desperate to stave off bankruptcy, companies in Korea, Japan and the countries of Southeast Asia looked westward for a foreign savior. Many of the early deals following the crisis involved parties who had known each other for a long time, either in some form of strategic alliance or as joint venture partners. Having built up their relationship, the two sides knew and trusted each other. Consequently, the Western firms were able to increase their equity share, buy out their partner or even make acquisitions, knowing exactly what they were getting, at a good price. Thus Blue Circle, the UK-based cement company, acquired two local rivals at the modest price of US$631.6 million, making itself the unassailable number one in Malaysia, where it had been present since 1953.

Other multinationals that had been waiting to break into industries previously closed to them were also able to move into the region by acquiring local companies that were in trouble. Those that had carefully prepared their positions got a bargain – a local company that was exactly the strategic fit they sought and potentially profitable. However, those that moved quickly in an opportunistic fashion, without doing the necessary research, were more likely to find themselves paying over the odds for companies that later turned out to be mired in hidden debts. The cycle would begin again.

A SWOT Analysis of Asia

Every Western manager is familiar with the concept of a SWOT analysis, an exercise in plotting the strengths and weaknesses, opportunities and threats in a company's external and internal environment, which generally prefaces important investment decisions. Out of this situational analysis arise objectives, strategies and actual plans to execute the chosen strategy.

Few multinationals would contemplate moving into a new market in the US or Europe without undertaking such an exercise. They require their business development planners to compile detailed dossiers of information about the country, the industry, its markets and consumers before reaching such crucial investment decisions. However, until recently, few companies put the same effort into Asia, despite the fact that they were stepping onto a notoriously uneven playing field where the local teams had a well-earned reputation for being sharp operators, where the culture was totally different from any they had known, where they could not communicate with local workers, managers and owners, and where operating practices were a mystery.

If Western firms are to build strength in Asia and give themselves options in the future, clearly they must approach their investment differently, and build on a solid foundation of information. What is more, having done this, companies *must act on it*. For the other unfortunate tendency has been for those companies that did put an effort into collecting information about the markets in Asia, paid for expensive reports on the political or economic risks and carefully plotted the data on a matrix of high and low desirability, to then ignore any negative indicators and go ahead with their investment anyway, on the grounds that "We can't be left behind."

This has frequently been the case with China, where the attrition rate of Western companies has been, and continues to be, tremendous. The reasons why joint ventures failed there have been well researched and widely publicized, but, indisputably, one of the key reasons was ignorance on the part of the foreign firm. Yet despite this, multinationals have continued to make the same mistake and enter the market without sufficient preparation. The information was there, but seemingly few bothered to look for it.

The External Environment

Many of the factors concerning the external environment are beyond the firm's control but will affect the business environment, and so need to be fed into the final decision-making process. The data that needs to be collected on the external environment – political, economic, legal structure, educational/ skill levels – is easily accessible. For example, reports on the economic outlook and main economic indicators for each country are regularly updated by the EIU in its various country reports and research papers.

One often ignored aspect in Asia is the social and health environment – think of the acute disruption caused by SARS and bird flu, the tsunami and the ever present threat of AIDS. Do you have emergency plans to deal with any future disasters that might arise? A relatively recent but potentially critical external threat that companies might have to deal with in some parts of Asia is the security of their operations. In Indonesia, for example, ExxonMobil's operations in Aceh province (where it needed a guard of 3,000 government troops) and Java have both been subject to terrorist threats, as has the US mining company Freeport-McMoRan Copper & Gold Inc. in Papua. Anti-US demonstrations from Islamic or radical groups exploiting nationalist sentiment can be another hazard. The cost of extra security and appeasing the local community can be considerable – besides the threat to a company's reputation if riots do break out or its managers are harmed in some way.

Information on government spending plans is also useful and easily obtained. Remember, most of the big conglomerates in Southeast Asia got big by investing in industries starred for growth in government plans. The governments of China, India, Vietnam, Indonesia and Malaysia all produce five-year plans that set out their economic priorities. It should not be beyond the wit of Western multinationals before drawing up their business plans to look at the published reports of the region's governments and check where future investment will be targeted, or where special deals or tax holidays may be on offer to help a backward region or get an industry going. However, a word of caution about statistical forecasts on growth rates, market potential and so on. Be very, very wary. Government forecasts in some Asian countries reflect aspirations more than reality.

Under pressure from bodies such as the International Monetary Fund (IMF) and the World Trade Organization (WTO), countries in the region are moving toward deregulation and privatization. But again check out the facts. Continued progress in this direction cannot be taken for granted since, in many places, strong resistance from the local population has led to a "one step forward, two steps back" scenario. Governments that give with one hand have been known to take it away with the other. Thus, when elected in 2001, Thai Prime Minister Thaksin Shinawatra proclaimed the country open to foreign investment. He then backtracked amid fears that the foreign investors would become too influential. Privatization was also slowed on earlier promises.

Privatization plans for other countries such as Indonesia, South Korea, China and India look good on the surface but again, beware. A little digging will reveal obstacles in the shape of entrenched vested interests in local government, business or bureaucratic circles, making for a still very uneven playing field. Look at which governments are dragging their feet when it comes to selling off assets, allowing powerful but heavily indebted local businessmen to use court cases and queries about contract issues to cause delay. Check also how many parties are likely to be involved in the final decision-making process. In China, it is usually necessary to obtain approval for a contract or joint venture at many bureaucratic levels, in strict hierarchical order. This can be an unexpected hurdle that can slow down negotiations for months, if not years.

The quality of your local staff will be crucial for the success of any venture, so it is worth collecting information on the education and skill levels to be expected and where to find good employees. Competition is fierce for the most skilled workers and managers, so investigate the best way to find them. Do you use headhunters (at what extra cost?) or poach them from other companies? Localization is becoming a critical issue in China especially, and the cost of keeping expatriate managers in place is highly expensive. So again, better investigate how much hiring and, more important, retaining local managers is likely to increase your budgets.

Political Risks

A working knowledge of the political environment is also important, especially in assessing potential risks. This does not mean compiling a history of the region, although being aware of the reasons for friction between Japan and South Korea or Japan and China, or the sometimes fractious relationship between Singapore and Malaysia can help to avoid mistakes. But it does mean tracking political changes in a country's leadership. When long-serving leaders like Mahathir Mohamad in Malaysia, or Singapore's Lee Kuan Yew step down, what changes might their predecessors make that will open up new business opportunities? Or when a new president takes over in China, what might be the implications for policies – more economic reform or less, political liberalization or authoritarianism?

Especially vital in China, and in countries such as Indonesia, where decentralizing pressures are growing, is the need to collect and monitor information on the political scene at every level – central, regional and local. This will help to identify the ministries, provincial bodies and organizations that are the most important when it comes to contacts and licenses for your particular industry. In China, it might also be useful to know which "princelings," the sons of powerful members of the Communist Party, are moving to control newly privatized companies. After the election of a new prime minister – in Thailand or Indonesia say – which of their relations or business networks might it be wise to cultivate? Who might be rehabilitated and become a powerful new figure on the business scene – and who might suddenly be less favored? Corruption is another risk to be weighed: it is a subject well documented in business journals and publications, particularly those of the corruption watch group Transparency International.

Legislation

Information about the legal framework, that is, foreign direct investment (FDI) rules, import tariffs and taxes and local content requirement are particularly crucial in Asia, since they vary from country to country and from sector to sector and are constantly changing. Monitor them to avoid missing out on sudden openings or spotting new obstacles placed by governments.

Advance information about moves toward the creation of an ASEAN (Association of South East Asian Nations) free trade zone and changing AFTA (ASEAN Free Trade Association) legislation with regard to import tariffs can be vital for cost projections. For example, the implementation of the Common Effective Preferential Tariff due in 2003 and 2010 will progressively bring down agricultural products on the sensitive list, so allowing foreign producers to match the prices of their local competitors.

China merits a SWOT analysis by itself here when it comes to changes, rules and risks. What are the latest FDI rules and how might they change tomorrow? Which new sectors are due to open up under China's WTO commitments? In which industries is a joint venture partner still obligatory – or can you now set up a wholly owned subsidiary and gain a measure of control over your business?

Another important input will be information about the country's labor laws: where can you hire and fire relatively easily, and where only after protracted negotiation? Coupled with this is knowledge about the strength and militancy of trade unions. In India, South Korea and Thailand, for example, they have strongly resisted privatization plans, and played a powerful role in stopping foreign companies from completing proposed investments. In April 2002, 10 million Indian public sector workers went on strike against legislation to make it easier to lay off workers. Make a note of these and other such developments in Asian countries. Strikes and confrontations are not what Western firms want to provoke. Their shareholders flinch from seeing company names being bandied around by workers brandishing banners characterizing them as "rapacious vultures."

The Competitive Arena

The industry/market/competitive structures and so on are another key data set. Since the economic crisis of 1997–98, industries in many parts of Asia have been restructured and many of the old conglomerates in South Korea, Indonesia and Thailand will claim to be reformed companies and model citizens when it comes to corporate governance. However, any restructuring claims by previously indebted conglomerates should be verified in as great a depth as possible. Which have real profitability? Is the sector you are interested in really safe to buy into, or is reform superficial?

One easy way to tell is to look at what everyone else is doing. If nobody else is buying into a certain sector, however attractive, there must be a good reason. This is particularly true of the banking industry in most Asian countries; for a long while in China, the Bank of China (ironically considered one of the best run) had no takers, while Indonesia's Bank of Central Asia, once the financial core of the mighty Salim family empire and 30 percent owned by the Soeharto family, was on sale for two years.

Gathering information about your competitors is always important, but in Asia this is made more complex by the number and variety of domestic competitors. Local competition in Asia can range from big conglomerates to myriad hole-in-the-wall operators who are ambitious to grow. Some of them will, so it is important to collect information on likely future competitors, especially those where the next US-educated, MBA-trained generation is taking over. Look out for changes in the business model as they try to implement some of the Western business methods to make them more competitive. But whether they are big or small, do not doubt that they will be well entrenched and ready to copy your products with lightening speed or fight keenly on price. Never underestimate them.

Some multinationals have set up excellent information systems to keep an eye on their local rivals. The shampoos, conditioners and hair coloring products of French group L'Oréal, for example, can be seen on sale all over Asia. To maintain the company's preeminent place in the market, each day hundreds of packages arrive at the hair care division's headquarters in Paris. They contain every new product on the shelves, each of which is analyzed to add to the information store about content, innovation, packaging and so on. Traditionally, Western firms have left the marketing side to their local partners but, for the future, they need to build up their own databases on consumer tastes and buying habits, for example the bestselling international and local products, how prices vary and how likely are price wars.

For those companies contemplating a joint venture, obviously every type of information will be needed in order to understand the different business culture they will be getting into – the potential partner's past history, how the businesses was built up, its assets (or those that are known), the background of its top managers, the skill levels of its employees, links with local/regional governments, reputation in the business community and so on. Check them out with their suppliers, distributors, competitors – in short talk to everyone you can. It will not be easy but could save you a lot of grief later on.

Domestic competitors represent only one set of rivals in Asia. An equally dangerous set will be other multinationals not just from the West but from other parts of Asia – specifically South Korea, Taiwan and Japan. They are experienced players in the region who have long regarded Southeast Asia as their "backyard." Multinationals tend to know a great deal about their fellow Western rivals, but are less well informed about these big Asian players, so it is worth looking into their past and present actions in the region. Japanese investment in Southeast Asia is well known, but in fact its investment in China is even greater. By the end of 2005, Japanese investment in China stood at a record US$6.5 billion, while 71 percent of Taiwan's FDI was in China. South Korean firms were also expanding rapidly into the country via the purchase of stakes in companies or licensing arrangements, as were some well-known Indian firms. Who are they and how do they operate? What new ingredient will they add to the business mix?

In such a volatile competitive environment, changes can happen quickly, so you need to keep a strict watch on what is happening in your industry. In particular, look out for signals from industry leaders. Companies, like birds, tend to flock together, so don't be left behind by failing to spot new investment moves. For example, check out the FDI and merger and acquisition (M&A) tables in the region, and monitor changes in investment patterns. A few years ago, the trend among foreign multinationals, such as Alcatel, IBM, Oracle and Microsoft among others, to move their research and development (R&D) operations to China (notwithstanding widespread intellectual property abuses in that country) signalled that China was making rapid progress up the value chain, changing the view of it as primarily a source of cheap labor and recipient of technology for manufacturing operations. More recently, renewed optimism about the business potential of Vietnam has been signalled by a rising tide of FDI – up to US$5 billion in 2005 – and announcements from firms such as Sony Corp., Samsung and Dell of substantial investment in new factories there. Such moves could change your own business plans. Similarly, an exodus of foreign firms from a particular country can signal that it is not the right time to invest there.

Marketing in Asia has generally been a weakness among multinationals, who have had to learn to adapt their products for different tastes, complexions, buying habits and so on. Western companies that are acutely aware of the differences between Italian and Swedish consumers have tended to regard Asia as one homogeneous market – a view that a little research could quickly correct. In many countries, there are two distinct markets – the vast majority living in the countryside and the smaller urban population, with its nascent middle class. Within the latter, different market segments exist or are emerging due to demographics and wealth creation – each requiring different products and marketing strategies.

Having identified your market or the site for your factory, better check out the surrounding infrastructure. How do you get your products to the markets you identify? For non-geography graduates, a little map work on Asia is always a good idea – especially when it comes to India and China. Where are the big markets? How far are the docks from your factory? What state are the railways/roads in? Are there toll charges? Where is the

nearest airport? Note the bordering countries. Three of Thailand's neigh-
bors are Myanmar, Vietnam and Laos – not known for their political or
economic stability, but with a heavy involvement in the drugs trade and
smuggling of contraband goods. How could that affect you?

All this information can then be tested against your own company's
internal resources: your financial, organizational and human resources,
core competencies, strategic objectives and so on. Where are the weaknesses, what are your strengths? What is the chance of building a long-
term, sustainable competitive advantage? Would it be better to wait – what
future changes might offer opportunities/threats/potential synergies? It is
all classic textbook stuff and, if thoroughly done, might help you to avoid
making an expensive mistake. If you really do know your enemy and
know yourself, you will be in good shape to move into Asia.

Information Sources

Information about any of the above can come from many sources. Fastest
and easiest, anyone with access to the Internet can discover an enormous
amount of background information about countries and companies in all
parts of the region. Read the local media. The *Bangkok Post*, Singapore's
Business Times, the *Jakarta Post*, the *Asian Wall Street Journal*, the *South
China Morning Post* and Malaysia's *The Star* are among the better
English-language publications in the region for local business coverage.
Reading the local media is the best way to get a feel for the country and its
business context – who is expanding or linking up with whom, who is
borrowing money, issuing a bond or looking for an injection of equity. One
expatriate had the bright idea of looking up the website of a key
competitor. He was amazed at the information to be found there:

> Even information about their brands and the perceptions behind them. We had
> been trying to work it out for ourselves, and there it was all the time. It would
> have saved a lot of expensive consultants' time if we had thought to look on the
> web beforehand.

Many books have been written about Asia – its business context, ethnic
Chinese entrepreneurs, brands and the region's politics. China's emergence onto the world's business stage has sparked off a torrent of literature
about how to do business there – many of which date quickly. But one
little known source is the archive of case studies written by business
school faculties around the world about the experiences of companies

investing in Asia, and on Asian companies themselves. Written for peda-
gogical purposes, the studies aim to teach managers about how business
works in Asia. Companies can save themselves a lot of time if, for a stan-
dardized and modest fee, they buy relevant case studies from the clearing
houses that collect and hold the cases that are written around the world.[2]
Highly detailed case studies can be readily bought, for example, on the
histories of Asian conglomerates or joint ventures in China. Many have a
teaching note to emphasize key lessons, and sometimes a later update.
Investors and companies could learn a lot for very little effort, but this is
perhaps too easy. Few companies avail themselves of this opportunity but
many more should.

Of course, these are all secondary sources of information. The best way
of all is to go directly into the field and collect it yourself. Set up an office
as a listening post, make contacts with locals, fellow expatriates, embassy
staff and tune into the gossip, get invited to the parties, watch what local
consumers are buying, drive out of town and see where the roads run out.
It will be worth your while if being Big in Asia is your aim.

Hitting the Ground Running is Preferable to Simply Hitting the Ground

The biggest challenge for many companies operating in Asia will be
simply how to make money out of the region. As always, opinions as to its
future prospects vary and the questions are endless. Will the China powerhouse continue, or will social disorder bring it to a halt? Will India really
be the next big market – and what about Vietnam? Will it finally be "open
for business" after so many false dawns, offering the skilled workforce and
teeming markets of China a decade ago? Whatever the reality, the return
you get in any Asian country will depend on making a wise investment,
and this will only be possible on the basis of good information.

In Strategy 8, the story of Lafarge, the French construction group, and
its entry into Southeast Asia demonstrates perfectly the importance of
preparation in determining a successful outcome. It shows how collecting
the right information and preparing the ground thoroughly can ensure that
you really do hit the ground running, ready to beat the competition and
make the right acquisitions at the right price. As a result, Lafarge is well
on the way to becoming Big in Asia.

Remember

- ■ Ignorance is not bliss. Ignorance means:
    - A weak negotiating position
    - Weakness in understanding the terms of a contract you sign
    - A weak position in the ongoing relationships with your partner
    - Weakness in anticipating future threats or opportunities
    - Few options.
- ■ Information gives:
    - Choices
    - Power
    - Leverage in negotiations
    - A long-term future
    - The potential to become Big in Asia.

Finally, also remember that:

- ■ To remain competitive and plan future moves with confidence, information collection never stops.

Notes

1   *Asian Wall Street Journal*, "Asian CEOs talk recovery," 2 February, 1999.
2   Websites: http//www.ecch.cranfield.ac.uk; http//www.ecchatbabson.org.

Know the Firm, Know the Family: Dealing with Asian Family Firms

WHAT'S IN THIS CHAPTER?

▷ Asian Business is Family Business
▷ Keeping it in the Family
▷ When Families Fight
▷ Complications Caused by Polygamy
▷ Dealing with Asian Family-owned Firms: What you Need to Know
▷ Things to Consider when Partnering an Asian Family Firm

Asian Business is Family Business

Asian business is family business, so if you want to be Big in Asia, you must be ready to do business with Asia's families. Yet much of the literature on modern firms is based on the assumption of wide ownership, but in Asia, ownership is anything but wide.

Most firms in Asia outside China and Japan are founded, owned and managed by single families. This means that existing management theory that relates to corporations and firms is largely misleading when applied to Asia.

Analysts' reports and even due diligence studies also often ignore the role of Asia's families. Analysts' reports, even those produced locally, might go into detail on P/E (price/earnings) ratios and other multiples, but then neglect to mention anything about companies' shareholders – the fact that there might be a single controlling shareholder and it is a family. Yet Asian families have an enormous influence on the structure and behavior of Asian firms. Sometimes, who owns a firm is more important than what it actually does.

Partly, the problem is that US researchers and MBA programs make the mistake of assuming that the US model applies to the rest of the world. It could not be more different in Asia. Most large American corporations do not have a single controlling shareholder, while most large Asian companies do. And it is not a large pension fund or some other hands-off investor but a family, with a whole range of motives, only one of which might be maximizing their rate of return. Indeed, internal accounting standards might be so poor and the companies so complex and lacking in transparency that even the controlling family might have little idea as to the actual rate of return. Many are happy so long as they have cash at their disposal whenever they want it, cash flow often being mistaken for profits in Asia.

A recent World Bank study analyzed 2,980 publicly traded companies in Hong Kong, Indonesia, Japan, Korea, Malaysia, the Philippines, Singapore, Taiwan and Thailand. It focused on the largest public companies in these countries.[1] The study found that more than half were controlled by a single shareholder, usually a family. Ownership was widest in Japan, where less than 10 percent of listed companies are now controlled by families. Elsewhere families controlled on average at least 60 percent of the large listed companies. There was also significant state control in Indonesia, Korea, Malaysia, Singapore and Thailand. The World Bank study also found that the smaller and older the firm, the more likely that it was controlled by a family. Separation of ownership from family control was also found to be rare. Asia's families want to manage the companies they own, which presents its own problems. Many may be entrepreneurs, but many are not managers. So, it's not only the food and the climate that foreign executives will find different in Asia.

Keeping it in the Family

The companies of Asian business families serve many purposes. Experience shows that they mean more than wealth alone. Witness the number of Asian families that fight to keep their companies long after they should have sold out had they wanted to keep their wealth intact. For many, the company is synonymous with the family.

Maintaining family control is paramount. That is not good news for minority shareholders or joint venture partners. It also means that something other than commercial factors are at play. And what that means is that the motives of outside investors (who generally rate return maximization as a priority) who wish to link up with Asian firms typically will differ from the motives of the business families.

In Asia, control of large groups of companies is enhanced by arranging the companies into pyramid structures, with a family-owned, private holding company at the top and subsidiaries beneath it, some of which are publicly traded. These companies in turn control other subsidiaries. The further down the pyramid, the more the family's equity is diluted but, due to clever use of voting rights, control is not. Consider a family that owns 51 percent of the equity and thus 51 percent of the voting rights in Company X. This company in turn is the largest single shareholder in Company Y with 20 percent equity. The rest of Y's equity is widely held and no other shareholder owns more than 2 percent of the remaining equity. Thus the family can control Company Y even though it has only 10 percent of its cash flow rights.

Typically, the better quality, higher yielding assets are nearer the top of the pyramid and those assets the family values less are nearer the bottom. Changes in how the family views an asset can be seen by how it is passed up and down the pyramid. Assets viewed as deteriorating in value are sold on down the pyramid so that the family's direct and indirect equity in them falls. But all the while, the family's control over them is likely to remain unchanged. Control over the group is further enhanced by deviations from the one-share-one-vote rule that allows voting rights to exceed cash flow rights.

The other important means of control of a group is to bind companies together through complex cross-shareholdings and related-party transactions. These make it difficult for individual companies to be sheared off from the rest of the group. It also makes it difficult for the group to be broken up in the event of a family dispute – many Asian business patriarchs deliberately leave behind intricately enmeshed groups to force the family to stay together. The strategy often works if for no other reason than because no one is able to unravel the family's corporate holdings. Elaborate cross-shareholdings also make the ultimate ownership of each unit difficult to ascertain, which has the effect of reducing group transparency and making it less vulnerable to takeover by outsiders.

The desire to keep companies under family control can mean that many families do not raise capital and bring in outside investors when their companies need it. Sometimes companies are pushed to the point of insolvency before their controlling families are ready to accept other shareholders. The result is that many Asian business families prefer to borrow rather than issue new shares that might see a dilution of their control. This pushes their gearing ratios beyond what is optimal, making them vulnerable at times of crisis. The desire to preserve family control is an indulgence that can mean that bondholders, creditors, minority shareholders and joint venture partners are forced to bear greater risk than they would otherwise.

Asian family-controlled firms exist for things beyond making profit

They also exist:

■ To give family members a job

■ To hold the family together

■ To honor the ancestral founders of the firm

■ For the family's prestige and honor.

These are things that most Asian business families care deeply about. They are motivations not cared for by most outside partners and investors or regulators.

Family-owned and managed companies pose problems everywhere. Look at the collapse of the Robert Maxwell-owned Mirror Group Newspapers in the UK. The UK government report in 2001 into the collapse highlighted a range of problems in the group that had as its source the group's family control.

Maxwell's son Kevin was quoted in the British media at the time as saying that no one should work for a family business. The temptation to flout the law to save the family empire is substantial:

In family-run businesses, the conflicts of interest with outside shareholders are so deep and so impossible to deal with that I don't think it is either safe or fair for family relations to be exposed to those types of pressures. If you are brought up in a family business, you view the continuity of that business as almost sacred, as a duty. You do everything you can to save it and you lose sight that you are just a manager, no different from the hired gun who you pay a large sum to … one's sense of duty to the family overrides everything.[2]

So problems with family-owned business are not unique to Asia; but what is unique, at least compared with the more mature economies of the West, is the degree of control that families have over Asia's corporate sector.

Some Asian family-run business groups are not profitable at all. They are not required to be. Some groups have become large and complex because the families behind them have become large and complex. Agility and flexibility have been sacrificed to keep the family working together. Working in the family business has become the only way to profit from it for some Asian families. This was the case for Li & Fung, one of Hong Kong's most prominent trading companies today. Brothers William and Victor Fung decided to modernize and streamline the company but first they had to buy out the interests of some 30 cousins so that they would have a clear run at achieving their aims. The company was not profitable in the latter years of its broad family control. It was also sluggish and old-fashioned. Today, it is profitable, agile and admired.

Some Asian business families do anything to avoid bankruptcy or shedding companies when they should. They do this to avoid the loss of prestige and "face" in the local business community, but also to uphold the honor of the family's ancestors. Many Asian business families would see it as unfilial to sell or liquidate a company that a grandfather or great-grandfather had founded. It is another important motivator in corporate Asia that is at odds with the interests of outsiders.

Unraveling Multi-Purpose Holdings

The unraveling of Malaysia's Multi-Purpose Holdings Bhd (MPHB), a group of companies controlled by Lim Thian Kiat (or T.K. Lim, as he is better known), around 1999 demonstrated what can happen to a group when a single shareholder arranges it not for transparency or profits but simply to exert control. Lim had structured MPHB in the pyramid manner described above. And the cement that he used to hold the pyramid together was a highly complex array of cross-shareholdings.

Lim acquired MPHB in 1989 through his family company, Kamunting Corp. He developed it into a sprawling conglomerate, building it up in such a way that he personally owned very little of most of its subsidiaries. MPHB grew to encompass a bank, several property companies, gaming and shipping. At least seven group members were listed on stock exchanges in the region. Using the classic pyramid structure of holding companies and cascading subsidiaries, Lim was able to control a great deal with very little equity, and a high proportion of the equity that he did have was borrowed. Lim had no direct and little indirect equity in companies at the base of the pyramid, but they were still part of the MPHB group and he was able to control them through cascading voting rights as if he did own them. Less than 10 percent of the equity in some of these companies was attributable to him.

Ultimately, the group suffered from poor management and high indebtedness. By the time of the Asian economic crisis, MPHB and Lim were in deep financial trouble. The size of the group and the size of its debts saw the Malaysian government step in. The then Finance Minister Daim Zainuddin gave Lim the option of facing bankruptcy proceedings, probable prosecution and probably being left with nothing, or going quietly, handing over control of the group to new managers and being left with his personal assets. He opted for the latter and departed Malaysia for London. The government did not buy into the group. Instead, Daim "invited" in several businessmen who he felt could sort out the troubles at MPHB.

They set about unraveling the group's highly complex ownership structure. The process of picking their way through the intricate mixture of cross-shareholdings and loan guarantees took around a year. The aim was to divide the group into its key components – stand-alone companies that could then be separately listed on the stock exchange as independent companies. As Lim's structure was unscrambled, the true extent of the group's borrowings became clear. What also became clear was how little equity Lim actually had in the group. He was able to control billions of dollars in assets with a personal stake measured only in the tens of millions.

When Families Fight

Family ownership and management means that much of corporate Asia is exposed to the risks of family infighting. When business families fight, they tend to take their eye off the ball when it comes to their business affairs. Carve-ups become inevitable and much time is spent trying to determine who owns what and who can have what. Rarely are breakups clean and quick. The elaborate structures of many family-owned groups are designed precisely to ensure that they will not be.

Corporate interests potentially face harm by such breakups. Splitting up the pie becomes the focus of the family's attention rather than expanding it. Having a local family that is embroiled in infighting as a business partner is a real risk in Asia and one that needs to be quantified. It is a problem not restricted to obscure, small firms in Asia's more immature markets. Blue-chip firms and families with excellent reputations are all as much at risk.

Among the more prominent Asian business groups whose controlling families have engaged in public brawling that has often led to negative media coverage and ended up in the courts are: India's Reliance Group; Malaysia's Tan Chong Group (the Tan family – the company is a prominent distributor of passenger motor vehicles in Asia); Singapore's Scotts Holdings (the Jumabhoy family – the company, which the family lost, owned property and serviced apartments); Wah Kwong Shipping (the Chao family – the company is one of Hong Kong's main shipping companies); and Singapore's Yeo Hip Seng Holdings (the Yeo family – the company is a beverages and condiments manufacturer). In the cases of the Jumabhoy and Yeo families, the infighting led to them losing control of the companies they had founded.

Each of these examples involves listed companies that have enjoyed some of the best reputations in their respective markets for shareholder responsibility. The assets of each have been first rate. But what let the side down was factionalism in the controlling families.

There is growing recognition of the problems of family control among Asian business families themselves. The problem is what to do about it. Restructuring Asian family firms is a growing business for management consultants.

Several of the bigger business families in the Philippines noticed that at their third-generation level there was much intra-family rivalry and squabbling. "They're all cousins now" was the observation – and cousins are not nearly as naturally cohesive as siblings. So in the mid-1990s, a Harvard Business School academic was hired to advise them in a five-day seminar in Manila on how to manage change in their family-run businesses. Word was sent to other big local business families and they too were invited to send along representatives and help to share the cost of the seminar. Around 10 of the biggest business families in the Philippines, including the Tuason, Elizalde, Zoebel/Ayala, Cojuangco and Soriano families, all participated, each sending along several representatives.

One of the attendees interviewed by the authors said that the academic presented two basic options. One was that the families could stay together. Strategies on how to manage this without fighting were then presented. The other option was to split up. Ways in which this could be achieved fairly and without acrimony were then looked at. The biggest issue is not necessarily how to divide assets but how to value them so that they can then be divided. Methods for this also were examined. Some of the families made some changes. Most opted to defer their decision making. Perhaps it was felt that changes made now would simply bring future squabbles forward.

Complications Caused by Polygamy

An added complication to family ownership and management in Asia is that many of Asia's earlier business generations were polygamous – the business founders had more than one wife concurrently. Polygamy is still practiced by some of Asia's biggest entrepreneurs today. It is not the fact of polygamy that is problematic but its results. Sets of rival children each grouped under their respective mothers attempting to assert their claims over one set of corporate assets are not helpful to the health of those assets.

Asia's royal families have long been polygamous. The current Sultan of Brunei has two official Queens. Thailand's King Mongkut – the king in *The King and I* – was astonishingly polygamous. He had 23 official wives and another 42 concubines. He had dozens of children as did many of his relatives and predecessors. There are thousands of Thais today who can lay claim to royal blood if not a royal title.

Other examples, in Asian business today, include:

- Eka Tjipta Widjaja, the founder of Indonesia's Sinar Mas Group (8 or possibly 12 wives and more than 40 children)
- Tiang Chirathivat, the founder of Thailand's Central Group (several wives, 26 children – 14 sons and 12 daughters – and more than 40 grandchildren)
- Srisakdi Charmonman, the head of Thailand's KSC (31 brothers and sisters and their children now account for an extended family of more than 300)
- Chew Choo Keng, the founder of Singapore's Khong Guan biscuits (5 wives, 23 children)
- Thaworn Phornpapha, the founder of Thailand's Siam Motors (3 wives and 13 children)

- Stanley Ho, the Hong Kong founder of the casino industry in Macau (at least 3 wives and 17 children).

Polygamy has its costs though. Large nuclear families are prone to factionalism if only because of their size. But this is more so when a family comprises an explosive mix of brothers, half-brothers, endless cousins and so on coupled with sometimes enormous corporate wealth.

Dealing with Asian Family-owned Firms: What you Need to Know

When outside companies seek to link up with Asian companies, it pays to determine if the local firms are controlled by a family. It pays not only to assess the health of the company but also the health of the family:

- Does the family have a history of infighting?
- What are the risks that infighting might break out?
- How complex is the family? Are there potentially rivalrous sets of half-siblings?
- Are ownership issues settled among the various branches of the family or is that yet to be determined?
- Is the family's equity in the company ascribable on an individual basis or a joint stock basis?
- Is there a clear succession for the current family head/CEO?
- If a successor has been chosen, will this choice hold after the death of the current patriarch or will it be challenged?
- If fighting does break out, is there a professional management team in place to pick up the slack as family members get on with attacking one another?
- If the family splits apart, how amenable are its corporate assets to being split apart? Will the breaks be easy or destructive to the businesses concerned?
- If you have joint ventures or MoUs (memorandums of understanding) with a family-controlled concern, are your agreements with the family holding company or with individual subsidiaries? If the former, what will happen if the family holding company is wound up?

These are legitimate questions if you intend to go into business with an Asian business family in any significant way.

Things to Consider when Partnering an Asian Family Firm

- Ensure that due diligence covers not just the state of the firm but the state of the family.

- Ask to meet various family members, get to know them and stay on good terms with them all.

- Don't just deal with family members. Also get to know the family's professional managers.

- Preferably sign agreements with companies other than family holding companies. If families fight, it is their family holding companies that are liquidated first.

- If the family is already factionalized, partner an entity that has clear individual owners if possible rather than one that is owned by the "family" as a whole.

- Attempt to get as clear as possible an explanation of the family's corporate holdings, including which companies are subsidiaries of what and where the cross-shareholdings are, so that you'll have an understanding of where your venture sits relative to the family's other assets should a family dispute arise and the assets are to be divided up.

Notes

1   Claessens, S., Djankov, S. and Lang, L. *Who Controls East Asian Corporations?*, World Bank, Washington, February 1999.
2   *Sunday Times*, "Kevin Maxwell: don't ever work for a family business," 1 April, 2001.

Strategy 3

Women in Asia:
Beyond the Stereotype

WHAT'S IN THIS CHAPTER?

▷ Why Women Matter

▷ The All-important Historical Context

▷ Asian Business Leaders (who are women)

▷ Muslim Women at the Top of Business and Government

▷ Women in China

▷ Corruption and Women

▷ Some Things to Consider

Why Women Matter

The view outside Asia of women in Asia is distorted. Certainly women have found themselves in subservient roles historically in many parts of Asia. But that has changed in many parts of Asia to a degree that's often not appreciated. The view that Asian women are demure and forced to accept lesser roles to men has been mixed with a view of some women in Asia in their roles as prostitutes (thanks largely to Bangkok's well-known Patpong sex strip), victims of sex traffickers or mail-order brides. This has helped to mask the important roles that many Asian women play at senior levels of government and business across Asia. This is important to remember, for when many Asian men are carrying on with excessive bravado and role playing for the sake of face, it's often the women who are getting on with the job.

Five things particularly have been important in raising the profile of women in Asian business. They are:

- *Economic growth* – many Asian economies have grown so quickly that employers have had no choice but to choose the best person for the job, rather than the best man. Economic growth is always one of the best remedies for discrimination.

  At lower levels, rapid growth has been important for mobilizing women into the paid workforce. For example, half of all female migrants in China go to Guangdong Province, to the Pearl River Delta, with Dongguan at its heart. Employers prefer young women for assembly line work because they are nimble and pay attention to detail. Dongguan city has a population of 1.5 million locals and more than 5 million migrants. Locals estimate that perhaps 70 percent of the population now is female.[1] It is Dongguan and the surrounding area that accounts for much of China's exports.

- *Family ownership* – most private sector companies in Asia are owned and run by families. Unlike Japan, where politicians are thrown into a panic at the thought of a female ascending to the Chrysanthemum throne, many ethnic Chinese entrepreneurs treat daughters as equal to sons. The Indonesian entrepreneur William Soeryadjaya had two sons and two daughters, Joyce and Judith, but, as Judith maintained, "never favored one child over the other in terms of opportunity or preference."[2] When Joyce Soeryadjaya married and moved to Hong Kong, she looked after the family's offshore interests there. Judith was more ambitious to take up the business mantle, not only running her father's private business interests, but also building up her own tourist and hotel business in Bali.

  The shortage of sons to manage companies when they grow has also meant that families have either had to bring daughters into management too or lose family control of their businesses. Failing that, they can choose not to expand. As a consequence, women can be found in executive and ownership roles across Asia, and most particularly in Thailand and Singapore.

- *Communism* – in China, Mongolia and elsewhere in Asia, Communism sought to abolish traditional submissive roles for women. Women were given senior positions in state-owned enterprises (SOEs) and, importantly, schooling for girls and not just boys was made compulsory. As a consequence, literacy is higher, for example, in Mongolia and North Korea today than it is in, say, Singapore.

- *Islam* – Islam, particularly as practiced in Southeast Asia, is a religion of tolerance and respect. It allows women significant roles in society, government and business. It is nothing like the repressive version of Islam that's practiced in, say, Saudi Arabia, where women must be veiled outside the home and are forbidden to drive.

- *Increased use of the Internet/the rise of the Web* – women have been swift to appreciate the gender neutrality of cyberspace and in particular the power of email to level the communications playing field. Being natural networkers, they have been swift to take advantage of email and the number of lists for female entrepreneurs has been booming. Webgirls International, for example, which began in New York but quickly expanded into Asia, provides a way for women to network, exchange jobs and business leads, form strategic alliances and so on. As one writer observed, "for those women who feel stifled in corporate environments, the explosion of internet on-line offers a wealth of opportunity to business-minded women that did not exist a decade ago."[3]

In Singapore, Cheryl Ng successfully started up Style Surfers, an online magazine containing a mix of fashion, women's issues, arts, travel, health and food articles and so on. As she observed: "We are starting to see the birth of the paperless society, and starting online is in line with this trend, as well as being economically viable for entrepreneurs like myself."[4] Women's organizations from Mongolia to Vietnam (The Vietnam Professional and Businesswoman's Network) and Nepal have set up sites that are opening up opportunities for Asian female entrepreneurs. Moreoever, they are operating not just in traditional female sectors such as lifestyle, health and beauty, but also competing to enter partnerships with foreign companies in industries such as textiles.

The All-important Historical Context

Many outsiders might be surprised to learn of the regard for women in Asia in history, particularly in indigenous communities in Southeast Asia. While it is not true to say that traditionally women have been equal to men in Southeast Asia, it is the case that men and women have had different but well-defined economic roles. Women had their own areas of competence but, significantly, those roles were respected and valued. Also, social institutions ensured that women were less economically dependent on men in Southeast Asia, particularly compared with the situation in, say, Europe.

Dowries were common across Southeast Asia as in India but, unlike India, dowry wealth passed from the male side to the female side. Even today, marriages among Malays in Malaysia, for example, typically feature the groom's parents giving gifts of gold to the bride. The tradition is sometimes misinterpreted. Rather than the gold representing a "purchase" price, it is in fact a transfer of capital to the bride. She owns it and retains it, allowing her to be less dependent on her husband than otherwise and, importantly, such wealth allows her to more easily exit the marriage if need be.

Everywhere, women are trapped in marriages because they cannot afford to leave. The saying that most women are only a husband away from poverty still holds in many parts of the world. But this was less the case in Southeast Asia, and, just as in the West, increasing divorce rates are not a sign of greater family breakdown or looser morals, but rather that more women than ever before are financially independent and so more able to leave unhappy marriages. Accordingly, divorce rates among the Muslim populations of Indonesia and Malaysia have been among the highest in the world. The majority Muslim populations of Malaysia and Indonesia, for example, had divorce rates of greater than 50 percent even into the 1960s.[5] This was not so much because Islam makes it easy for men to get rid of unwanted wives but because the tradition of wives having their own capital made it easy for them to leave. This has meant that while divorce was common in Southeast Asia, marriages tended to be happier. The relative ease of divorce on both sides and its social acceptance also meant that marriages tended to be monogamous. All this has meant that the traditional view of women in Southeast Asia is one based on greater respect and equality. Women traditionally have been accorded more respect as individual beings, far more so than, say, in India, China or Japan.

Traditionally in Southeast Asia, property was held by both the husband and the wife and administered jointly, rather than by the husband alone as was the case in China and India. And children have tended to have an equal claim in inheritance regardless of sex but with one very important exception: the Minangkabau people of west Sumatra (Indonesia) and peninsular Malaysia (particularly Negri Sembilan state). They are matrilineal – the men inherit nothing, everything passes to the daughters. This is still practiced.

Indeed, when one of the authors recently took a taxi at Jakarta International Airport, the usual conversation that you have with Indonesians (are you married?, how many children do you have?, and so on) took an unusual turn. The driver revealed that he had four sons. "Well done!" said your author. "Well done?" replied the taxi driver. "It's terrible. I'm Minangakabau!" Meaning that rather than being desperate for sons as is usual among poor people in the developing world everywhere, he was desperate for a daughter – someone to inherit his wife's property. He intended to keep having children until he eventually had a daughter.

Even in India, where women are still encouraged to remain in traditional roles, there are cultural vestiges that can be built on. Traditionally, Hindus consider the age of 60 to be the halfway point in a man's life. When a man turns 60, celebrations are held and if his wife is still alive, their marriage is reenacted. The wife is celebrated and is seen as auspicious because wives are held responsible for their husband's longevity. Occasionally, younger women might seek blessings from these older women.

Asian Business Leaders (who are women)

Increasingly, women senior executives and CEOs are becoming less of a rarity across Asia. The 2005 *Wall Street Journal* global "Top 50 Women to Watch" list included six who were based in Asia. They were:

- Singapore's Ho Ching, CEO of the Singapore government holding company Temasek Holdings
- Japan's Izumi Kobayashi, president of Merrill Lynch Japan Securities, Japan's most profitable foreign brokerage firm
- China's Xie Qihua, chairwoman of Shanghai Baosteel, China's largest steel producer
- Japan's Yoshie Motohiro, managing director of Nissan Motor India, the first woman at Nissan to run an overseas subsidiary
- China's Wu Xiaoling, deputy governor of the People's Bank of China, and so the most powerful woman in Chinese finance
- Japan's Kazuyo Katsuma, a telecom analyst at J.P. Morgan Chase Japan.

The previous year's list named several of these plus:

- Japan's Fumiko Hayashi, BMW Tokyo president
- China's Yang Mianmian, CEO of Haier Group
- South Korea's Yoon Song Yee, senior executive at SK Telecom
- South Korea's Kim Sung Joo, owner of Sungjoo Group, a luxury goods retailing concern.

The Leading Women Entrepreneurs of the World awards were held in Asia, in Bangkok, for the first time in 2006. Ten Thai women entrepreneurs were shortlisted. And of the 20 global award winners in 2005, two were Thai. Other famous Thai businesswomen include Oradee Sahavacharin and Jirapat Sirijit. The former was responsible for Thailand becoming the world's top orchid supplier. Starting with a program in orchid-tissue culture in 1978, her cloning techniques helped to pioneer an export industry worth US$32 million by 2000. Of the younger generation, Jirapat Sirijit is, at 30 years old, the youngest chief executive in the Thai retail sector. She is responsible for the 1,200-shop Union Mall that opened in Bangkok in January 2006. Shopping malls are big business in Thailand and competition is keen, but Jirapat, who has already managed another Bangkok mall, aims to make Union the most popular mall in Thailand within three years.

These women are important as role models to other women in their respective countries.

Muslim Women at the Top of Business and Government

Women play a role that is both full and prominent in Malaysia and Indonesia, East Asia's two biggest Islamic countries. It is common to see women in senior management positions in both the civil service and the private sectors in these countries.

In the professional and managerial category in Malaysia's federal public sector, almost 43 percent of officers are women. Given that women do take time out to have babies and raise young children when men don't, such a high figure is extraordinary. Nik Zainiah Nik Abd Rahman, for example, has three grown-up children and is a grandmother. She is also director-general of the National Productivity Corporation (Malaysia), a member of several international organizations and an expert in the field of productivity enhancement, quality improvement, competitiveness, SME development and women entrepreneurship. There are also several women who serve as secretary-generals of ministries. In higher education, the number of female students at the institutions of higher learning is more than 50 percent of the total enrolment. Affirmative action policies for women might be needed in the US but clearly not in Malaysia.

In early 2001, Malaysian Prime Minister Mahathir Mohamad appointed Zeti Akhtar Aziz as the governor of Bank Negara, Malaysia's central bank. The fact that she was a women barely rated a mention in the Malaysian media, and yet it is one of the few occasions on which a woman has been appointed to head her country's central bank. It hasn't happened in the US, Australia or the UK, but it did happen in largely Islamic Malaysia.

And then there is Rafidah Aziz, Malaysia's long-serving minister for international trade and industry. Not for her the demure role of the stereotypical Islamic woman. Her ferocity and determination have won her wide respect in Malaysia. Malaysia's preparedness to have women serve not only in prominent positions but also those that are hard edged such as finance and trade will come as a surprise to many. In the West, the tendency has been to give prominent women responsibilities in areas that are traditionally seen as "nurturing" such as welfare, education or health.

Over in Indonesia, women have served as ministers in the various cabinets for years and between 2001 and 2004, the country had its first female president, Megawati Sukarnoputri. True, she gained the position largely on the back of the popularity of her father, President Sukarno, but it said a lot about Indonesia, the world's most populous Islamic country, that it was prepared to accept a female head of government and state.

Indonesia also commemorates female emancipation in an annual national public holiday, called Kartini Day. It is named after Raden Ajeng Kartini, a Javanese woman who wrote about her plight as a noble woman (Raden is an honorific) in nineteenth-century Java and became a symbol to others.

One woman who has succeeded in both business and politics is Rini Soewandi – variously described as a clever lady who reached the top of Indonesia's notoriously greasy business pole and a tough, ruthless executive. Born into a well-known Indonesian banking family, Rini graduated from Wellesley College in the US and made an immediate impact during her early career at Citibank where "she could out-compete everybody."[6] Within seven years, she rose to be vice president but, in 1989, hitting the glass ceiling for local executives, she left to join PT Astra International, then Indonesia's second largest conglomerate, as general manager of the finance division. Within two years she was finance director, a job previously earmarked for another (male) high-flyer, and the only woman on the Astra board. As she observed in an interview at the time: "There is no limit because I am a woman, and more talented women are coming up through the Astra ranks ... Women often perform better than men. They are better educated and a lot more loyal."[7] In fact, when Rini became chief executive and president director of Astra International in 1998, she was succeeded as finance director by another woman, Dorys Herlambang.

Rini's time as CEO was no sinecure, and her actions proved that she understood what heading such a big organization implied for her personally: "You must be ready to be unpopular. Maybe even hated by people."[8]

Astra was debt-ridden and its businesses had hit turbulent times (her first task was to fire 25,000 people – 20 percent of the workforce) but Rini won widespread acclaim as Astra became the first major Indonesian company to restructure its debt. One prominent banker praised her, saying: "the deal will be held up as a benchmark in the region for other restructuring."[9]

However, she then became involved in a bitter struggle with the government-controlled Indonesian Bank Restructuring Agency (IBRA), where ironically she had served a short term as deputy chairman. Many applauded her firm stance against the head of IBRA – refusing to give the group of companies, then bidding for a 40 percent controlling stake in Astra, full access to the firm's books on the grounds that it would violate capital market laws. This time Rini lost and, ousted finally from Astra, she moved to be executive director of an Internet portal operator, where she was joined on the board by her former colleague at Astra, Dorys.

A few years later she was back at the top, but now immersed in politics as she toured the world, first as minister for energy and later minister of industry and trade. She maintained that being a woman had helped rather than hindered her career: "Because there are so few of us, people don't see women as a threat in corporate Indonesia … I have never felt discriminated against."[10] Probably nobody would dare.

Women play substantial roles in commerce and public administration in Singapore and the Philippines, which has had two women presidents. In 2005, Olivia Lum, group chief executive, president and founder of Hyflux, a water treatment company, was the first woman ever to be named Singapore's businessperson of the year. Under her leadership, Hyflux has become an important regional player, with growing sales in both China and India.

Women are less visible in Korea and Japan where society is more male and macho-oriented. A Labor Ministry survey found that many Japanese companies did not promote women to management positions due to their "lack of knowledge and judgment." The big drinking culture of business socializing in these two countries also discourages women's effective participation in the workforce at a professional level.

However, in Korea, Silver Kim, CEO of the executive search firm Sterling Resources Group, has tried to push the profile of women via the Businesswoman's Roundtable she founded in 2003. This is a networking forum for women entrepreneurs and businesswomen to share their experience and knowledge. Membership can only be claimed by women with at least five years in a senior executive position, or who are the founding CEOs of a new business. In such a male-dominated society, it represents a revolutionary move.

In Japan, Mari Matsunaga is credited with the successful launch of i-mode by the Japanese mobile services firm NTT DoCoMo in 1999. A journalist with 20 years' experience working with Recruit, Mari was persuaded to join the DoCoMo team and provide ideas for the content of the services it would offer on its mobile phones. Although initially uncomfortable in the hierarchical, male-dominated culture of NTT, she overcame opposition to her innovative proposals on content and price, and was responsible for creating the famous i-mode identity. I-mode was a runaway success and less than a year after launch, DoCoMo had a subscription base of three million – three months earlier than the original target. By August 2000, the number had risen to 10 million and it was estimated that a third of Internet users in Japan were using i-mode to access the Internet. Matsunaga and Keiichi Enoki, DoCoMo's chief, were on the cover of *Business Week* and in October 2000, *Fortune* named Mari Matsunaga Asia's number one businesswoman.[11]

One reason why women in Asia can be found in senior professional roles, often at a relatively young age, is because home help is cheap and there are few labor law restrictions on it. Maids and nannies free up local professional women so that the breaks in their careers when they have children need not be as great as they are for many women in the West, where home help can be prohibitively expensive.

Women in China

Traditionally women have had a difficult time in China. The most overt practice that kept women dependent on men was foot binding, if for no other reason than it rendered them physically immobile, reducing them to ornaments while their husbands took concubines and minor wives.

Then along came Mao-Tse-tung who famously proclaimed that "China's women hold up half the sky." He wrote that, "In order to build a great socialist society, it is of the utmost importance to rouse the broad masses of women to join in productive activity"[12] and certainly, under the Communists, the role of women expanded, even if this did not always lead to an improvement in their lives.

Nevertheless, for the first time, women were given roles in public administration and formal commerce, allowed to seek divorce and hold land. Mao appointed women to his cabinets and imposed employment quotas for women at all levels of government administration, although with the exception of his second wife, the notorious Jiang Qing, women generally found themselves relegated to subordinate positions in the party leadership. Money was pumped into sports for women. The strong showing by China's female athletes at the various Olympic Games since is a continuing legacy of that.

Big strides were made in female literacy too. A hundred years ago almost no women in China could read or write, but today 86.5 percent of all adult women are literate, and over 50 percent are educated up to middle school (see Figure 3.1). In India, the figure for female literacy is just 48.3 percent.

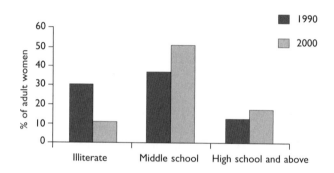

Figure 3.1 Changes in female literacy and education in China, 1990–2000
Source: National Bureau of Statistics of China.

Although the position of women in the cities has been much improved, little has changed for many women in rural areas. They are cashless, dependent and many are still subjected to arranged marriages. So they have flooded in their millions from rural hinterlands into China's coastal provinces to seek factory jobs and a better life.

These women have been at the forefront of China's export revolution. The toys, the computer components, the television sets and all the other merchandise exports that China produces are put together on assembly lines at which women have an obvious and often a dominating presence. They work long hours, often in trying conditions, in return for a modicum of financial freedom and independence. Yet there are signs that the entrepreneurial spirit is causing more of them to reject working in such poor conditions and return home to set up their own businesses in the service sector.

Examples are proliferating of women leaving the factories to start their own businesses, a process hastened by the need of many SOEs to trim their staff as China's economy restructures, and often those who are fired first are women. "If the state-owned companies don't want us any more, we'll just go out and start our own firms," was the attitude of Senna Li, who in 2001 set up her own travel agency.[13]

The trend for women to become their own boss is most noticeable in the cities, notably Shanghai, a city with a population of 12 million. A survey conducted by 18 multinational corporations in October 2002 found that there were more female than male managers in joint venture companies, while a third of all the companies in Shanghai were headed by female presidents. One of them was the entrepreneurial Jiang Shia, named as one of the top 10 model workers in the nation, a rare change from the usual honoring of agricultural workers. Laid off from the no. 4 textile factory in 1994, she spotted a business opportunity in the growing popularity of imported bottled water. With a city-government grant she started off her own bottled water operation, which, by 2003, was one of the most profitable parts of the giant Shanghai Mechanical and Electrical trading company. "Maybe at first people thought I was a secretary, but now they all know who's the boss," she said.[14] The increased status and wealth of such pioneers is further marked by the fact that, in Shanghai, young single women are buying up apartments formerly marketed as bachelor pads.

One well-known journalist is Hu Shuli, editor of the twice-monthly magazine *Caijing* (finance and business), which combines investigative journalism with critical commentaries on the Chinese authorities. Hu learned her trade in the US, including a year at Stanford University, and in China where she spent 10 years working for the official *Worker's Daily*. Dubbed "the most dangerous woman in China" for her exposure of abuses in the stock market, she believes it is *Caijing*'s mission to stop China succumbing to the crony capitalism so pervasive in Asia, "We want to influence decision-makers, not reflect what they think. That makes us very different from the official papers that write what they are told to and the commercial papers, which pander to readers."[15] It is a brave stance, given the uncertain environment in which the media operates in China. When the Chinese authorities feel threatened, press freedom is usually the first victim.

These women bear out the findings of a recent official report on the background of successful women entrepreneurs and high-level managers, which found that they fell into four categories. The first consisted of women who had become major shareholders in restructured SOEs and subsequently become senior managers with a large say in running the company. The second were women who had set up their own small businesses after training with the help of a grant, and the third were professional women who had obtained doctorates and higher education abroad and then returned to China to start up their own business, usually technology based. The final group consisted of women who had been laid off from SOEs and then set up their own small business, for example producing home-cooked, traditional food, and so supported themselves and their families.

In 2005, readers of a government-backed popular magazine *Chinese Women* voted for their 10 most influential women in China. Their choice was based on four criteria: that she had made an outstanding contribution to society, must represent an important aspect of today's China, must have achieved something significant in her field and, finally, must have influenced the Chinese public by her actions. Four of the top 10 were high-ranking politicians and three came from the academic world (one had helped to train Chinese astronauts, the second carried out research into bird flu and the third was a famous biologist). The final three were respectively a singer of traditional ballads, the presenter of a Beijing-based radio call-in program (Xiang Fei), who had persuaded two killers to give themselves up to the police, and one businesswoman Jiang Peizen – director and CEO of Golden Throat, a company producing traditional herbal medicines and well known for its cough mixture.

The choices probably reflect the key interests of women in China today, influenced by what they read or see in the media. The All-China Women's Federation, a quasi-government organization, is strident in representing what it sees as Chinese women's interests to the government of China. It looks at health, labor rights and education matters typically but also raises more symbolic issues. It was instrumental in pushing for the inclusion of women in China's space program, for example.

But old habits die hard. Rules can be changed overnight, but culture is less malleable. Xinran, a former public radio show personality, who for several years hosted a talk-back radio show on women's issues in China, writes about the stories she collected in that role in her book *The Good Women of China*. The accounts might be apocryphal but are nonetheless harrowing. They paint appalling pictures of women who are disempowered and deprived of respect and opportunity because of their sex, despite the Communist Party's attempts to end such discrimination. Very often laws are not enforced and old ways triumph.

This is especially so outside China's main cities. Rules on quotas are overturned or simply ignored. Bribes paid to officials ensure that they look the other way. Finding employment in the private sector is hard for women due to rampant discrimination, although conditions there are not good. A 2005 opinion poll found that 40 percent of women in private and foreign-owned businesses and 70 percent of women working in service industries claimed to have suffered sexual harassment. Passed in September 2005, the Law on the Protection of the Rights and Interests of Women banned sexual harassment against women for the first time and decreed that equality between the sexes was "a basic state policy." Time will tell if this heralds real change.

Perhaps most revealing of all are the Chinese characters that make up certain words. As Xinran points out, when the character for "female" is paired with that for "housework," the result is the Chinese word for "woman." When it is paired with the character for "kindness," the result is "mother." Paired with the character for "son" and the word that's created is "good." And so there, embedded in the written language that all Chinese in China use, are powerful subliminal reminders about the traditional role of women in Chinese society.

So the position of women in China – all 600 million of them – is replete with contradictions. Tradition dictates a subservient role. The Communist Party under Mao sought to overturn this via quotas and other regulations. The downsizing of the state sector is undermining these affirmative action measures. Today, women make up more than 60 percent of the country's agricultural workforce, but occupy only 20 percent in the national parliament. But Chinese women are now finding a new role on the front line of China's export revolution. And there are some leading lights; such as the already mentioned Xie Qihua, chairwoman of China's biggest steel producer, Shanghai Baosteel; her counterpart at Haier, Yang Mianmian; Wu Xiaoling, the deputy governor of the central bank; and Mary Ma, chief financial officer of Lenovo, who played a leading role in the company's 2005 purchase of IBM's PC operations.

Critics should remember that progress in Europe has also failed to live up to its promises. In the UK, despite the 30-year-old Sex Discrimination Act, women still make up only 11 percent of directors and 9 percent of the judiciary. In France, where equality was made part of the constitution in 1946, the average net salary of women in 2005 was 21 percent less than that for men.

Corruption and Women

Anecdotally, women are less likely to behave corruptly than men when acting in an official capacity. Also anecdotally, they are better at complying with corporate governance measures. Whereas men might be seen to be visionary and "big picture" in business, women are more likely to be careful to comply with regulations and auditing requirements. So in a list detailing the personal wealth of former ministers drawn up by the

Corruption Eradication Commission in Indonesia in 2005, Rini Soewandi was the only one whose personal assets had dropped during her term of office, down from Rp73.987 billion and US$351,361 million in 2001, to Rp48.072 billion, with debts of US$1.236 million in 2004. By contrast, all the other (male) ministers saw their assets increase considerably during their time in office. As a former tourism and culture minister declared, "I'm grateful that after being a minister, I now have plenty of savings."[16] And in 2006, even Indonesia's former religious affairs minister was jailed for massive corruption. Tens of millions of dollars disappeared from the fund set up to allow pilgrims to make the haj to Mecca during his administration.

Hu Shuli, editor of *Caijing*, banned her reporters from accepting "transportation fees" and other such "gifts" from the companies they covered, and, perhaps not surprisingly, it was a woman who blew the whistle on ex-President Estrada in the Philippines. Clarissa Ocampo was the vice president of Equitable PCI bank who testified that Estrada had been using the alias José Velarde to hide funds suspected of being illegally obtained. She had to be protected by eight bodyguards until she appeared in court, and afterward was flown to the US to await the verdict. "I was very, very scared," she recalled.[17]

In Asia, this can mean that companies should consider having more women in their auditing teams, and when it comes to negotiating with government officials in countries such as Indonesia, Vietnam and India that are noted for corruption, they might be wise to maneuver their way to ensure that they deal with female officials.

As companies move from manufacturing into services, they will meet more female executives and they would be wise to never underestimate the potential of businesswomen in Asia.

Some Things to Consider

- Before going to Asia, shed Old World notions about women in Asia if you want to be Big in Asia. Quite simply, there are already many women who are Big in Asia, and eventually you will have to do business with them.

- Don't underestimate the strengths of female managers in Asia, their skills and their diligence. The locals don't. That's why accounting and audit teams in much of Asia are dominated by local women.

- Got a problem with corruption in your management ranks? Fire the culprits and replace them with women.

Notes

1 *Wall Street Journal*, "At 18, Min finds a path to success in migration wave," 8 November, 2004.

2 Butler, C. *Dare to Do*, McGraw-Hill Education, 2002 p6.

3 *Asian Women On-line: Making a Net Impact*, Barry Lee Brisco, courtesy of WomenAsia. com.

4 Ibid.

5 Reid, A., *Southeast Asia in the Age of Commerce 1450–1680*, vol 1: *The Lands Below the Winds*, Silkworm Books, 1988, p153.

6 *Far Eastern Economic Review*, "Rini Soewandi has made both friends and enemies," 10 February, 2000.

7 Interview with Charlotte Butler, Jakarta 1998 (unpublished).

8 *Asiaweek*, Cover story, 8 October, 1999.

9 *The Challenges to Establishing Good Governance*, MCGA Quarterly report, vol 31, 2001.

10 Op cit., *Far Eastern Economic Review*, 10 February, 2000.

11 "NTT DoCoMo and i-mode," by Professor Masaaki Hirano, Waseda Business School.

12 Introductory note to "Women have gone to the Labour Front" (1955) *The Socialist Upsurge in China's Countryside*, Chinese edn, vol 14.

13 *TIME Asia* magazine, "Shanghai's strong women," 21 July, 2003.

14 Ibid.

15 *The Economist*, "Keeping an eye on business," 27 May, 2004.

16 *Jakarta Post*, "Ex-ministers 'richer for the experience,'" 25 February, 2005.

17 *Business Week*, "Stars of Asia," 2 July, 2001.

Strategy 4

Understand Asia's Overseas Chinese

WHAT'S IN THIS CHAPTER?	
	▷ Asia's Movers and Shakers
	▷ Chinese are not just Chinese
	▷ What's in a Name?
	▷ Why the Success in Business?
	▷ Occupations and Dialects
	▷ Chinese Associations
	▷ Contacting Asia's Chinese Chambers of Commerce

Asia's Movers and Shakers

The influence of ethnic Chinese businesspeople in Asia is now well known. Approximately 30 million ethnic Chinese live in Hong Kong and Southeast Asia today. They control companies and capital far in excess of that suggested by their numbers, to the point where doing business in Asia outside Korea and Japan usually means doing it with an overseas Chinese business partner. The name might be Thai, Indonesian or another local variant, but, more often than not, the local will still be ethnically Chinese (Table 4.1). Everyone knew the founder of Bangkok Bank as Chin Sophonpanich, for example, but Chin Pik Chin was his original, Chinese name.

Table 4.1 Southeast Asia's Chinese

Country	Total population	Ethnic Chinese % (estimated)
Indonesia	242 million	2.2
Malaysia	24.0 million	26.0
The Philippines	87.9 million	2.0
Singapore	4.4 million	76.0
Brunei	370,000	13.0
Cambodia	13.6 million	2.0
Myanmar (Burma)	42.9 million	3.0
Vietnam	83.5 million	3.0
Laos	5.9 million	0.5
Thailand	65.4 million	10.0

No one ever got Big in Asia by being ignorant of the detail. Certainly not the overseas Chinese. As we shall see, being better than almost anyone else at getting information is how they have made their fortunes. An important step to success in Asia is to understand the overseas Chinese – their business, their culture and the many differences among them.

The wealth of Asia's overseas Chinese received a battering during the region's economic crisis in 1997–98. Many went into the economic crisis highly leveraged and with their debts unhedged. During the crisis, debts ballooned in local currency terms, asset prices collapsed and banks and finance companies were shut down, nationalized or merged. The Indonesian corporate scene had been almost entirely owned by local Chinese, if not foreign or state-owned. But many Chinese had to pledge their assets in return for state-sponsored bailouts of their banks. Chinese elsewhere suffered too, although in lesser degrees. They have been weakened in absolute terms, but in relative terms, their dominance remains intact.

Many of Indonesia's big Chinese families all but relocated to Singapore after the economic crisis and with political uncertainty, legal problems and harassment at home. The Salims (Salim Group), the Gondokusumos (Dharmala Group), the Widjajas (Sinar Mas Group) and the Nursalims (Gadjah Tunggal Group) were among those to shift family members to Singapore, from where they continued to manage their Indonesian interests.

Chinese are not just Chinese

The forebears of the majority of Asia's overseas Chinese emigrated from China comparatively recently – mostly in the nineteenth and early twentieth centuries. They were economic migrants and their departure from

China often coincided with famines or civil strife. Today China has 29
provinces, but the great majority of Asia's overseas Chinese ancestrally
come from just three of them: Guangdong and Fujian Provinces on the
South China Sea in the bottom southeast corner of China and Hainan
Province, an island off the southern tip of Guangdong. China might have
over a billion people but the overseas Chinese have cultural, family and
language ties with relatively few of them. So it is true that many of Asia's
overseas Chinese have ancestral and family connections that can be useful
in opening doors but those particular connections are not at all broad.

Asia's overseas Chinese are not a monolithic group. Many are now
second, third or more generation residents of the countries in which they
live and so have taken on many of the local ways and culture as their own.
Also, there are important differences among the Chinese in any given location and between the Chinese outside China and those in mainland China.
Understanding these differences is essential to understanding the overseas
Chinese as businesspeople.

The native tongue of almost three-quarters of all Chinese who live in
China is Mandarin (or *Putonghua*, as it is called in Hong Kong), but it is
the ancestral tongue of perhaps less than 5 percent of Hong Kong and
Southeast Asia's Chinese. Mandarin is the language of northern China, not
southeastern China where most Southeast Asian and Hong Kong Chinese
have their origins.

All speakers of Mandarin or one of the many Chinese dialects share the
same written language but pronunciations can differ so much that most of
the dialects of southeastern China – and hence the dialects of most Southeast
Asian and Hong Kong Chinese – are not intelligible to Mandarin speakers.

The main ancestral languages of Asia's overseas Chinese are Hokkien,
Cantonese, Hakka, Teochiu, Fuzhou/Hokchia, Hainanese and Henghua,
probably in that order:[1]

- *Hokkien* is the dialect for those with origins in southern Fujian
  Province. Hokkien is the dominant ancestral dialect of Singapore's
  Chinese and the Chinese in the Philippines. The Quek family of
  Malaysia and their cousins, the Kweks of Singapore, both of which own
  business groups called Hong Leong in both countries, are among Asia's
  richest overseas Hokkiens. The Tan family of the Philippines, who
  founded Jolibee Foods, is also Hokkien.

- *Cantonese* is the ancestral dialect of those with origins in much of
  Guangdong and Hong Kong. Cantonese speakers dominate Hong Kong
  and the Chinese communities of Kuala Lumpur (but almost nowhere

else in Malaysia) and Saigon. Ronnie Chan of Hong Kong's Hang Lung property group is a prominent Cantonese businessman.

- *Hakka* (or Keh) is the language of a group of Chinese who in recent centuries have been sprinkled throughout northern Guangdong, southern Fujian and further inland. This dialect group further divides into subdialect groups such as Huizhou, Taipu, Fengshun, Meixian, Popo and Yongding. They have no single ancestral homeland in China due to their past continual migrations. Hakka are found everywhere but do not form a majority of the Chinese in any particular country. They do dominate in some regions though, for example in the Malaysian state of Sabah where almost 60 percent of the local Chinese are Hakka. The Lamsam family of Bangkok who founded the Thai Farmers Bank is a prominent Hakka family.

- *Teochiu* (or Chiu Chow [Chaozhou] as it is spelled in Hong Kong) is the dialect of those from the Shantou area of northern Guangdong. Most Thai Chinese (perhaps 80 percent) are Teochiu and it is the second most prominent ancestral dialect among Singapore's Chinese. The five big entrepreneurial families of Bangkok are the Wang-Lee, Sophonpanich, Tejaphaibul, Srifeungfung and Chearavanont families. Not only are they all ethnic Chinese but they are all Teochiu. Hong Kong's Li Ka-Shing is Asia's best-known Teochiu/Chiu Chow businessman. Eka Tjandranegara, founder of Indonesia's Mulia Group, is another prominent Teochiu.

- *Fuzhou* is the ancestral dialect of those from around Fuzhou city in the northern tip of Fujian, and *Hokchia* is the closely related dialect of those from the area around nearby Fuqing. Members of these groups can be found everywhere but most of Southeast Asia's Fuzhou Chinese are to be found in Malaysia, particularly Sarawak, and most of the Hokchia are to be found in Indonesia. The Fuzhou and Hokchia are numerically a very small group, but are disproportionately represented among the ranks of the highly successful overseas Chinese businessmen. Hong Kong-based Malaysian Robert Kuok is perhaps the most prominent overseas Fuzhou businessman. Indonesia's Liem Sioe Liong who founded the Salim Group is an important Hokchia.

- *Hainanese* (or Kheng Chew) is the language of those from Hainan Province. There are Hainanese Chinese across Southeast Asia but they are always in a minority. The Thai Chinese businessman Sondhi Limthongal, who founded Thailand's M Group, is Hainanese.

- *Henghua* is the language of the smallest group who ancestrally come from the Putian area, close to Fuzhou in China. They are found in small

numbers across Southeast Asia. Indonesia's Sjamsul Nursalim (founder
of the giant Gadjah Tunggal Group) and Mochtar Riady (founder of the
equally large Lippo Group) are prominent Henghua.

However, it should not be assumed that all Chinese in Southeast Asia
can actually speak or read their ancestral dialect or in fact any Chinese.
Many cannot – many have no Chinese language abilities whatsoever. A
high proportion of Indonesian Chinese are in this category. Some Indonesian Chinese are not even aware of what their ancestral dialect is. William
Soeryadjaya, the founder of Astra Group, Indonesia's largest listed
company, is one prominent Indonesian Chinese who cannot speak
Chinese – Dutch is his preferred language and that of several of his key
senior executives.

Chinese who have been in their countries of residence for many generations and have become highly· acculturated with local ways, such as
William Soeryadjaya, are called the *Peranakan* in Indonesia and the *Babas*
in Malaysia and Singapore. But acculturation need not mean assimilation.
There is much resentment in Indonesia against all Chinese. The Chinese
are most assimilated in Thailand, where many have intermarried with
ethnic Thais. Many and maybe most Bangkok people can claim some
Chinese ancestry, including King Bhumipol Adulyadej himself whose
mother was half-Chinese. Elsewhere, intermarriage has been less
common. In Malaysia, it is rare but that is changing. Marriages between
Malay men and Chinese women who convert to Islam and take Muslim
names are becoming more common. Wan Azizah Wan Ismail is ethnically
Chinese. She married former Deputy Prime Minister Anwar Ibrahim and is
now an opposition politician in her own right.

There is one other important migrant Chinese group in Asia and that is
the Shanghainese of Taiwan and Hong Kong. They fled mainland China in
1949 in the wake of Mao's Communist takeover. Many were successful
industrialists in Shanghai but left with little of their wealth intact. They
started anew and today some of the wealthiest families in Hong Kong and
Taiwan are actually old Shanghainese families, whose ancestral dialect is
Shanghainese.

They have become important investors again in Shanghai and Ningbo.
Typically they rebuilt their fortunes in textiles and clothing – Hong Kong
owed its initial prosperity to the textiles industry built up by the Shanghainese refugees. Almost all cotton spinning mills in Hong Kong or
those owned by Hong Kong investors in nearby Guangdong are actually
owned by migrant Shanghainese. Peter Woo of the Wharf/Wheelock
Group, David Wong of Dah Sing Financial Holdings, and Henry Tang of

the Winsor Textile Group are among the prominent Shanghai-descended businesspeople in Hong Kong today. Shipping in Hong Kong is controlled by three big Hong Kong Shanghainese families – the family of the late Y.K. Pao (World-Wide Shipping), the family of C.Y. Tung (Orient Overseas) and Frank Chao and his family (Wah Kwong Shipping). Tung Chee Hwa, Hong Kong's first chief executive and son of C.Y. Tung, is of Shanghainese descent. In Taiwan, one of the richest families, the Hsu family, is originally from Shanghai. They own the massive Far Eastern Group, which includes Far Eastern International Bank, Far Eastern Textiles, Asia Cement, U-Marine Shipping and Far Eastern Department Stores. It is important to remember that most Chinese in Hong Kong and Taiwan are the children or grandchildren of refugees. Hong Kong and Taiwan are not their places of ancestry.

What's in a Name?

Quite a lot, if you are Chinese. Overseas Chinese tend to have traditional surnames, which, when rendered in English, reflect their ancestral dialect and thus their place of Chinese ancestry. There are more than 6,000 possible Chinese surnames, although many have died out. There are far fewer surnames among Asia's overseas Chinese because their ancestral homes are mostly in the southeast corner of China. There are around 500 surnames in use among Singapore's Chinese but there are several that are particularly common. The three most common are Tan (9.9 percent of all Singapore's Chinese), Lim (6.9 percent) and Lee (4.6 percent). Each of these is the Hokkien pronunciation, reflecting the dominance of the Hokkien among Singapore's Chinese. The same Chinese characters used to denote Tan are pronounced as Chen in Mandarin, Chan in Cantonese and Ting in Fuzhou. Thus someone who has the surname that's spoken as Tan will have the same Chinese characters as someone who is Fuzhou and who calls themselves Ting. Both the surnames read the same but are spoken differently. Wong, one of the most popular surnames in Hong Kong, is the Cantonese rendering of Ong in Hokkien or Heng in Teochiu.

When Chinese meet each other for the first time, they are often eager to know each other's surname. Pronunciations differ so widely that they often need to write their names to show each other the actual Chinese characters. If they share the same surname, they are "kinsmen" and right away they share a bond. Traditionally, Chinese with the same surnames were forbidden to marry as it was believed that they had the same ancestor.

Chinese surnames can reveal a lot. Any recognition of this and interest shown in the ancestral origins of many Chinese is often met with surprise and delight. After all, it is something that interests many Chinese.

Why the Success in Business?

Asia's overseas Chinese have been so successful in business largely for two reasons. Many of Asia's ethnic Chinese businesspeople have a dual role. They are well-entrenched citizens in their home countries, but they also operate at a regional level, using their family, clan, dialect and other ties with Chinese in other countries to invest and trade. These international networks of family relations and friends allow them to operate across markets. Shortages in one market can be matched with excesses in another. Trade is nothing if it's not about leveraging information ahead of competitors. The networks allow for that information to be gathered in and used.

This tendency to do business on the basis of connections means that Chinese businesses often become eclectic and unwieldy. Consider a typical Chinese shop in any Chinatown. It might be filled with a bizarre array of items – packets of seeds along with pairs of rubber gloves, children's toys and woks. Decisions on stock purchasing are driven not so much by customers' needs but with which suppliers the owner has personal connections. Thus the range of stock is driven by supply rather than demand. Now upscale that shop a few thousand times and you have a typical Chinese-owned conglomerate, its scope of opportunities determined not by strategy and complementarity but by opportunity. Such a structure is optimal only in certain economies at particular stages of immaturity.

The second factor in the commercial success of Asia's overseas Chinese is that they have institutions that allow them to operate in environments where legal protection is poor. By doing business within their communities and having additional legal contract enforcement mechanisms, such as a highly developed sense of face, whereby being a bad debtor is simply too humiliating for oneself and one's family, and having chambers of commerce within which disputes can be settled without recourse to the law, the overseas Chinese are at a significant competitive advantage to other ethnic groups that do not have these mechanisms.

The overseas Chinese tend to be among the first investors in "new" or opening markets (such as Myanmar, Vietnam and Cambodia) or dominate old markets (Indonesia, the Philippines and Thailand) where legal systems are marred by corruption and poor drafting of laws.

East Timorese Chinese were among the first investors back into East Timor after the country seceded from Indonesia and the UN set up a provisional government. Many families had fled with the Indonesian invasion of 1975 and had not been back for 25 years. One family, the Japes, had settled in the northern Australian city of Darwin where they had set up local hardware and bedding franchises. They set up a store selling furnishings, hardware and home appliances in Dili shortly after the UN's arrival, and relied on extended family members to run it.

Once legal systems develop so that all groups can do business on the same basis, then the overseas Chinese lose much of their comparative advantage. That is why Western multinationals do well in Singapore (with its first-rate legal system) and why Australia's 3 percent ethnic Chinese community does not control 70 percent of that country's private, corporate capital.

The overseas Chinese have also been adept at filling market niches – gaps in economies where there is a demand for some product or service to be supplied but where local social and cultural constraints inhibit that demand being fulfilled. For example, Islamic laws prohibit usury but the Chinese have no such religious constraints, and so early on became the moneylenders across Malaysia and Indonesia. Hindu restrictions on "unclean" occupations dealing with dead cattle have seen Hakka Chinese in Kolkata (Calcutta) dominate the city's leather industries, with most of its several hundred tanneries being run by the small local Chinese community.

Local investment flows around Asia often can be explained by looking at the ancestral and historical links of Asia's overseas Chinese. For example, trade and investment flow across the Straits of Malacca between Medan in Indonesia and Penang in Malaysia largely because both places are dominated overwhelmingly by Hokkien Chinese. Taiwan invested billions of dollars in Penang's massive electronic components industry because the local infrastructure is good and the government offers lucrative incentives, but also because the Chinese in Taiwan and Penang overwhelmingly share a common Hokkien ancestry. Singapore and Hong Kong have been the biggest investors in Myanmar in recent years, because it was to Singapore and Hong Kong that many Burmese Chinese fled in the 1960s and they are now taking advantage of the Myanmar government's new pro-market policies to invest in their old homeland. And then of course many of Asia's overseas Chinese have used local knowledge and connections to invest in their ancestral homes in China itself.

Occupations and Dialects

Historically, overseas Chinese of certain dialects dominated particular occupations. For example, opticians, Chinese herbalists, tailors, pawnbrokers and tin miners in Malaysia and Singapore usually were Hakka Chinese. Electrical shops were run by the Hokkien and rice export-import agencies, antique and curio shops and fishmongers by the Teochiu. These linkages have tended to break down but are still important to explain some patterns observed in overseas Chinese business today. The Henghua Chinese were traditionally found in occupations associated with transport. They owned bicycle shops and were even bus drivers. The Gadjah Tunggal Group is Indonesia's largest manufacturer of rubber tyres. (Incidentally, its tyres are the number one imported tyre to the UK today.) The company had its start in this sector by making tyres for rickshaws. The owner and founder of Gadjah Tunggal is Sjamsul Nursalim, a Henghua Chinese. The family started in the business because of its traditional association with the Henghuas – other Henghuas were already in it so the Nursalims followed.

One traditional occupation–dialect linkage that still holds is the prominence of Teochiu traders in the cross-border trade for rice, fresh fruit, vegetables, poultry and seafood across Southeast Asia and Hong Kong. Much of it is sourced from Thailand, where Teochiu Chinese are dominant, and then distributed around Asia by local Teochiu traders. Also, cold storage facilities are often owned by Teochiu businesspeople. Teochiu families also control much of the integrated poultry raising and processing in Thailand, Malaysia and Indonesia. If your business is in these sectors, you can expect to find yourself dealing with the Teochiu.

Chinese Associations

Traditionally, Asia's overseas Chinese have been great joiners of clubs, chambers and societies. Partly it is a function of their having been a migrant minority culture. Migrant minorities tend to form themselves into self-help organizations to deal with an uncertain or even hostile new environment. But also the number and variety of organizations suggest how fractured and non-monolithic overseas Chinese communities are. This is because many traditional overseas Chinese organizations are based around Chinese ancestral origins, their dialect group or their surname or clans. Guilds were also popular for both controlling entry into a sector and the worship of the craft's patron deities.

Some of these groups have formed international bodies that meet annually or biennially at massive conventions. For example, world Fujian conventions have been held that have drawn together thousands of Chinese, who have their ancestral origins in China's Fujian Province, for several days of feasting, seminars and networking. Overseas Hakkas, Hainanese and Fuzhous have held similar events. Every two years, a World Chinese Entrepreneurs' Convention takes place. (The 2007 convention will be held in Kobe, Japan, where there is a small but significant Chinese community. The 2005 convention was held in Seoul and in 2003 it was held in Kuala Lumpur. The inaugural convention was staged in 1991 in Singapore.) These have met with mixed success depending on the quality of the organizing skills of the host Chinese chamber but they always attract thousands of participants. Non-Chinese attend as well – eager to make new business contacts in the overseas Chinese business community.

Then there are the Chinese chambers of commerce. Historically, these regulated the business affairs of the community and adjudicated in disputes. The chambers provided venues where legal disputes could be solved "in-house." Today they are important around Asia to act as a single voice to lobby government, promote business within the community and assist with international trade promotion. There are many local Chinese chambers of commerce across Asia but there is usually a main chamber in each country (see below).

Many have websites, their own newsletters that often accept advertisements from outsiders and some offer associate membership to non-Chinese. It is always worth making contact with the local Chinese chamber but it is surprising how few Western businesspeople do so on coming to Asia. Some chambers are better resourced and organized and more welcoming than others, but they do provide a route into the wealthiest sector of the business community in every East Asian country bar Korea and Japan.

The younger generation of overseas Chinese businesspeople tend not to join or at least not be active in the more traditional Chinese associations. Instead they join other groupings. Rotary and other service clubs have taken off in some parts of Asia. Various local industry and trade associations that need not be exclusively Chinese are also important. Classmate and alumni associations are very important among the younger generation of foreign-educated overseas Chinese. Such associations allow networks started at overseas tertiary education institutions to be maintained. This is important, for many parents send their children to US, British and Australian institutions for both education and networking opportunities with other well-to-do Asian classmates. Associations such as these are also more accepting of non-Chinese. In fact, many of the new generation of overseas Chinese find traditional Chinese organizations too limiting. They want to grow their contacts and businesses in the Chinese community but also beyond it.

Contacting Asia's Chinese Chambers of Commerce

Covering all bases in Asia means also covering the local Chinese chambers of commerce. As has been mentioned, they are not strictly for Chinese – indeed some are welcoming to non-Chinese. The chambers exist for the benefit of the local Chinese business community rather than as clubs designed to exclude outsiders. The following list gives names and addresses of the main chambers in Asia:

Brunei
Chinese Chamber of Commerce
72 Jalan Roberts
2–4 Floor
Bandar Seri Begawan 1902
Brunei

Myanmar (Burma)
Myanmar Chinese Chamber of Commerce & Industry
No. 84, 8th Street
Lanmadaw Tsp
Yangon
Myanmar
Tel: 951 222223, 951 223445
Fax: 951 226635

Hong Kong
Chinese General Chamber of Commerce in Hong Kong
4/F, 24–25 Connaught Road, Central
Hong Kong
Tel: 852 2525 6385
Fax: 852 2845 2610
website: www.cgcc.org.hk
email: cgcc@cgcc.org.hk

Malaysia
Associated Chinese Chambers of Commerce and Industry of Malaysia
8/F Office Tower, Plaza Berjaya
12 Jalan Imbi,
55100 Kuala Lumpur
Malaysia
Tel: 603 2452503

Fax: 603 2452562
website: www.acccim.org.my
email: acccim@acccim.org.my

The Philippines

Federation of Filipino Chinese Chambers of Commerce and Industry
6F. Federation Center
Muelle De Binondo St
Manila
Philippines
Tel: 632 2419201
Fax: 632 2422361

Singapore

Singapore Chinese Chamber of Commerce and Industry
47 Hill Street # 09-00
Singapore 179365
Tel: 65 3378381
Fax: 65 3390605
website: www.sccci.org.sg/
email: corporate@sccci.org.sg

Thailand

Thai Chinese Chamber of Commerce
233 South Sathorn Road
Bangkok 10120
Thailand
Tel: 662 6758574
Fax: 662 2123916

Note

1   This list is amended and extended from Backman, M., *Asian Eclipse: Exposing the Dark Side of Business in Asia*, John Wiley & Sons, 2001.

Strategy 5

Understand Asia's Overseas Indians

WHAT'S IN THIS CHAPTER?

▷ The Overseas Indian Century has Arrived
▷ Asia's Overseas Indians
   The Ismaili Khojas and the Gujarati Hindus Overseas
   The Sindhis
   The Jains Overseas
   The Parsis
   The Sikhs
   The Tamils
▷ Overseas Indians in the West
▷ Networked Investment
▷ Indian Chambers of Commerce in Asia

The Overseas Indian Century has Arrived

Globalization, the proliferation of English as the world language of business, the rise of the service sector and the importance of technology – all things that favor Indians and overseas Indians – mean that the importance of the overseas Indians is changing relative to that of the overseas Chinese. In short, the overseas Chinese are losing ground. As a commercial diaspora, overseas Indians – as many as 25 million Indians live outside India – have never been as important as they are now, and their influence is increasing.

India is also becoming more important to the world economy as its high-tech sectors compete on cost and quality better than almost anyone else. Business processing (BP) functions increasingly are being outsourced to firms in India. India is now a mainstream option when it comes to North American corporates outsourcing their back-office functions. General Electric, British Airways, P&O Nedland, ABN Amro, ING, American Express, Agilent Technologies and Cap Gemini are among the many big names to have shifted some or most of their BP operations to India. Even the Washington-based World Bank has moved most of its global accounting operations including payroll processing to Chennai (Madras) in India. Now more than ever it is time to learn about the emergent power of the Indian diaspora in business.

Overseas Indians are adding management and high-tech capabilities to their traditional capabilities in trading. Very few multinational corporations have expatriate CEOs in India. The skills base and English-language proficiency in India is such that it is not necessary. The CEOs sourced locally are usually highly educated professionals rather than members of the old Indian business families. There are also plenty of examples of Indians who are the CEOs of multinational corporations worldwide, as we shall see.

But Indians are not just Indians. Like the overseas Chinese, there are many cultural, language and religious differences among them. Indeed, Indians tended to migrate not as Indians but as Jains, Gujaratis, Sikhs, Muslims, Tamils and so on, and they settled on that basis. These differences that Indians themselves recognize.

Indians, again like the overseas Chinese, have traditional surnames that convey a considerable amount about their ancestral origins. Most Indians can identify which Indian state another is from, whether they are a Jain, a Parsi, a Tamil, which Hindu caste and so on, simply by that person's surname. With that comes a whole host of other assumptions and information.

The differences among Indians help to explain a lot about where and with whom they do business. Hiring practices can also be explained by looking at Indian subgroups, for it is often when Indians and overseas Indian firms choose their staff that group loyalty is at its most apparent.

The clan networks among overseas Indians are weaker than those of the overseas Chinese. Overseas Indians also have a less sentimental attachment to their places of ancestry. They are more likely to invest in India if they think they will make a profit rather than out of some sense of duty. Of course, networks are always useful for reducing information costs and alerting businesspeople to unexploited opportunities here and risks there, so, as with the overseas Chinese, ethnicity and ancestry drive a certain amount of Indian trade and investment.

Relationships among Indians tend to lack the emotional aspects of the *guanxi* (personal connections) of the Chinese. Their relationship building is grounded in more practical considerations and focused on recognizable payoffs. Friends may not see each other for years but when they do it is as if they have never been apart. Relationships are more easily built, because they tend to be built less with a shared history in mind but with a view to future rewards. The more clearly defined those rewards are, the more intense the relationship building will be. However, treacherous behavior is met with permanent estrangement. Pragmatism only goes so far and grudges can run deep.

The explicit "what's in it for me" attitude has deep cultural underpinnings, built up by a long history in India of a broad system of patronage that also cuts deeply into all levels of society. But it is one that other cultures find grating. Local resentment toward Indians across Asia can be high, particularly in their role as employers. (Ethnic Indian businesspeople have a reputation for sharp business practices in Bangkok as in other Asian cities. "If you see a snake and an Indian, hit the Indian first" goes a common Thai saying.) This is a problem that many Indian expatriate managers must come to terms with when they are posted to East Asia.

In the words of one Western businessman who sells high-end food products across Asia:

> Doing business with Indians and in India is different to doing it with the overseas Chinese or in China. In China and Southeast Asia one must first establish the trust and the relationship, then matters relating to making business come next. And only then, once the relationship has been developed and the scope of the business to be done has been determined is the matter of contracts raised. In India it's about making money first. Developing the relationship follows and then comes discussion about contracts.

The need for very clear rewards means that India and many overseas Indian communities are beset with an all-embracing patronage system, in which little is done on principle alone. Samy Vellu, the head of the Malaysian Indian Congress, Malaysia's main Indian political party and a member of the ruling coalition, is both public works minister and sits atop an extensive and deep network of patronage. The network reaches all layers of local Indian society to deliver the majority of Malaysian Indian voters to the ruling coalition. Vellu is often blamed for the nepotism and patronage that is part of Indian politics in Malaysia but he is a product of the culture in which he must work, so change, if it is desired, will be slow.

Traditionally, Indian family businesses are joint stock companies with each son or family member jointly owning all the assets. This can lead to some spectacular bust-ups when Indian families fight. Assets not being assigned to individual family members as a matter of course means that if they want to take their inheritance and strike out on their own, it must first be determined how the family's assets are to be divided. A recent spectacular case of an overseas Indian family breaking apart, with the family losing control of the family firm, was the Jumabhoy family of Singapore, which had built up the retail and property group Scotts Holdings. The family fought and Scotts is now owned by a Singapore government-linked company.

While corporate structures of many overseas Indian family-run firms lag behind when it comes to modernization, overseas Indians are at the forefront of adopting new technology. The Internet has become an important way for overseas Indians to stay in touch with their own subgroups and developments in their ancestral regions in India in a way that far exceeds the use of the Internet by the overseas Chinese. Overseas Indian sites have proliferated. They are well maintained, well resourced and up to date. They are an excellent means for Indians to stay informed about each other and for outsiders to have a window on the astonishing vibrancy of overseas Indian business.

Asia's Overseas Indians

Indians are spread across Asia, but in far smaller numbers than the overseas Chinese. The main communities in East Asia today are:

- *Hong Kong:* where there are about 80,000 Indians
- *Malaysia:* where there are about 1.8 million ethnic Indians
- *Singapore:* where there are about 250,000 ethnic Indians
- *Thailand:* where there are possibly as many as 100,000 ethnic Indians
- *Myanmar:* where there are possibly several million ethnic Indians. Today Indians are more plentiful than Chinese on the streets in Yangon (Rangoon).

There are other small Indian communities in the Philippines and Indonesia, and even in Korea and Japan. Overseas Indians can be divided again according to several very different commercial minorities.

Indians ain't just Indians

Some key commercial minorities in India:

- Ismaili Khojas
- Gujarati Hindus
- Sindhis
- Jains
- Parsis
- Sikhs
- Tamils

The Ismaili Khojas and the Gujarati Hindus Overseas

A large proportion of ethnic Indians outside India have their ancestral origins in India's Gujarat State. For example, around 40 percent of the Indians in the New York area are from here. But, more particularly, many are from the Kutch region, a dry, barren area with few economic activities. Kutch, a small princely state in the northwest of Gujarat adjacent to what was Sind, has given rise to a surprising number of global commercial Indian networks. Many of the Kutchi merchants who emigrated to trade anywhere from Asia to East Africa often came from only a handful of villages. Among them were Lohana Hindus, Bhatia Hindus, Muslim Ismaili Khojas, Bohras Muslims and Sunni Memons. Indians are not just Indians, but nor are Indian Gujaratis simply Gujaratis. The story is far more complex.

The Indians who settled in East Africa tended to be Ismaili Khojas and Gujarati Hindus. The Ismaili Khojas, who today number 15–20 million, were economic migrants. Many went to Zanzibar and Uganda. Ismaili merchants formed trading networks that linked Bombay with Zanzibar, Kampala, London and the Middle East, particularly Oman. Spices, textiles and ivory were traded.

The "Africanization" campaigns of the 1970s saw tens of thousands of Indians expelled but rarely did they go to India. The dictator Idi Amin forced out thousands from Uganda in 1972. He made the point that only a third of Uganda's Indians had taken out Ugandan citizenship. Many in fact held British passports and so 27,200 Ugandan Indians resettled in Britain. Others fanned out across the world, so that today there are Ismaili Khoja and Gujarati Hindu communities in many countries. There are 45,000 Ismailis in Canada, many from Uganda. Those who sought refuge in the

UK took up the businesses they left behind in Africa – shopkeeping and small-scale trading. Today ethnic Indians run as many as 60 percent of all independent retail stores in the UK.

The Khojas are a subset of the Nizaris who are a subset of the Ismailis. The Ismailis in turn are a subset of the Shiite Islamic sect and the Shiites are a breakaway group from the dominant Sunni Islamic sect. Today, the Nizaris are the dominant group within the Ismaili community, and the two terms now tend to be used interchangeably.

The Aga Khan is the spiritual leader of the Nizaris and thus the Indian Ismaili Khojas. There is even an Ismaili flag and this is used when the Aga Khan visits friendly countries. The Aga Khan used what influence he had with prime ministers and presidents around the world to have third countries accept Khoja refugees from Africa after their expulsion in the 1970s.

Earlier Aga Khans were based in Iran, then India and now France. Nizari Ismailis are exhorted to save and to pay a monthly tithe from their savings. The tithes are paid to the Aga Khan, and although historically they have been used for charitable works in the Nizari Ismaili community, the sums collected were regarded as the personal property of the Aga Khan.

Today, the Aga Khan, who lives outside Paris, is supposedly one of the wealthiest men in the world. The various Aga Khans' private fortunes have made them independent of the tithes of their followers so that the tithes can be distributed as charity. The Aga Khan and his charitable foundations claim to give around US$100 million away each year to development projects in developing countries.

The most prominent business family in East Asia today with Ismaili Khoja roots is Singapore's Jumabhoy family, the founders of Scotts Holdings and the Ascott serviced apartment group. The family's patriarch Rajabali Jumabhoy (who died in 1998) arrived in Singapore from Kutch in 1918. He imported dates from Persia and exported timber from Java. He amassed a small fortune that he used to branch into other businesses. In 1952, the elder Jumabhoy passed control of what was, by then, the family's property business to his son Ameer Rajabali Jumabhoy, and in turn Ameer's two sons, Rafiq and Iqbal, became involved. Outside Scotts, the Jumabhoys held the A&W Restaurants fast-food franchise in Singapore, substantial duty-free shopping concessions at Singapore's Changi Airport and commenced real estate development outside New Delhi. Today, the family's wealth is much diminished after it lost control of Scotts Holdings in 1998 due to family infighting. The various Jumabhoys now pursue business activities independently of one another.

The Sindhis

Another important Indian diaspora are the Sindhis – Hindu Indians from what is now Pakistan. Most left the province of Sind when it became the new Islamic nation of Pakistan. But others left well before then to become merchants and traders as far afield as China and Africa. There are Sindhis everywhere, from Asia to North America to Europe. Many overseas Sindhis have "ani" as the suffix to their surnames, as in Mirchandani or Tolani.

The most prominent Sindhi-owned business group in India is the Escort Group owned by Rajan Nanda. Escort has three main divisions: telecommunications, construction equipment manufacturing and motorcycle manufacturing. While Sindhis in India are by definition a migrant group, they are comfortable and fit in well with the majority Hindu culture. They do not face the acculturation pressures faced by migrants elsewhere.

The most prominent overseas Sindhi business family in the world is the billionaire London-based Hinduja family, with interests in finance, oil and telecoms. Initially, the family made its fortune not in India but in Tehran, before settling in London. The Hindujas first became well known to average Britons when they were linked to a political controversy over "cash for passports," as the tabloid press put it.

In East Asia, Hong Kong's Harilela family is the most prominent Sindhi business family. They originated from Hyderabad. Lilaram Harilela was the family patriarch. He had six sons and today they run the family's business, headed by second son Hari. The family started in trading and then in the 1970s made its wealth in tailoring. They then diversified into property, electronics and software.

The family ventured into hotels with the construction of Hong Kong's Imperial Hotel and then the 650-room Holiday Inn Golden Mile. They now own Holiday Inns in Hong Kong, Singapore, Bangkok and Penang, the Sheraton Belgravia in London, a Quality Hotel in Montreal, Canada, a Westin Resort in Macau, the W Hotel in Sydney, the Grand Stanford Intercontinental Hotel in Hong Kong and the transit hotel at Singapore's Changi Airport. The hotel interests are all privately owned by the Harilela family. Even the left-luggage service at Changi Airport is operated by a Harilela-owned company.

The Harilelas jointly own their business interests in the joint stock arrangement that is common among Hindu Indian families. This communal arrangement follows through to their living arrangements. More than 40 members of the family – the six brothers, their sisters and all the wives and children – live in one large compound in Kowloon,

Hong Kong. It has almost 90 bedrooms and garage space for more than 30 cars. Members of the younger generation are not encouraged to move out on their own, instead more wings have been added to allow them more privacy.

The controversial brothers Raj and Asok Kumar of Singapore are from another prominent East Asian Sindhi family. They own the Royal Brothers property group in Singapore. Their father founded a chain of silk stores in Singapore in 1947. The brothers' speculation in property at one stage included a chain of hotels in Australia and New Zealand, around 400 shop units in Singapore and Mumbai's Searock Hotel. However, their fortune waned when they were charged in 1997 with attempting to bribe a senior banker.

Another prominent Sindhi family in Singapore are the Melwanis, who own the popular Modestos restaurant in Singapore, among a wide portfolio of investments. They are also major shareholders in Malaysia's Melium Group, a fashion and lifestyle-based group of companies.

The Jains Overseas

Another Indian subgroup is the Jains. The Jain religion is a subsect of Hinduism but is more like Buddhism, with its emphasis on not harming living creatures. Jains are strict vegetarians. They are also remarkably clannish. There are worldwide Jain conventions, such as the Eleventh Biennial Jain Convention that was held in Chicago in July 2001. Religious observances and celebrations are another force that binds the Jain diaspora.

There are about 3.5 million Jains in India (concentrated in Rajasthan, Gujarat and Mumbai) and a small number overseas. Jains are viewed in India as disproportionately commercially successful and are often compared with Europe's Jews.

But the overseas Jains also exert an influence that is way out of proportion to their numbers. They have done this by capturing a large part of the world diamond trade. Many of the overseas Jains involved in the diamond trade are from Palanpur, a town on the Gujarat-Rajasthan border. With such a specific ancestry, many sharing the similar surname of Mehta, it is common today to find diamond traders from London to Israel with the surname of Mehta.

The international diamond trade works on secrecy, trust and strong cross-border connections. It had been the preserve of a small, powerful group of Hassidic Jews until the 1980s when the Jains moved in. Almost all the Jain firms involved in the business are owned and run by families and the diamonds are handled internationally via networks of brothers and cousins that span Europe, the US and Asia.

Jain diamond merchants and cutters now dominate the diamond trade in Tel Aviv and Antwerp and they control about half the world's gem-quality, cut-diamond market. Rough gems are imported by Jain-owned firms in Mumbai from dealers in Antwerp, London, New York and Tel Aviv, from where they are taken to Jain-owned cutting and polishing factories in Gujarat and then back to Mumbai and reexported to gem centers around the world. Bangkok too is becoming more prominent in the diamond cutting and polishing trade, with the small Jain community there handling much of the business.

The Gembel Group is one of Belgium's more prominent diamond cutters and exporters. Based in Antwerp, it was founded in 1956 by Kirtilal Manilal Mehta, an Indian-born Jain. He claimed to have helped 1,800 other Jains set up their own diamond businesses in Antwerp. Gembel now has a network of offices in Belgium, New York, Israel and Mumbai and each is managed by a Mehta family member.

B. Vijaykumar & Co. is another Jain-owned diamond firm. It is India's largest importer of rough diamonds and was founded by the Jain businessman Vijay Shah. The company has cutting and polishing factories in Bangkok, Antwerp, Tel Aviv, Mumbai, Surat and Palanpur, collectively employing 22,000 people.

The way in which the Jains have moved in on the multi-billion-dollar diamond trade and turned it on its head in less than three decades is remarkable. Jain entrepreneurs have gone right to the heart of the old Hassidic diamond networks – even placing family members in Tel Aviv itself – to capture the industry. The Jains have given the established diamond firms such as De Beers and Argyle Diamonds a whole new cultural setting to get used to.

The Parsis

The Parsis are another subgroup. They are from India but ethnically are not Indian. They are descended from Parsi families who migrated to Bombay from Persia in the eighth century, to escape Muslim persecution. Their religion is known as Zoroastrianism, one of the world's oldest religions but one that is now close to dying out.

There are probably no more than 140,000 Parsis worldwide (about 80,000 live in Mumbai). They are a tiny, close-knit community and their commercial influence has been out of all proportion to their numbers. Initially, the Bombay Parsis were involved in spinning and dyeing. The giant Bombay Dyeing and Manufacturing Company is still owned by the Mumbai Parsi Wadia family. Financing is another Parsi activity. Wealth from spinning and financing was put into property so that, by 1855, Parsi families were believed to own approximately half the island of Bombay. Property developers today wanting to move into Mumbai find that more often than not they must deal with Parsi landlords.

Several of India's most famous business families are Parsis, including the Tata, Modi and Wadia families. The Tata Group, controlled by the Tata family, is India's largest industrial group, with sales of at least US$15 billion annually and encompassing around 30 listed companies and many more private ones. It is not a bad result for a family that is not strictly ethnically Indian. The massive Mumbai-based Godrej Group is another prominent Parsi-owned enterprise, owned by the Godrej family. It is an important producer in India of non-perishable consumer goods.

Prime Minister Indira Gandhi's husband, Feroze Gandhi, was a Parsi. Prior to the marriage, he had spelt his surname Ghandy. The later rendering appears to have been an opportunistic and erroneous attempt to suggest a link to Mahatma Gandhi. The late Freddie Mercury, lead singer of the rock group Queen, was a Parsi. His real name was Farookh Bulsara and he was born in Zanzibar to a local Parsi family. World-renowned conductor Zubin Mehta is another Parsi.

Traditionally Parsis have been involved in money lending outside India. The Parsi linkage with money handling is why the finance column in the now-defunct Hong Kong-based weekly magazine, the *Far Eastern Economic Review,* was called Shroff; Shroff being a common Parsi surname. It is also why offices in Hong Kong that handle small payments such as parking fees in high-rise car parks are called Shroff offices. Parsi Road in Singapore runs between Singapore's Monetary Authority building and its car park, a further allusion to the historic money-handling role of the Parsis.

The Parsis were especially prominent in business in Hong Kong. Twelve of the 62 founding members of the Hong Kong General Chamber of Commerce were Parsis. Most of the rest were British. (There were no founding Chinese members, local or otherwise.) Many Parsi surnames particularly in Hong Kong have "jee" as a suffix. Ruttonjee Estates is a big commercial property company in Hong Kong, owned by the Parsi Shroff and Ruttonjee families. These families still maintain close links with the Parsi community in Mumbai. Today, however, there are thought to be just 200 Parsis left in Hong Kong.

The Sikhs

There are about 14 million Sikhs in India, mostly in the Punjab region, but they are found all over India. The Sikh religion is comparatively modern (about 350 years old) and was established to combine elements of Islam with Hinduism – Sikhs cremate their dead, for example, but are opposed to idol worship. Observant Sikh men do not cut their hair, keeping it twisted over their heads and hidden in a turban. Not all Sikh men do this and so today there are many Sikhs who have the appearance of other Indians. However, all Sikh males have the surname Singh, although it may not always be used. All Sikh women have the surname Kaur.

Sikhs in India are yet another small group that is disproportionately wealthy. They tend to be involved in commercial activities with a mechanical emphasis. Many are sports fanatics in and outside India and choose businesses that have a linkage to sport. Local Sikh families run most sports goods stores in Kuala Lumpur. Similarly, East Asia's biggest regional chain of sports goods stores is Royal Sporting House, founded in Singapore by local Sikh J.S. Gill. Today there are more than 200 Royal Sporting House stores across Asia and the group manages Lacoste, Golf House, Greg Norman, Reebok and Nautica stores in Singapore, all of which have a sports focus.

Thailand's Sikh community is prominent in that country, although numerically small – about 25,000 – and most are in Bangkok. Tailoring in Thailand is an occupation dominated by Sikhs, especially in Bangkok, Phuket and Pattaya. They run the tailoring stores, import the necessary fabrics and contract out the actual tailoring mostly to ethnic Thais.

Sura Chansrichawla is Thailand's most prominent Sikh businessman. He controlled Thailand's Laem Thong Bank before losing it in the wake of Asia's financial crisis of 1997–98. The bank had been brought to the point of collapse by Sura after he had it extend huge loans to his other business interests. He also founded Thai Prasit Insurance Co., which he sold in April 2000. He has claimed to have owned seven hotels in India. Today, Sura concentrates on real estate holdings and, true to the typical Sikh interest in sports, is well known as a big donor to sports development in Thailand.

Kartar Singh Thakral is another prominent Southeast Asian Sikh. He was born in Bangkok and went to Singapore with his father in 1952 to set up a textile trading business. He made Singapore his home and he now holds Singapore citizenship. His business interests are in property and electronics, spanning Singapore, India, China and Australia. Among Thakral's Australian hotel assets are the Sofitel in Brisbane, the Menzies

Sydney, the Hilton on the Park in Melbourne and the Novotel on Collins, also in Melbourne. Thakral is the patron of the Singapore Sikh Welfare Council.

The Tamils

Southern Indians, particularly Tamils, dominate Malaysia's Indian community today. In fact more than half Malaysia's Indians, or about one million, are Tamil. The forebears of the vast majority came from what is now Sri Lanka. They came during the colonial period to work as indentured laborers in the rubber plantations. A small group came from mainland India. They were better off and better educated and tended to take jobs in the colonial civil service.

Today, Malaysia's Tamil community tends to be among the poorest Malaysians and many still live on rubber plantations where salaries and government services are poor. They do not have a strong voice in government and their relative poverty is a perpetual social and political issue in Malaysia. There are around 111,000 Tamils living in Singapore, where they tend to work as laborers, security guards and shop assistants.

The best-known Tamil businessman in East Asia today is Malaysia's T. Ananda Krishnan. He built his billion-dollar fortune from oil trading in Malaysia, telecommunications and property. He built Kuala Lumpur's twin Petronas Towers, for a while the tallest buildings in the world. He keeps a very low profile, is rarely photographed and almost never appears in the media. He was on good terms with Malaysia's former Prime Minister Mahathir Mohamad, which helped to smooth his way to the upper echelons of Malaysian business. *Forbes* magazine assessed Ananda Krishnan's wealth in 2005 to be US$4 billion.

The most prominent ethnic Indian conglomerate in Indonesia was the synthetic textiles-based Texmaco Group, founded by the Marimutu family and headed by Marimutu Sinivasan. The Marimutus are also of Tamil descent. Texmaco owns several massive factories in Indonesia and invested heavily in India prior to Asia's and its own financial crises. The Marimutu family intended to build a US$700 million power plant in India, for example. They paid US$48 million in 1997 for UK-based clothes manufacturer SR Gent, which supplies clothes to the UK retailer Marks & Spencer. Texmaco's management is dominated by Marimutu family members and other ethnic Tamils, notwithstanding its massive operations in Indonesia. By 2006, the Marimutu family had lost control of much of Texmaco. The family's financial difficulties had become accute. Marimutu Manimaren, the younger brother of Marimutu Sinivasan, chairman of Texmaco, threw himself to his death from the window of a central Jakata hotel tower in August 2003.

Overseas Indians in the West

London is an important focus of the old Indian diaspora and from there the Indian linkages and networks spiral back to India, Africa, the Caribbean, Hong Kong and the rest of Asia. Indians are prominent in the Americas as well. Ethnic Indians run almost half of all small motels across the US. One of the oldest Indian names in business in the US is Amar Bose who founded the Bose Corporation in the 1950s. Today the Massachusetts-based company is the world's largest manufacturer of high-quality loudspeakers, and state-of-the-art Bose sound systems are sold around the world.

The US is also the focus of recent migrations from India, particularly California's Silicon Valley. The overseas Indians of old were traders and shopkeepers. The new generation of overseas Indians are professionals, who do not need to have their own companies and are comfortable working for others. So, today, ethnic Indian professionals can be found heading up some of the world's most important corporations, as shown in Table 5.1. Their surnames suggest more than that they are simply of Indian descent. Jim Wadia is a Parsi, and Pradman Kaul's surname suggests that he is ancestrally from the Kashmir region, for example.

Research by AnnaLee Saxenian at the University of California, Berkeley indicates that about one-third of the engineers in Silicon Valley are of Indian descent, while 7 percent of the high-tech firms are led by Indian CEOs. Two of the most prominent are Vinod Khosla, co-founder of Sun Microsystems, and Sabeer Bhatia who founded Hotmail and sold it to Microsoft for US$400 million.

Many Indians also work in the financial sector as fund managers, analysts and stockbrokers. Accordingly, Indians were prominent among the victims of the 2001 terrorist attacks on New York's World Trade Center. And they have not missed out on the post-Enron rash of corporate scandals either. Sanjay Kumar was indicted on securities fraud charges in 2004 in relation to his conduct at Computer Associates. Victor Menzes settled insider trading charges with a US$2.7 million payment in February 2006 in relation to his time with Citigroup.

Table 5.1 Recent Indian heads of worldwide multinational corporations

Name	Company	Period	Place of birth
Rajat Gupta	CEO, McKinsey	1994–2003	Kolkata, India
Jamshed "Jim" Wadia	Worldwide Managing Partner, Arthur Andersen; Chief Operating Officer, Linklaters	1997–2000 2001–2004	India
Arun Netravali	President, Bell Labs	1999–2001	Karnataka, India
Sanjay Kumar	President and CEO, Computer Associates	2000–2004	Colombo, Sri Lanka
Rana Talwar	CEO, Standard Chartered Bank	1997–2001	India
Aman Mehta	CEO, HSBC	1998–2003	India
Rono Dutta	President, United Airlines	1999–2002	India
Rakesh Gangwal	President and CEO, US Airways	1998–2001	Kolkata, India
Victor Menezes	Chairman and CEO, Citibank	2000–2004	Pune, India
Shailesh Mehta	CEO, Providian Financial Corporation	1994–2001	India
Pradman Kaul	Chairman and CEO, Hughes Network Systems	1990–	India
Rajiv Gupta	Chairman and CEO, Rohm & Haas	1999–	Mumbai, India
Ramani Ayer	CEO, Hartford Financial Services	1997–	India
Arun Sarin	CEO, Vodafone	2002–	India
Indra Nooyi	CEO, PepsiCo	2006–	India

But the star overseas Indian entrepreneur in the world today is Lakshmi Mittal, owner and chairman of Mittal Steel, who is based in London. *Forbes* magazine ranked him in 2005 as the world's third richest person, with a personal fortune of at least US$25 billion. Other epithets have followed: the world's richest non-American, the richest UK resident, the richest Indian, even the world's richest vegetarian.

He is a member of the Agarwal caste within India's Marwari community, which is centered on Rajasthan. The Marwaris are well known in India as entrepreneurs and traders. They have their own language, a dialect of Hindi. The Birla family, which founded the Aditya Birla Group, one of India's biggest conglomerates, is also Marwari. By 2006, Mittal Steel was the world's biggest steel producer, accounting for around 5.4 percent of world steel production and with operations in 14 countries. In 2006, it embarked on a successful multi-billion dollar takeover of Arcelor, the Europe-based number two producer of steel in the world.

Networked Investment

Examples of cross-border joint ventures between overseas Indians are not as common as among overseas Chinese, but they do happen. Singapore's Jhunjhnuwala family owns Singapore's Hind Development Group. The company had its start in 1997 when it acquired the Oberoi Imperial Hotel in Singapore from India's Oberoi family. Today the Jhunjhnuwala family is involved in property development in Singapore, Hong Kong and Australia and running northern Indian food restaurants in Singapore. The family has around 50 members today in Singapore. Originally from India, they were based in Burma until the 1960s' exodus when the Burmese government nationalized industry. The family acquired listed industrial paint-maker Shalimar Paints in India in 1988, but it was the early acquisition of the Imperial Hotel from fellow Indians that provided their real start in business.

Two Indian families founded the G. Premjee Group in 1868 in Burma, principally to trade in rice. They moved to Bangkok in 1918 and today the group employs more than 2,000 people in 200 subsidiaries involved in trading, shipping, tourism and real estate. Singapore's Jumabhoy family chose Shah's G. Premjee Group as its local partner for its Bangkok Palm Court serviced apartment development – another example of cross-border overseas Indians linking up. The Group still sources rice from Thailand, Myanmar, India, China and Pakistan and sells it to East Africa via local Indian importers there. Its listed Precious Shipping is Thailand's largest shipowner. Nearly all the Group's top executives are Indian. In 1999, G. Premjee Group's Thai Indian head Kirit united with India's Ballarpur Industries and its president Lalit Mohan Thapar to oust the expatriate American management of Thailand's Phoenix Pulp & Paper.

Thailand's Sikh businessman Sura Chansrichawla (mentioned above) co-owns Bangkok's Holiday Inn Silom Hotel with the Hong Kong-based Indian Harilela family – another example of cross-border overseas Indian cooperation. The Harilelas were part of an initial rescue bid to pump funds into Sura's Laem Thong Bank as it faltered with the Asian crisis in 1998. (The bank was ultimately absorbed into a state-owned bank which itself was then sold to a Singapore bank.)

The Silicon Valley Technology Group, founded in San Jose by Anil and Sucheta Kapuria, also benefited from finance from the Harilelas in its early days.

Indorama Group (also known as the Irama Unggal Group) is another Indonesian Indian-controlled conglomerate and, like Texmaco, it concentrates on textiles. It is owned by the low-profile Lohia family and has

expanded across Asia using Indian family members and Indian expatriates in its offices in Indonesia, Thailand, Turkey, India and Sri Lanka.
Polyester and worsted yarn is produced in Thailand, Indonesia, India and
Sri Lanka. It is a case of an overseas Indian family expanding to wherever
it has family and personal connections. It has around US$600 million in
assets. The Lohias bought Thailand's ailing Siam Polyester in 1998 for
approximately US$5 million and installed a family member to oversee it.

Indian Chambers of Commerce in Asia

There are Indian chambers of commerce across Asia as there are Chinese
chambers. They provide good starting points for outsiders wanting to
access the local Indian business community, and also good entry points for
newly arrived Indian businesspeople.

The main body in Hong Kong is the Indian Chamber of Commerce Hong
Kong. It was established in 1952 and today has hundreds of members. It is
a member of the Council of Hong Kong Indian Associations.

The main body in Malaysia is the Malaysian Associated Indian
Chamber of Commerce and Industry. In Singapore, it is the Singapore
Indian Chamber of Commerce and Industry. In Myanmar, it is the
Myanmar India Business Club; in Korea, the Indian Merchants Assoc-
iation; in Japan, the Indian Chamber of Commerce; and in the Philippines,
the Filipino-India Chamber of Commerce.

Indonesia has an organization called the Gandhi Seva Loka. It is a well-
funded foundation for Indonesian Sindhis. It recently built modern, three-
storey premises in central Jakarta, called the Graha Sindhu (Sindhi House).
The foundation acts as a Sindhi chamber of commerce and cultural center.

In 1999, a move was made to unite these bodies at a regional level and
so the Asia Pacific Indian Chambers of Commerce and Industry (APICCI)
was formed in Singapore. The founding members of this new body
comprise all the Indian chambers above plus chambers in India itself,
Japan and Korea.

There are also Indian chambers of commerce in many other parts of the
world. Perhaps the most renowned of the American chambers is IndUS
Entrepreneurs. It comprises a large group of mostly Silicon Valley-based
ethnic Indian entrepreneurs. Its main function is to hold monthly meetings for networking. There are chapters in Atlanta, Austin, Bangalore,
Boston, Chicago, Chennai, Dallas, Delhi, Hyderabad, Los Angeles,
Mumbai, New York, Seattle, and Vancouver BC, thus providing a formal
basis for networking across North America and India.

The overseas Chinese were Asia's most important commercial diaspora in the twentieth century. Southeast Asia's share of the Asian economic miracle was their doing with the help of largely benign government policy.

But it will be the overseas Indians who will be this century's important diaspora in Asia. And probably the most important economic diaspora in the world.

Ignore them at your peril!

Dealing with Information Ambiguity, Local Consultants and Accounting Firms

WHAT'S IN THIS CHAPTER?

▷ Information: Asia's Scarcest Commodity

▷ Local Business Consultants

▷ Caveat Emptor: Auditing in Asia

▷ Conduct Unbecoming? Western Investment Banks in Asia

    Second-guessing the Investment Banks

    Some Questions You Should Ask of Local Auditors

    Some Questions You Should Ask Local Business Consultants

    A Note on Consultants' Out-of-pocket Expenses

▷ Economizing on Information

Information: Asia's Scarcest Commodity

Getting good information in most of Asia is not easy. Due diligence reports with gaping holes, local partners with fingers in many pies (most of which are kept hidden), vaguely specified contracts, companies with three or more sets of books, rumors that are never confirmed or dismissed – such are the joys of operating in Asia. Information is like gold in Asia – it's valuable, scarce and no one ever has enough. And when legal structures are poor in Asia, remedying mistakes can be difficult. So it pays to do your research first. But how do you get good, timely and reliable information?

The media in Asia is often poorly resourced and compromised by its owners' other businesses. Journalists from Thailand and China to

Indonesia and the Philippines are paid so poorly that many accept payments either not to write bad news stories or provide companies with only favorable coverage.

Asian entrepreneurs generally prefer low or no profiles and nor are their businesses transparent. Statutory filings are rarely required and, even if they are, the requirements may not be complied with.

Government statistics are poor in much of Asia and in China particularly are more for propaganda purposes than recording reality. It all adds up to an information-poor environment. When information is available, it is often tainted or simply fabricated.

Due diligence reports out of China, for example, might come with documents, some of which are not even photocopies, but handwritten copies of documents that have been sighted. Managers will need to make their own judgments about the reliability and reputation of the due diligence firm they are dealing with to decide if they should accept this sort of "evidence." Sometimes there's no choice.

Managers in Asia must learn to operate with not as much information as they typically have at home and learn to interpret what they do have. "Bad news never travels up" is an adage nowhere more true than in Asia. The reticence of employees in Asia to report bad news to superiors can mean that managers – and joint venture partners – may be left in the dark until it's too late. Information *about* companies is often hard to get but also information *within* companies may not flow as it should.

Head offices must also understand that their Asian offices may not be able to supply all the information they would normally receive from more mature markets. If they don't, opportunities may be lost. In this regard, regional managers in Asia will need to learn as much about managing head office expectations on this as operating in an information-scarce environment.

Business intelligence gathering has become big business in Asia. New York-based Kroll Worldwide is one of the market leaders. It was one of the first to tackle business information constraints in Asia in a serious and professional manner. Former CIA (Central Intelligence Agency), FBI (Federal Bureau of Investigation) and ASIO (Australian Security Intelligence Organization) officers were initially among its staff. The company's Asian operations specialize in providing corporate due diligence assessments, particularly in China, investigating fraud by joint venture partners and helping to enforce copyright protection.

Another company is the Hong Kong-based Hill & Associates. Most of the principals of the company are former senior officers of the Hong Kong police force. There are one or two former FBI officers too. The company specializes in IP protection, advising on the physical security of Asia-based personnel and general investigation. It also provides bodyguard protection for Hong Kong's billionaire businessmen and their families. Like Kroll, Hill & Associates has offices around Asia.

Apart from these two companies, there are many local companies willing to offer local "intelligence"-gathering services, devise market entry strategies and so on.

Local Business Consultants

One way to solve the information gap in Asia is to hire local business consultants. But many are not all that they're cracked up to be and some, with their vested interests, are simply downright dangerous. Many are Western expatriates who like Asia, didn't want to go home, decided to stay and set up in business, running business partner matching services and providing market entry advice.

Local consulting firms face problems like any other firms in Asia. They face difficulties in hiring local employees who are able to think creatively and analytically and who have the ability to be skeptical of whatever information they come across as part of their corporate and industrial research. And many of the local firms that do not have the backing of an international brand name accordingly attract lower fees and thus cannot usually afford local staff of sufficient calibre.

So instead of hard-edged research, they often congregate at the lower end of the spectrum, offering the types of service that the bigger names don't want to soil themselves with. They can "buy" data from government officials on your behalf, find you the "right" local business partner and help you to get around the US Foreign Corrupt Practices Act.

One of the biggest problems when it comes to engaging local consultants is that of faked data. Research staff, unable to find the information needed or who simply want to cut corners, might be tempted to make it up. This is especially so in an information-scarce environment that makes obtaining supplementary data for cross-verification purposes expensive, if not impossible, to obtain. Japanese firms tend to go through the research results they pay for and strip them apart, wanting to know how the information was collected, by whom and from where. Western clients tend not to do this and routinely accept research reports from local consultants at face value. They shouldn't.

How to avoid such problems? Of course there are smaller companies that are genuinely reputable and try the best they can with limited resources. Another possibility is to approach big name firms. These tend to hire good local talent, pay them accordingly and, most importantly, train them. One risk, however, is that these larger firms use their big names to pull in clients but then subcontract work to small local consulting firms whose calibre and staff they have little control over.

A US$100,000 research project, for example, might be awarded to the consulting arm of one of the big international accounting firms. One of the reasons why the firm is given the project is because of its big name and reputation ("no one has ever been fired for choosing McKinseys" as some say). The client is prepared to pay to have the brightest and the best working on its brief. But the accounting firm then seeks to subcontract out the entire project to a smaller local research firm – the sort of firm the principal client had hoped to avoid. In turn, the smaller firm seeks to break up the brief and further allocate it to several more small firms – all without the principal client's knowledge. Each step in the chain requires its cut and before long perhaps almost two-thirds of the total fee is chewed up by cascading margins.

The vested interests of local consultants can pose more problems. What are the family and equity connections of the owner and the staff that can affect the advice they give to clients? Another more potent problem is confidentiality. Information is bought and sold in Asia like nowhere else. But information need not be sold for confidences to be broken. Idle secretarial chatter between firms in Asia can be a big problem. One expatriate employee in Jakarta was approached by a headhunting firm for a position elsewhere. The potential candidate was not particularly interested but handed over his CV anyway. A secretary in the client firm was friendly with the expatriate's existing employer's wife and wasted no time in telling her that the expatriate was looking for work elsewhere. He wasn't, but suffered accordingly. Similarly, no consulting assignment in Asia, or anywhere for that matter, should be awarded without the consultants agreeing to strict confidentiality provisions. And yet, it's amazing how often Western firms are willing to accept standards in Asia that are far lower than what they would expect elsewhere when it comes to these sorts of provision.

Caveat Emptor: Auditing in Asia

Hire an external auditor, pay him hundreds of thousands of dollars and then call him "independent" – the practice is bizarre anywhere and nowhere more so than in Asia. Audits are not just audits. Managers intent on investing in companies in Asia need to assess the professionalism of the auditor as well as the audited accounts.

The first problem is that accounting standards differ from country to country. A profitable company in one jurisdiction might well be unprofitable in another, depending on what is permitted as income, costs, assets and so on. Hong Kong's Pacific Century Cyberworks, for example, reported a loss of US$884.6 million in Hong Kong for the year 2000 under Hong Kong's accounting rules. One unit's American depository receipts were listed on the New York Stock Exchange, so it was required to report its results under US standards as well. And its loss under US rules was more than double the Hong Kong figure, at US$1,867.9 million – two very different results for the one company. Worldwide harmonization of accounting standards is in sight, but in the meantime, managers need to be aware of the potential for these sorts of discrepancy.

Western accounting firms have been instrumental in moving Asia's corporate governance standards further along the track to modernity. But, given Asia's economic crisis, have they been doing a good enough job? And if the Enron–Arthur Andersen debacle of 2002 can happen in the relatively well-regulated US market, then what does an auditing report mean in China, Indonesia, Thailand or India, even if it is conducted by a worldwide accounting firm?

Local auditing firms without worldwide reputations to protect should be immediately suspect, particularly in economies where regulatory and supervisory systems are weak. China is the classic case. There are many cases of local accounting firms helping to cook the books in China. Sometimes it is the accountants that initiate the "service." China's official news agency Xinhua reported in 2001 that accountants working at the Hubei Lihua accounting firm had helped eight listed A grade share companies to falsify their accounts since 1998. The fraud, as reported, was not terribly sophisticated. It simply involved the accounting staff signing off on accounts "regardless of their truth." They did so for money.[1]

But then how much better are audits conducted by international accounting firms? The name might be global but the staff and the practice generally are local. The fiasco over the adequacy of the audits conducted by Deloitte Touche Tohmatsu in Hong Kong of locally listed "red chip" Guangnan (Holdings) Ltd is a case in point. Audits commissioned from KPMG suggested discrepancies in Guangnan's audited accounts of some US$1.07 billion. These were followed in 1999 by the unprecedented withdrawal by Deloitte of its 1997 audit report of Guangnan.

The debacle over Asia Pulp & Paper (APP), a listed Singapore-based company, and several of its listed Indonesian subsidiaries provides another example. APP and its listed units were audited by the Singapore and Jakarta offices of Arthur Andersen. APP became the subject of the largest emerging market's debt work-out in history. It had around US$14 billion in debts by early 2002. Derivatives that led to US$220 million in losses went unnoticed in its audited accounts for three-and-a-half years and when they were finally noticed it took another five months before they were disclosed publicly. Even APP's chief financial officer said that the company's accounts, as audited by Arthur Andersen for the years 1997, 1998 and 1999, "should not be relied upon." Almost US$200 million was deposited by an Indonesian-based APP unit in a related-party bank that was misnamed in the audited accounts. And a billion dollars had been siphoned off by five mysterious British Virgin Islands companies that appear to be linked to Indonesia's Sinar Mas Group, which controls the company. The five companies, with names that almost no one has heard of, were responsible for almost a third of APP's "sales" in 1999. By mid-2002, none of the money owing had been paid and the five companies had ceased operating. Disgruntled US bondholders and shareholders commenced legal proceedings in 2001 against Andersen auditors in relation to the audits of APP in Indonesia, Singapore and New York.

Sidharta, Sidharta & Harsono, the Indonesian version of KPMG, was pursued in 2002 by the US Securities and Exchange Commission (SEC) and the Justice Department, under the Foreign Corrupt Practices Act, for allegedly being the conduit through which a US$75,000 bribe was paid to an Indonesian tax official to provide a favorable tax assessment for US energy firm Baker Hughes. The matter only came to light after Baker Hughes' head office itself reported it to US authorities.

SGV, the Andersen affiliate in the Philippines, was reprimanded for "unethical conduct" by the local accountant's professional body in 2000, after it unilaterally withdrew three years' worth of audit reports for a local listed firm, Victorias Milling Co., which later went bankrupt. Andersen-SGV had certified the inventory without actually checking it. The figures were later found to be massively fraudulent. In early 2002, SGV was ordered by the Central Bank of the Philippines to conduct "tighter" bank audits after central bank officials disagreed with SGV's assessments.

It is not as if investors haven't had enough warning that all may not be well with auditing in Asia. In 1982, the collapse of the Carrian Group in Hong Kong led to a massive negligence action against Carrian's auditors and the prosecution of several members of its staff.

But is auditing in Asia worse than anywhere else? Auditing in Asia is not easy. There is a culture of secrecy, a suspicion of outsiders such as external auditors and a failure on the part of many majority owners to even understand their obligations once they list their companies on a local stock exchange. Too many fail to recognize that listing "their" company means that it is no longer exactly that. The number of listed companies in Asia issuing annual reports in which their auditors express a qualified opinion or a fundamental uncertainty is rising. But, if anything, the numbers should probably be higher.

That even the local offices of the big international accounting firms are seen as potentially compromised was demonstrated best by the Indonesian government in the wake of Asia's economic crisis. Most of Indonesia's big conglomerates and nearly all its banks were technically insolvent by 1998. The government created the Indonesian Bank Restructuring Agency (IBRA) to help sort the mess out. The first task was to find out just how bad things were. But IBRA did not invite local auditors in to do the work. Instead they bypassed Jakarta and engaged auditors in the Australian and London offices of what was then the big five.

In Asia, perhaps more than anywhere else, listed companies habitually shop around for the most agreeable auditor. In the US, a listed company's decision to change auditors is a decision not taken lightly – it rightfully begs the question of whether the company has something to hide. The same degree of apprehension is yet to develop in much of Asia.

Yet another complication rarely thought about is what happens to local affiliates when the world's major accounting firms merge? The 1987 merger of Klynveld Main Goerdeler with Peat Marwick to form KPMG is one example. Once the merger occurs, it is assumed that all the obstacles must have been ironed out. That might well be the case as far as the key participants are concerned, but the merger between two major world accounting firms may mean that unfriendly local affiliates are dragged into the process as well. For example, when Price Waterhouse and Coopers & Lybrand merged in 1998, it meant that their Jakarta affiliates, Hadi, Susanto & Co. and Sidharta & Sidharta, also had to merge. Too bad if the two firms have a long-standing rivalry and even hatred of one another. The problems can take years to sort out, as KPMG found after it was formed. Inappropriate mergers at the local level in Asia are simply asking for trouble.

There is no doubt that the big international accounting firms in Asia have been instrumental in exposing enormous corporate frauds and impropriety across Asia, but it should never be assumed that there is a single standard of quality across all branches in all countries. Nor should it be assumed that branches faithfully replicate those in, say, the US. In many Asian countries, foreign accounting firms are required or have been encouraged to take local partners. Not all the marriages are seamless. Typically, these mixed marriages employ Western expatriates but rarely are they employed in the lucrative and sensitive auditing divisions. More usually, and particularly when it is the local partner that is ascendant, they are restricted to the taxation and consulting divisions.

When so much else has failed in Asia, be it government and stock market rules and regulations, or systems of internal corporate governance, it is too much to assume that auditing can pick up all this slack. It is also too much to expect that the professionalism of the sector can be maintained when so much of the environment in which it must operate has been so compromised when it comes to modern standards of ethics and corporate governance.

Conduct Unbecoming? Western Investment Banks in Asia

Investment banks are another source of corporate information. They have been useful in modernizing corporate Asia, but there are limits to this usefulness. Many of the big investment banks have helped local firms to issue new shares and bonds and have assisted them with other services. They also offer investment advice to institutional and retail investors but rarely, if ever, do they declare the work that they have done, are doing, are bidding for or are likely to bid for in relation to the companies they analyse. What incentive does an investment bank have to rate the stock of a company from which it is earning millions of dollars in fees as a "sell"? The lack of transparency relating to this practice and the perversions in advice that have resulted are every bit as unseemly as the worst corporate governance excesses in Asia.

Part of the problem is the Asian inability to brook any criticism whatsoever. The concept of face has been so highly developed that many owners and senior managers see any criticism, no matter how minor, as major. Criticism is not seen merely as restricted to that practice being criticized but is seen as a general affront; an assault on their credibility, authority and standing. Thus research reports that report fairly on companies' good and bad points are simply unacceptable to many in corporate Asia and they habitually move their business accordingly.

Second-guessing the Investment Banks

1. Undertake the research yourself or commission some. All the statutory corporate filings need to be examined. Particular attention needs to be paid to related-party transactions.

2. Ask the investment bank or brokerage that has issued the research what, if any, commercial relationship it has with the company under research or that it expects to gain. View the efficacy of its research only in light of its answers to this question.

3. Take a lead from institutional investors. Generally, they have their own in-house research that is independent of the potential conflicts of interest of the research teams of brokerages and investment banks. If they are buying into an issue, presumably they see it as well priced.

Some Questions You Should Ask of Local Auditors

1. What commercial relationships do they have with the companies that you are interested in? Do they, for example, contract the company for any services, or rent any property from them?

2. In respect of accounting firms in Thailand, Indonesia, China and the Philippines, are there any Western expatriates who work in the auditing division or are all the staff local? If the company does employ Western expatriates, in what divisions are they and if there are none in auditing, why?

3. If the accounting firm is a member of the big four, is the local office a joint venture or is it operated outright by the big four firm?

4. Can the firm guarantee that none of its audit staff trade in the shares of the company in which you are interested?

Some Questions You Should Ask Local Business Consultants

1. If you are to commission a study from a local consulting company, ask for the names and CVs of all the staff who will work on the study. Is it possible to meet each of the staff? Who will be leading the research team? What are that person's qualifications?

2. Who are recent past clients? Would any be willing to discuss their experience of using the consulting firm's services?

3. Can the consulting company guarantee that it is not currently engaged by any competitors?

4. Can it guarantee that none of its research staff have family or any other links with competitors?

5. Who is the ultimate owner of the consulting company? Do any of the shareholders have any other businesses that might pose conflicts of interest for the work you wish to assign to the company?

6. Will the consulting firm be undertaking all the work or does it intend to subcontract all or part of the project? Does it guarantee that it will undertake all the work itself?

A Note on Consultants' Out-of-pocket Expenses

Consultants almost always charge for two items – their time and "out-of-pocket expenses" (OPEs as they're called in the business). These are the costs they incur, such as travel expenses, data purchasing costs and so on, that are directly attributable to your project. Often the contract will include some sort of cap for OPEs such as "OPEs will not be more than 20 percent of the total agreed professional fee without the written approval of the client." If it does not, you should insist on it.

Clients rarely seem to question OPEs in Asia. They should. These are routinely padded out and become a back-door way for consultants to earn extra fees. One assignment undertaken for a major American client by a Southeast Asian office of one of the world's big accounting firms included US$58,000 for OPEs. The main consultant later admitted to one of the authors that the accounting firm had documentary evidence for less than US$5,000. The rest was padding. This is fraud. Clients do not accept these sorts of things in New York, Sydney or London, so why do they accept it in Asia?

You should *always* insist that OPEs are capped and that they will be paid upon receipt and verification of all the supporting documentation for the claim. Claims for expenses that cannot be verified or reasonably justified should not be honored. Allowance will need to be made for those expenses for which supporting documentation cannot be obtained, such as unofficial payments to government officials for obtaining statistical information, but typically these should be relatively trivial.

Economizing on Information

Information makes the difference, not simply between success and failure in Asia, but between success and losses that can be ruinous. Saving money on upfront research is a false economy.

There is no need to rush into Asia. It will still be there tomorrow. Gains that might be won by getting in early and cheaply might be lost by having gone in from a position of ignorance.

There are surprising differences between the nationalities of foreign investors when it comes to gathering information. Large and well-resourced American companies sometimes send in wave after wave of research teams. They keep them in-country for maybe three months at a time while they learn and conduct their research. It is expensive but better than using local consultants who might be an unknown quantity. The local consultants, if used at all, can be hired simply to set up local appointments. Many large companies find that this is a sensible division of labor.

When American companies, for example, commission local consultants to do research, they tend to ask few – too few – questions about how the research was conducted. Rarely do they test finalized research reports for their veracity, but they should.

Japanese firms often conduct their research in-house. When they do commission work from outside consultants, they are utterly meticulous in questioning the consultants about how the research was conducted, the appropriateness of the methodology, who undertook the research, their qualifications and so on. Nothing is taken at face value, nothing is trusted and everything is questioned. The contrast of this with the ease with which American managers accept the findings of externally produced research reports is startling.

UK firms tend to stick to the consultants they know. Names they are comfortable with such as the EIU and the big four accounting firms are used. Australian firms, being smaller and less well resourced, tend to economize on their research. They are not used to paying the big consultants' fees that American and European companies pay. They are more likely to hire expatriate Australian staff in Asia who come with on-the-ground experience. Such staff are used as a substitute for commissioning research reports.

Note

1   *Business Times,* "Accounting firm helped to cook books: Xinhua," 21 August, 2001.

Strategy 7

Network like a Local, Negotiate like a Westerner

WHAT'S IN THIS CHAPTER?

▷ Why Do Relationships Matter?

▷ Can non-Chinese Utilize Overseas Chinese Networks?

▷ Culture Counts But Not That Much

▷ Developing Relationships and Connections in Asia

▷ Choosing a Local Partner: Some Basics

▷ Negotiating in Asia: Some Suggestions

▷ Don't Dirty your Nest

Why Do Relationships Matter?

There are three things that really matter when it comes to doing business in Asia. They are (in no particular order):

1. Relationships
2. Relationships
3. Relationships.

The US popstar Cyndi Lauper had a hit in the 1980s called *Money Changes Everything*. The Asian version could well have been "Connections Change Everything." They really do. Knowing the right people can solve most problems in much of Asia.

But why do connections and relationships matter? They matter because from China to Indonesia and much of what lies in between, legal protection is weak. And when laws are weak, businesspeople need to find other ways to protect themselves. Typically, they do business only with those they trust and are comfortable with. So the first step to being Big in Asia is to develop good connections – a good local network. A general rule of thumb is that the weaker the local legal system, the more needed are well-founded local personal connections to trade and invest successfully. Thus, they are very necessary in Indonesia and China, less so in Malaysia and Korea, and less still in Singapore.

> At one time, *guanxi* was sufficient to win deals. Then it became necessary but not sufficient. Now we're between that phase and the time when *guanxi* will no longer be necessary.

So said telecoms consultant Duncan Clark in relation to winning contracts to manage telecom IPOs (initial public offerings) in China.[1] Having friends matters everywhere. But the path to economic modernity means that friendships and relationships become less important to doing business over time.

Having a wide network of friends and colleagues also provides the means for collecting information and, as we have said, much of Asia is an information-poor environment. Opportunities come and go but without a good network, you will simply never hear about them. Or if you do, you will often lack the means to access them.

Connections open doors and keep them open. By way of example, almost all expatriates who work in Indonesia do so officially in only one capacity, that of "technical adviser." The idea is that Indonesians should manage all businesses operating locally and the expatriates are there merely to advise. Of course, it is a farce and everyone knows it. There is a chronic shortage of human capital in Indonesia and outside managers are needed there perhaps more than any other country in the region. The Ministries of Manpower and Immigration and the police are able to call in any expatriate and accuse them of acting beyond the limited confines of their work permits. At that point, exorbitant bribes might be demanded. But if the expatriate has connections higher up in any of these bodies, or is connected with someone who can intervene on their behalf, then the harassment can be stopped. If not, the expatriates can be thrown out of Indonesia, as has happened.

Connections help with solving day-to-day problems but they are necessary at every level of business. Having a lot of friends means having a
wide set of potential business opportunities. Not having many friends can
constrain the growth of a business. So social structures in Asia have developed to allow people to meet and greet easily, to circulate socially.
Weddings tend to be big lavish affairs with thousands of guests. There is a
lot of emphasis on eating out in restaurants and taking the whole family.
Business after all is a family affair. Chambers of commerce are popular as
are social clubs such as the Rotary and so on. All this allows people to
catch up with each other, to maintain friendships and develop new ones.
And with friendships comes business.

In a business environment that is defined by overlapping webs of
personal connections and loyalties, who's who takes on vital importance. It
is essential that newcomers to Asia get on top of who the big names are in
the local corporate scene and how they all fit together. Whereas the
business community in the West is a community of companies, the business
community in Asia is a community of people. In the West, companies tend
to do business with one another. In Asia, the deals are all done between
personalities. So when, in 2000, Hong Kong's China Cyberport bought a
stake in the Kerry Group, it was not of itself big news. The real story was
that Oei Hong Leong of Indonesia's billionaire Widjaja family had bought a
stake in the private family holding company of billionaire trader Robert
Kuok. That was the big news. It's a different mindset.

The people who own and run Asian firms determine the firms' integrity.
Goodwill is attached to the owners rather than the firms themselves. Many
businesspeople in Asia will even be unfamiliar with trading and company
names because of this tendency to think more in terms of the people
behind the companies rather than the companies themselves. Westerners,
on the other hand, tend to recognize company names but have little idea
who owns a company or the name of its CEO. Personalities and people
matter in Asia, and so does news about them. Corporate gossip is everything. Often the media cannot be relied upon to convey accurately the
latest corporate goings on in Asia. In countries such as Thailand, the
Philippines and Indonesia, bad news is often kept out of the media by
paying journalists and editors not to run it. Reliable credit checks and due
diligence assessments are hard to come by, so good managers in Asia have
little choice but to keep their ears to the ground; to stay attuned to whatever gossip is going around. Who is having problems meeting their orders,
debts and other commitments is essential information but is only likely to
be spread by word of mouth.

Not knowing the names and backgrounds of the people behind the big companies in New York, London or Sydney is, at best, barely necessary and, at worst, ignorance. In Asia, it's unforgivable. Who's who and who is doing what to whom is the lifeblood of conversation in Asian business circles, and for good reason. There's little point sending a business development manager to Asia who is not gregarious.

Can non-Chinese Utilize Overseas Chinese Networks?

Can non-Chinese utilize the cross-border connections that many, although not all, overseas Chinese have? It's all very well hearing that the Chinese do business on the basis of personal connections or *guanxi*, a term that has become much overused, but what practical relevance to a non-Chinese are the networks of the overseas Chinese?

They can work for non-Chinese but, like everything in Asia, it takes time. Consider this example. One Perth-based businessman had been doing business for many years with a local ethnic Chinese timber importer. This man had lived in Australia for almost 20 years but was Malaysian by birth. The two had a business relationship of several years standing but had also become friends, not close but they did enjoy each other's company. The Australian businessman decided that he wanted to expand his business into a new area – importing children's clothing to Australia. He wanted to buy in Asia, probably Thailand, but didn't know how to go about it. One day he mentioned this in passing to his Chinese friend. "I can help you," he said, and right away began making telephone calls to associates in Chiang Mai in northern Thailand. Everything was arranged after just three phone calls. The Australian would go to Chiang Mai where a local Chinese businessman, a friend of the Perth Chinese man, would meet him at the airport. This friend would take care of everything. The Australian didn't know what to expect but decided to go to Chiang Mai and just see what would happen.

He arrived in Chiang Mai and received a welcome that could not have been more effusive and helpful. He was taken around factories and shops and wined and dined. His host, the friend of his Chinese friend back in Australia, would not allow him to pay for a thing. He provided cars, guides and personally accompanied him as much as he could over the course of a week. The Australian was taken to factories all around northern Thailand and introduced to all the right people – everywhere doors opened. The locals even took care of the shipping and customs.

It was a successful trip to Thailand – stunningly so – and it was all due to cross-border Chinese connections. The non-Chinese Australian was given access to and benefited from these connections. However, the key to this story is that he had a long-standing relationship with the local Chinese businessman that was built on both business and friendship over several years. The Chiang Mai businessman was not doing the Australian a favor, rather he was doing it for his Chinese friend back in Australia.

Many people claim to have "connections" or "relationships" but it is their quality that matters rather than the quantity. Knowing someone in Asia or having had a few dinners with them does not constitute being strongly connected to them. It helps to get one to the right door, but don't expect the door to swing open – at least not yet.

Culture Counts But Not That Much

How important to business success in Asia is an understanding of the local social etiquette? Contrary to popular belief, the answer is, probably not much. Business guides tend to overemphasize the cultural aspects of doing business in Asia. "Don't touch Asians on the head," "don't point with your feet," "don't touch locals on the back" and so on – forget all that. Common sense is what matters – listen and be sensitive to the needs and reactions of others and you'll go a long way. Talk with people, not at them. Be a sensitive conversationalist. This is very important in Asia where people tend to be taught not to be self-promoting but self-effacing in how they present themselves in person.

Everyone expects those from other cultures to get it wrong. Businessmen, Asian or otherwise, just want to make money. Million-dollar deals, or, for that matter, deals of any size, are not going to fall through because a visitor to a foreign country handed out his business card in the wrong way. Equally, no one is going to be a success in Asia simply because they have mastered all the local social mores and habits. All cultures make allowances for guests. Minor cultural trespasses are readily forgiven, if noticed at all. Businesspeople in Asia are no more unforgiving of minor cultural errors than Westerners are of them. Besides, if you are from the West, people can reasonably expect that you will behave like a Westerner – and Westerners are generally admired across Asia.

Of course, efforts to get it right are appreciated but at the end of the day making money is what counts. Small cultural errors are important between Asians and will be seen as the insult that they are probably intended to be. But it's a different story when they occur between Asians and visitors to the region. Western sensitivities to the minutiae of cross-cultural nuances derive more from political correctness trends at home than any codes of behavior particularly demanded of foreigners in Asia. Of course, Western business-people should not go to Asia and be loud, aggressive and backslapping, but then that sort of behavior is not necessarily acceptable back home either.

In any event, times are changing and Asia's business elite increasingly are Western-educated and speak English, which is fast becoming Asia's language of business. Knowledge of Asia is rising in the West too. Both sides are becoming more comfortable with each other. It is the practicalities of doing business that really count rather than the vagaries of cultural nuances.

Developing Relationships and Connections in Asia

Having exchanged a business card with someone does not mean that you have a "relationship" with them. It simply means that you have met. Similarly, having met a lot of people in Asia does not mean that you are well connected. Good relationships in Asia are something that should endure over the years, which means that they must be built on solid foundations.

There was once a conference on doing business in Asia that featured a session in which audience members were given 20 minutes to meet as many attendees as possible and, after the 20 minutes, the individual who had collected the most business cards was declared the winner. It sent out entirely the wrong message. Quantity of connections at the expense of quality is not the approach if you want to be Big in Asia.

There are no quick and easy rules to forging relationships in Asia. They take time if they are to be worth something. Similarly, simply because someone has spent a lot of time in Asia does not mean that they are well connected. Someone might have lived in Jakarta for 25 years, for example, but that does not mean that the locals respect that person or that they can open doors. Asia is full of long-term residents from the West who have not so much run to Asia as run from the West. If they had trouble making it in their own countries, what hope do they have in someone else's? Expatriates like these can be more dangerous than helpful, particularly when they dress themselves up as consultants.

Asian and particularly ethnic Chinese businesspeople are always looking to forge new connections and relationships. But they don't do this with specific business goals in mind. The friendships are ends unto themselves. Networks of friendships are forged and then business opportunities are allowed to arise. It's an organic process, which does not happen the other way around – friendships are not developed to cover a specific business opportunity.

This confused many Americans during the "Donorgate" scandal in which Indonesian Chinese businessman James Riady made illegal donations in respect of President Clinton's election campaigns. "Why would the Riadys donate this money – they don't have many businesses in the US," was a common theme in the media. But this was looking at it from a Western perspective. Businesspeople from Asia generally prefer to develop relationships first and then invest. They do not invest and then attempt to develop relationships to protect or enhance investments already made. India presents an exception to this rule. As mentioned earlier, Indians like clear upfront indications about the benefits they can expect. "Why should I see you? What will it mean for me?" might be a typical response in India. Once the answer to that is made clear, the relationship building can commence.

The most important rule for developing relationships in Asia is not to rush into talking about business right away. Locals will understand that someone from a large American or British firm who is not based in Asia has only limited time and they may make some allowances for that. But it is still necessary to forge good relations where possible. Repeat visits and plenty of follow-up are important. Remember, people in Asia tend to see business as something that occurs between people rather than companies. It is the people who give the companies definition rather than the other way round. There is an element of that in Western business too but it is heightened in Asia. So, taking an interest in the local parties outside work is essential. Taking the trouble to learn about their personal interests and their families is a good idea. Take time to notice things, to care about things. This is how a contact is converted into a colleague.

How does an outsider know when they have been accepted in Asia and that associates are no longer just that but are now part of their network? There's no easy answer. But one indication might be when the locals themselves suggest opportunities that could be embarked on together and when they personally invite you to functions and events that are important to them in their private lives.

Choosing a Local Partner: Some Basics

A local partner can make sense in those markets that are difficult, complex and lack transparency. In some sectors in some countries (such as accounting in Thailand and mining in Indonesia), a local partner might even be required by law. However, having a local partner is not a universal panacea. In fact, it can prove a disaster. There are plenty of foreign companies who opted for local partners in China and Indonesia that led to the destruction of the venture, when possibly the company might have performed better going it alone. So, if taking a local partner is necessary or seems sensible, it's worth the time and the expense to choose the right one. Here are some things to consider:[2]

- *Make sure that you have similar objectives to your partner.* You might be looking to achieve market share but your partner might be interested in quick profits. Differing objectives are a common reason why joint ventures come unstuck.

- *Make sure that you have similar plans for the venture as your partner.* For example, you might intend the venture to stay focused, whereas your partner might want it to diversify; you might be planning for a single factory, but your partner might be hoping for six across the country.

- *Make sure that your partner isn't involved in other businesses that will present a conflict of interest for your venture.* You don't want to discover that your partner is reluctant to move into certain areas because he is already producing in that area, or is related to someone who is.

- *You need to feel comfortable with your partner.* To feel comfortable you need to know as much about them as possible. You must be able to trust your partner. You do not want to discover some time after agreeing to a joint venture that your local partner is actually a front for some general or a local politician's youngest son.

- *Your partner must be well thought of locally.* You need a partner who can deal with the local bureaucracy and speed things up. You do not want to be tarred by your partner's pre-existing business problems and bad blood with the local authorities or business community.

- *You need to consider how much information you will share with your partner and how safe it will be.* Asia is littered with examples of joint ventures in which the local side simply wanted to use the venture to gain technology transfer and other know-how and once this was gained, created a dispute with the foreign party so that they could be free of their contractual obligations to start up on their own.

- *You might want to consider paying for a due diligence check on your prospective partner.* What is their actual corporate structure? What related parties are there? What other joint ventures do they have and how have their other partners been treated? Who are all the equity participants and who are the real ultimate owners? What sort of general reputation do its principals enjoy, do they have criminal records, what are their outstanding tax obligations, their bank and other debts? What is its financial position? What are its sources of financing? Does it face any pending legal action? Has it been involved in any practices which, if continued, would lead to a possible contravention of the US Foreign Corrupt Practices Act or similar laws on the part of the foreign party? What is the structure of the family behind it and are there any internal family conflicts? Is there a myriad of cousins, half-brothers and half-sisters among whom trouble could flare in future? What are the other corporate activities of the immediate and the extended family? With whom are they close and who are their enemies? Are they politically neutral or politically aligned? How would a change of government affect their business prospects?

- *Your partner should be able to add to the business.* It's always tempting to sign on with a local partner who is already in the business that you are in, simply because they know the business locally. It is far better if they can also bring to the business something that you do not have – such as a good distribution network, useful land holdings or good local access to raw materials.

The most important ingredient to finding the right local partner in Asia is time, followed by research. It takes many visits if the entrant company does not have local representatives. All too often joint ventures are signed too early and thus between incompatible partners, simply because of pressure at home to deliver a signed and sealed joint venture in Asia. Too often, foreign firms in Asia sign joint venture agreements too early because of a need to be seen by head office to have made "concrete" progress or improve someone's immediate career advancement prospects.

Even after a joint venture is established, sound relationships must be established between the staff on either side. The trust of the local staff must be gained and everyone must feel comfortable and able to share information and news, be it good or bad.

It is not uncommon to take two or three years to find a suitable local partner in Asia and then another year for the two partners to properly enmesh and the staff on both sides to establish good working relationships.

If negotiations fail and a joint venture does not materialize, all is not lost. What might well have been gained are useful relationships and they should not be discarded. Maintain them and they might prove to be helpful later. The Asian side at least will see such relationships as a positive outcome in themselves.

Negotiating in Asia: Some Suggestions

Typically, businesspeople will find that it is members of the owning family with whom they work when dealing with smaller overseas Chinese-owned firms. In larger overseas Chinese firms, initial negotiations will be with employees. Members of the controlling family will be introduced as negotiations proceed. At that point, negotiations will gather pace noticeably, or the fact that a family member has suddenly become involved signals that the local side believes that the negotiations are close to nearing completion.

Things can be a little different in India. Negotiations will be more formal than elsewhere and more regard will be paid to hierarchy and process. To quote one Western businessman who does business there:

> India is still a very class-ridden society. Determining each rank of the locals with whom negotiations are to be conducted is very important. I find it prudent to always ask for a list of the locals' names and their position in the company before the meetings begin. That also helps with working out the seating arrangements. Small things like who sits where can matter a lot in India. These things are less important in China and Southeast Asia. We are always expected to make the first presentation, which gives them the advantage of reading the situation better. They do not like surprises and always want briefings ahead of meetings.

When planning for negotiations in Asia, be it for trade or investment, the following should also be considered:[3]

- *Never economize on information and research.* Enter negotiations well briefed on the market that you are interested in and the people with whom you are to negotiate.

- *Never negotiate alone.* It is far better to have two main negotiators, but they must present a unified front and never disagree with each other in front of the opposite side. Disagreements can be handled during requested adjournments. Almost certainly the local side will outnumber the non-local side, and there might be some people in the room whose reason for being there is not obvious. Ask who they are and what their position is.

- *Keep the same negotiating team.* Negotiations can go on for months and sometimes even longer, so keep the same negotiating team. Relationship building and trust are important for both parties and negotiations can take longer when new negotiators are brought in because trust will need to be established with each new team member.

■ *Do not send in the final decision maker,* or at least suggest that you need to refer decisions to some absent decision maker. The local side will always want to defer decisions up the line and you can do the same. This buys more time and allows for decisions to be made outside the room and not in the heat of the moment.

■ *Negotiations in Asia take a lot of time.* This is partly strategic – single negotiation sessions might be drawn out for five or more hours in a deliberate attempt to wear down the opposite negotiating party. Things that you thought had been agreed might be reopened just when everything looks clear cut. So sufficient time must be allowed. One way around shifting decisions is to keep records of all decisions and have both parties sign off on them, reconfirming them after they have been checked with the higher authority.

Negotiations can also take a lot of time because many in Asia typically are not direct. Issues can be raised with a great deal of preamble and the matter of contention is not always clear. Important matters might be raised in the most oblique ways, so it is important to listen very carefully and deal with each point at the time, one at a time. Be mindful also that if negotiations are to be conducted in English, for many Asian people that is their second language.

Discussion might be oblique but it might not always be polite. Some negotiators in mainland China tell of actually having been yelled at and abused by the opposite side – usually by just one individual in what looks like a rehearsed "good guy, bad guy" routine. One response is to call for a temporary halt to proceedings and only agree to return to the negotiating table once the other side agrees to adopt a more civil and appropriate mode of behavior.

Don't Dirty your Nest

The web of overlapping networks that define business in Asia mean that information is exchanged rapidly. This can mean that commercial in-confidence information once leaked can spread quickly. Similarly, news of a falling out between partners can spread quickly. The local business sector can close ranks and the party deemed to be at fault quickly frozen out. Thus, it is important that not only are relationships made in Asia but that they are kept. Failing that, when relationships end, care should be taken that all sides do not lose face or that the relationship dissolves into acrimony. Because there is a tendency in Asia for everyone to be related to everyone else, falling out with a partner can have serious knock-on consequences.

When the impeachment trial of Philippines' President Joseph Estrada was before the Philippines' Senate in January 2001, one of the 22 senators was Miriam Defensor-Santiago. The previous year, her brother Benjamin Defensor was made head of the Philippines' air force. Her husband, Narciso, had been appointed interior undersecretary. Her sister, Peachy Defensor, was appointed environment undersecretary. Estrada is also the godfather of one of Senator Defensor-Santiago's adopted daughters. Asked if any of this would influence her vote, Senator Defensor-Santiago was reported in the media to have said, "Of course not."

Everyone knows that relationships are important to running a business in Asia, be it the presidency of the Philippines or more commonplace ventures. Many senior business figures in Asia are related to other prominent figures by blood or by marriage. The connections in Asia are often not obvious to outsiders but they can be a minefield for the unwary.

The mix of marriages and blood relations in Asia can make for some complex webs. Here are a few examples that involve some of Asia's biggest business names:

- Quek Leng Chan, head of Malaysia's massive Hong Leong Group, is a cousin of Kwek Leng Beng, head of Singapore's Hong Leong Group. (The two groups are separate but share the same name. *Hong* means good and plentiful; *leong* means great prosperity.) Kwek is a shareholder in Hotel Properties, controlled by Ong Beng Seng. Until 2005, Ong was a substantial shareholder of NatSteel. David Fu, Ong's brother-in-law, served as a director. Fu's cousin, David Ban, the co-owner of the worldwide franchise rights for Japanese fast-food chain Genki Sushi outside Japan, Taiwan and Hawaii, also served as a director. Lee Suan Yew is a past director of Hotel Properties. His brother is Lee Kuan Yew, Singapore's former prime minister. Their brother Freddy Lee is a former chairman of Vickers Ballas of which Ong was a major shareholder.

  Dennis Lee, the chairman of Singapore food company Cerebos Pacific up until his death in 2003, was another of Lee Kuan Yew's brothers. Dennis's wife, Gloria Lee, is the founder of one of Singapore's most prominent stockbrokerages Kim Eng Securities.

Lee Kuan Yew's mother, Lee Chin Koon, was a cousin of the late Wee Kim Wee, Singapore's former ambassador to Malaysia and later a president of the Republic of Singapore. Lee's son Lee Hsien Yang is a recent past head of Singapore Telecom. Singapore Telecom is controlled by Temasek Holdings, which is headed by Ho Ching, who is maried to Lee Hsien Loong, Lee Hsien Yang's brother, who is prime minister of Singapore.

- Natseel was acquired in 2005 by Tata Steel, part of India's Tata Group which is headed by Ratan Tata. Pallonji Shapoorji Mistry, the largest individual shareholder in Tata Sons, is the father-in-law of Ratan Tata's half-brother Noel Tata. Ratan is very close to Nuslia Wadia, chairman of the massive Bombay Dyeing and Manufacturing Company. In turn, Wadia is the son of Dina Wadia, the only daughter of Mohammad Ali Jinnah, the founder of Pakistan. Tata controls Tata Consulting Services (TCS), India's biggest software company. The wife of Narayana Murthy, chairman of Infosys, one of TCS' main competitors, is the sister of the wife of Gururaj Deshpande, founder of Sycamore Networks.

- The sister of the Gunawan brothers who founded Indonesia's Panin Bank is Suryawaty Lidya, who married Mochtar Riady, the founder of Indonesia's Lippo Group. Mochtar Riady controls the Matahari department store chain, which was founded by Hari Darmawan. Hari is related by marriage to Ong Tjoe Kim, who owns Singapore's Metro department store chain.

- Listed Singapore companies Van der Horst and L&M are controlled by Indonesia's Edward Soeryadjaya. Edward is married to Atilah Rapatriarti, whose brother is married to Sukmawati, a sister of Indonesia's former President Megawati Sukarnoputri. His late first wife also was the adopted daughter of Megawati's father's third wife. L&M director Bambang Sukmonohadi is the father-in-law of Megawati's only daughter.

There are also plenty of linkages between companies. Firms routinely take equity stakes in one another and rarely is any company in Asia completely independent of other companies. Take the time to look at the notes to any annual report of a listed Asian firm and chances are you will see a whole raft of transactions with related parties – companies that you never knew existed. Asia's corporate scene is not so much a constellation of independent bodies as it is in the West but a tightly bound web in which everyone is linked to everyone else. And that has real implications as to how business should be approached in Asia.

Notes

1 As reported in *Asiaweek*, 29 December, 2000.
2 Some of the points in this section have been adapted from a speech given by John Coates, then general manager commercial for Amcor Fibre Packaging Asia, "Amcor's direct investment experience in Indonesia," 31 August, 1995.
3 Adapted in part from a speech given by John Coates, ibid.

Taking the M&A Route?

WHAT'S IN THIS CHAPTER?	
	▷ M&A Madness Part I
	▷ Disillusion
	▷ M&A Madness Part II
	▷ A Seamless Process
	The Pitfalls
	▷ Lafarge Gets Big in Asia
	A Strategic Objective
	The Preparation Period
	Information Gathering
	Acquisition Mania
	Lafarge in Action
	Profitability
	▷ Key Lessons

M&A Madness Part I

The Asian crash of 1997–98 provided an unparalleled opportunity for multi-nationals to move into the region. Foreign companies (not just Western but those from other Asian countries too) had been shut out of whole categories of industries during the boom years of the 1990s. Now they found the door not just unlocked but, in some cases, wide open. Desperate for outside invest-ment to save them from bankruptcy, governments in South Korea and the countries of Southeast Asia declared themselves open for business. For Western firms, outright acquisition seemed to offer the perfect way to bypass all the problems associated with minority shareholdings or joint ventures. Conditions seemed ideal, as pressure from the IMF forced countries in the region to promise privatization and deregulation. When some of its most famous conglomerates began to restructure and put assets up for sale, foreign companies at last saw the opportunity to take real control of their Asian operations, rather than being at the mercy of a local partner.

There is no such thing as a bad asset – bad assets are simply ones that are overpriced. Reality was at last catching up with asset valuations in Asia. With valuations of companies at historic lows, Western managers were granted a once-in-a-lifetime opportunity to buy at bargain-basement rates. In some sectors, such as hotels and cement, assets were actually trading at a significant discount to replacement values.

Under cover of those fashionable slogans, globalization, liberalization and privatization, Western firms set up M&A task forces and began bidding; their moves were heralded with great fanfare in the local and international press, although in fact they often lacked in-depth preparation.

Sometimes the intense competition between Western firms increased prices. One American manager recalled how the ethnic Chinese owner of a firm in the Philippines skilfully played his company off against a European competitor. The American firm thought it was close to a deal, and the US manager was about to leave for the airport to lead the due diligence team in the Philippines when a phone call told him that the Chinese owner had called it off. Three hours later it was on again, then off, and the US manager finally flew out the next day to join a team of 30 people ready to start work. They then sat around for a week while nothing happened, until the Chinese owner finally said the deal was dead. As they later learned, he had actually sold out to the European firm: "He just used us to push the price up."

Further north, meanwhile, the Ministry of Finance and Economy in hitherto xenophobic South Korea announced that foreigners would be allowed to make hostile M&As under a revised law. The country's *chaebol*, the huge conglomerates that had led South Korea's economic miracle, began a series of minuets as one potential foreign partner after another came forward to try and make a deal. Anything seemed possible when, in September 1999, the South Korean government signed an agreement to sell a controlling stake in Korea First Bank to Newbridge Capital Ltd, a US-based investment firm. Analysts hailed the US$525 million deal as the first step in President Kim Dae Jung's efforts to reform the economy. In fact, it was only finalized after Newbridge was indemnified against future debts, an issue over which other deals later faltered. For the moment, however, the party continued.

Figures on M&A activity in Asia between 1998 and 2000 illustrate both foreign investors' initial enthusiasm and their later caution. In 1998, US acquisitions reached a value of $8 billion, double that of the previous year. In 2000, the headline was "Asia hits M&A record," with transactions worth $76.5 billion announced in the first quarter alone, although the figures were inflated by a couple of big telecoms deals.[1] But this turned out to be the peak year. In 2001, the value of announced deals was down 46 percent on the previous year and during the first two months of 2002, *M&A Asia* reported a "tortoise-like pace" compared with the previous two years; the number of European deals was down two-thirds on the previous year, from 37 to 12.[2] The decline continued for the rest of the year, part of the global slump following the events of 9/11 in the US. In the end, the volume of activity in Asia (excluding Japan) for 2002 fell 12.6 percent to US$100.6 billion.

Disillusion

The more cautious approach was the result of mounting disillusion among investors about the value of the assets for which they were bidding. Many potential deals foundered during the process of due diligence, as the real extent of companies' debts became clear. Early in 2002, after 18 months of negotiation, American International Group (AIG), the world's largest insurer, dropped out of a consortium planning to invest US$846 million in Hyundai Securities and two affiliates. This would have been the biggest ever transaction for South Korea's financial services industry, but in the end the prospect of hidden debt traps proved too risky a gamble for AIG to take. The company returned to South Korea in 2003 and finally gained control of Hanaro Telecom, but only after a long and bitter battle with the LG Group, Hanaro's biggest shareholder. Even then, LG said it might take action to try and nullify the shareholder vote in AIG's favor. Another high-profile victim was the US firm Micron Technology, which for six months pursued a possible $3.4 billion merger with Korea's Hynix Semiconductor. The deal would have created the world's largest chip-maker, but it turned out to be yet another long-running saga. Labor unions and minority shareholders held up the deal, which finally collapsed in May 2002.

By then, Western firms had been further discouraged by the lack of progress on restructuring in countries such as Indonesia and Thailand. In the former country, IBRA promised much, but became embroiled in scandal and lacked transparency. It also suffered from regular changes in its senior management – it had seven chairmen in four years – and only achieved one big sale, that of PT Astra International in March 2000.

Three years later, when IBRA finally got around to selling stakes in assets seized from other major conglomerates such as the Salim Group, or the Riady family's Lippo Bank, the sales were overshadowed by rumors that the original owners were in fact buying them back via proxy bidders, and at bargain prices. Not surprisingly, foreign investors were steering well clear of this apparently rigged auction.

Local opposition also played a part in preventing deals – often for years. When, in 1998, Cemex, the Mexican cement group, took a 25 percent equity stake in the Indonesian cement group SMGR (Semen Gresik), it thought it had an agreement with the central government to increase its holding later to a 51 percent controlling share. However, the plan ran into tremendous opposition from the provincial governments involved, notably that of west Sumatra. The projected foreign takeover became part of the wider issue of independence from Jakarta, and to locals seemed to threaten a long-standing source of income and patronage.

When Susilo Bambang Yudhoyono became president in 2004, he declared he wanted to make Indonesia a country where foreigners could do business, and promised to resolve the Cemex impasse and another long-running dispute involving ExxonMobil within 100 days. Cemex finally hoped for a settlement, but no. The opposition of managers, workers and local politicians proved as strong as ever and, over a year later, Cemex was still waiting. While the struggle continued, Cemex was unable to institute any reforms in the companies and was forced to watch its investment dwindle.

The ExxonMobil deal, which was being blocked by the state oil company Pertamina, was finally resolved after only a six-year delay. Pertamina's tactics to delay an extension (first discussed in 2001) of a contract to develop vital oilfields were a classic example of the frustrations of operating in Indonesia: "They say 'OK' in front of the government and when they go back to the office they are just trying to buy time so they can do what they want."[3] In March 2006, the two sides finally signed a deal, but only after the president had sacked half Pertamina's bosses.

Hostility to foreign investment has also clouded deals in Thailand and South Korea, where shareholders and unions have constantly combined to vilify Western firms and defeat acquisition attempts. As one analyst observed: "The Koreans don't see any of the deals as win–win. They think that if the foreigners get it, then Korea is losing."

The sad truth is that the majority of M&A deals in Asia fall far short of their promise and unravel – sometimes in spectacular fashion. China in particular, the biggest hunting ground for M&A targets, has been the scene of many well-documented disasters (see Strategy 24). Some of the highest profile deals have become major disappointments for acquirers and their shareholders. Too often, the original forecasts have had to be drastically reduced, and what was touted as a new global contender turns out to be something rather less. The high failure rate is not, however, just an Asian phenomenon; many M&A deals in the West also end in tears. According to research carried out by academics and consultants, 60–70 percent of *all* mergers fail, 67 percent of them in the first five years.[4]

M&A Madness Part II

Perhaps surprisingly given the above, by October 2005, banner headlines were again announcing "Asia M&A heads for new record" – already 57 percent up on the whole of the previous year.[5] Investment bankers were jubilant, forecasting "a bull run." The rise was due to strong growth in China, plus a large number of deals in South Korea. A triumph of hope over experience, or a sign that Western companies were confident that the business landscape was now more favorable?

Sadly not. For behind the figures lay the information that many of the South Korean deals, for example, were being "driven by foreigners selling out of investments made in the aftermath of the 1997–98 Asian financial crisis."[6] One of those exiting the country was Newbridge Capital, which sold Korea First Bank to Standard Chartered for US$3.2 billion. Neither had other inhibiting factors disappeared. In 2006, fervent opposition to the takeover bid of the US investor Carl Icahn for the tobacco and ginseng company KT&G forced the South Korean government to reassure foreign investors yet again that they were welcome. And Cemex was still waiting as the Indonesian government announced once more that it was trying to nego-tiate a settlement. The Mexican company's patience finally ran out and, in May 2006, it was set to sell its stake to a local group and exit the country. If the whole sorry muddle was not a discouraging enough signal to would-be investors, even this attempt at a clean break was threatened by the maneu-verings of local politicians who clamored to sell the stake to a consortium of SOEs. An agreement was finally reached in July 2006. "I think Cemex is very happy to be leaving Indonesia," commented one local executive.[7]

Even Vietnam, by then seen as the next favorable place for investment, given its low-cost but skilled labor force, saw industrial action breaking out. In January 2006, a workers' protest over wages and conditions was only settled by a rise in the minimum wage in foreign-owned factories. This led the European Chamber of Commerce to write and remind the Vietnamese prime minister that investors had gone to Vietnam because "the workforce is not prone to industrial action."

Despite all this, M&A figures show that Western companies remain upbeat about the long-term prospects for the region as a whole, although in the short term, their main efforts will undoubtedly continue to focus on China. With sectors such as banking and financial services scheduled to open up to comply with WTO commitments, the Chinese magnet still exercises a powerful attraction. However, foreign investors should weigh all the risks fully before jumping at the first acquisition target that appears.

One that did so was a US private equity firm that entered negotiations to acquire the assets of a Chinese manufacturer in a city north of Hong Kong. At first it seemed like a dream deal. The target made products popular in the US and, with annual revenues of about US$25 million and earnings before interest, tax depreciation and amortization (EBITDA) of around US$6 million, the US$31 million price tag seemed reasonable. However, before the deal was actually signed, a number of fault lines appeared that made the US buyer pause:

- First was the discovery that the manufacturing operation was actually located in an area zoned for agricultural use only. Although assured that such violations were common in China, and that the local authorities had never yet raised objections, the buyer was concerned.

- Next it emerged that the target company's real estate included many long-term ground leases, some due to expire within the next year. The seller maintained that renewing the leases would not be a problem but, again, the buyer was unconvinced. He asked the Chinese seller to covenant to locate new land if the leases were not renewed. He also asked for a reduction in the price – which was refused.

- Midway through the negotiations, the buyer realized that the seller's financials were audited based on generally accepted accounting practices (GAAP) in Hong Kong, which differed from the US GAAP that the buyer had used to evaluate the company. The buyer asked the seller to represent and warrant that the financials were in accordance with US GAAP. The seller refused.

- The Chinese company had unpaid unemployment taxes. The seller argued that in China it was common practice to negotiate payment only when local officials asked. The buyer became even more uneasy. This was not how it was done in the US.

In the event, the buyer backed out of the deal. He was not reassured by promises that local officials would continue to treat him as they had the Chinese owner, and he was uncomfortable with the perceived risk in such an unfamiliar business environment. Perhaps by doing so he lost an excellent opportunity. Or perhaps he avoided heavy losses and a big headache. But at least he realized the extent of the gulf between local practices and those in the US and decided the deal was not for him. Other companies might benefit from adopting a little bit of his caution when assessing their own M&A targets.[8]

A Seamless Process

Fortunately, many multinationals have succeeded in making a good deal, and are busy implementing post-acquisition strategies to bring their new assets up to speed. What did they do so right? What are the "dos and don'ts" of making an acquisition? Where are the most common pitfalls?

Ideally, the acquisition process should be a seamless one, in which the end is foreseen and planned for from the beginning. From target to post-merger integration (PMI) should be one long process in which what is done before the deal is as important as what happens during any negotiations. What you do after – the PMI plan – should emerge, almost by osmosis, along the way. Doing one stage at a time with different sets of people involved works against the possibility of this happening. Unfortunately, due to time pressures or lack of people experienced in the acquisition process, it is the way many companies act.

The Pitfalls

A lack of clear vision

Why are we doing this? Where is the strategic fit? What synergies do we expect from it? What do we want to gain – market share, a strategic foothold or economies of scale?

Without satisfactory answers to questions such as these, companies will be groping in the dark. The logic of going ahead with an acquisition must be clear and compelling. Along with this go realistic expectations about what can be achieved. This in turn implies careful planning to identify targets that fit into the company's overall strategy. Grabbing at an apparent bargain for the sake of it spells disaster from the start.

Inadequate due diligence

Doing due diligence does not, of course, mean merely checking out the books, although in a region known for creative accounting (a PwC study found that South Korea, for example, had one of the most opaque standards of accounting and corporate governance of the 35 countries it surveyed), this is essential.[9] One experienced member of an international due diligence team remarked that he often had to go by instinct, backed by an assessment of the plant or businesses for sale, how much it would take to get factories up to speed, current market prices for products and so on. But sometimes, he said, "You just shut your eyes and go for it."

Different valuations are another common reason for deals failing. During the ongoing negotiations between General Motors (GM) and Daewoo, when GM tried to reduce the price, the US partners reportedly complained that the Korean negotiators thought not of the company's present value, but how much they had invested in the past. The Koreans complained that the Americans were going to get valuable assets at far below equity. In fact Ford, the original preferred bidder for Daewoo, had already closed talks after a closer inspection of the books. But GM was convinced it had sound strategic reasons for the deal and pressed on. Negotiations on price between GM and Daewoo dragged out the deal for two years. There were rumors that the GM team had uncovered W2 trillion of contingent debt, something denied by the Daewoo team, who accused GM of using the rumors as leverage to reduce the price. The deal was finally signed in April 2002, after both sides had made concessions. In Asia, you can never overdo due diligence.

Poor cultural due diligence

In Asia, due diligence must also include the cultural aspects of the deal – the human resources (HR) available to both sides, the management culture and the cultural fit. Is there likely to be a clash between the values and beliefs of the two sides that will cause problems? Will good staff stay to work for the new owners? Research has consistently underlined the crucial role of HR issues in the outcome of the acquisition process. For example, an impression of opportunistic buying rather than a commitment to build something for the future will not help your cause. In 1998, Thailand's Bank of Asia reportedly chose ABN Amro as its new majority shareholder because it agreed to keep the bank's name and top executives and so "left it with its dignity intact." Such cultural sensitivity can go a long way to give you the good publicity to clinch a negotiation and get off to a good start in the relationship. Sadly, although ABN Amro avoided this pitfall, other problems eventually caused the demise of the venture at the end of 2004.

In many companies, the cultural process is spearheaded by the HR division, which consolidates all the information on the target company and produces a list of key issues for due diligence. A useful move is for members of the due diligence team to study the local culture to learn what to say and how to act before they go into the company. For this, local consultants can be used.

A due diligence team is usually made up of experienced staff in systems, HR, finance, acquisitions, commercial, operations and administration, selected by head office. The key is to take the best from each area and fly them in for the time it takes (anything from a few weeks to 18 months) to carry out the procedure. The information collection should be a two-way process; the targeted company needs to learn about the acquirers – why it is interested in the company and what it hopes to achieve if and when it takes over.

The importance of cultural knowledge and sensitivity is illustrated by the following true story. One experienced due diligence finance director was sent out to Indonesia to finalize a deal. After a few hours on his first day at the potential acquisition firm, he left his team working to go and answer a call of nature. Following the signs down a series of narrow corridors, he came to what he assumed was the washroom. He looked through a door and saw that the room contained a pipe running round the wall, with holes at regular intervals through which passed running water into a gutter. He relieved himself and returned to work. When he arrived the next morning, it was to find that the workforce had called a huge demonstration, and that the owner was threatening to call off the deal because "someone had urinated in the room where the Moslem workers wash before going to prayers."

Poor integration

Poor integration stems from mistakes made at the beginning of the process. Perhaps the company did not take care to understand fully how the assets would fit, perhaps it bought at too high a price, perhaps early management contacts were hostile, in which case the PMI phase will fail. To avoid this, work to a clear PMI strategy, covering all the key issues thrown up during the negotiating process, using your best and most experienced managers. The culmination should be the integration of the acquisition into your regional and global structures.

Finally, take a long-term – seven–ten years – Asian view of your investment. It will demonstrate that you are beginning to understand the culture.

What may pass unnoticed in all this emphasis on Western acquisitions is the amount of M&A activity taking place among Asian companies. New giants are being created in China, and domestic deals in many countries of the region are creating strong competitors for the future, both in Asian and Western markets. Western companies cannot afford to be left out, or continue making such a mess of their acquisitions. With M&A activity in southeast Asia on the rise again following the record US$5 billion paid by Philip Morris in 2005 to acquire Sampoerna, an Indonesian clove cigarette company, perhaps they might usefully study the following business case of how one European company made an acquisition that, up until today, seemed to work.

Lafarge Gets Big in Asia

A Strategic Objective

In the aftermath of Asia's economic crisis, Lafarge,[10] the French construction group, took part in an assault on cement manufacturing companies in the region, which had become the objects of a fierce acquisition battle between the largest Western cement producers. Lafarge had less exposure to emerging markets than its nearest competitors, such as the UK-based Blue Circle or the Swiss group Holderbank (later Holcim). Consequently, how to be first in any acquisition spree that came along was a key preoccupation of the global strategists at the Lafarge headquarters in Paris.

The Preparation Period

Although it had been present in Southeast Asia since the 1980s when it opened an office in Singapore, the region's weight within the Lafarge portfolio remained minute. During the 1990s, with the industry growing at 10 percent annually, the company decided to step up its efforts there, setting up industrial facilities and opening sales offices. However, along with other multinational players, it had concluded that, pre-crisis, acquisitions were too expensive in ASEAN, and virtually impossible in northern Asia. The Southeast Asian cement manufacturers were doing so well that they had no reason to sell or take a partner.

Information Gathering

During these years, the HQ strategy team kept a close eye on the region, studying the main players, building up a network of relationships and compiling a dossier on the dynamics of each market. Systematically, its managers gathered industry knowledge specific to each country – the intensity of the competition, the evolution of prices, whether they were controlled by the government (in which case deregulation might be an imminent possibility) and so on. They identified where the local industry was protected by import bans or tariffs, and made some preliminary calculations about how prices were likely to evolve. Finally, they ranked the countries of the region in order of attractiveness for investment.

As a result, Lafarge probably knew the region's markets far better than any of the local producers, who had no time for such careful calculations. They were reveling in the growth conditions they were experiencing, busy counting their profits and expanding like there was no tomorrow with the help of huge bank loans. But Lafarge understood that the oversupply situation building up in the region would sooner or later lead to a collapse in prices. Its planners counted on making acquisitions during this counter-cycle.

In 1996, a new business development manager was sent to Singapore to study the markets in greater depth. He was not surprised to see acquaintances from every other big cement company setting up offices to carry out the same task. They all smelled big profits in the air, if only they could get access to the local markets.

When it arrived, the 1997–98 economic crisis made the overcapacity problem far more severe for the locals, and acquisition easier for foreign firms. In this case, events played straight into their hands.

Acquisition Mania

The regional economic crisis and subsequent downturn completely changed the game for foreign players such as Lafarge. The local producers found themselves caught in a trap of their own making. They had all borrowed heavily – mostly in dollars – in order to fund expansion. When the crisis came, they were hit by a triple whammy. Their hard currency debts exploded in local currency terms and yet most of their earnings were in local currencies. The sector had borrowed on the basis that it would continue to experience high growth, but instead it experienced a sharp contraction. And the local currency earnings themselves collapsed. Asia's cement firms had been walking a narrow path between growth and debt, and they now found themselves utterly overwhelmed by events that pushed most of them into insolvency. The only hope for most was to find a rich investor.

The usual outcome of this would be to allow foreign firms to pick up such failing companies for a song but, in fact, the intensity of the competition between the multinationals to complete deals while the window of opportunity was open led to far higher acquisition costs. And this despite the fact that cheap exports from neighboring countries were flooding in, making overcapacity even worse. Taiwan and Japan were dumping their excess, China was pushing up its own cement production; it was a frenzied time. So although the region's economies were collapsing, the cement industry was at a standstill and prices were dropping like stones – there were no cheap bargains to be had.

Lafarge in Action

Its thorough study of the region had given Lafarge a very good idea of which companies it was really interested in. Its business development team had already identified those with the right fundamentals, that is, those with sound infrastructure and potential for growth when cement demand once more turned around.

So, once the crisis took effect, the team only had to get out the list, check the targets and see what was available. In fact, during the first months of panic, Lafarge had many calls from cement firms throughout the region, begging it to take a share or buy them out. But it neither made a move nor committed itself until the local company had been checked against its hit list, and several were rejected straightaway. As soon as anyone called, the head of the Lafarge team knew who they were and whether he was interested in them or not.

In making its acquisitions, Lafarge used a variety of approaches, depending on the circumstances and the information in the dossiers it had built up. In some cases, it went for a strategic partnership with a company that wanted someone to share its debts, and took an equity stake. Alternatively, in the case of local companies that had only moved into cement as an opportunistic move, Lafarge bought them outright. There were different patterns and Lafarge adapted to each individual case.

Once Lafarge decided to move, its managers took care to handle negotiations as sensitively as possible. Since cement was a young industry in the region, many of the founding fathers were still in charge of the target companies. Having done their cultural due diligence, the Lafarge team was well aware of what it meant in terms of loss of face for such a family to sell out, so they treated them with appropriate deference and sensitivity. They spent time with the heads of these companies to talk through the deal and convince them of the wisdom of taking a strategic partner. In view of all the bad publicity in some countries about Westerners being sharks coming to gobble them up, this was very important. Lafarge argued that it was the only sensible decision to take, and especially emphasized the need to keep local managers in place, since they knew the market and its own managers did not. Its catch phrase was "Let's build something together for the future." Once the deal was done, the Lafarge managers moved very circumspectly, always leaving the local management to continue running the plants – as long as they were good.

The negotiations were run from the Lafarge office in Singapore, backed by the HQ team that followed progress from Paris. Lafarge had one local and three expatriate managers on the ground, but once the due diligence stage was reached, HQ sent in finance, human and legal resources to compile as complete a picture as possible of the target company within the time limit.

These people, too, were keenly aware that, in Asia, due diligence was another part of the relationship-building exercise, during which it was important to show that they understood the company. The team leader emphasized to those carrying out the due diligence process: "This is a polite and culturally sensitive exercise, don't act like tax inspectors!" The Lafarge philosophy was that the success of the due diligence process depended as much on what you did before the deal as after – it was the culmination of all your efforts. So the time its managers spent getting to know the company and building up trust was not wasted and, of course, by doing it this way, they rarely missed anything.

Inevitably, there were some hard negotiations on price. The Lafarge valuation included a calculation of the quality of the plant – how expensive it would be to keep it going while it got production prices down and so on. Generally, the team had already identified where improvements could be made in its investment targets and these were packaged ready to hand on to the post-acquisition team. These were based on the objectives of reducing production costs and improving the quality of the asset, so the plant would be ready for action once demand rose again.

Profitability

The Lafarge strategy in the region was both aggressive and cautious, and followed the clear investment guidelines laid down by head office. The golden rule for this was, first and foremost, profitability. Lafarge has very stringent profitability criteria for any acquisition; it must be EVA (economic value added) positive within three years. If the business development team did not believe this could be achieved, it would not make the deal. Thus Lafarge turned down possible acquisitions in Malaysia and

Thailand because they did not meet this requirement. Lafarge was interested in expansion, but not at any price.

Its strategy was also guided by the need to participate in the consolidation of a market, which was being whittled down to a few major players, of whom Lafarge was clearly determined to be number one. But at the same time, those acquisitions had to provide synergies with positions it already held, synergies either within the local domestic market or through trading between various countries in order to produce best delivered costs. Finally, Lafarge looked for future growth possibilities – companies with good limestone reserves that would allow future low-cost expansion.

Knowing that the present oversupply situation in Asia would not vanish overnight, Lafarge planned to use the intervening time to make sure that the integration process went smoothly. The aim was to ensure that its new plants were running as efficiently as possible when the market picked up. Each country would recover in its own time. In the meantime, Lafarge continued to build up its assets in order to become Big in Asia.

Key Lessons

■ Set a clear strategic direction
■ Evaluate potential targets carefully:
  ■ Their business portfolio
  ■ Their human resources
  ■ Their potential profitability
■ Define objectives
■ Decide on negotiation strategy and tactics
■ Fully brief the financial and cultural due diligence team
■ Implement a seamless process, from target to PMI.

Notes

1 *Financial Times*, "Asia hits M&A record," 11 April, 2000, p18.
2 *M&A Asia*, "Recent deals & joint ventures," February 2002, pp16, 19.
3 *Financial Times*, "Exxon is blocked on Indonesian venture," 16 September, 2005 p5.
4 *Financial Times*, "Exposing the truth behind merger myths," 25 March, 2002, p30.
5 *Financial Times*, "Asia M&A heads for new record," 17 October, 2005 p23.
6 *Wall Street Journal Europe*, "Asian deals extend past China," 9 May, 2005, pA6.
7 *Financial Times*, "Cemex retreats from Indonesia with sale of stake," 25 July, 2006.
8 *China Business Review*, "Chinese M&A: Green light or red flag?," N.T. Avedissian, Sept–Oct 2005, pp26–7.
9 *The Economist*, "Korean murk," 31 March, 2001, pp89–90.
10 Taken from "Lafarge in Asia," a case study by Charlotte Butler and Professor Peter Williamson, INSEAD-EAC, 2001.

Managing Partnerships with Southeast Asian Firms

WHAT'S IN THIS CHAPTER?

▷ Horror Stories
▷ Why a Partnership?
▷ Understanding the Chinese Family Firm
    A New Generation
▷ Partners to Avoid
▷ Know the Key Players
    PT Astra International
▷ Key Factors in a Partnership
    Clear Objectives
    Shared Objectives
    Control
    Leverage your Power
    Build up Trust and Commitment
    Know When to Withdraw
▷ Key Lessons

Horror Stories

Whenever a group of Western managers with Asian experience gather together, talk almost invariably turns to horror stories about Asian firms they have known and the pitfalls of doing business with them. This is because, for many Western companies, managing business relationships in Southeast Asia proves to be a confusing, frustrating and mostly loss-making affair. Yet success in managing these relationships will be critical to the outcome of your Asian investment.

In great part, this attitude stems from the feeling of powerlessness that overcomes many Western businesspeople during their everyday transactions in Asia, whether they are dealing with joint venture partners, suppliers, distributors, local politicians or ministry officials, customs people or bankers. This helplessness in turn arises from their discomfort at operating in such a foreign environment. The best antidote to this is to forge your own competitive edge, one that will give you sufficient power to balance this otherwise unequal relationship. Unfortunately, this comes only after gaining a working knowledge of Asia's very different business culture. Before you can join with corporate Asia successfully, you must understand the firms and, most importantly, the people behind them.

Why a Partnership?

For most firms, their experience of managing relationships in Asia comes from being in some kind of strategic alliance or partnership with a local firm. For many years, the most popular route to enter Asia has been via a joint venture. In many countries, this was the only legal way open to foreign firms. More practically, it was the only way that gave any hope of gaining access to protected or difficult markets. Moving into such unknown territory, it made sense to take a local partner to spread the risk and provide the capabilities and resources lacking in the foreign firm. These capabilities included, most famously, access to the networks or *guanxi* – political and business – necessary to negotiate with local politicians or officials to gain licenses or operating concessions, and to deal with what were often euphemistically termed "speedy service" payments. A local partner could also provide access to marketing and distribution networks and the workers and managers to run them. In return, Asian companies usually sought access to technology and an injection of financial resources, although in theory the financial burden was shared by the partners. In summary, Western firms provided the cash and the locals the connections.

Such partnerships had the advantage of providing a learning curve for the foreign company involved. Over the years they would build up experience of the business environment and, once they had learned the ropes, they could either branch out on their own with a wholly owned operation or perhaps buy the partnership out, so taking over a going concern they knew well.

However, this theory rarely worked in practice. Many partnerships fell short of their promise; research shows that over 70 percent ended in failure within 10 years. The most common reason for failure was a mismatch between the foreign investor and the local partner or, as a Japanese saying puts it more picturesquely, because the two partners found themselves "lying in the same bed but dreaming different dreams." Many joint ventures formed in the aftermath of the Asian economic crisis were based on necessity – the desperation of the Asian partner to find a foreign savior – rather than any shared vision or real synergies. Inevitably, like many marriages made in haste, they later fell apart.

For the majority of Western companies entering Southeast Asia, the partner dreaming different dreams was one of the local Chinese family-owned and managed firms that accounted for between half and three-quarters of all listed companies on the stock exchanges in Hong Kong, Taiwan and Southeast Asia. The unique nature of these firms was beyond the experience of most Western businesspeople, and the secretive way in which they operated militated against any balanced relationship between the partners from the start. Building up the trust and commitment required for a successful relationship required a different mindset in order to understand this very different business model. Unfortunately, by the time most foreign firms grasped this essential fact, it was too late and the relationship had irretrievably broken down. Therefore an understanding of how these firms operate, both pre-crisis and since, is important to any firm hoping to become Big in Asia.

Understanding the Chinese Family Firm

The founders of most of the sprawling conglomerates that dominated business in Southeast Asia were ethnic Chinese entrepreneurs. Starting out as traders with very little during the 1970s or earlier, they built up diversified empires assisted by strong *guanxi* – the close political and business connections that brought them opportunities and sometimes even concessions and monopolies.

Power in these conglomerates was firmly centralized in the hands of the founder. Surrounding him, the senior management ranks were the preserve of close family members (sons and daughters, brothers and nephews) or old friends. The latter group was usually there not by virtue of any particular management skills, but because they had been with the patriarch from the early days, when life was hard, and had been part of the early struggles when the founder was making the deals that helped to make his fortune. This shared history as schoolmates or fellow traders guaranteed them a place in the sun for life, part of the trusted inner clan.

As Western managers would eventually discover to their great frustration, however powerful they might be in their own milieu, rarely could

they be part of this magic circle. They would always be heard with courtesy, but would never be able to influence key decisions. Any close relationship would have to be built up slowly, over time, as Douglas Daft,
chairman of Coca-Cola explained when speaking of his relationship with
Robert Kuok, former chairman of Hong Kong-based Kerry Holdings,
which was one of Coke's major bottling partners in China:

> We had a lot of common ground and, I think, liked each other. That led to the
> ability to discuss and develop a business relationship. Essentially that relationship
> was on trust ... without that relationship it would have been months of dialogue
> between parties at different levels to reach an agreement on the way the
> business would be structured. [1]

However, to reach that level of trust required a heavy investment of time
and effort that few Western managers were able to make.

The autocratic and centralized leadership style also came as a rude
surprise to many Western managers. Business meetings, for example,
tended to be not so much open discussions of financial forecasts or
strategic issues but the occasion for rubber stamping a decision already
taken by the inner circle. One Western businessman recalled his shock
at the sheer terror inspired by one patriarch at meetings, even when
discussing relatively non-contentious issues. Bullies are not unknown in
Western business circles, but the atmosphere of fear around the table, he
recalled, was palpable. The local managers were so intimidated that
they did not dare to tell the truth about the progress of a project, or the
fact that the target date for completion might be missed. Another time,
there was complete silence, nobody spoke until the chief had made his
own opinion clear, after which everyone rushed to agree with it. Alternatively, when the head of the firm tried the tactic of waiting to speak
last in a debate so as not to influence the decision, everyone could see
the knuckles of his hand going white with the effort to stop interrupting.
On one occasion, everyone turned up for an 8am meeting but the chief
was delayed. Nobody dared move until 1pm, when the meeting was
finally canceled.

Another characteristic that could mislead Western firms was the lack
of ostentation shown by many of the most successful founders. In the
West, success tends to be obvious, with expensive offices, perhaps even
a corporate jet; in Asia, many of the richest men in the region often keep
a low profile. This is because coming from poor backgrounds and being
a minority in countries where they have often been scapegoats and
subject to violence when the hard times came – as occurred in Indonesia

at the fall of Soeharto – they have learned to be discreet about parading their wealth, so that foreign firms can be deceived about the true extent of their resources.

For many years one very powerful and successful ethnic Chinese entrepreneur kept his head office in a run-down part of town. Its anonymous entrance was in a busy commercial street, above a grocery store. To reach the offices, visitors were forced to climb a rickety, uneven staircase, and frequently found themselves tripping on steps added in at random to avoid the total number of stairs amounting to an unlucky number. A walk through a narrow passage led to a bare meeting room, whose decoration reflected utility rather than gloss, and through whose thin partition walls could be heard the clack of typewriters and shouting. Tea was served by people who could occasionally be seen shuffling round in carpet slippers.

Such an alien context prevented several would-be investors accepting a partnership with the entrepreneur. But such cultural dissonance is part and parcel of Asia, and can cause opportunities to be missed. Lacking the cultural reference to assess such a context, Westerners tend to judge on external appearance alone, and so they severely underestimated the substance behind the run-down office. As the entrepreneur observed: "They never understood how things are done in our part of the world." Cynically, he added that later, when his entourage had moved into a brand new plaza, built by himself in the central part of town, the queue of applicants for a partnership was a long one. Still, none of this need imply that Western businesspeople are necessarily inept. When corporate transparency is poor, the state of a company's offices might become a proxy for its creditworthiness, albeit an obviously poor one.

The culture of secrecy that characterizes ethnic Chinese firms is another hurdle that Westerners have had to face. It meant that the key facet of the relationship would be ignorance on the part of the foreign investor about the local partner's businesses, particularly his financial affairs and the true extent of his business interests. Often, the original stake on which the founder's fortune was based came from trading deals, made quickly with money borrowed from family or friends. Money came in and went out, and only the founder knew how many deals were cooking at a time. This habit of not letting the left hand know what the right was doing died hard, and made it almost impossible for foreign investors to track the route of any investment meant for a joint venture operation, even in companies known for their integrity. As one Western banker observed of such companies:

> They could lose anything anywhere, and you could drive yourself nuts trying to follow investment A through to B via C and D, not to mention E and F.

However, the two most worrying practices for Westerners have been the cronyism and nepotism associated with their way of doing business. The practice of giving contracts, jobs or easy loans to friends, associates and other well-connected individuals is again something foreign firms have found hard to accept in their partners. Post-crisis, these practices were condemned and the need to reform the Asian way of doing business widely discussed. The new emphasis was to be on restructuring, focus and professional management, transparency and corporate governance. However, the definition of these in a Southeast Asian context may not be immediately recognizable to Western businessmen. When Thaksin Shinawatra became prime minister of Thailand in 2001, he promised to bring "CEO-style management to government." Few observers, apart perhaps from his family and business friends, would claim that his subsequent performance has brought transparency and corporate governance to the country's political or business affairs.

A New Generation

For the implementation of these desirable outcomes, many put their faith in the new generation beginning to take over from their founding fathers, or creating their own empires. Educated in Europe and the US, usually with MBA qualifications, foreign partners have generally found them easier to deal with, since they share a common vocabulary and tend to be more open to outside investment. The handover of power to the next generation has in some cases been hastened by changing technology and the need for firms to become more internationally competitive. The older generation of entrepreneurs who founded the firms tend to be less comfortable with high-tech projects and financial services, or dealing with non-Chinese partners, than their offspring.

However, the instincts of many of these younger men, just like their fathers, are still to trust schoolmates and family members. In 2002, Fred Ma was appointed group chief financial officer of PCCW, founded by Richard Li, second son of Li Ka-Shing. Ma, who had joined the company in May 2001, replaced one of the most senior men to stay on after the takeover of C&W in August 2000. A Hong Kong native, Ma attended the University of Hong Kong at the same time as Anthony Leung, Hong Kong's financial secretary. The two are still friends and golf partners, together with Canning Fok, group MD at Li's father's company, Hutchison Whampoa.

Moreover, in many cases, although their fathers have "retired" from business, deference to age means that the old patriarch still exerts great influence. In one sense, they never retire – the culture in which they operate prohibits it. Robert Kuok, the Malaysian-Chinese tycoon and founder of Hong Kong-based Kerry Holdings has an empire that includes the international hotel chain Shangri-La. An international trader in commodities, the group also has interests in the media and property development and a manufacturing base in China. In theory, Kuok retired and handed over key businesses to his two sons, two nephews and a nephew-in-law. However, he remains head of the steering committee that watches over the group. Li Ka-shing, founder of Hong Kong's Cheung Kong Holdings, has appointed his son Victor to succeed him, but nobody doubts that he will remain the guiding power as long as he lives. Dhanin Chearavanont, head of the Thai agribusiness colossus Charoen Pokphand, still dominates the two businesses, cable TV and telecoms, which, theoretically, he has given to his two sons to head and develop.

Contracts can still be blocked by cronyism, things still get done through relationships, just as the old school tie connects managers in the UK or the meritocracy of the *grandes écoles* executives in France. Asian businessmen still use their connections to achieve their goals, and trust only their family and a close circle of old friends.

So despite the sale of some assets and superficial restructuring, many of the same patterns of doing business are still discernible, even post-1997. The pressure of the old guard, however discredited, is still immense, as the slowing or reversal of reform attempts in Indonesia and Thailand demonstrates. Prachai Leophairatana, the founder of Thai Petrochemical Industries (TPI), resisted every step of the way the financial restructuring of his empire, in debt to the tune of US$3.7 billion and declared insolvent in 2000. When the Western accountant met 3,000 of his employees to explain the restructuring plan, he discovered that the microphone had been turned off and, when he did speak, he was heckled. Before a meeting of the TPI creditors, thousands of TPI employees turned up, waving banners castigating "Norman the bloodsucker."[2] In October 2004, seven years after its indebtedness first appeared, Prachai was still battling to keep control of the cement company, denouncing the restructuring plan as "unfair" and demanding to be given back management of TPI. Building a positive relationship with such determined businesspeople is not easy.

So, once you have understood the rules of the game, how do you build a more equal and lasting partnership in the future? One of the keys is to select the right partner in the first place.

Partners to Avoid

Experience has shown that, in Southeast Asia, partnership with state-run companies, or with powerful political or military figures can be time-wasting and unexpectedly costly. The former can also bring problems that you may be unable to resolve, such as a corporate culture that is simply too different from yours. The latter will always have the upper hand, and should the relationship deteriorate seriously, they may mobilize regulatory, legislative and even judicial enforcement against you. Moreover, political allegiances may change and you could easily find yourself tied in with the wrong side.

Similarly, it can be safer to avoid government projects. Governments and their agencies are often only interested in gaining access to technological expertise, and may drop you as soon as it becomes convenient, or may break undertakings if under financial pressure, as has been the case in Indonesia (see Strategy 25 for more on this.)

By and large, the safest strategy is to maintain good relations with the host government of the country you are in but, if you have the choice, never enter into a joint venture with it or its agencies.

Know the Key Players

Take time to look at the key players in the region. The best approach by far when it comes to forging the right links in Southeast Asia is either to link up with someone who has real business strength and a genuine interest in making the relationship work or, alternatively, with someone who may be an up-and-coming power and has a small but strategic business. If you get in early with such budding entrepreneurs, you will have a friend for life and grow with them.

Knowing who the key players are in the region is the first step in selecting a suitable partner. This is not always easy. Many are notoriously publicity shy. Successful Western businesspeople might write books and give interviews to the media, but you will be unlikely to pick up Li Ka-Shing's top 10 business tips at WHSmith in Singapore's Changi Airport.

Therefore, collecting good information on any potential partner and the business context is essential (see Strategies 1 and 7). Look at the skill base of its managers, its relationship with the government (which may be a positive or negative factor) its financial credibility and so on. Talk to bankers, suppliers, customers, competitors and other foreign investors as much as you can. Such preparation will pay off, as Tesco found when it entered the Thai food retail market via a partnership with the Charoen Pokphand (CP) Group, one of Thailand's biggest conglomerates. A well-known joke relates that "the Thai civil service rankings are known as C levels, with C1 being the lowest, then C2 up to C11. After C11 comes CP.[3] The joke circulated after yet another government official left the Thai civil service to join CP, and illustrates the nature of the group's excellent connections. Tesco took the CP stake only after it had sent out four teams to explore opportunities in Thailand, Taiwan, Malaysia and South Korea. The partnership worked well; Tesco helped CP to develop a competence in food processing and Tesco got the marketing and distribution for its superstores business. Everyone gained, which is how joint ventures should work, but rarely do.

Much of this information will, of course, be circumstantial and difficult to verify, given the secretive nature of the beast. The only financial accounts that you can trust will be those of any publicly listed companies, which tend to be newly established and so "clean." But remember that the boundary between public and private assets is blurred, and that the most profitable companies in any group typically will be wholly under family control. However, what will be public knowledge is their past record in conducting relationships with foreign partners. If you find a company that has successfully sustained a number of long-standing joint ventures and has built up the business of both themselves and their partner, it is surely a safer bet than most. One of the better known groups that has managed relationships successfully with outside firms for many years is Indonesia's PT Astra International.

PT Astra International

In Indonesia, a long preferred joint venture partner has been Indonesia's PT Astra. In the murky political and business environment of that country, Astra, with its marketing and distribution expertise, has shone like a beacon for many foreign firms seeking to enter the country. Astra also had the advantage of a professional management, trained in both Japanese and Western business methods. It has long been one of Southeast Asia's most admired companies.[4]

Known for keeping its distance from the government circle, Astra grew to be the second biggest conglomerate in Indonesia through long-running joint ventures with Japanese firms such as Toyota, Honda, Komatsu, Daihatsu, Fuji and Xerox, plus the North American-based GE Credit

Corporation and Digital Corporation, all the main European auto manufacturers and Taiwanese and South Korean firms. For anyone contemplating a partnership in Indonesia, Astra was the first port of call.

Astra chose its partners carefully, selecting the best one for the industry it wished to enter and learn about. Its skill in conducting these relationships was demonstrated by the fact that although many of the ventures began in the 1970s, they were still going strong over 30 years later, despite the political ups and downs of both the company and the country. The group also had long-standing and excellent relations with foreign bankers, such as Citibank, Chase Manhattan, Société Générale, Nomura Securities, and was consistently singled out as the only company they could trust and do business with. Post-crisis, a stake in Astra that had been seized from delinquent debtors was the first big sale actually completed by IBRA, a 23 percent slice going to Singapore's Cycle & Carriage Ltd. The strength of the company was demonstrated by the fact that there were several consortia of bidders, all eager to buy a group with such a good record and strong business partnerships. It was, and remains, Indonesia's only genuinely blue-chip, private sector company; its flagship Toyota and Honda ventures still dominating the auto and motorcycle markets and attracting substantial investment from them.

Key Factors in a Partnership

Clear Objectives

Before entering any partnership, it is important to know exactly what you hope to gain from it. Is it a short-term opportunistic move, or a long-term investment to build a position in the market? Is it a preparatory stage for an acquisition or expansion, do you hope to buy out the partner eventually and take over, or sell your stake at a profit?

The answer will determine both the size of your investment and the strategy you adopt. Westerners tend to think primarily in financial terms. They have their shareholders to please and so usually their key measure for success is how long it will take to achieve profitability. Few can afford to lose money over a long period if a partnership turns out badly. So decide how big a gamble to make at the beginning, and have an exit strategy prepared if it all goes wrong.

Shared Objectives

When you have decided your own objectives, make sure your partner shares them. Otherwise, failure and disillusionment is inevitable. When the US investment bank Goldman Sachs pulled out of a joint venture with the Thai Dusit Thani hotel group in 2003, it blamed "differences in strategic vision." In 2002, France Telecom's mobile phone unit Orange thought it had made the perfect match with Thailand's TelecomAsia. Orange would provide the marketing and technological expertise, TelecomAsia the local knowledge and *guanxi*. Two years later, the venture fell apart over "competing strategic visions between its Thai and Western managers."[5]

Similarly, remember that keeping their shareholders happy is a Western obsession that family-owned firms are unlikely to share. Generally they prefer to reinvest to build up market share. If a quick profit is paramount, then don't enter a joint venture in Southeast Asia.

Control

This is one of the most difficult issues and one that can cause most friction with a Southeast Asian partner. Someone who has spent a lifetime being in total control and respected by everyone around them is not likely to share it willingly. This fact alone tends to make Southeast Asian family companies difficult joint venture partners. Rarely do they have a culture of sharing control – especially with foreign managers. They are also apt to believe that they know best when it comes to local issues such as marketing tactics. Many Western firms have been shocked at how little managerial control they were able to exercise once the venture was up and running.

Thus it is important to determine from the beginning who is responsible for what. Partnerships are supposedly about complementary skills not competition, so if your strength is technological expertise and your partner's is distribution, a division of responsibilities should be easy. If you are the more experienced partner in a new venture, then make sure you are able to exercise control.

Another important point is to make sure that you are kept fully informed by putting in key people, for example a finance manager or a good production manager, to report on what is happening. Make sure that senior people make regular visits and, most importantly, check that the composition of the board gives you real power and that you will not merely be a cipher. And remember, never equate control with any legal power you might think you have. As many discover too late, a strong equity share, seats on the board and even government promises by no means guarantee control. They all help, but might not be enough.

Leverage your Power

Southeast Asian firms are like businesses elsewhere – they do not enter into joint ventures or business partnerships out of altruism. Ideally, they would prefer to keep the business in the family. They need you for a reason. This power that you have is there to be exploited.

So decide where your power lies – in brand names (which are becoming increasingly important in the region), technology or access to international markets – and leverage it to the full. Use it to negotiate very hard on partnership issues, especially when it comes to control. For example, during their highly successful operations in partnership with PT Astra, neither Toyota nor Honda ever transferred state-of-the-art technology, but drip fed the Astra subsidiaries with older technology, despite the company's wish to go into production on its own account. By so doing, the two Japanese companies kept the upper hand in the relationship.

Build up Trust and Commitment

Trust and mutual respect are the basis of any successful partnership. In Asia, it comes from long-term relationships, not only by working together, but by giving assistance with family matters. For example, you might be asked for help in sending children abroad for education, or looking after relatives visiting abroad for the first time. A positive response to any such requests will be greatly appreciated and will help to cement the relationship. The UK company Inchcape, which had many partnerships in Asia and other parts of the world, kept a list of half-term holiday dates for main schools at which its partners had children, and made sure they were looked after. It was a gesture that paid off in forging strong relationships.

Trust also comes from shared adversity as well as success. Asians do not like people who "take away the umbrella when it rains" any more than anyone else, so staying in through the bad times as well as the good will show that you are committed to making the partnership work – and will not be forgotten. In any business, changing market conditions will require additional resources, probably financial but also perhaps in terms of personnel. Discussing such issues and showing that you are willing to give something extra will also help to establish the partnership.

Don't try to run the venture at arm's length. The more you discuss and manage problems together, the stronger the bond will be. Send in good people to work with them on a permanent basis, not technical or production staff who fly in and out. This will be taken as a sign of commitment.

Make sure that your interests in other markets don't impinge and spoil this partnership. The Virgin Group's mobile phone business in Asia, for example, was launched in partnership with Singtel, while Singapore Airlines (SIA) took a 49 percent stake in Virgin Atlantic. However, the relationship became strained when SIA's Australian partner, Ansett, collapsed, partly due to competition from Virgin Blue, an Australian domestic airline set up by the Virgin Group.

Know When to Withdraw

Even in the euphoria of signing the contract, have an exit strategy prepared and make sure that, if you threaten to withdraw, you really mean it and can get out with bearable losses, and a fund of experience and knowledge that you can leverage next time you venture into Southeast Asia. But remember that every time you dissolve a partnership, it will diminish any store of trust or reputation you may have built up in the country. So make sure it really is the last alternative.

Key Lessons

The secret of managing a good partnership in Southeast Asia is:

- Find the right partner to start with
- Understand his business model
- Have a clear idea of what you expect from the partnership
- Build commitment and trust
- Lay down clear rules on control
- Keep a close eye on operations
- Have a good, pre-prepared exit strategy.

Notes

1 *Far Eastern Economic Review*, "Coke's new formula," 20 April 2000, pp64–5.
2 *Business Week*, "Fixing the debt mess," 12 February, 2001, p18.
3 Taken from "De-mythologizing Charoen Pokphand: an interpretive picture of the CP Group's growth and diversification," Paul Handley.
4 See *"Dare to Do: The Story of William Soeryadjaya and PT Astra International,"* Charlotte Butler, McGraw-Hill Education (Asia), 2002.
5 *Far Eastern Economic Review*, "Thailand's rocky road," Shawn W. Crisp, September 23, 2004, pp39–40.

Managing Partnerships with Japanese and South Korean Firms

WHAT'S IN THIS CHAPTER?

▷ The Model
▷ Japan
    MITI and the *Keiretsu*
    Cultural Obstacles
    The Japanese Consumer
    Failure ...
    ... But Some Successes
    A New Model?
▷ Wal-Mart in Japan
▷ South Korea
    The *Chaebol*
    A Different Culture
    The British Frog in the Field
▷ Key Lessons
    In Japan
    In South Korea

The Model

The economies of Japan and South Korea are each dominated by distinct forms of business organization – in Japan the *keiretsu* and in South Korea the *chaebol*. One of the unique features of these business models is that they were born out of a centrally directed industrialization policy, so that for decades, the strong government backing and protection they received made them practically invincible in their home markets. However, buffeted by economic downturn and the pressures of globalization, the business environment in both countries has begun to change, giving foreign firms the opportunity to enter even these most difficult of Asian markets.

Japan

Writing as long ago as 1993, a business school professor noted that:

> As a market, Japan is still perceived by many foreign firms as a nightmare rather than as an opportunity, despite 120 million affluent customers. The rules appear to be different and rigged against them.

Nearly fifteen years later, foreign firms are still discovering the truth of this statement. Despite the economic difficulties of the intervening years, the Japanese way of doing business still retains enough unique features to defeat their best efforts to enter and build a business there. The reasons for this are both historic and cultural. Politically, the government has long kept a directing hand, while the perceived collusion between the main corporate groupings, or *keiretsu* networks, in order to repel outside competition is still evident.

MITI and the *Keiretsu*

Universally acknowledged as the driving force behind Japan's industrial and economic success in the 1970s and 80s, the Ministry of International Trade and Industry (MITI), together with the powerful Ministry of Finance, was long seen as one of the villains of the piece because of its control of Japanese companies through what it euphemistically called "administrative guidance." Having chosen certain industries for nurture and development, it then set goals and "encouraged" growth along the lines it had selected. Although theoretically free to accept or ignore this guidance, the threat of "undesirable outcomes" ensured that MITI's advice was usually followed.

MITI's weaponry also included various policies seemingly designed to exclude foreign enterprises from the domestic market. These included informal rules such as not allowing foreigners more than a 50 percent share in joint ventures, restricting the number and voting rights of foreigners on the boards of Japanese firms and, in the last resort, excluding any foreign participation that had not obtained its permission.

The offspring of MITI's work were the *keiretsu*, a term mainly associated with bank-centered financial groupings. The big six that came into being in the 1950s were those based on the Fuji, Sanwa, Mitsubishi, Mitsui,

Dai Ichi and Sumitomo banks. In accordance with MITI policies at that time, each bank group acquired or created within it a range of companies covering all the government-designated growth industries. A typical group would consist of several firms operating in different industries, centered on a main bank, a main manufacturer and a general trading company.

The overall strategy of the *keiretsu* was growth. The bank played the critical role in expansion by providing capital for the group members. It owned a significant number of shares in the group firms and often took part in management. To protect the *keiretsu* firms from hostile takeovers or unfriendly shareholders, cross-shareholdings between group members was common. The shares were held long term, leaving few to be traded on the open market. This stable shareholding structure enabled the companies to concentrate on developing new products and markets rather than worrying about short-term dividends.

The intra-firm relationships and alleged willingness of *keiretsu* to cooperate led non-Japanese competitors to portray them as representing a barrier to entry into Japanese markets and a major reason for high prices. But, in fact, a high degree of competition existed between *keiretsu*, which were keen rivals in individual industries, where the leading firms were of more or less equal size and totally committed to winning and keeping market leadership. What is not disputable, however, is the way this very particular business environment has long made it difficult for Western firms to compete successfully there.

Even today, although the power of both MITI (now metamorphosed into the Ministry of Economy, Trade and Industry – METI) and the *keiretsu* has diminished, their influence is still discernible in certain situations. MITI, for example, has been known to step in when there are concerns about protecting the country's technological assets. Thus, to prevent Japanese technology being transferred abroad along with manufacturing facilities – notably to China where technology may be quickly copied – METI persuaded the electronics giant NEC to sell its plasma-display businesses to a local firm rather than to a foreign investor. Similarly, the continued strength of *keiretsu* ties was demonstrated when the Mitsubishi Group rescued the ailing Mitsubishi Motors, while the car maker Toyota was said to have used its huge cash reserves to help bail out troubled companies with whom it had close links.

Cultural Obstacles

Another barrier to entry has been the distinctive Japanese business culture, which represents a blend of all the cultural and religious influences guiding

Japan over centuries. From Shintoism comes the ideas of harmony and ritual, from Buddha, the concept of space and not offending, from Confucius, the idea of roles and place, from *nemawashi* the idea of informal canvassing for support before a meeting, and from the US business guru, Deming, the idea of continual improvement. Such a culture makes the negotiation and decision-making process in Japan very different from the Western norm. As Coca-Cola President Douglas Daft discovered during his time in Japan, the negotiating table is not the place where minds can be changed. "Before the Japanese have reached a consensus," he noted, "they can't negotiate. After consensus is attained on the other side, there is nothing to negotiate." Over time, Daft learned how to communicate in Japan:

> and I don't mean speak Japanese. For example if I want to have a meeting with the chairman of a company, first of all someone goes and talks through what the meeting will be all about. By the time we get there, both parties know if there are any controversial issues and what the outcome of the meeting will be.[1]

Not every Western manager or indeed other Asian managers had the time to understand and adapt to such a different environment.

Another particular feature of the business culture was the belief in lifetime employment; this meant Japanese managers regarded the company they first joined as their only company and an extension of their family. Such a strong bond made it difficult for local managers to transfer their loyalty to another company, even if it was Japanese. Being taken over by a foreign firm was unthinkable and seen as a great loss of face. Foreign firms therefore found it hard to attract good locals to work for them, to sack workers in companies they acquired or to sell off poor performing divisions. Even recently, asked if he was prepared to consider forming an alliance with a non-Japanese bank, one senior Japanese banker reportedly replied: "I do not want to become a subsidiary of the Americans."[2]

The Japanese Consumer

Apart from these structural and cultural obstacles, Western companies have also been handicapped by their failure to understand the notoriously difficult Japanese consumer. Discerning and demanding, Japanese customers insist on extremely high standards of quality and service that many Western firms find difficult to meet. In addition, foreign entrants found themselves operating in fiercely competitive markets, where it was difficult to differentiate their products from those of domestic players. After that loomed another very high hurdle; getting their products on the shelves given the tight local distribution networks. To all these problems, the obvious solution was to take a local partner. Unfortunately, few joint ventures between foreign and Japanese firms lasted long, largely due to disagreements over control. Add to this the high property prices and living costs that meant companies trying to enter Japan needed deep pockets, and it is not surprising that the convenient excuse, "Japan is too difficult, too different," was readily employed by Western firms to excuse their failure.

Failure …

High-profile failures of Western retailers who tried in vain to do all the right things seem to indicate that this view is still valid. In 1999, Boots, the UK health and beauty retailer, formed a joint venture with the trading house Mitsubishi. Boots usually spends two years preparing entry into a new market but, for Japan, it took over three until it felt it had found the right partner. This potentially powerful ally, it believed, would give an unknown foreign entrant credibility, besides supplying government and legal contacts, advising on adaptation to the local market and providing logistical help.

In Japan, opening up in the right area is critical and, with Mitsubishi's help, Boots opened four stores in prime locations. It also reformulated over 2,000 products to gain a Japanese license and changed the packaging of its products to cater to the Japanese preference for fancier wrapping, as well as introducing seating at its cosmetics counter. "Japanese customers are extremely demanding," noted the president of Boots Japan in October 2000.[3] "You have to get things more right in Japan than anywhere else. You need to have patience, you need to rethink every aspect of your business." Yet despite its meticulous preparation and cautious approach, the venture failed and Boots withdrew in July 2001.

The experience of the UK's Vodafone is another vivid illustration of the importance of satisfying local tastes. In 2004, Vodafone spent US$14 billion to expand into Japan, the world's biggest mobile phone market. Vodafone relied on its massive scale and global brand image to succeed where others had failed and, at first, events seemed to endorse this strategy. Vodafone quickly became the darling of the market, with a phone that offered cutting-edge services such as photo-mail. Most importantly, the model was taken up by the trendsetting Shibuya girls, one of Japan's most important market segments, whose tastes in fashion, technology and films are copied throughout the country. Unfortunately, the phone was sold only in Japan, and when Vodafone's global strategy led it to discontinue the model in favor of standardized 3G handsets, the fickle Japanese customers deserted in droves to the next innovation.[4]

As every effort to win back customers failed, the company lagged behind local competitors NTT DoCoMo and KDDI who, to add insult to injury, launched their own versions of Vodafone's winning model. After two more years, Vodafone conceded defeat and agreed to sell its 97.7 percent stake in Vodafone Japan to Softbank Corp. of Tokyo for a sum that would not allow it to recoup its investment. The deal later turned into a bidding war that still left Vodafone bruised – and brooding on the lesson that, in Japan, global branding does not work.

... But Some Successes

And yet American firms, such as Coca-Cola and IBM, and French luxury goods companies, such as Cartier and LVMH, have had a long and profitable presence in Japan. More recently, Apple Computer Inc. successfully sold 14 million iPod portable music devices there in the last quarter of 2005 – its best sales since 2001 when it introduced the iPod.

Many pharmaceutical firms also have a long history in Japan. It is the most important market in Asia for foreign pharmaceutical companies, being second in size to that of the US. In the past, the government's support for a strong domestic drugs industry put high hurdles in the way of foreign entrants, including regulatory requirements that made it hard for foreign firms to license medicines and sell them. Despite this, the US pharmaceutical firm American Home Products has been present for 50 years and Pfizer is the largest pharmaceuticals firm operating in Japan, albeit with a market share of only 3.3 percent. Novartis and Merck have also been successful, although on a much smaller scale than they would normally expect.

By 2000, all the signs were that the market was slowly opening up, and that foreign firms were gaining approval more quickly and easily. However, when AstraZeneca tried to launch a new cancer treatment in June 2002, it "shot itself in the foot" by not giving enough information on side effects, resulting in screaming headlines calling the drug "a killer," following reports of death from side effects among people taking the treatment. Observers judged that AstraZeneca had "failed to take account of the peculiarities of the Japanese market, and marketed the drug too aggressively to doctors not used to prescribing this type of medicine."[5] Although the drug was later approved, the episode was a PR disaster for AstraZeneca.

Despite such episodes, international pressure to normalize its markets is slowly bringing change to Japan. A decade of stagnation since the bursting of the economic bubble has brought down costs and made markets more accessible, and even hiring local staff has become easier. Having seen their elders laid off in the recession, the younger generation are more prepared to look to Western companies where they can progress more quickly than under the old seniority system, or even accept the introduction of Western-style work practices into traditional Japanese firms.

Nikko Asset Management, Japan's third largest fund manager, has recently been restructured by two US managers. They introduced Western-style incentive plans such as performance-related pay and a share savings plan to help to attract new young talent, and replaced underperforming managers by younger, more motivated executives. However, they wisely took a cautious approach to layoffs to avoid affecting staff morale, and ensured that the changes were well communicated throughout the firm via meetings, surveys and suggestion boxes. Similarly, the appointment of Sir Howard Stringer as Sony's chief executive in March 2005 seems further proof that Japanese companies are looking to change. Given that Stringer speaks no Japanese and planned to run the company from New York rather than Tokyo, the appointment looked even more remarkable.

A New Model?

As Japan continues to open up, and encouraged by the success of partnerships such as Renault–Nissan, Western companies are again looking at its markets more seriously. The pioneering Renault–Nissan alliance was seen as "mission impossible" when it was signed in March 1999. A tie-up with Nissan had already been rejected by both Ford and Daimler in the belief that "only a mad Frenchman would do this sort of thing." Yet the partnership has confounded every pessimistic forecast that it would be defeated by cultural clashes and strong opposition from the Japanese workforce.

Other examples of tie-ups that bring genuine benefit to both sides indicate that this may become the model for other firms in the future. In April 2002, Ericsson, the Swedish telecoms equipment maker, was discussing a joint venture mobile phone operation with Sony of Japan. The deal was labeled "a dream combination of Ericsson's technology and Sony's consumer electronics know-how, brand and marketing skills."

Another successful example of this model has been the partnership between the Swiss drug maker Roche and Chugai, Japan's tenth largest pharmaceuticals company, which began life as a friendly merger in December 2001. The two companies had no prior links, but agreed to a pioneering partnership without full union. Formal control was held by Roche but management was arm's-length. The deal, described as "a marriage of equals between partners with strong mutual respect" has been a success. With the extra drugs introduced into its portfolio by Roche, Chugai reinforced its position in the Japanese market, becoming the country's third largest pharmaceutical company. For Roche, the benefit has been the creation of a strong distribution network. Speaking in April 2006, the chief executive of Chugai observed that:

> Usually in Japan, acquisitions are about a strong company resuing a weak one, but Chugai was relatively strong. Roche invested in a company with a traditional research infrastructure. They had a clear understanding: they want us to develop too.[6]

Finally, in 2004, the Swedish home furnishings group IKEA announced it would make a second attempt to enter Japan, 30 years after its first ended in failure largely because, as the chief executive of IKEA Japan observed: "In 1974, I do not think they were ready for IKEA ... with flat packages and asking consumers to put things together."[7] This time, the company planned to open 8–12 stores in Japan, purchasing two big parcels of land outside Tokyo in preparation – a rare vote of confidence since most foreign firms prefer to lease land. Evidently, the group felt that the times were more favorable, since it aimed to "try and change the way the Japanese live." If IKEA can get Japanese consumers to spend their precious leisure time assembling their own kitchens rather than playing golf or shopping at Prada, it really will signal a revolutionary change in consumer habits.

Overall, the evidence does suggest that Western companies are sensing a weakening of resistance to the entry of foreign firms into Japan. Perhaps at last it is time to be Big in Japan. Certainly, this seems to be the Wal-Mart view. In January 2003, the company announced it was making a big push into the market via a controlling stake in its Japanese partner Seiyu. The challenge was described as "how to find a way to meet the fastidious Japanese consumer expectations for service and quality while maintaining their streamlined cost structure, despite high labor costs and a multi-layered distribution system."[8] What actually happened gives an instructive insight into the problems that foreign firms can still encounter when trying to enter Japan.

Wal-Mart in Japan

"Japan is a challenging market, but it's also a very significant growth opportunity," said Greg Penner, CFO of Wal-Mart Japan. "We'll get the building blocks in place first – the systems, the financials, and the merchandising – and then we'll move toward the US model." (*Business Week*, May 2004)

The cookies were too sweet, and 30–40 percent of them were broken ... We are a fish-eating culture. Japanese consumers like fresh food, whereas Americans prefer processed foods. (Yasuyuki Sasaki, director of Equity Research, Crédit Suisse First Boston)[9]

Due to its peculiarities, the Japanese retail market is famed as one of the world's most difficult to crack. Even though the Japanese may be among the world's wealthiest consumers, with a GDP per capita of US$32,000, they have, on average, only 33m^2 of living space per capita. This is 45 percent less than the living space enjoyed by Americans. Since refrigerators and storage space in Japanese homes are limited, Japanese consumers do not or cannot buy goods in bulk.

Wal-Mart spent four years studying the market before concluding that it needed a local partner. In March 2002, Wal-Mart invested in Seiyu, a prominent Japanese retailing chain, purchasing an initial 6.1 percent of the company. Within 18 months, it had acquired over 38 percent of the company, with an option to increase this to 67 percent by 2007. It had significantly restructured both its relationships with suppliers and its in-store look and feel, and had imparted some of the Wal-Mart culture. In 2003, Noriyuki Watanabe, Seiyu's chairman of the board, stated: "Seiyu has already adopted Wal-Mart's three basic beliefs."

The Competitive Environment

Despite high-profile bankruptcies of local players in 2002, Japan's retail sector remains overcrowded and the competition cutthroat. However, the industry has been restructuring: in 2000, market deregulation measures relaxed the Large-Scale Retail Store Location Law, which had prevented large-scale retail developments and protected the small retailers.

Wal-Mart faced stiff competition from local retailers who were revamping their systems and rushing to outdo the US giant, revolutionizing Japan's backward retail system in the process. Retailers were pressing suppliers to sell to them directly – a step toward breaking the stranglehold of middlemen over the supply chain. Wal-Mart itself held several meetings with more than 500 Seiyu suppliers to discuss buying directly, dangling before them the carrot of carrying their products in Wal-Mart stores world-wide. It showed wholesalers and suppliers how to lower their prices by shaving costs and forecasting demand. Retailers were also trying to move the wage-fixing process from a seniority-based to a merit-based system.

Competitors responded to the Wal-Mart threat by building their own megastores, with large areas for parking, pouring millions into computer systems and slashing prices. They even copied Wal-Mart's "Buy American" principle by launching a "Made in Japan" campaign to win over Japan's consumers. Wal-Mart's two main rivals were Aeon and Ito-Yokado.

Aeon, the parent company of Jusco, was Japan's second largest super-market chain, with US$25.8 billion sales in 2002. Operating 368 stores, it was the most aggressive and innovative big retailer in Japan. Its new Jusco stores looked just like Wal-Mart's and copied its labor-saving tricks, such as displaying clothes on hangers instead of folding them.

Ito-Yokado, Japan's largest supermarket chain, had no plans to build super-centers because land costs were too high. The company found it hard to envisage that Japanese consumers would appreciate Wal-Mart's emphasis on price and efficiency over its own offering based on service and quality. In the 1990s, Ito-Yokado had stocked Wal-Mart biscuits in its stores, only to find them shunned by consumers because of their sickly taste (to the Japanese palate) and poor quality (some 40 percent of the biscuits were said to be broken). Therefore Ito-Yokado chose not to reduce its store staff or its prices but instead to emphasize higher quality, together with a "Made in Japan" campaign.

Wal-Mart's Progress

Despite adopting a cautious and methodical approach to the market, Wal-Mart's results in Japan proved disappointing. The company first carefully remodeled the 416-store Seiyu chain, and then reduced prices and tackled cultural hurdles such as trying to work out how far it could cut costs without alienating Japan's quality-conscious consumers. "We have to do it step by step," said John Menzer, chief executive of Wal-Mart's international division, a reflection of Wal-Mart's desire to avoid the type of costly mistakes made previously when it had moved too quickly in other countries.

Wal-Mart's best effort was the four-storey Seiyu store in Futamatagawa, where sales went up 15 percent after the remodeling, although only about 500 of the store's 50,000 items were sold at rock-bottom prices. Wal-Mart tried to boost sales by persuading customers to use shopping carts rather than the baskets favored by Japanese customers.

But overall, Wal-Mart failed to win over demanding shoppers who remained suspicious of its low prices. Japanese customers are known to demand the freshest food and orderly stores. "The lower price on sashimi doesn't mean it's a few days old, but that Wal-Mart got a better price on it," noted Masao Kiuchi, president of Seiyu. The emphasis on fresh produce also means that there is high demand for perishable goods and less for processed food, the typical staple of Western discount stores. Moreover, customers and employees alike had trouble understanding some of Wal-Mart's terms, like "rollbacks," which describe items with long-term price cuts.

Perhaps the one ray of hope for Wal-Mart lay in the emerging smart-shopping trend in Japan. After decades of obsession with expensive designer brands, Japanese consumers were beginning to turn to discount stores, factory outlets and "100 yen" stores where almost everything was the equivalent of about US$1. If this trend continued, then Wal-Mart's low prices could catch on with these most finicky of buyers.

In the meantime, the venture was not yet making money and at the end of 2005 still lagged in fourth place in the market. Seiyu's chief executive had stepped down and Wal-Mart's board was discussing whether or not to turn the company into a fully fledged facility. A local retail analyst estimated that Seiyu would not become profitable until 2007. Perhaps the most telling epitaph on Wal-Mart's progress in Japan so far came from Seiyu's new chief executive, Noriyuki Watanabe, who commented: "Most businessmen know the Wal-Mart brand in Japan. But most housewives still don't."[10]

South Korea

The economic change that lifted South Korea from poverty to affluence in one generation, making it the world's 11th largest trading nation and, in 1996, the first Asian tiger to join the rich man's club, the OECD (Organization for Economic Cooperation and Development), was led by its family-owned business groups or *chaebol*. Their initiator, General Park, who ran the country until his assassination in 1979, based his economic policy on the Japanese model.

The *Chaebol*

Through a series of five-year plans, Park built national champions or *chaebol* who entered selected industrial sectors. In the 1970s, for example, Daewoo, a *chaebol* then specializing in textiles, was ordered to take over a machine-tool maker and a shipyard, besides entering the automotive sector.

Park's strategy was based on encouraging the growth of heavy industry, at first steel and shipbuilding, together with an export orientation to supplement the small domestic market. In the 1970s, the focus was on metals, machinery and chemicals industries, but the next decade saw a move for companies to develop their own technology and market their brands outside Korea. The state rewarded firms investing in these areas by giving them cheap loans and other subsidies. The strategy resulted in growth of 10 percent a year and an economy dominated by five big, family-run *chaebol* – Hyundai, Samsung, LG, Daewoo and Sunkyong. By 1998, they accounted for over a third of the country's entire sales and almost half of all exports. Their tentacles reached into every business from shipbuilding and car making to semiconductors, consumer electronics and satellite broadcasting.

Like Japan, South Korean firms had a particular business culture, characterized by a quasi-militaristic organization and a paternalistic management style that demanded a high degree of loyalty and obedience from its workers. Promoted according to seniority, they worked long hours in return for lifetime employment. After 1987, the growing power of the trade unions gave the country a reputation for labor militancy.

The cosy arrangement between the *chaebol*, the politicians and the bureaucracy resulted in a market that Western firms found almost impossible to enter. Moreover, in Korea, the cultural heritage led to the development of a more overtly hostile business environment, in which the *chaebol* became synonymous with a nationalistic, almost xenophobic outlook.

Foreign firms who did try to enter the market were faced by government restrictions on their owning controlling stakes in joint ventures in "strategic industries." Those that did take minority partnerships found that the *chaebol* were prone to use their investment either to prop up weak subsidiaries or to increase market share. Either way, there were few dividends for investors. An EIU survey found that, in 1996, wholly owned foreign firms reported more than double the operating profit of joint ventures.[11] Perhaps not surprisingly, analysts noted that the usual life span of a Korean joint venture was four to seven years, compared with several decades in other countries.

In December 1992, the newly elected President Kim Young Sam refocused the attention of the *chaebol* on *segyewha* or globalization. Ever obedient to the government's wish, the largest *chaebol* issued almost daily announcements of the establishment of overseas plants, alliances and takeovers as they invested in North America, Europe and neighboring countries in the Asia-Pacific region. The pace of investment was fast; by the first half of 1996, investments abroad amounted to US$9.5 billion, of which US$1.7 billion was destined for Asia and half of that for the fast-growing China market.

The economic crisis of 1997 saw an abrupt halt to this spending. Their traditionally high gearing, with debts sometimes averaging four times their equity, had long put a question mark over the financial stability of the *chaebol*. The crisis revealed a history of reckless borrowing and an abuse of corporate governance that surprised even their fiercest critics. Subsequently, the IMF rescue package of US$58 billion, signed by new President Kim Dae Jung in 1998, imposed a wide range of reforms on the corporate and banking sectors. Daewoo was allowed to collapse in 1999 and Hyundai, once the largest group, was dismantled into five mini-groups. As a result of the opening of the capital markets to foreigners, over half the stock in companies such as Samsung Electronics was bought by foreign investors, who by 2001 also held 30 percent of shares traded on the Korean stock exchange.

In the years following the financial crisis, South Korea proved to be the most lucrative M&A market in Asia as foreign investors moved quickly to buy the assets of the dismembered *chaebol*. Many rejoiced at their apparent demise, anticipating it would open up the economy and allow small and medium-sized, more entrepreneurial companies to emerge. South Korea itself won wide praise for making one of the fastest recoveries from the 1997 crisis, paying off its loan three years ahead of schedule.

However, five years after the crisis, the depth of the restructuring of the *chaebol* and the bad-loan-ridden banks from whom they had borrowed was still not clear. All the indications were that change ran only skin deep, and that the behavior of the *chaebol* had not really altered. In 2002, the top 30 groups still controlled 617 affiliates and a lack of transparency in accounting remained a serious problem. This was underlined in March 2003, when ten executives of the SK Group, the third largest conglomerate, were charged with accounting fraud. The group's vice chairman was later jailed for three years. Meanwhile the fugitive founder of Daewoo, Kim Woo-choong, remained at large until June 2005 when he finally returned to Korea to face charges of fraud and embezzlement. In May 2006 he was sentenced to 10 years in prison, ordered to forfeit US$22 billion and pay a W10 million fine.

There is a widespread perception that while *chaebol* such as LG, Posco (about two-thirds foreign owned) and Kookmin Bank (85 percent foreign owned) have made progress on corporate governance, reform has been merely cosmetic in *chaebol* that remain influenced by the founding family. As with the *keiretsu*, there is still tendancy for them to bail each other out in time of trouble: in 2004, for example, SK Corp. went to the aid of its affiliate SK Network, while the Korean government – notwithstanding its stated commitment to reform – itself organized the rescue of the LG group's failing LG card business.

Other old habits also seem to be dying hard. In October 2005, the chairman of Samsung Group, the biggest and best-known *chaebol*, faced court action over an attempt to transfer control of the group to his son and other family members. Two Samsung executives were given suspended prison sentences for the same offence. In June 2006, the head of the Hyundai motor group, Chung Eui-sun, went on trial charged with embezzlement and breach of trust. He was said to have created a US$107 million slush fund to pay politicians and officials for business favors.

In an increasingly common act of penance, Chung and his son apologized to the South Korean people and promised to give 60 percent of their stake in an affiliate company to charity. The same path was followed by Samsung, which donated US$1 billion to society in atonement for its misdemeanors, and the US private equity fund Lone Star, owner of half the Korean Exchange Bank (KEB), which it had bought in 2003 when it was on the verge of bankruptcy. Lone Star admitted that its former country head had broken the country's laws, apologized and promised to donate US$105 million to Korean society. At a press conference, the company's executives were confronted with a dozen KEB union members holding up signs declaring "Let's break down Lone Star, which ridicules Korea."[12]

So what are the prospects for better corporate governance in South Korean firms? Perhaps the one ray of hope is that Korean companies are increasingly being held to account by shareholders, and the appointment of more outside directors is bringing greater transparency. However, clearly corruption and cronyism have not been stamped out, but still represent considerable obstacles to the ambitions of any foreign firm wishing to enter this highly attractive market. To these hurdles must be added another enduring feature of Korean business life; the Korean culture and the way it influences the conduct of local managers.

A Different Culture

The influence of Confucianism in South Korea means that Koreans place a heavy emphasis on duty and harmony, based on respect for hierarchical relationships and obedience to authority. This is reflected in their negotiating stance: Koreans tend to present themselves in a team organized vertically by rank and gender, and it is important to identify the leader from the start. The need to maintain harmony is a crucial goal throughout any negotiations. However, this has not stopped the Koreans from gaining a reputation as extremely tough negotiators. One of their favorite tactics is to go over the detail of any proposition over and over again in order to wear down the opposition. "The Korean culture," remarked one veteran negotiator, "doesn't allow for a win–win situation. It's kill or be killed."

This attitude arises out of the mental scars caused by South Korea's long history of foreign invasion and occupation that has left its people with an "us and them" mentality that equates foreign ownership with imperialism. There is an ingrained attitude that Korea will only succeed by keeping foreigners out, hence the strong antipathy toward selling to outsiders. Among the reactions after the IMF bailout, for example, was the staging of public burning of foreign goods, the vandalism of foreign cars and a boycott of foreign imports in favor of "Buy Korean." As soon as foreigners show any interest in buying into a business or making an acquisition, the Koreans believe that they are selling it too cheaply.

Against this background, the many foreign firms that entered South Korea after 1997 looking to pick up a bargain have had a hard time finding one. Even after identifying a possible partner, the lack of transparency and the hostility and threats from the labor unions have made any negotiation a protracted and sometimes unpleasant process. HSBC, Deutsche Bank and Ford all invested a lot of time and money to make deals with supposedly debt-laden and desperate local companies, only to withdraw, defeated by the complexity of the deals and the difficulty of gauging the true extent of the company's indebtedness. Other companies found their efforts strangled in red tape. In 1998, the US-based Dow Corning decided to give up its plan for a US$2.8 billion silicone plant, which would have been the largest foreign project in Korea, and build it in Malaysia instead.

Even foreign companies that do persevere have not found that the situation improves with time. GM negotiated long and hard to take over part of Daewoo Motor Co. and by early 2003, felt that its investment was paying off (see Strategy 8). But in September that year it was forced to give its workers a 14.8 percent pay rise to avert a strike that would have jeopardized all its plans for the future. The next year saw yet another strike in search of a further double digit rise. Despite this, Nick Reilly, the chief executive of GM Daewoo, noted that Korean car workers were more highly skilled and worked longer hours than their British counterparts, and that labor relations in South Korea were not as bad as press reports suggested. It should also be noted that even domestic firms are not immune to union militancy. In 2005 Hyundai union members, who have walked out every year since the union was established, struck for two weeks to gain a 6.9 percent pay rise and shorter working hours.

Again and again, Western firms have found it impossible to break into markets dominated by strong domestic competitors. In 2006, first Carrefour then Wal-Mart exited the retail market, defeated by local players with connections to the big *chaebol* and the preferences of Korean consumers for service over price. The Danish brewer Carlsberg also sold out the stake it had first acquired in 1999. All three companies said they planned to concentrate on the China market instead. Other multinationals, including McDonald's, Coca-Cola, Google and Nokia, were also struggling to adapt to this very parochial market.

Another stumbling block has been the mismatch in expectations between venture partners. In 1996 the US firm GE Capital went ahead with a joint venture with Sindoh Ricoh, which makes copiers and fax machines. GE planned to expand later and move into financial services but, unfortunately, its 51 percent stakeholding partner did not want to step outside its known consumer business. The venture broke down.

Similarly, a US investment bank which entered into a securities joint venture with a Korean *chaebol* discovered very quickly that the two were a long way apart when it came to their understanding of what the business entailed. Among the factors that led to the breakdown, the most telling was the experience of the US manager drafted in from New York to head the venture. In his first week, he was surprised to learn that one of his Korean staff had been sacked for losing $2 million on a deal. The US manager protested that in such a high-risk business this was considered peanuts, and was by no means a sacking offence. The same person could lose $2 million today but might make $8 million tomorrow – such losses were part of the game. His argument was not accepted. Within a few months the venture was dissolved; the gap in the understanding of the two sides about the meaning of risk proved unbridgeable.

A study of the business context in South Korea, published in 2006, concluded that:

in spite of the efforts by the Korean government and society to improve the business environment in the wake of the 1997 financial crisis, foreign business people in Korea hold in general a negative view on progress ... They consider that the major spheres ... including government–business relations, labor relations, business relations with Korean counterparts, and Koreans' parochial attitudes have not really improved.[13]

Certainly, hostility toward the efforts of foreign firms to invest in the country remains strong. At the end of 2004, the Ulsan Chamber of Commerce launched a "Buy SK Corp." campaign, urging every citizen to buy 10 shares to preempt a hostile bid by a Monaco-based investment fund. When Citibank bid for the country's sixth largest lender, Koram Bank, the chief executive of Korea's biggest bank announced he had put his staff "on a war footing." After the acquisition went through, Citibank suffered a series of strikes. When Lone Star entered negotiations to sell the Korean Exchange Bank to Kookmin, it was accused of draining Korea of its wealth by making excess profits. The phrase "vulture capital" overshadowed both this and US investor Carl Icahn's hostile bid for KT&G tobacco company early in 2006. Such adverse headlines prompted the Korean finance minister in May 2006 to assert that despite "some nationalism in some sectors of the economy," the government still welcomed foreign investment.

As these examples demonstrate, in many ways, South Korea is still a rigid and largely closed society. Consequently, foreign firms remain disadvantaged by a system in which the *chaebol* still benefit from unfair advantages and rely on personal relationships for business dealings. Add to this a government bureaucracy characterized by a lack of transparency and consistency, plus the cronyism and excessive discretionary power of local administrators, and the playing field becomes even more stacked against them. The *coup de grâce* is delivered by union militancy and strong anti-foreign sentiment, backed up by a hostile press ready to attack foreign companies on the slightest pretext.

However, the situation is not all doom and gloom. Slowly, South Korea is changing as a younger, talented generation realize that lifetime employment is no longer on offer. There is a move toward a more flexible labor market in which people change jobs and are willing to work for foreign firms that offer better career prospects. Foreign investors are growing in influence: in 2006, about 45 percent of the Korean stock exchange was owned by foreign investors. For Taiwan and Japan the figures were 31 percent and 23 percent respectively. Perhaps the rise of foreign car sales in the country is a sign that the "hermit kingdom" is finally beginning to open up. According to the president of BMW Korea, "Driving a BMW has become a symbol of success in Korea."[14]

Finally, a story to demonstrate that it is possible to manage a successful partnership with a Korean firm. Dongsuh, a joint venture that began in 1984, illustrates some of the key points to watch in order to build up a harmonious, enduring relationship.

The British Frog in the Field

Dongsuh Industrial Company Ltd[15] was the offspring of the British automotive components group T&N and Yoo Sung Enterprise Co. Ltd, a piston ring and cylinder liner producer. The South Korean firm was a well-respected mini-conglomerate, founded by Hong Woo Ryu in 1960 to produce cylinder kits for the nascent South Korean automotive industry. By 1996, the group consisted of six companies, all producing component parts for domestic car makers. Of these, Dongsuh was the jewel in Ryu's crown. Despite his 72 years, Ryu was still the active chairman of Dongsuh. One of his five sons, Si-Hoon, had just been promoted to managing director and was being groomed to take over on the retirement of then President W.K. (Simon) Min.

The 50/50 joint venture to make pistons was signed on 13 December, 1984. The name of the new company, "Dongsuh" was chosen by Ryu to illustrate that the venture would be a marriage between the East (Dong) and the West (Suh). In 1984, Dongsuh's board was composed of two directors from each side, plus Ryu as chairman with the casting vote. By 1997, the board was made up of Ryu, his two sons and Simon Min for the Korean side, with three representatives (one of them a finance director) representing T&N. The board met twice a year.

As Simon Min recalled, from the start there was a gentleman's agreement that management should be the responsibility of the Koreans, while the British firm would restrict itself to technical support. For the first three years, a UK engineer was located almost permanently at Dongsuh to provide support to the production engineering side, especially during visits to customers. This close contact continued.

The company operated from a site on a new industrial estate outside Seoul and, from the very first day, "everything went like a dream." As the South Korean car industry grew, so Dongsuh grew with it, to become an enormous success story. After making a loss in the first two years, the company broke even in the third year and, from then on, its profits increased steadily to provide a 15 percent dividend annually. In the 12 years of operations, sales expanded twenty times (enough to pay royalties and fund all its subsequent growth and new machinery) and T&N, whose initial investment was US$1.4 million, had "never put in a bean since."

According to Simon Min, apart from labor disputes, Dongsuh had encountered no major problems, nor had there been any tensions in the relationship with T&N. He attributed this to the excellent understanding and friendship that developed over the years between Ryu and Sandy Barr, the T&N director of licensing and joint ventures responsible for handling the Anglo-Korean relationship until 1992.

The growth of Dongsuh

When it was established, Dongsuh produced only 20,000 pistons a month. By 1996, it had grown 25 times and was producing 500,000 pistons a month, or 6.5 million pistons a year. Of this total, 2.8 million pistons were for diesel and 3.7 million for gasoline passenger cars. It also produced 3 million gudgeon pins for Hyundai.

In 1997, Dongsuh was the number one piston manufacturer in South Korea, with a 40 percent share of a market dominated by four companies. Its nearest competitor Dong Yang (in which Mahle GmbH had a 45 percent share) had 30 percent of the market and the other two companies shared the balance. Dongsuh's products were distributed through three main channels to its four principal customers: Hyundai, Daewoo, Kia and YPR. Demand, observed Simon Min, had never been a problem for Dongsuh, rather, the difficulty had been to meet it.

Technology

Technology transfer, a frequent cause of friction in many joint venture relationships, has never been an issue. At the outset, 11 British engineers worked alongside their Korean colleagues and "made every effort to transfer technology as quickly as possible and make sure everything was understood." Fortunately, recalled Min, "the learning curve was very sharp and so we could go very fast. This experience formed an unbreakable trust between us and T&N, and again gave us confidence."

Indeed, the years have seen a reverse technology transfer take place, for which Si-Hoon was given much of the credit. He had worked closely with a UK engineer in overseeing the automation of Dongsuh and, under his guidance, Dongsuh developed its own innovative production engineering processes. These so impressed T&N that they had been deployed in their other operations round the world.

Relationships

T&N's strategy toward all its joint ventures was to treat them, as far as possible, like wholly owned subsidiaries. While exercising fairly strict financial control by requiring monthly statements and regular full accounts, T&N was always concerned not to appear to usurp authority but, instead, exercise control or influence through building good relationships.

It was a delicate line to tread but in Dongsuh, thanks mainly to Sandy Barr's close affinity with Ryu and Simon Min, it had been achieved. Brian Ruddy, who took over Barr's role, noted that: "At T&N, we worry a lot about our relationships."

When trying to explain why the relationship had been so successful, Mr Min placed a heavy emphasis on the word "trust." "We established trust between us through good communications. When two partners are a long distance from each other, small things can quickly become big problems. But both partners made every effort to avoid this." As Min spoke both English and German, communications were never a problem and, he recalled:

> We would telex each other two or three times a day at the beginning and telephone every evening. I reported every little thing that happened, just to keep Sandy informed. He visited us twice a month at first, and we quickly became the best of friends. Whenever we had a problem, he would try to solve it for us. Even if he didn't succeed, we knew he had done his best.

In a video made to celebrate Sandy Barr's retirement, Min calculated that Barr's travels to and from Dongsuh amounted to circumnavigating the globe seven and a half times, "and in those days, the trip was not so easy." In turn, Min made regular visits to the UK.

Si-Hoon explained the difference in outlook he had noted between the British and YPR's Japanese joint venture partners:

> We have a saying that the Japanese approach is like a frog in a well. All it sees is the sky in a round shape. The British are more like frogs in the field, they see the total view and they are more open. That is why we have confidence in them.

Key Lessons

Setting up and running joint ventures in Japan and South Korea requires patience and commitment.

■ In Japan:

- Don't simply try to transfer Western models
- Always keep local management and listen to them
- Study the customer and remember: quality, quality, quality – from the product to the packaging and beyond.

■ In South Korea:

- Go for a majority share or wholly owned venture
- When drawing up the contract, insert clauses to absolve you from responsibility for any future debt that may be uncovered
- Put in a good finance director you can trust
- Set aside a fund to cover charitable donations "to Korean society" – just in case you run into trouble.

Notes

1 *Far Eastern Economic Review,* "Coke's new formula," 20 April, 2000, pp64–5.
2 *Financial Times,* "Culture clashes prove biggest hurdle to international links," 24 January, 2002, p15.
3 *Financial Times,* "The Japanese face of Boots," 4 October, 2000.
4 *Financial Times,* "Small but perfectly funded," 12 October, 2005, p5.
5 *Financial Times,* "Hard lessons from Japan's drugs market," 24 June, 2003, p11.
6 *Financial Times,* "A model experiment in Japan," A. Jack, 21 April, 2006, p8.
7 *Financial Times,* "Confidence has been renewed," M. Sanchanta, 24 March, 2004, p4.
8 *Financial Times,* "Retailers set sights on Japan," 13 December, 2002, p24.
9 Taken from the case study "Walmart in Asia," Claudia Gehlen and Professors Neil Jones and Philippe Lasserre, INSEAD-Singapore, 2005.
10 *Financial Times,* "Japan's high supermarket stakes," M. Sanchanta, 19 September, 2005, p18.
11 *The Economist,* "Look before you leap," 14 March, 1998, p78.
12 *Financial Times,* "Lone Star goes hunting goodwill in South Korea," A. Fifeld, 20 April, 2006, p15.
13 *Asia Pacific Business Review,* "Recent changes in Korea's business environment: views of foreign business people in Korea,", O. Yul Kwon, vol 12, No 1, pp77–94, January 2006.
14 *Financial Times,* "Foreign cars gain traction in South Korea," Song Jung-a, 23 March, 2004, p11.
15 Taken from the case study "Dongsuh Industrial Co. Ltd." by Charlotte Butler and Professor Henri-Claude de Bettignies, INSEAD-EAC, 1997.

China or India?

WHAT'S IN THIS CHAPTER?

▷ India Mania
▷ The Same Yet Different
▷ Useful and Useless Government
   Inflexible Labor
▷ Infrastructure, Infrastructure, Infrastructure
▷ The Chinese Way
▷ A Tale of Two Cities
▷ Corruption
▷ Bankruptcy
▷ The Courts
▷ India as a Market
▷ Made in India?

India Mania

At the World Economic Forum held in Davos in January 2006, India was, as its slogan announced, "Everywhere." Politicians and global business leaders alike queued to pay homage to a new star on the world stage. Phrases like "economic powerhouse" and "the Indian century" appeared in the media and, suddenly, India was all things to all people – for politicians, a strategic ally in the region, for business, the perfect destination for outsourcing ambitions, a source of R&D innovation and a second potentially huge market stocked with middle-class consumers ready and willing to spend. The Taj Mahal was used as a backdrop by designer Roberto Cavalli at Milan Fashion Week, the windows of New York's famous store, Bergdorf Goodman, reflected Indian designs, silk and gold embroidery and fabrics, and Bollywood films continued to be big box office.

According to some pundits, China would soon be eclipsed by this new economic giant that, to all its other attractions, added the sure card of being "the world's biggest democracy." India was China with the additional advantages of English language capability and a younger population. Impeccable credentials. But were these claims rooted in reality? Or was this merely a repeat of the hyperbole that greeted China's entry into the business world only a few decades ago, born out of a desire to find "the next best thing" or perhaps an alternative to the Chinese leviathan? When it comes to business potential, how does India really measure up to China? And how close are perception and reality when it comes to India's apparent arrival?

The Same Yet Different

Table 11.1 India and China compared

	India	China
Population	1.08 billion	1.31 billion
Approximate number of people who can afford Western-style levels of consumption	20 million	100 million
Median age	24.66 years	32.26 years
Annual population growth	1.4%	0.58%
Sex ratio – males/females	1.06/1	1.06/1
Life expectancy at birth	64.35 years	72.27 years
GDP per capita (PPP basis)	US$3,400	US$6,200
Estimated number of Internet users	28 million	130 million
Estimated military expenditure	US$18.86 billion (2005)	US$67.49 billion (2004)
Total adult literacy	59.5%	90.9%
Total adult female literacy	48.3%	86.5%
Perceived corruption according to Transparency International	Equal 88 (out of 158 countries; the higher the rank, the greater perceived corruption)	Equal 78
Estimated cumulative foreign investment	US$25 billion	US$900 billion
Annual graduates four-year engineering degree	112,000	351,000
Share of world trade	>1%	6%
Labor force in agriculture	60%	48%

Note: many of these figures are not or cannot be precise; their main function is to show relative magnitudes.

In many ways, the recent development of both India and China has followed a similar path. Both have experienced strong growth rates: India's economy grew by an annual average of 8 percent between 2003–06. China's averaged 10 percent a year during the same period. Both have shown an even stronger rise in domestic consumption and offer low-cost, well-educated pools of labor. Consequently, both have become magnets for FDI – China has been the number one destination since 2003 and India leapt from 15th place in 2002 to third by 2005. Together they have attracted the bulk of the world's offshore activity (see Strategy 17) and are evolving beyond straightforward call center activity in the case of India, to become R&D hubs: out of the 885 R&D-oriented greenfield FDI projects announced in Asia between 2002–04, over 80 percent were concentrated in China and India.

Both can lay claim to having at least several world-class, highly competitive companies: China's include Lenovo (PCs), Haier (white goods), TCL (electronics) and telecoms player Huawei, while India's include software giants Infosys and Wipro, Ranbaxy (pharmaceuticals), Bajaj Auto (components) and the Birla Group's flagship Hindalco (non-ferrous metals). Firms from both countries are beginning to undertake some M&A activity and in some areas are now being touted as strategic partners – especially when it comes to the search for oil supplies. In January 2006, the first trip abroad for the new Saudi king was to India and China, and in the same month China and India announced a joint bid for a Syrian oilfield. The two are also opening factories within each other's borders, and bilateral trade, just $339 million in 1992, is expected to grow to $20 billion by 2008. Haier and TCL are sourcing goods in India, and Huawei has set up an R&D center in Bangalore. Tata Consultancy Services, Tata Steel and Tata Motors are already established in China, as are Ranbaxy and the Birla Group, while Wipro (IT) has set up a development center in Shanghai.

There is a general consensus as to their relative merits. Foreign businessmen have long been mesmerized by China for its market size, access to export markets, government incentives, favorable cost structure and infrastructure. Its weaknesses are considered to be poor English skills, weak IPR and a lack of managerial talent. India's most frequently cited relative strengths are a sizable pool of educated workers, management talent, rule of law, cultural affinity and regulatory environment. Its weaknesses usually center on its slow-moving government and dismal infrastructure.

Both countries face similar challenges – underemployment, rural poverty and the threat of social unrest, overregulation, an underdeveloped banking system, corruption, environmental damage and the threat to its population's health posed by AIDS. Future development in both countries will be constrained by a lack of raw materials, notably oil and steel. In order to remedy these lacunae, both are themselves becoming sources of FDI. Chinese companies have been active in Latin America, Africa, Central Asia and Australia and Indian companies in Russia and Africa. Both are eager for recognition of their technical prowess and weight as world players. Both have space programs, for example.

Despite all this, when it comes to international trade, the comparative advantages of India and China could not be starker. India specializes in supplying services to the outside world. China specializes in supplying light manufactures. Why should this be so?

One reason for the prominence of services exports is the ability of many but by no means all Indians to converse in English. However, far more important has been their different approaches to remedying their structural weaknesses and exploiting their low-cost strengths. When it comes to reform, China's progress has been rapid and effective while India has moved at a glacial pace. China's government has been prescriptive and proactive, while India's federal and state governments have often been inept, intrusive and corrupt, so much so that Indian entrepreneurs have found that the only way to succeed globally from within India is to export something that government officials cannot see and intrude upon: services. And besides, India's ports are a disgrace.

Useful and Useless Government

Take their comparative performance with regard to reducing poverty, an area where both governments frequently voice concern. In India, as in China, the fruits of economic success have been limited to the urban population of a few high growth areas – Mumbai, Bangalore, Delhi and the southern corridor. Roughly 70 percent of the Indian population live in the countryside, vulnerable to the vagaries of the monsoon and with little opportunity to improve their lives. Impoverished states such as Bihar – the poorest, most corrupt and most caste-ridden in the country – and Orissa have been left way behind.

According to the World Bank, between 1980 and 2000, the number of people in India living on less than $1 a day (adjusted to reflect purchasing power) fell by just 70 million. During the same period, the number in China dropped by around 400 million.

This difference stems partly from the fact that India is a dynamic but fractious democracy. By 2006 for example, the ruling coalition, led by the Congress Party, relied for its parliamentary majority on several Communist parties that opposed many reforms. So rather than being cooperative partners, they often acted like an opposition group. For example, in 2005, the Left-leaning coalition parties forced the government to abandon plans to sell stakes in 13 state-owned companies to strategic investors. The contrast with the Chinese governments' treatment of its state-owned enterprises, half of which have been privatized in the decade since 1995, could hardly be starker (see Strategy 24).

As a result, the hand of government over the Indian economy still lies heavy; privatization began in 1991 but even in 2004, seven of the country's ten biggest companies (measured by sales) were still majority owned by the state. State-owned banks control nine-tenths of deposits and the railways employ more people than any other commercial organization in the world.

Both China and India work to five-year plans. The difference is the speed at which the plans are implemented. In India, promised key reforms, notably in the labor and power sectors, are routinely delayed largely due to opposition from the Left. The result is that the regulatory jungle, the "license Raj," lives on and continues to impede progress: a 2004 study found that each industrial unit was still visited by 40–60 inspectors in the course of a month, and that Indian managers spent 16 percent of their time dealing with government officials.[1] That isn't prudent supervision. It's harassment.

Inflexible Labor

Foreign investors and local entrepreneurs have long waited in vain for the deregulation of India's labor market and an end to production being reserved for the small-scale sector (around 670 items, including 21 textile or hosiery products, are still reserved for small-scale producers). Labor laws in India are notoriously inflexible. The Industrial Disputes Act restricts the ability of managers of firms with more than 100 employees to fire staff. Such firms require government approval before they can make dismissals. Typically, that permission is not forthcoming, and if it is, it must be paid for by paying off the appropriate officials. The direct financial cost may not be great, but the cost of the time spent negotiating often is. Long, drawn-out dismissals waste managerial time and are not conducive to good staff morale.

The impact of such rules on India's competitiveness and flexibility was sharply illustrated by events in the textile industry. When global textile quotas ended on 1 January, 2005, India, with its huge domestic cotton industry, spinning and weaving experience and cheap labor costs, should have benefited more than any other country. Instead, it was Chinese companies that took full advantage (as the ensuing trade row with the EU and US demonstrated). Its exports jumped by 59 percent in the first quarter of 2005, as against India's miserly 5 percent growth. A significant reason for India's poor showing was that its textile firms were reluctant to expand employment to meet the increased demand because of the difficulties of laying them off subsequently, and could not ask existing workers to work longer hours since employees can only do a maximum of 45 minutes overtime a day.

The power sector is another black area. The 2003 Electricity Act was supposed to usher in a new era of power reforms but captive interests have prevailed to strangle it. At the beginning of 2006, India faced a shortfall of over 7.5 percent in energy requirements, and over 11 percent of peak demand. The cost of power for an industrial user in India has been calculated at more than twice that in China, where electricity production is three times higher.

Some cautious progress was made toward opening up some industries in 2005, when the government allowed foreign firms to enter the construction and property industries. India also signed an open skies agreement with the US and passed a patent law that met WTO standards. But politics and organized interests combined to keep many FDI restrictions in place. Banking liberalization is not scheduled until 2009 and in the insurance sector, foreign insurers can only buy 26 percent of their Indian counterparts. Until recently, foreign firms wishing to set up shop could only do so via franchise operations, as Pizza Hut and Benetton have done.

Perhaps the most closely watched sector for signs of liberalization has been India's US$200 billion retail industry. The big global players, Carrefour, Tesco and Wal-Mart are eager to enter India and offer consumers the modern supermarkets most have never experienced. However, the government fears for the future of the vast sprawl of 9 million small shops if ever they were exposed to such intense competition. "The issue is being looked at closely" has been the constant refrain, and domestic retail groups have asked for another two or three years in which to prepare for liberalization. In January 2006, a new measure was passed that enables foreign firms to take a 51 percent investment in single brand retail operations, meaning they will finally be able to operate their own stores. Cynics (or realists?) are waiting to see how openly the new policy will be applied. Meanwhile, Carrefour for one has revolutionized retailing in China.

Infrastructure, Infrastructure, Infrastructure

The state of India and China's infrastructure demonstrates the most glaring disparity between the effectiveness of the two governments. In India, infrastructure development is often something that's only ever talked about. State legislatures are notorious for slowing down and stopping development. As a result, by and large, India's infrastructure is abysmal. It adds to the costs of operating in India and, according to many despairing businessmen, threatens future growth. In February 2006, Rajeev Chandrasekhar, an ex-telecoms entrepreneur, summed up one of the major problems: "Business has been growing feverishly in India, now it is heading like a rocket into a dead end. That dead end is a lack of transportation infrastructure."[2]

In India, roads, rail, sea and air all tell the same sorry tale of poor management and lack of investment. Both the badly run state-owned railway network, comprising 63,000 km of track and the 3.3 million km road network (only 57 percent of which is paved), slow the passage of manufactured goods. In the inefficient and congested ports, India's lead time for an export consignment to the US is 7–12 weeks. In China it is 3–4 weeks.

In 2004, the Indian government did finally make a start on modernization, with a 15-year project to widen and pave about 65,000 km of otherwise decrepit, narrow national highways. It is a huge undertaking that will cost tens of billions of dollars. The first stage to be completed will be highways that cut across and ring India, linking Chennai, Mumbai, New Delhi and Kolkata, at a cost of more than US$6 billion. This will see a significant reduction in distribution delays and costs and enhance economic efficiency. By contrast, China has been spending almost US$24 billion a year on improving its highways in recent years. In 2005, it built 129,748 km of road.

Very few Indians have the means to fly. At the beginning of 2006, Indian airlines collectively owned less than 200 jets. But if 10 percent were to fly routinely, then India would probably need around 2,000 jets. But could India's 330-odd airports cope? As it is they are in an appalling state. A popular joke has it that Mumbai's Sahar Airport exists for the sole purpose of making Delhi's Indira Ghandi International Airport look good. Terminals are inadequate, necessitating aircraft spending more time on the ground and less time in the air as ground staff struggle to cope with out-of-date facilities. Airports are undercapitalized; most are not privatized and suggestions that they should be are typically met by strikes on the part of thousands of airport staff. Indian airports have become places to sleep, because that's what passengers are often forced to do in them while they wait out delays. Mumbai's airport even has daybeds along its concourses where other airports have conventional seating.

Cargo carriers such as FedEx are prevented by law from flying domestically. They must fly to Mumbai or New Delhi and then continue by road. It is a ridiculous situation for a county that aims to be developed by 2020. It's little wonder that India's services sector has become the star export earner: services don't need to be physically carried. Hopes have been raised by the award of privatization mandates for Mumbai and Delhi.

Telecommunications is one sector in which India has had some success. By 2005, it had more than 115 million mobile phone subscribers. But is it really a success? Many subscribers resort to getting a mobile phone because the landline rollout is so slow that it's either a mobile or nothing. In any event, mobile phone penetration rates are far greater in China where mobile operators are earning huge revenues (Figure 11.1).

Perhaps the worst example of the government's self-destructive approach has been in Bangalore – India's so-called Silicon Valley. Home to 1,500 IT companies and the star that first put India on the global business map, Bangalore is an acclaimed disaster area. "Its roads are grid locked, rubbish goes uncollected, sewage pollutes the water and bare power lines run through the slums."[3] It is so dire that the heads of leading firms such as Wipro and Infosys are investing elsewhere in the country. They are totally frustrated by the lack of action from the state government, which seems more concerned with debating a name change for the city (part of the general rejection of anglicized place names) than with remedying the situation.

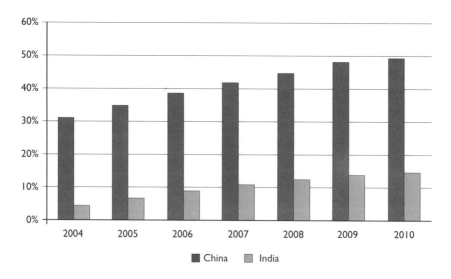

Figure 11.1 China and India: mobile phone market penetration, 2004–10

One estimate of the investment in infrastructure needed by India in the decade to 2015 is US$440 billion. But it's extremely unlikely that anything like this sum will be invested, given persistent public sector budget deficits and the recurring alienation of private investors in Indian infrastructure projects.

The Chinese Way

China's government, bureaucrats and party officials have also been intrusive, meddling and corrupt, but on average less so than in India. And there has been far greater emphasis on infrastructure development in China. Far more attention is paid to outcomes rather than processes, and as a consequence, once the party hierarchy commands that a toll road or a new airport be developed, generally it is. Thus while the project for a new international airport in Bangalore, begun in 2000, was still under discussion in 2006 (the Infosys chairman having resigned as head of the group overseeing the construction in disgust), by then China had built 130 airports handling over 1 million passengers a year. It further plans 55 new international airports to be built by 2020.

Tonne-kilometers of freight hauled on railways is about 4.5 times greater than in India, and air-freight tonne-kilometers flown in China is almost ten times higher. Container traffic shipped through ports is 16 times more in China. The relative quality of China's infrastructure, particularly in the dynamic coastal regions where most export-centered manufacturing occurs, helps to cut business costs and enhance predictability.

In China, the New Economic Zones, such as those in Guangdong's Pearl River Delta, opened up to foreign investors in 1980, played a huge role in the country's economic success and have now been superseded by development everywhere. In India, the government was forced to water down its proposal to set up similar schemes. In January 2006, the Chinese government proposed the creation of a pan-Pearl River Delta region, which will link up the nine southern provinces, together with Hong Kong and Macau, to promote sustained economic growth in the region. The provinces will cooperate on infrastructure development, transport, trade and economic policy and so on. Cooperation on energy will be one priority. In India, proposals for new power plants have tended to lead to litigation rather than energy.

In 2003, India's then Privatization Minister Arun Shourie, frustrated at endless hold-ups to his program of reforms, said that "If the rates of growth of India and China continue to differ by the margins of the past

15 years, within the next 15 years the Chinese economy will be six times that of India." Pluralism and democracy are factors, but China's preparedness to accept foreign investment compared with India's is another.

In short, there is much hyperbole about India, largely on account of its IT outsourcing sector. The reality is that this sector employs relatively few Indians compared with the overall population. Most Indians remain poor. Per capita income on a PPP basis is half that of China's. And infrastructure is a disgrace in practically every area. There has been progress but the real point of comparison should be with India's competitors and not with its past.

A Tale of Two Cities

Shanghai is the financial capital of China. And Mumbai is the financial capital of India. As financial capitals, they are windows to the world. And windows to their own domestic economies. The views could not be more different.

Shanghai is an astonishing place. It may not have the most resilient and transparent economy, its real estate market inevitably will be characterized by boom and bust, and it has grown too fast, but it is there. Pudong, on the opposite side of the Huangpu River to The Bund, was swampy marshland in 1990. Now it is home to something that verges on Manhattan.

The Jin Mao Tower dominates Pudong. It is China's tallest and the world's third tallest building (or it was when it was completed). It contains what is described as the world's highest hotel, a Grand Hyatt, which starts at the 54th floor. If you go to the 88th floor, you see in every direction literally hundreds of square kilometers of tall office and residential towers. In fact, Shanghai today is home to more than 4,000 buildings that are 18-storeys or more high, almost twice that of New York. The speed with which this has happened compounds the shock. More than two-thirds of these towers have been built since 1994.

Shanghai's Pudong International Airport is world class. By 2010, it will have three runways and double its 2006 capacity. The expressway from Shanghai to the airport is wide and impressive and alongside it runs the extraordinary Maglev train. The German-designed, magnetically propelled train reaches speeds of 430 kilometers an hour and is the fastest commercial passenger train on earth. It can do the 30-km journey to the airport in just eight minutes. No other city in the world has one.

The first ever Chinese Formula One Grand Prix was staged by Shanghai in September 2004 at a state-of-the-art track at Anting, 30 kilometers outside Shanghai.

And then there is Mumbai. Arriving at its airport can be something of a shock. Go outside, find a decrepit cash machine to get local currency, hop into a tiny, rusted taxi and things go from bad to worse. Slums immediately border the airport from which the most decrepit, congested road imaginable leading from any international airport snakes into downtown Mumbai.

Life in Mumbai is fraught and tense. And it's getting more so. Soon, the city will have a population greater than all of Australia. And by 2020 its population is forecast to be 28.5 million.[4]

The city is prone to flooding. One of its worst ever floods occurred in August 2005 after almost unprecedented rainfall. More than 400 people drowned, were smothered in landslides or killed in stampedes. The airport was closed for two days. The city's creaking infrastructure was tested and failed: eight days after the floods commenced, many areas remained under water, this when Mumbai is located by the sea which presumably should aid rapid drainage. Many areas were without electricity for a week and mobile telephone and even landline coverage remained sporadic for much of that time.

Mumbai simply looks run-down, a legacy of rent controls which mean that building owners have little incentive to repair their buildings. Tenancy laws greatly favor tenants and evictions are almost impossible to obtain. Shopping centers and supermarkets barely exist, certainly not in downtown Mumbai. This adds to the city's run-down feel.

Mumbai and Shanghai are worlds apart. Just as India and China are.

Corruption

Transparency International, in its annual survey of corruption perceptions, found in 2005 that India was perceived to be more corrupt than China, although among all countries about which perceptions were surveyed, the two were roughly in the middle rankings, meaning that, broadly, they are not dissimilar when it comes to corruption.

One likely reason why India is seen as more corrupt than China is because there are more bureaucratic procedures in India and so there are simply more opportunities for officials to behave corruptly and hold up proceedings until they receive the required inducements. The World Bank, for example, found in 2005 that it takes 71 days to start a business in India but 48 days to do so in China.[5] One reason is the greater number of approvals required.

Petty corruption is a constant annoyance. A 2005 study backed by Transparency International estimated that Indians collectively pay around US$4.6 billion annually to low-level officials. A survey of 14,000 people in 20 Indian states found that more than 80 percent of them had bribed a policeman in the last year, and a quarter had paid bribes in government hospitals to get better service.[6] Ordinary people in China face similar impositions not just when dealing with government officials, but often even in the workplace. It is not unusual in SOEs for employees to bribe supervisors to ensure that they are allocated to more interesting or less demanding jobs. Students bribe teachers so that they receive a good recommendation and so on.

Some Indian businessmen have voiced their concerns about the depth of corruption permeating society. Writing in January 2006, the chairman of Infosys concluded that "corruption is now an accepted phenomenon in the psyche of Indians from all walks of life." Moreover, it was "the most powerful inhibitor of economic progress," affecting small companies who cannot afford the increased costs, enabling larger firms to create monopolies or improve their market share and inhibiting GDP growth rate. Researchers claim that if corruption had been controlled, India would have had an average GDP growth rate of 8 percent in the last two decades of the twentieth century, rather than the 6.1 percent achieved.

Is there any hope of India rooting out this evil? It will take a huge effort of leadership among politicians, bureaucrats and business leaders and, at the moment, the will does not appear sufficiently strong. It is anticipated that change in India will come as the next generation of Indian MBA-trained managers takes over the running of the family-controlled empires so prominent in Indian business, or when investment gives foreign firms more influence over their Indian operations and they begin to demand corporate governance, professional management, transparency and so on. But that day may still be some way off.

And China? Despite recent moves to improve China's image, a 2005 OECD report described corruption there as "severe and widespread."[7] Apart from the threat to the country's economic progress, corruption was also seen as a "danger to legitimacy for Beijing because there was much popular dissatisfaction with corrupt officials, particularly in rural areas." The Ministry of Commerce estimated that during the past two decades, 4,000 corrupt officials had fled China taking with them roughly US$50 billion. A graphic indication for foreign investors of what they might expect could be the announcement of the governor of the northeast China Liaoning Province. He noted that to revitalize the economy, he would be using all possible measures to "smash the scourge of official corruption ... and ... emancipate the economy from bribery, favoritism, Mafia influences and other abuses."[8] That's promising rhetoric.

Bankruptcy

Bankruptcy and liquidation procedures in India are notoriously cumbersome. Even companies that have made losses for years must attempt remediation under the auspices of the Board for Industrial and Financial Reconstruction. And that is a problem because the board must have unanimity to proceed with closure. Any stakeholder such as a creditor, union or owner can block restructuring plans or company closure. This means that winding up companies is difficult and costly. According to one recent estimate, more than 60 percent of liquidation cases before the high courts had been in process for more than 10 years. Such delays tie up creditors' capital for years, preventing it from being used more efficiently elsewhere.

Bankruptcy procedures in China are if anything more problematic. At the start of 2006, a bankruptcy law was in place but it dated from 1988. Accordingly, it was hopelessly out of date so that bankruptcy was rarely a viable option for otherwise rebuffed commercial creditors. A revised law has been drafted but has not been passed. It had been expected to have been passed in 2005. But its passage was held up by debate about what to do with laid-off workers. Even if and when it is passed, the question then will be about enforcement of decisions, just as it is in other countries with poor legal systems such as Indonesia. Will China's new bankruptcy code be of help to outsiders, assuming it's passed? As is usual in China, only if the government and local Communist Party officials want it to be and then on a case-by-case basis.

The Courts

The judiciary in India is relatively independent but it is underresourced. The backlog of cases to be heard can run into many millions across the country. This means delays of sometimes years before a case may be heard. Appeal processes serve to amplify such delays. Lengthy waiting times mean that India's courts are not a good place to solve commercial disputes and so most companies prefer arbitration if major contracts are involved.

The judiciary in China has little independence or resources. The law in China is not applied equally when it is applied. The 60 million Communist Party members, the judiciary and the police all feel themselves to be above the law. Judges are nominated by local and provincial party committees and approved by local people's congresses. The congresses provide the salaries, housing and other benefits for judges, many of whom have little or no legal training but instead are ex-military personnel. They are expected to discuss sensitive cases with members of their local Communist Party political-legal committees before making rulings. There is not even a pretence that judges are in any way independent. Having said this, legal procedures are improving, particularly with regard to commercial disputes and particularly intellectual property infringement. This has come about largely from international pressure. But foreign companies now find that while they might obtain a reasonable decision from a commercial court, enforcement then becomes the problem, so many victories are pyrrhic.

India as a Market

China's billion potential consumers have long exercised a magnetic attraction over foreign business (see Strategy 24). But what about India? Doesn't it also have a billion potential consumers? Increasingly, foreign investors are focusing on reports of a consumption boom breaking out among the new middle class and a young generation of IT workers who are willing to spend on foreign brands, and who are optimistic about the their own and the country's future. In 2005, a year that saw the highest number of jobs created since 2000 and the biggest salary rises, 70 percent of the Indian population was under 36. Between 1995 and 2004, the credit card subscriber base grew by 35 percent annually. Other portents also look promising. In 1975, Indian consumers had a choice of three car models. By 2004 there were 90. By 2006, India was thought to be the second largest market for cell phones and among the top 15 for airline passengers.

The luxury end of the market has been encouraged by the changing rules in the retail sector. In February 2006, Christian Dior opened its first franchise shop in India in New Delhi, in the wake of other brands including Chanel, Cartier, Fendi, Dolce & Gabbana. According to a report published in February 2006, there are 1.6 million households in India earning $100,000 or more a year and spending $9,000 a year on high-end designer goods, translating into a market worth $14.4 billion.[9] The number of households in that segment is said to be growing by 14 percent each year. To supply their needs, 93 new shopping malls are planned by 2007, and developers are rushing to build luxury apartments and open new restaurants. But it must be remembered that while the number of rich in India is growing, it remains a puddle rather than a pool; a rich puddle beside a sea of poverty. Malls might well be busy but often with sightseers rather than shoppers.

Made in India?

"China has world-class manufacturing, India has third-world manufacturing" is a tag that has long summed up India's manufacturing image. But although services still dominate India's exports sector, there are signs that manufacturing is finally beginning to take off. Manufacturing has "started to enjoy its fastest growth in memory, expanding at 9.8 percent in the five months to August (2005) compared with a year earlier, and business confidence indices are at their highest levels since 1995."[10] Manufacturers might have further taken heart from reports early in 2006 that China's manufacturing competitiveness was being eroded by rising energy and labor costs so that it was "no longer the most cost-effective country in the region."[11] Exports in the seven months to October 2005, of which 75 percent were manufactured products, were up 22 percent. However, that year India's exports accounted for 0.8 percent of world merchandise, China's for 6.4 percent.

Foreign manufacturers are cautiously optimistic. Flexitronics, the world's second biggest electronic manufacturing player, spent US$1 billion on acquisitions in India in 2005. Its chairman believes that "India is climbing the (manufacturing) league table fast" as a base for the large-scale production of goods such as computers and mobile phones.[12] In 2006 GE, so often disappointed by its India business in the past, indicated its readiness to invest billions of dollars if proposed infrastructure growth actually materialized, while Dell India has declared it aims to become the world's biggest PC manufacturer.

Considerable excitement has centered on the telecoms industry. In 2005, industry analysts forecast that over the next twelve months 2 million new mobile subscribers would sign up each month, making India the world's fastest growing mobile telecoms market. In fact, the numbers fell short of this target but, given the market potential, all the big players, Alcatel, Motorola and Nokia, have started operations there. To encourage local production, the government has imposed a 4 percent duty on all imported handsets. Old habits die hard.

Drugs manufacturing is another bright spot, largely on account of the large existing domestic market, which allows the sector massive economies of scale without even having to export. However, before exports can really take off, India still has some significant IPR issues to solve in this area.

In the short term, high-tech manufacturing based on India's reputation as a software and R&D hub has the most promising prospects. India's R&D capabilities are highly rated sources of innovation for Western firms such as Intel, Motorola and Cisco, which in November 2005 announced a $1.6 billion investment in India, mostly in R&D. By 2006, over 150 international companies were doing research in India. China trailed with only 40 companies.

But generally, India's manufacturing sector has a long way to go before it can compete with China. Not just improvements in infrastructure and modernizing factories are needed but new manufacturing techniques, which will in turn require heavy investment in training. Exporting goods requires efficient ports largely free of corruption and spoilage and, again, India falls far short of China.

When it Comes to China or India, Remember:

■ Two legs are better than one – so have a foot in both camps
■ All the mistakes you made when you went into China – don't repeat them in India
■ India's middle class is still only about 15 percent of the population – so don't expect a consumer boom, whatever the pundits predict
■ China's pool of middle-class consumers is bigger and richer but still barely amounts to the equivalent of a medium-sized European country
■ Both India and China might well be great places to invest. But are they great places to make money? The vast majority of outside investors will find that the answer is no.

Finally, some cogent words of advice from Sunni Bharti Mittal, chairman of Bharti Enterprises. Based on his long experience, he offers that "If you want to invest in India, go where the government has no role."[13]

Notes

1 *The Economist*, "Can India work?," 12 June, 2004, pp67–9.
2 *Financial Times*, Comment and Analysis, 13 February, 2006, p11.
3 *Financial Times*, "India and globalisation," special report, 26 January, 2006.
4 BBC News, "Bombay faces population boom," 30 December, 2000.
5 *International Herald Tribune*, "Giants unchained? Not so fast," P. Bardhan, 3 November, 2005.
6 *Guardian*, "Corrupt practices cost ordinary citizens £2.7bn, says watchdog," 2 July, 2005.
7 *Financial Times*, "OECD concern over impact of graft in China", 28 September, 2005, p5.
8 *Financial Times*, "Curbing corruption 'vital' for China's north-east rustbelt," 9 January, 2004.
9 *Financial Times*, "Christian Dior hopes to bag Indian demand," A. Jain, 21 February, 2006, p11.
10 *Financial Times*, "Back to the future," J. Johnson, 30 November, 2005, p11.
11 *Financial Times*, "China's competitiveness hit by energy and labor costs," T. Mitchell, 23 March, 2006, p1.
12 *Financial Times*, "India's fight to slay the dragon," 18 May, 2006.
13 *Financial Times*, "India's phones-to-farms operator", J. Johnson and K. Merchant, 19 October, 2005, p10.

Strategy 12

Avoid Post-acquisition Trauma

WHAT'S IN THIS CHAPTER?

▷ Beyond the Point of No Return
▷ What Type of Changes?
▷ The Post-merger Integration Process
▷ Cultural Change
▷ Human Resource Issues
  Downsizing
  Finding a Skilled Workforce
▷ Transparency
▷ Processes and Systems
  Quality Improvement
▷ Coordination Mechanisms
▷ Key Lessons

Beyond the Point of No Return

So, you have made your acquisitions and are now part of the Asian business scene. Perhaps you have bought a company outright, perhaps you are the majority owner of one or more companies. Maybe you paid a little too much, maybe you got a bargain – or think you did. But now it is time to make the investment pay back and, for most, that means serious planning and thought about how to manage and organize these new operations. And this in turn means making changes.

This is not to say that multinationals and other smaller investors are necessarily making poor investment decisions. In most cases, the business they buy into is a good one with potential. The company is perhaps the market leader or one of the top three in its industry, and probably turned in improved results annually before the 1997–98 economic crisis. On the other hand, often deals are signed quickly in the heat of the competitive situation or to take advantage of preferential tax situations. Due diligence is done as well as possible, and the market research looks promising. But, as we have seen, information about these areas can never be 100 percent reliable and faults are almost bound to appear later.

In all cases, with an eye to the future, Western companies will invariably aim for greater efficiency to improve the results and competitiveness of their Asian possessions via an injection of Western business methods and technical know-how. Maintaining the status quo is not an option. If you want to be Big in Asia, that probably indicates the need for big changes. But how you manage those changes in order to integrate your acquisition successfully will be vital to the success or failure of your investment. Siemens Corporation, the German electrical engineering and electronics firm, has a wide experience of cross-border acquisitions. Interviewed in 2002, its CEO Heinrich von Pierer declared that:

> To fully integrate the companies that we have in our portfolio is the decisive factor in the success of an acquisition. This boosts productivity and optimizes the new unit's potential together with our own competencies. Integration teams usually start structuring the acquisition process, but the real work comes in the postmerger period.[1]

Of course, in a perfect world, you will have made the right acquisition at the right price for the right reasons and will have a detailed integration plan ready to put into effect – no fears for your future. However, in real life, nothing is perfect, and the figures for disappointment or withdrawal by companies that have failed to make their acquisitions pay are chastening. In which case, a few hints on what to do and what not to do may be useful in avoiding that awful state of post-acquisition *tristesse*.

What Type of Changes?

The type and depth of the changes necessary will vary from one country and one industry sector to another. At one end of the spectrum, taking over a mainland Chinese SOE, used to operating within a planned economy and all that that entails, means taking over a largely unskilled workforce imbued with a "featherbedded" culture of lifetime employment and no sense of personal involvement in issues such as quality or productivity. The barriers to change in such a company are daunting and can take years to break down, so be prepared for the long haul.

At the other end of the scale, an acquisition in, say, Malaysia will have a head start in terms of trained workers who are good English speakers and used to maintaining relatively high operating standards. In between, Thailand, Indonesia and Hong Kong offer a range of cultural and business environments that may throw up greater or fewer obstacles to growth. Of course, buying out a local partner will give you the benefit of advance knowledge of a firm and a pool of managers who have built up contacts with their local colleagues. Their experience will make it easier to bridge the change of ownership, but does not necessarily mean that there will be fewer changes to make.

The Post-merger Integration Process

Following the acquisition, many experienced companies move straight-away to implement a post-merger integration (PMI) plan. This plan is based on reports from everyone who participated in the acquisition process but, primarily, from the work of the due diligence team. These reports normally contain an assessment of the new possession and a list of proposed areas for improvement. During the next stage, these reports are analyzed and combined in a single document by a specially constituted PMI committee, whose membership includes corporate strategists, business development planners, Asian experts, financial, operational and product managers. The single document that emerges from this operation is then circulated among senior executives and any problems identified are benchmarked against the company's own operations. If it appears that the acquired company has a better method of doing something, the difference can be noted and adopted to the benefit of the rest of the company.

In a parallel phase, the PMI plan sets targets for the acquisition, based on its present and future capabilities, and the company's objectives for its Asian investment. These objectives should also fit within the company's overall global strategy. The outcome should include a fairly detailed business plan for the short and medium term, targets for production, which products for which markets and so on.

Once this framework has been established and the list of improvements and the business plan finalized, then operational teams – even if only two or three people – can be despatched to begin the process of change. In the past, some Western firms have been content to let local managers continue to run their Asian operations, merely sending out technical advisers on short-term missions to transfer technology, and a senior executive to attend board meetings. But trying to run an Asian acquisition (or even a joint venture) at arm's length is one of the surest ways to ruin. Western companies must send in their own "best" people to lead the company and control crucial functions such as finance. "Best" in this sense means people who possess excellent business and management skills, and are also attuned to the cultural sensitivities of the host country. Their task is to bridge the gaps between the two companies, to blend the different organizations and cultures to achieve enhanced performance, which requires a high degree of skill.

Sending in new people definitely does not imply a clear-out of the existing management team. Good local managers will be vital to the future and, in any case, it is hardly motivating to acquired firms if their people feel threatened or unappreciated by the new owners, especially if they are foreign. Again the PMI plan should have identified their strengths and weaknesses and indicated where management needs to be improved. So the long-term aim of the Western team is to introduce training programs where necessary to improve staff skills, raise standards in administration and production and, the biggest challenge of all, change the prevailing culture to match that of the new owners.

One useful tactic is to identify staff with influence in the acquired company – managers and personnel – and build performance incentives for them into the plan to get them "on-side." Hopefully, these key people will then influence those around them at different levels of the company to accept change more readily, and there will there be a good chance of implementing the business plan successfully. The advantage for a company that develops such procedures is that they are able to work quickly to turn the company around. Of course, this does presuppose a high-quality team, with experience of managing change in different cultures – unfortunately quite a rarity, even in sophisticated multinationals. Where possible, it might be wise to co-opt local staff from the acquired firm into the team to give their insights into previous performance, explain cultural differences and generally act as a bridge between the two sides.

The usual areas targeted for improvement are HR, transparency, product quality and efficiency. However, success in changing these depends very much on how well the post-acquisition team is able to begin changing the corporate culture and induce the troops to accept new ways of working.

Cultural Change

To implement cultural change is difficult even within a mature market context – think of the potential problems arising from a French acquisition of an English company. Then think of what it means for a Western firm to try and introduce change into an Asian acquisition, whose local managers are used to deferring utterly to seniority and hierarchy, have developed their own close-knit networks and might operate in a culture where bribery is a fact of life. To alter Confucian social structures and habits of obedience and respect for authority that have been entrenched for the last 2,500 years could well be classed as the thirteenth Herculean labor.

Real change – as opposed to superficial lip-service – means shattering the status quo and replacing it by a new culture marked by very un-Asian characteristics such as individualism, self-assertiveness, initiative and personal responsibility. Most of all, Western companies talk about implementing a winning culture, one that is competitive and with a strong will to win. They aim for global strategies and the spread of global best practices, but many of these sit very uncomfortably with Asian habits and ways of thinking. To introduce such a changed mindset is a long process, requiring great skill on the part of management and needing continual reinforcement. However, unless it is tackled with some success, tensions between the two cultures will severely impede the development of the company. The subject is dealt with in greater detail in Strategy 16.

One way of getting staff to think differently about their company may be through changing its image. A rebranding exercise, based on the known strengths of the investing firm, can bring great benefits both in changing customer perceptions and giving staff a new pride in their company. After ABN Amro acquired Thailand's Bank of Asia, its first step was to undertake a thorough rebranding exercise. While this was a delicate and sensitive issue to handle, it paid off within a year. Being allied to a foreign and "trustworthy" bank was appreciated by its employees, which helped the bank to increase its market share.

If changing the local management culture is an enormous hurdle, managing the ordinary factory workers is perhaps an even greater challenge. Just as in Europe, huge cultural differences exist between the local populations of the different countries in Asia.

These cultural differences can radically affect the training process, as one British expatriate, who had been happily teaching machine operators in Malaysia, found. The Malay workers had some engineering experience and were familiar with the basic language and technical skills necessary, so were easy to train. When he moved to a plant in Indonesia, he found a totally different proposition. There he was faced by high-school graduates with little foundation on which he could build. Working on a site in Kalimantan, all went well until a group of Bataks from Sumatra arrived. They were better trained, but their high-handed attitude toward the locals caused tensions. Their more aggressive approach disrupted workplace harmony to the point where the situation erupted in rioting.

Workplaces with different cultures that may prove antagonistic to one another need careful managers who understand the different cultures and know how to get things done. This is not usually the case with the expatriates sent in to head the company and fill key posts. Therefore, to ensure that orders are carried out and factories run smoothly, multinationals must have a good middle layer of managers, supervisors and team bosses. In addition to local managers already in place, some companies recruit Indian or Filipino expats to fill these roles. Less expensive than their Western counterparts, they are often highly qualified. However, even here there can be problems.

Many firms have found that South African managers are the best solution. Their home experience in managing employees from different tribal groups gives them a distinct advantage, plus the fact that they tend to be more comfortable than many US or European managers with the concept of being a "father" figure to the workers. Many have a long working experience in South Africa, but left their home country for political reasons and are seeking short-term contracts to fill in the years up to their retirement. This factor is another plus for companies hiring them. Since age is respected in Asia, local workers often find change easier to accept from a senior figure than a brash young manager in a hurry.

In the long term, the extent of cultural change and the ability to manage local workers is a major determinant in the success or failure of an acquisition. However, the trick is to know what can be altered or leveled up, and which parts to leave alone so that the acquired company feels it has some autonomy left. As Heinrich von Pierer noted:

> I think it's important that the buying company does not try to overrun and completely change the corporate culture in the acquired company. We at Siemens always strive to establish ourselves as good corporate citizens in all our local markets … Whilst a rigorous, success-oriented culture throughout the company is important for big corporations like us, it's equally important to give individual units entrepreneurial freedom in their daily operations.[2]

If there is a discernible trend toward improvement, some diversity in practice is not serious, and a happy workforce is more likely to deliver the desired results. One of the key factors here will be communication between management and employees – why you are making the changes, how this will make them part of a winning team and why this is a useful aim.

Human Resource Issues

Human resources (HR) can make or break an acquisition; in every survey on key issues for Western companies moving into Asia, they topped the list of problems. Downsizing, finding good quality people and staff development are crucial issues and potentially the biggest barriers to growth if not dealt with effectively.

Downsizing

Before the economic crisis, of course, staff retention was the important issue, since the too few good people were easily enticed away by higher paying competitors. After 1997, the situation changed dramatically; for example Marks & Spencer, the UK retailer, found that its annual staff losses dropped from 30 percent in 1995 to almost zero post-crisis. Since then, the problem has been how to lay off staff without provoking demonstrations, bad feelings or even violence, since rejection is often taken personally. Following the economic downturn, the suicide rate increased in Japan and Korea, while the murder rate rose dramatically in Thailand where at least one manager was murdered by a sacked employee. It has been said that "When a Korean loses his job he kills himself. When a Thai loses his job, he kills his wife." Glib though this might seem, it does suggest the degree to which employment is linked with self-worth in Asia.

Compared with Western staffing levels, most Asian companies are over-resourced, and one of the first aims of a company making an acquisition is to reduce the headcount. However, any downsizing needs to be carefully managed, according to local labor laws and through negotiation with regional or local governments. This applies especially to China, India and Indonesia, which have particularly strict labor laws.

One Thai owner found a way to cut down his distribution and sales force for one business from 100 to just 5 people that mixed Western "rationalism" with Asian "paternalism":

First of all I sat down with them and gave them the facts and figures. They saw that we just weren't able to go on because we were dealing with imported products and with the devaluation of the baht, we couldn't sell them at the high prices we got before. They understood, and we paid them all compensation. We parted amicably. Some workers I was able to move to other parts of the business, some I have let have a van to run a small business themselves. They pay us the cost of running the van and we source essential foods such as rice or fish sauce for them. These are all easy to sell from a van, and most are making a living.[3]

However, one Western expatriate who tried to get rid of an unsatisfactory finance director in a culturally sensitive way did not find it so easy. First he tried promoting the manager way beyond his capabilities in the hope that, overwhelmed by his new responsibilities, he would lose face and resign. In fact, although clearly under stress, the manager merely avoided meetings at which he might be exposed and showed no sign of leaving. The MD then promoted someone else who was well qualified and actually did the work, hoping that the rest of the finance team would see this as unfair and put pressure on the first manager to leave. However, when asked, they said that they were "happy to work round him."

Examples such as these demonstrate what a sensitive issue this is and why it must be handled carefully. Few ordinary workers would believe that a rich Western firm did not have the financial resources to keep workers on, so downsizing merely confirms Western firms' reputations for being uncaring and ruthless. Perhaps the most effective way to deal with layoffs is to work with local managers to map out a strategy for any layoffs, and try to keep the news quiet for as long as possible, to avoid sparking protests and riots. Generous compensation complying with, or even exceeding, the legal limits is a must. Some companies try to cushion the blow by hiring outside firms to give counseling and help in writing CVs so that workers can find other jobs. This approach will protect the firm's reputation and make it easier to attract workers back later.

Finding a Skilled Workforce

The other side of the coin is finding the skilled, well-trained local staff needed to run your acquisition. Recruitment of factory workers in many Southeast Asian countries tends to follow a pattern in which those hired will in turn recruit other members of their family. This reflects a culture in which people most trust those who are related to them This was the experience of the Belgian logistics and high-tech services company Katoen Natie (KTN), following its entry into Thailand. For the first three years, its operations were led by a Flemish manager sent out from its Antwerp headquarters. As KTN has no human resource management (HRM) department, he was directly responsible for local recruitment and so initially hired the 50 people needed at start up via press advertisements and a local employment company that helped with screening applicants. As KTN's vice president Dirk Lannoo recalled, the staffing then followed a typical Thai cultural pattern: "one guy we hired had a nephew, and it went from there – we got the whole family."[4]

For the first three years the operation ran well. Then the original Flemish manager moved to head KTN's Canadian operations and was replaced by a young, locally hired manager who had previously worked for a major electronics firm. Unfortunately, the Thai workforce did not think the new recruit was mature enough to lead them and people began to leave. KTN was forced to find another head and this time chose an old Asia hand with a long track record working for multinationals in the region and, above all, in Thailand. He was able to offer the Thai staff the maturity they sought and the workforce stabilized once more.

However, the HR issue that gives foreign firms the biggest headache is finding – and keeping – well-qualified, professional local managers. This scarce commodity is dealt with separately in Strategy 15.

Transparency

Despite carrying out due diligence, companies can never be sure of what exactly they are buying into in Asia. They can only hope that the cupboard does not contain too many skeletons. Gaining control of financial data and bringing more transparency into the company's finances is almost always the number one priority once they have deciphered the balance sheet. Only then can they go forward with confidence. An expatriate finance manager, able to install and maintain strict systems and processes, is the swiftest and surest solution. In the long term, it is a cultural issue that time and training will change, as managers used to working in the Asian way get used to the idea of openness and accountability.

One example illustrates how fraught an issue this can be. A Scottish managing director with 30 years' experience, mostly in Malaysia, was hired to identify the problems of a newly acquired, badly performing agribusiness division in Indonesia and turn it around.[5] He quickly decided that the accounting system needed a complete overhaul. Although the division produced numerous sets of figures from the units, none of them made sense.

An outside accountant's report confirmed that the system needed to be changed completely, and a new one was drafted. A memo was circulated, calling for a meeting of all division managers in order to present the new accounting format and the rationale for change. Both the finance manager and the heads of the individual agribusinesses were present. Within a few minutes, the Scottish manager knew that he was facing a solid block of resistance – nobody was going to accept the new format. Exchanges became quite heated, as the managers refused to accept his arguments and accused him of being a one-man show, not consulting them and so on.

The Scottish manager called a five-minute break to allow tempers to cool, then began again, patiently explaining why the system had to be changed and answering all criticisms. He also said he would not give in, that whether it took an hour or 24 hours, the meeting would not end until the new format was accepted. In an ever more hostile atmosphere, one manager finally rose to his feet and, in what the Scottish manager afterward realized was probably the only time in his life he had given an honest opinion in a meeting with his boss, actually shouted: "We do not want this. Don't you realize that if we change, people can understand our figures? We want no one to understand our figures."

Processes and Systems

Processes and systems are at the heart of change and vital to the success of the integration process. First and foremost is the need to ensure that the acquired company's production processes are in line with those of the investing firm. Technological incompatibility, of IT platforms for example, can be a particularly thorny issue that needs to be sorted out straightaway. Delays are likely to lead to more expense later on, so it is better to make the investment in the early days while the change process is in full swing.

Ideally, the due diligence process will have itemized all the areas in the product process that need to be changed and committed the necessary resources for training and the replacement or updating of equipment. This is important where equipment, originally of good quality and technically sophisticated, has been badly installed and poorly maintained during its life. Improving production will almost inevitably mean new management, since often plant managers will have been long established and surrounded by employees who are friends or relatives.

Another frequent obstacle to change is the manufacturing culture in Asia. Any attempt to talk of increased production to meet changed economic circumstances, a keener competitive environment or future challenges is likely to be met by blank incomprehension. As far as existing managers and workers might be concerned, the factory has increased output over the years and that is quite sufficient. There may also be a strong union presence. To get workers to accept new practices or feel able to suggest ways of improving systems will take time and patience. Again, the key is training; taking a few key people for special courses and then cascading the new processes down.

A useful approach is to lead by example and work directly with the workforce. One European manager trying to improve production at a factory in China gained the respect and interest of the workforce by working alongside them, "getting his hands dirty." It also meant he could keep an eye on what they were doing. Another experienced Dutch expatriate found himself pulling on cables in the rain and mud on a factory site in Indonesia but, again, he found that it was the best way of demonstrating how to do the job. Yet another, senior Australian manager, who had been more or less office-bound for many years, was surprised to find himself hanging upside down from the roof joists, doing electrical work to keep the newly acquired factory going. It's usually more important for expatriate Western managers to be seen doing such tasks than it is for local Asian managers.

Quality Improvement

ISO 9000 registration is becoming increasingly sought after throughout Asia. However, it is often difficult to get local managers to take working toward it seriously, since it means a lot of documentation work or written procedures that are alien. A faster first step is to set up a quality control department staffed by trained workers. Previously, many factories either lacked such a department or it functioned badly.

Coordination Mechanisms

Once a company has several acquisitions in different countries in the region, it faces the problem of how to organize the relationship between them in order to leverage value. An extension of this is how to organize the relationship between the Asian subsidiaries and the home base. The problem is how to strike a balance between too loose a rein, which can result in subsidiaries wasting resources competing with each other and fighting turf wars, and too strict a mechanism that merely adds a further layer of bureaucracy with expensive overheads. Out of the various formal coordinating mechanisms tried in the past, the two most popular solutions have been regional headquarters and country managers.

During the 1990s, regional headquarters (RHQs), usually based in Hong Kong or Singapore, became fashionable. Through them, companies hoped to capture synergies and square the circle of the ongoing battle between geography, function and product. This frequently resulted in hostilities, when the demands of global product managers clashed with those of local managers more attuned to the sensitivities of their particular markets. However, there were advantages. Having a senior manager based out in the region, it was argued, would send a strong signal that the company was committed to its Asian investment. In addition, the regional base could act as a funnel for continued information collection and begin to formulate a regional strategy to increase the pace of growth.

Unfortunately, many of these RHQs only added an extra layer to the organizational and administrative hierarchy out in the region, an unwelcome development for hard-pressed subsidiary heads. Regional directors, moreover, ended up spending a vast amount of time in the air, either between the subsidiaries or flying back to home base for meetings. Generally, these structures proved neither successful in becoming a focus for investment in the region, nor in resolving the local/product manager clash. With the Asian currency crisis, many of them were closed down. Three years later there was a move to reopen RHQs, but this time in Hong Kong rather than Singapore, a sign of the changing direction in Asian investment. But by 2003, the pull of China was proving irresistible and the next round of moves left Hong Kong losing out to Shanghai and Beijing.

The appointment of country managers, tasked to look after geographical and political dimensions, was another attempt by multinationals to ensure that local responsiveness was not swamped by the emphasis on globalization. However, as several companies found when they tried the experiment, in any fight involving product and geography, product won hands down, and the hapless country managers, lacking any real authority, found themselves quite powerless and irrelevant.

In the end, the verdict on attempts to impose a coordinating mechanism across subsidiaries in Asia seems to be that, while it is important to make sure that managers in a region meet to get to know each other and exchange information, imposing a formal structure is not necessarily the most effective, and certainly not the cheapest, way to do so. Regular meetings in subgroups or task forces and workshops, in the presence of senior managers from the center who are there to listen as much as advise, seem to be a better first step to building a mechanism that can actually deliver something of value and help bed down new acquisitions.

Key Lessons

■ Have a clear, well-designed PMI plan
■ Send out the best people you can to implement it
■ Communicate what you are doing and why
■ Mobilize the commitment and resources for change
■ Be patient. Remember the Japanese proverb: "It takes ten years to grow a tree, but it takes a century to educate people."

Notes

1 *Academy of Management Executive*, "Siemens CEO Heinrich von Pierer on cross-border acquisitions," M. Javidan, 2002, **16**(1).
2 Ibid.
3 Taken from "Champaca Survives?," case study by Charlotte Butler, INSEAD-EAC, 1999.
4 Taken from "Katoen Natie enters Asia," case study by Charlotte Butler and Dirk Van den Berghe, INSEAD-EAC, 2005.
5 Taken from "Changing the Figures," case study by Charlotte Butler and Professor Henri-Claude de Bettignies, INSEAD-EAC, 1994.

Strategy 13

Send the Right People

WHAT'S IN THIS CHAPTER?

▷ Day One

▷ The Family

▷ The Importance of Being an Expatriate

▷ Getting the Best

▷ A Square Peg for a Square Hole

▷ What Support Systems?

▷ Key Lessons

    Send the Best

    Empowerment

    An International Cadre

    Start Preparing Now

Day One

So here you are on your first day of your posting, installed in an office which could be in a tower block in downtown Jakarta or Central District in Hong Kong, in a special economic zone near Shanghai, a portakabin on a building site in Sumatra or perhaps overlooking a factory floor on a new industrial estate on the edge of Bangkok. If you really drew the short straw, your office might be in a run-down, former SOE building on the banks of the Yangtse, with the smell of the rubbish drifting by and an over-flowing spittoon in the corner of the meeting room – a sign of a long-standing local habit that you may or may not get used to.

Whatever the case, it certainly isn't home. You flew in with your family yesterday, and the heat and smells hit you forcefully as you climbed into the limousine at the airport, and the landscape as you drove into town was definitely not European or American. You are excited about the challenge as the job was presented, but now that reality kicks in, you are feeling rather isolated and daunted. If this is your first time in Asia, so you should be.

Perhaps your company has just acquired a local firm or transformed a long-standing joint venture into a wholly owned subsidiary and sent you out to lead the integration process; your job is to change the culture, expand production and generally make it more of a strategic fit. Perhaps you are taking over a joint venture that is not delivering and are there to "sort it out," or maybe you are taking over from another colleague on a three-year rotational assignment in an Asian subsidiary. Whatever the case, responsibility for your home company's investment is now yours alone – the business development team and due diligence experts have moved their caravanserai on to the next target, the HR director and the head of Asian operations who sent you there are far away back at headquarters.

Of course, you have the long-term corporate strategy to guide you, and within it your own particular mission and targets plus spreadsheets showing financial growth projections for the next five years. But what looked to be a straightforward, clearly structured business development plan back at head office or in the sanitized surroundings of RHQ in Singapore or Hong Kong can take on a very different picture once you are actually in place and it is implementation time. Now you have to make the projected figures turn into the actual profits that will help to make your company Big in Asia.

At the micro-level, how its Asian operations are managed will be the key to the return that a company obtains on its investment there. Yet it is remarkable how poorly prepared are most expatriate managers sent out to run them. This is because appointments are generally made in a hurry, with time for only a minimal briefing. The lucky ones might get a trip out to visit the company before deciding whether or not to accept a posting to Asia but, in the days of budget cuts, this is becoming less and less likely. Some multinationals make an attempt to give their managers information about the country and the job – perhaps even sending them on a cultural course – but the reality of what it will mean to manage in such a different cultural context is not easily conveyed in a classroom. Often there is little overlap between the departing expatriate and the new arrival, so there is no time for a proper handover. The new manager inherits an unknown situ-

ation and then has to spend the next 12 months on a voyage of discovery –
whom to trust, what to do, how to go about it; all a terrible waste of a
highly expensive resource.

The Family

Another dimension that is often ignored in sending someone off on a
foreign posting is the effect on their family. Spouses are suddenly trans-
ported into a new environment, cut off from all their familiar support
systems and finding themselves coping alone, with a partner who is
working long days. Of course, for some, the expatriate lifestyle can be
luxurious compared with conditions at home, especially for those based
in Hong Kong or Singapore. Those benefiting from contracts stipulating
large apartments, club membership and so on can have a wonderful time
and, for most spouses, the perks of Asia include a nice apartment or
a house with a pool, an amah for the children and even a cook and
a driver.

But even these can turn out to be flawed. In all probability, the kitchen
is overrun with cockroaches, stomach upsets are rife and the amah is
spoiling the children. A young mother cannot take her baby out for a walk
in Bangkok or Jakarta – even if there was a pavement, it would be impossible to maneuver a pram along it and the air, polluted by fumes from a
thousand exhausts, will soon give the baby a nasty cough. Often there is
little scope for spouses who might want to work and, in the resulting
vacuum, boredom and loneliness can put a heavy strain on a marriage.
Alternatively, spouses who move to remote locations in the forests of
Indonesia or Thailand may find themselves living in rudimentary accom-
modation on a factory site, where watching TV is a challenge as the gener-
ator usually breaks down several times a day. And if you become ill, the
hospital is some distance away.

More than ever before, therefore, it is important for multinationals to
consider carefully which people to choose for a posting to Asia and what
sort of preparation to give them beforehand. Beyond that, they must also
think about another critical but often neglected side of managing in Asia,
how to organize the relationship between the multinational head office and
its expatriate managers once they are in place. Unfortunately, in the excitement of planning and implementing strategies for growth in Asia, these
issues are usually somewhat neglected, with negative consequences for the
success of the posting for both sides.

The Importance of Being an Expatriate

In the past, Asia was not high on the list of investment targets for Western multinationals. Even during the boom years of the 1990s, firms were slow to understand the growth possibilities of the region, and later held exaggerated expectations. Their emphasis was on gaining a foothold to keep up with their competitors and making short-term profits, rather than building up a good cadre of managers with Asian expertise who could run the business for long-term growth and solidly based prosperity. Those expatriate managers sent to Asia often found themselves overwhelmed by the number of VIP visitors from headquarters – main board members, corporate strategists, even the chairman – demanding a guided tour of "our Asian interests."

In the wake of the currency crisis of 1997, the instinct of many Western multinationals was to withdraw until the better times came round again, perhaps leaving a lone manager in charge of a scaled-down operation. Others saw the crisis as providing unparalleled acquisition opportunities at bargain basement prices but, as many of them now realize having read it so often in the business press, making an acquisition turned out to be only the opening paragraph of the story.

Then a few years later, along came the China boom and the stampede of Western companies to enter this new market. Substantial investment in China, together with recent renewed interest in acquiring Southeast Asian operations, means that success in the region is now much more important to Western multinationals as it will be an important factor in their future profitability. Yet operating in this environment remains a huge challenge, so if they are to achieve the sort of returns on these investments that their shareholders require, they will have to manage their Asian operations more effectively than ever they have in the past.

This means exerting a measure of control and introducing new management methods to raise standards and integrate these acquisitions into their global empire. To accomplish this vital task, they need to send expatriate managers able to drive organizational and cultural change, train the local workforce and make quality improvements in production, straighten out the finances and so on. In China especially, there are also sensitive relations with local governments to handle and the huge marketing and distribution problems associated with operating there. All this means that companies will have to rely on expatriate managers as never before, putting a tremendous strain on their HR capacity. Moreover, given the difficulties of localizing (see Strategy 15), this situation is likely to continue for some time to come. So for the senior management of companies hoping to get Big in Asia, the message is clear: a vital factor in the success or failure of your investment will be the calibre of your expatriate managers on the ground. The importance of being an expatriate in Asia has never been so crucial.

Getting the Best

Unfortunately, HR departments have not, in the past, been spoilt for choice when selecting candidates for an Asian posting. Given the ambivalent attitude of Western multinationals toward their regional operations over recent years, this is not really surprising. Taking their cue from head office, neither corporate HR departments nor ambitious young managers have seen Asia as a plum job, a chance to perform in a highly strategic part of the corporate empire.

Rather, it has been a road to nowhere – less a case of making your mark than of blowing your future in some forgotten country few can readily find on a map. The success of Douglas Daft, who took over as CEO of Coca-Cola after 20 years developing its operations in Asia, beginning in Indonesia in the 1970s, is still an exception rather than the rule. More likely is the reaction experienced by a young manager sent out to South Korea early in 2000, who was asked by his neighbor on the plane out to Seoul: "Where did you screw up in your last job?" One oil company refused to let its executives take familiarization trips, on the grounds that "If the manager knew where he was going, he would never take the job."

More often, a posting to Asia has been seen as an opportunity to get rid of someone considered a maverick, someone who "doesn't fit in," or even as a punishment. In the 1980s and early 1990s, many companies sent young, inexperienced managers who were considered dispensable or, at the other end of the age scale, people who were approaching retirement, to while away their last working years. Only in the late 1990s did potential high-flyers begin to take an interest in an Asian posting, a trend that quickly died down again with the Asian crash.

This is because, despite their much vaunted claims to be global, Asia still represented only a small percentage of the portfolio for many Western multinationals. The weight of their interests and therefore the perceived glory lay in the US or Europe, and even Eastern Europe or Latin America were viewed as higher up the corporate wish list by ambitious managers. Not unnaturally, therefore, they focused their hopes on a tour of duty where their efforts were most likely to bring them to the attention of top management. Asian operations were still a long way from the center of power at headquarters, and managers sent there feared being forgotten. Perhaps they too often saw returnees fail to reintegrate success-fully, or even be paid off as "there is nothing for you here," to want to copy them.

But this attitude is changing fast as Asia rises ever higher on the corporate radar. Increasingly, a China posting is being actively sought by ambitious managers eager to make their mark. It is where the action is. Given the difficulties of finding good local managers in China, expatriate managers will be needed out there for some time to come. But these are a very expensive item, so companies can no longer afford to send in inexpe-rienced people doomed to failure as they struggle to cope with this most inhospitable of competitive environments. They must be sure they send in the best. This means identifying the particular qualities that will make a manager most suited to making your company Big in Asia.

A Square Peg for a Square Hole

So what skills are needed to be an effective manager in Asia? If you are the HR director of a large multinational, what factors should you keep in mind when choosing who should run your operations there? Too often in the past, head office selectors have failed to appreciate that not everyone can adapt to a new culture, and that the qualities that make for a good manager in the aggressive markets of the US or Europe will not necessarily be appropriate or effective in the more consensual environment of Asia.

As many expatriate managers have discovered, in Asia none of their usual standards apply when it comes to assessing market potential or financial worth, and as for managing local people, all their previous exper-ience counts for nothing. Those used to working within formal structures that give security, or who in the past relied on the strict application of financial ratios before making a decision, must learn to operate in an ambiguous and volatile environment. In Asia, hard information is difficult if not impossible to come by, events can change rapidly and taking risks is a natural part of doing business. Someone who manages by the rule book, has a strong individual streak or is an aggressive exponent of Western management concepts is unlikely to thrive in such a different environment, or to have more than a temporary success.

Nowhere else are political and negotiating skills so vital. Life in Asia, observed one seasoned expatriate, is "one long negotiation." This will include negotiating with local politicians, city or regional government representatives and officials at every level, from ministries to foreign investment boards or trade councils, through unions and local suppliers down to the customs officer, not counting the daily negotiations needed to manage the workforce, its local managers and perhaps the joint venture partner. And remember, this must be done via an interpreter whom you must trust to convey the exact sense of your words. Chances are you will be unable to communicate directly with anyone except your personal secretary and most senior managers, and you cannot rely on the local newspaper to find out what is happening or what is being written about your company.

Any list of qualities and skills necessary for managing in Asia would probably include the following; resourceful, entrepreneurial, gregarious, patient and tolerant, a creative attitude to systems, a team player with good communication, negotiating and political skills, self-reliant, able to cope with high stress levels, build consensus, think on your feet, establish trust, and convince people to act in a way that is radically different from their previous habits in their working lives. Not an easy profile to fulfil.

And all this is only to be able to deal with the local environment; an equally heavy strain may be connected with the demands of the home base. For the expatriate is in place not just to manage a company but also to fulfil the targets and expectations of the corporate center. These will probably encompass a variety of dimensions from increased production, improved quality and faster delivery to cutting costs or manpower while expanding the business and, of course, increasing profits, all in the shortest possible time. But London or Houston will probably have little understanding of the reality of the business environment in which you are competing, or the true potential of its local company. Thus these targets may be ill-conceived or unrealistic and almost certainly will fail to take into account the long-term view that building a business in Asia requires, since the expectations of the home stock market and its shareholders will not allow it such a luxury. Little wonder that expatriates often find themselves torn in two as they try to satisfy the interests of such diametrically opposed stakeholders, to be a success in headquarters' terms while they themselves are adapting to a new culture and struggling to come to grips with a foreign business environment.

To avoid such conflicts, HQ need to ensure effective communications between themselves and their overseas managers. No longer is it enough to send them off with a cheery wave and a "See you in three years' time." They need to be in regular and close contact to ensure that their demands are based on a true evaluation of the situation. This means giving careful consideration to what sort of information they collect and analyze before setting targets for their Asian subsidiaries, and to the backup that they provide to help their expatriates do their jobs in good and bad times. What kind of support systems should head office put in place to ensure smooth communications between itself and its overseas managers?

What Support Systems?

The ideal support effort supplied by HQ would probably include a specific coordination team at the center, headed by an "Asian champion" who has pull at the highest level and consisting of people familiar with the business and cultural context. This team would be ready and able to, for example, respond quickly to appeals for help or information, perhaps negotiate with product groupings to arrange any special prices needed, send out any technical advisers necessary, supply training requests and, of course, boost the morale of those in the field. Such a system would be an expatriate's dream. Unfortunately, it rarely exists.

More typical is the experience of one German manager who found himself based in a factory in a small outpost in China, where he was at odds with his Japanese and Chinese joint venture partners over vital resource decisions and had little real power. Daily meetings deteriorated to a shouting match – albeit slowly due to the need for three-way interpreters. Often he went back to his hotel room in tears of frustration to drown his sorrows with Tsingtao beer in the empty hotel bar, knowing that his feelings about what should be done were not shared back at head office.

It is generally accepted that a company's attitude to managing its overseas operations reflects what has become known as its "administrative heritage"; how it organized itself in the past. This can either be a source of key competencies or represent a brake on the company's ability to change, and tends to be identified with the centralization/decentralization debate. Companies favoring the former try to maintain strict control over what their expatriate managers are doing via control of capital expenditure (cap ex) and budgets, those following the latter adopt a more laissez-faire attitude, whereby local chairmen are given a fair amount of autonomy over how they run their operations. Neither one is ideal and carried to extremes can be damaging.

Unilever, for example, has historically taken a decentralized approach, encouraging a culture of strong, local, self-sufficient operations overseas. This gave it great strength in terms of local responsiveness and knowledge. Managers had wide scope to act within the overall corporate plan and were able to take decisions quickly. Consequently, the company was able to build on its long connections in the region and, during the boom times, experienced successful and rapid growth in both Southeast Asia and China.

One company that has successfully combined decentralization with good support systems is the Belgian high-tech services company Katoen Natie (KTN).[1] KTN's independent business units form the foundation of the group. They are supported by a very small Antwerp-based headquarters, which has neither an HR nor a strategy function. Centralization comes via the reporting system, which allows headquarters to keep track of KTN's 100 logistics platforms throughout the world. At KTN, delagation is a key word that is actually put into practice.

Thus, after its entry into Thailand, KTN sent out a 29-year-old, single Flemish manager to start up the operations, together with a fellow engineer (married and only a year older) to oversee the investment. Neither had ever worked in the region before but, despite this lack of experience and their youth, KTN's vice president Dirk Lannoo had confidence in them since "They both had a good grounding in KTN." The operation got off to a good start and the first manager spent three very successful years before moving to head KTN's Canadian operations. KTN's Thai auto business was also launched by a young (33-year-old) Flemish manager, who was already working in the auto sector.

Commenting on KTN's policy of entrusting new investments to young managers, Lannoo emphasized that

> We send out people who have had a good training in the company in Belgium. Our culture and management are strong points for us – they must understand the company, its strategy and philosophy, and last and very important have a strong network. Because when they have a problem in Thailand or wherever, they must know the right person to call.

The right person is usually found among KTN's business support groups. These are people who have the know-how, skills, experience and networks to support operations anywhere in the world. They can either work from Antwerp or travel out to the business units. Their three main activities are making quotations, helping fine-tune operations and acting as a help desk for KTN worldwide:

> Just because you sign a contract and start operations, it doesn't mean that everything will run perfectly. So when there is a problem, or a need to upgrade or fine-tune an operation, the support team provides the experienced people who can help with this. And the help desk is there to help with any problems that arise with the machinery, computers and so on.

Of course, unfettered entrepreneurism can be dangerous if it leads to the building of fiefdoms, run by managers who take no notice of the center. In the case of KTN, leaving so much latitude to far-flung managers could invite the risk of HQ being unaware of serious problems that might arise and stay hidden. Lannoo acknowledged that

> I'm sure we don't know everything that is going on and we can still get surprises, but so far we have not had any really nasty surprises. From the management point of view, if we wanted to control everything, we would have to hire another 50 people to act as controllers and have more reporting – weekly/daily, form filling etc. This would cost a lot of money and would also kill enthusiasm and entrepreneurship. We try to strike a balance between maintaining adequate control whilst not killing initiative because, after all, we are a company that believes in entrepreneurism and innovation … The other way, that I have seen operating in US and British companies, is to have a very centralized and strict reporting and control system. But it means that, really, it is the controllers who are running the company.

Centralization, as Lannoo noted, implies a much greater restriction on the freedom of local expatriate managers to act in this entrepreneurial manner. It is usually associated with excessive bureaucracy at the center and phrases such as "finance driven" and "risk averse" to describe senior management. In particular, it implies the imposition of strict controls (especially of finance) and formal systems, manifested by an emphasis on regular requests for information and weekly or monthly form filling to produce short-term targets with a heavy emphasis on rates of return.

Such a culture is often not applicable in an Asian context. Where local managers are so constrained by having to refer back every decision and wait for an answer, their frustration can be immense. "If death came from Spain, we should all be immortal" was the famous remark made concerning Philip II of Spain's notorious inability to prioritize and give a swift reply to his ambassadors abroad. Managers waiting for urgent answers to demands for permission to do deals or spend beyond a cap-ex level set so low as to be excessively restrictive know exactly how they felt. If a response is swift and demonstrates an understanding of the situation, well and good, but, as one Unilever manager remarked, "the windows of opportunity in Asia are small and close up very quickly," so waiting for permission might mean the loss of a golden chance.

A senior manager from another Western company put the view more succinctly: "I find it hard to understand how somebody sitting in London can second-guess the guys who are in the market every day, 2,000 miles away."

Key Lessons

Send the Best

If a company is serious about becoming bigger in Asia, then its expatriate managers must be the highest quality available. This means, first, attracting talented people for Asian postings and, second, investing in training them before they go out to the region.

To achieve the first goal, it must be made clear that a posting in Asia is not a second-class appointment, but a route to career advancement within the company, and that only the best need apply. For the second, corporate HR directors must better prepare managers before they leave the home country so that they are aware of some of the differences and difficulties they are likely to face. Siemens is one of many multinationals that has its own management training center where people can receive training and information before they go out to run Asian operations. Unprepared managers are more likely to fail, which sends back the wrong message to their peers. HR departments must also ensure that career plans include re-entry strategies for managers coming back from Asia, signalling that such experience really is considered important for future promotion.

Unfortunately, even after all the publicity and debate about the need to enter new markets such as China and India and the prefixing of "global" to their company name, many multinationals remain dominated by a Western-centric outlook at the higher levels. Boards and executive committees still tend to be dominated by people with little knowledge or experience of managing in Asia. Promoting staff who have served in the region and giving them high visibility positions at headquarters would send out a powerful signal that Asia is the route to the top. Of course, the strongest signal would be to put an Asian manager on the board, but few companies have dared to go this far – yet.

Empowerment

Empowerment is not the same as leaving managers to sink or swim alone in their Asian postings. Rather, it means a recognition that a degree of autonomy is important in the countries of the region, where local contacts and knowledge count far more than in other parts of the world and therefore a certain latitude in decision making must be left to the man on the spot, even though this might impinge on the interests of the global products division. It also implies putting in a structure and backup systems, with experienced people in place at the center able both to respond to requests and supply help or informed advice as needed. Local managers can find themselves quite isolated at times, and in case of trouble need to know that there are reliable allies back home.

An International Cadre

One step further on from this might be the development of an international cadre of managers, experienced in different cultures and able to act quickly and effectively, while avoiding the extremes of going native or remaining stuck in their own cultural habits. Some companies, such as Unilever and Lafarge, have already tried this; Lafarge has developed an entry level for managers when they reach 35–40 years to train and take on an international role. Unilever, finding that many local managers in Asia were reluctant to move out of the region, concentrated on giving them the opportunity to change jobs within neighboring countries, so developing a regional cadre.

Start Preparing Now

No company that wants to be global can afford to ignore Asia, most are currently trying desperately to become bigger in China. In this ever more cutthroat competitive arena, a crucial factor in distinguishing winners from losers will be the ability of their people to manage there and the corporate center to give the right support in terms of human, financial and organizational resources. Start training your managers and spreading the right message now.

How "ready" is your company to send staff to Asia?

1. Is Asia considered a good ladder to promotion?

2. Is commitment to the region clear?

3. Are support systems at the corporate center well adapted to ensure mutual confidence?

4. Are there informal and formal networks for spreading information about managing in Asia?

5. Do HR directors have reentry strategies for career planning for those returning from Asian postings?

6. Is managing in Asia a component of executive training programs?

Note

1 Taken from "Katoen Natie enters Asia," case study by Charlotte Butler and Dirk Van den Berghe, INSEAD-EAC, 2005.

Strategy 14

Cross the Cultural Divide

WHAT'S IN THIS CHAPTER?	
	▷ The Asian Employee, the Western Expatriate and the Clash
	Workplace Factions
	Bad News
	Local Labor Departments
	▷ Expatriates Under Pressure: Working for a Local Firm in Asia
	▷ Islam in the Asian Workplace
	▷ Strategies for Coping

The Asian Employee, the Western Expatriate and the Clash

Managing local staff and their expectations is a key to being Big in Asia. If you're an expatriate, managing a team that is outside your own culture might well be one of the hardest things you will ever do in your career. Many who have worked as expatriates in Asia say that their time there was among the most rewarding of their careers. Their time may not have always been happy, and was probably often frustrating, but most would agree that it was always interesting.

Stereotypes are not always accurate but they do contain more than a grain of truth, which is why they arise. Table 14.1 shows a comparison

Table 14.1 Comparison between local employees and Western expatriates

The traditional Asian employee	The Western expatriate
Is most comfortable if there are strict orders to follow	Sees strict orders as insulting and undermining of personal integrity
Works to rule – a job is done well if the rules are followed	Results driven – a job is done well if the desired goals have been achieved
Prefers strict instructions, close supervision and unlikely to take the risks associated with creativity	Self-starting, likes to take initiative and demonstrate creativity
Views orders as commands to be followed	Views orders as suggestions to be modified and improved upon
Believes that loyalty to one's superiors and the firm counts above all else	Believes that hard work and honesty count above all else
Prefers teamwork and a lot of supervision	Prefers small or no teams and as little supervision as possible
Views the employer as a "father"	Views the employer as a colleague
Prefers either no performance-based pay or only if it is averaged across the team	Likes performance-based pay to be linked to own efforts
Prefer little or no work travel	Likes work travel
Prefers lots of small vacation leave periods	Prefers few but long vacation leave periods
Will resign rather than air a workplace grievance	Is quick to voice workplace grievances
Will rarely voice an opinion in a meeting, particularly in front of local work colleagues – meetings are to hear what superiors have to say	Likes the dynamism and debate of work meetings – meetings are an opportunity for input and voicing concerns
Accepts boredom in the workplace if it is a consequence of following superior's orders	Would rather resign than be bored
Output must be monitored closely for quality	Able to self-monitor output for quality
Able to operate with only partial knowledge about the company	Wants to be privy to everything that goes on in the firm
Has difficulty delivering bad news or complaints to superiors even if it means telling half-truths	Happy to deliver bad news to anyone in the interests of transparency

between common attributes of locals and Westerners in Asia in their roles as employees. Few workplaces in Asia where locals and Westerners are employed are as harmonious as they could be.

Workplace Factions

The workplace might split into factions when relations between locals and expatriate employees are not carefully managed, with local employees on one side and expatriates on the other. This can happen particularly when there are frustrations on either side – the expatriates might be viewed by the locals as apt to look down on them and the expatriates might have developed a poor regard for the skills of the locals and, as a result, are frustrated.

The salary and promotion expectations of local employees require careful management. Often in countries such as Indonesia, Vietnam and Thailand, local employees do not appreciate the gap between their technical skills and those of the typical Asian or Western expatriate. Consequently, the expatriates might seem overpaid to the local staff who do not recognize the relative extent of the expatriates' skills. A view might develop that the expatriates are paid more simply because they are expatriates, American, "white" or whatever. This is a potentially dangerous workplace issue that must be handled carefully and sensitively.

Hiring new and very good local staff members can help. If they are good, the expatriates will gravitate to them, demonstrating that the issue that might be at the heart of the expatriate's dissatisfaction is skills related and not race related. Occasionally, disharmony between foreign and local staff can be the result of one or a few local staff agitating against the expatriate staff, stirring up concern among the locals. Managers need to identify who the agitators are and work out the best way to neutralize their activities. Access to training opportunities is one way of closing the skills gap, rewarding good local employees and developing a more dynamic and harmonious working environment.

Bad News

How information is shared is a big issue in Asian firms. It is one of the most important commodities in the workplace, so managers must be careful to have structures in place to facilitate its circulation. Bad news brings blame and loss of face, so it is the most difficult form of information to have delivered in a timely fashion. Often the rot will set in, more junior staff will know about it but don't feel able to tell anyone about it. It's usually only discovered after the damage has been done.

Bringing bad news can cause a loss of face. It can be seen as confronting a superior even though the messenger might only be just that – the carrier of the message. Consequently, shooting the messenger is a common practice in Asia. "Why would you tell me this if you did not believe it yourself?" It's an unfortunate bind. The messenger acts out of loyalty, but his actions are interpreted as disloyalty.

Anonymous poison-pen letters are one way in which local staff might voice their concerns. But rarely will it be the excellent employees who resort to this technique. The letters are usually slanderous. Their anonymity adds to the general lack of transparency rather than helps it.

Local Labor Departments

One big surprise for many outsiders who come to Asia is that labor laws in most countries are not nearly as liberal as the Western media portrays them to be. While trade unions may not be powerful, local labor laws can be highly restrictive. Indonesia's are among the most restrictive in Asia. The Department of Manpower frequently intervenes on behalf of local employees, particularly if it is an obviously wealthy Western firm that is the employer. Overzealous labor ministry officials might be seeking bribes to halt their harassment. It happens. The best way to deal with these issues is to appoint a trusted local member of staff to manage relations with the labor ministry. That person's responsibilities include the need to develop good relations with officials, keep abreast of all new regulations to ensure that they are not contravened and learn about the structure of the ministry so that the company can protect itself particularly, say, if vexatious former employees wish to mobilize the ministry to cause trouble for their former employers.

Expatriates Under Pressure: Working for a Local Firm in Asia

There are four types of professional in Asia. There are locals who are educated locally and those who are Western educated. There are Westerners who work in the Asian offices of Western firms, and there are the Western expatriates who work in Asian firms.

The latter group is ignored by almost all the literature on management in Asia. Almost all guides on how to cope as a Western expatriate in Asia assume that you will be working for a Western company. The difficulties faced by expatriates who work for a local firm in Asia are little appreciated and understood.

Many leave for Asia expecting the good life of an expatriate and assuming that they will be valued employees in an organization eager to modernize and utilize their skills. Most are disappointed, while many return home bewildered, disappointed and angry.

Why should this be so? Outside Japan and mainland China, most firms in Asia – big or small – are owned and managed by families, and the companies are run as extensions of the families. Western expatriates in Asian firms face the problem that, while they are employees and probably highly paid ones, they will almost always be viewed as outsiders. Their seniority will be judged not by any formal internal organization chart but by their perceived closeness to the controlling family.

Rarely will they command the trust and respect in these companies that is commensurate with their level and position, as compared with working back home. For many it is a rude shock. Management at home is participative. But in the Asian firm they must get used to following orders, never really knowing what's going on and get used to not trying to find out. Many Western expatriates in Asian firms soon discover that they are grossly overpaid, given their lack of empowerment.

Many find that when they first arrive, the more junior local employees are appropriately deferential. But after some time, and if it becomes clear that they do not enjoy the full confidence of the controlling family, their position in the unofficial hierarchy starts to slide. They might even find themselves a target for anti-expatriate or anti-Western feeling when it becomes clear that they lack a powerful patron within the organization. Many an expatriate responds by working harder, feeling that their increased work effort will win the day. But they've missed the point. A valued employee is not one who is necessarily productive. It's loyalty to the controlling family that counts rather than to the firm or the other shareholders.

Added complications come from the lack of transparency within the firm. Asian firms often do not have formal internal codes of conduct and written rules. Everything depends on the whim of senior management and the founding family. Written rules mean inflexibility and a ceding of control – and Asian corporate patriarchs usually have little desire to share power with a rule book.

A newspaper column by one of the authors of *Big in Asia* on the difficulties of working as a Western expatriate for local firms in Asia drew many responses from readers who wanted to share their experiences. Nearly all spoke of feeling "disempowered" in their jobs in Asia and the deep frustration and distress that caused.

Asian employees are comfortable with a higher degree of workplace supervision than are Westerners. The paradox of the Asian workplace is that absolute loyalty above all else is demanded of employees by management and yet that demand for loyalty does not translate into the workplace being a high-trust environment. Everything must be micromanaged and initiative is discouraged.

One former expatriate in Hong Kong who had been working for a local firm said that after returning to a job in the West she was shown the stationery cupboard at her new workplace and told to help herself. "I nearly burst into tears," she said. "The previous job [in Asia] had me fill out a form for every pen and I was told that I was showing disloyalty to the company for using three writing pads over four months to the total value of US$2.50." She felt undervalued and underutilized for much of her time in Asia. Big achievements were ignored and instead she felt that she was measured on little things such as her stationery use. She reported that occasionally she would get together with other former expatriates and they would discuss their experiences over a drink but she abandoned this. It was "too emotionally draining." She, like other Western expatriates who had spent time in Asia working for local firms, was still too angry to relive the experiences.

Another former expatriate who had worked for a local firm in Japan described the experience as "feudal" and the managers as "bureaucrats rather than managers." He felt undervalued, not trusted and valued not as a potential long-term employee but merely for his short-term, "stopgap" capabilities. In that regard, another former expatriate described having been employed by a local firm in Hong Kong to help it to restructure. The changes that he suggested should be made were used as an excuse to fire eight staff and with that the expatriate's usefulness evaporated, he was starved of work and he resigned to flee the boredom.

Many expatriates talk of the importance of trust. It seems their productivity is never doubted. But it's not all about gaining the trust of management only. Many Western expatriates find that they must battle on two fronts – above and beneath them. Said another former expatriate:

> Expats are not trusted because of their short-term contribution, which lends itself to a self-reinforcing cycle. The power rests with those who stay in the company, have developed links with the more junior staff and thus gain their loyalty. Locals who are Western educated understand this and adapt accordingly.

Expatriates in local firms in Asia tend to either resign early or stay because of the financial benefits and because typically their title is more superior than what they could achieve at home, and they want to "leverage" it for a better job next time around. Rarely, however, are Western expatriates in Asian firms happy. So why do so many Asian firms bother hiring expensive Western expatriates but then don't bother to get the best out of them?

Expatriate staff are often used for their stopgap capabilities. They can go in, tread on the toes that need to be trodden on, in a way that hierarchy-aware locals won't dare to, and then be dispensed with. This makes them ideal for troubleshooting. But also it makes them short-term employees. Again, there is a mismatch of expectations. They expect that the reforms they make will see them rewarded but instead they might be shown the door. Their job is done and with them can go the blame for the inevitable unpleasantness that change in the workplace brings.

At other times they are hired by Asian firms to provide prestige or present a Western face when it's time to seek loans from Western banks or deal with Western fund managers. In this case, they need not be terribly productive at all. Their job really is to be corporate window dressing. Their job is to make the Asian firm look modern, professionally run and sophisticated. They might not be empowered and it might still be the controlling family that calls all the shots but it's the mirage that counts.

Whatever the case, rarely are Western expatriates who go to work for Asian firms in Asia prepared for the mental maze of their new workplaces. Some have a very fulfilling time but many leave Asia feeling that their skills and time have been wasted. Their experience is often completely different from the typical Western expatriate who goes to Asia to work for the local branch of a Western company.

Islam in the Asian Workplace

Where do most of the world's Muslims live? The Middle East? Wrong. The answer is Asia. The countries with the four largest Islamic populations are all in Asia. They are Indonesia (with about 212 million Muslims), Pakistan (158 million), India (145 million) and Bangladesh (120 million). The biggest Muslim populations in the Middle East are to be found in Iran and Egypt, with 67 million and 78 million Muslims respectively. Other countries such as Libya, which has a population of just 5.8 million – almost all of whom are Muslim, might be good at grabbing press headlines but they are tiny in comparison.

With a Muslim population of up to 30 million, there are possibly more Muslims in China than there are in Saudi Arabia, Lebanon, Libya, Bahrain and the United Arab Emirates put together. About 60 percent of Malaysia's population is Muslim and there are Muslims in Singapore, Brunei, the southern Philippines, southern Thailand and western Myanmar. Many of the Indians in Malaysia are Muslims too. Locally, they are known as the Mamak people.

There are five prescribed prayer times each day for observant Muslims. Many companies in Malaysia and Indonesia provide a small prayer room for this, rather than have their employees leave the premises to pray.

Ramadan – the Islamic fasting month – has a lot of significance for Muslims, even if they are not regular mosque goers. Many who are not still choose to fast. The fasting involves not eating, drinking, smoking or having sexual relations during the daylight hours. Ill people, menstruating women and travellers are exempted from fasting for that period of the fasting month that they are affected but time lost should be made up for later. The abstinence is to teach self-discipline and develop empathy with the poor.

Inevitably, fasting has a serious impact on employee productivity. Employees who at other times of the year are happy to miss prayers may become more devout during the month and pray five times each day. It is a time of the year that requires considerable forbearance on the part of employers, as many staff are irritable, productivity is low and for the first few days at least it is not uncommon to see staff practically collapsed on their desks by mid to late afternoon. Headaches cannot be relieved by aspirin because that would mean eating.

Despite the fasting, food consumption rises during Ramadan and cold-storage companies in Indonesia, Malaysia and Brunei usually carry excess capacity throughout the year so that they can cope with the huge rise in demand for space during Ramadan. How is this so? Each night during the month, many Muslims break the fast together after sundown and do so in a festive atmosphere that involves consuming a great deal of food. People take it in turns to hold an open house at which large trays of pre-prepared food are offered to friends and relatives. It provides an excellent networking opportunity and local Chinese and even some Western expatriates often turn up at their Muslim business partners and colleagues' homes to break the fast with them. The open nature of the festivities means that many use it as an opportunity to drop in on senior business figures or government officials whom ordinarily they cannot get to see.

Ramadan ends with a celebration known as Hari Raya in Malaysia and Idul Fitri in Indonesia. It is a time when Muslims spend time with their families first and then go visiting friends and other relatives. Almost all Muslim employees will want time off for this period, which is Islam's most important holiday.

Deepavali (also known as Diwali in northern India) is the most significant religious holiday for Hindus. It is celebrated on the new moon of the seventh month of the Hindu calendar – October or November). So companies that employ Hindu Indian staff, be they in Malaysia, Hong Kong, Indonesia or elsewhere, will need to take account of the likely desire of those staff to want to take holidays at this time. Deepavali is a time for new beginnings. Many Hindus see it as an auspicious time to begin a new enterprise or open a new bank savings account. And on the first day of Deepavali, most Hindus wear a complete set of new clothes.

Similarly, the most important date on the Chinese calendar is Chinese or Lunar New Year. Most Chinese employees will want to go home to spend the week with their parents – so Malaysian Chinese employees working in Singapore will want to go back to Malaysia and so on. It is a time that is spent with the family and is analogous to Christmas.

Strategies for Coping

■ As a Western expatriate in a local firm in Asia:

- Greatly lower your expectations about what you will achieve. This is the most important rule.

- Think carefully about the real reasons why you have been brought in and then operate with those in mind.

- Be prepared to sacrifice productivity for shows of loyalty. Opt for loyalty if there is a conflict between the two. Ultimately those who are trusted will be able to achieve more.

- Identify the locals who are the "power centers" in the hierarchy both beneath and above you and attempt to form visibly good relations with them.

- Learn to be a team player and share your skills.

- Try not to mix only with other expatriates in the workplace.

- Don't expect that all severance conditions will be honored without a fight even if they are contractual.

■ As a manager of local employees in Asia:

- Adopt a paternalistic, caring attitude, but remain aloof. Generally, you will not be able to be good friends with your local staff and also be their manager. In most of Asia, it's one or the other.

- Deliver bad news or orders that are likely to be viewed negatively within the framework of your concern for the employee, for example "We have decided to move you to this new position so that you will have fewer responsibilities, which we thought would allow you to spend more time with your family," is better than "we're downgrading your position because you are not delivering."

- Try not to allow local employees to lose face in front of their local colleagues. Deliver admonishments in private and in a caring, paternal manner.

- Set very clear tasks, with measurable milestones on the way to achieving the final goal. Remember to check back on those milestones.

- Singling out high-performing staff for praise might be counter-productive. It might be interpreted as an attack on everyone else and the singled out staff might feel to blame rather than proud. Try to congratulate a team, even if it means that some in the team are not deserving.

- Bad news rarely travels up, so look carefully for clues about staff dissatisfaction. Don't expect staff to complain about other local staff and managers even if they have a real grievance, and even when they are taken aside and given full opportunity to voice their concerns in private. They might still deny there is a problem.

- Treat unexplained resignations in any particular area as a possible sign that there are management problems in that area and staff are unhappy. Investigate carefully.

- Be prepared to set aside more time than you would prefer to monitor staff output. Be sure to give feedback – praise where it is warranted and suggestions for improvement.

- Be aware of all the local religious holidays and the obligations that these might impose on staff.

- If local staff must be fired, try to arrange for the severance to be as friendly as possible. Aggrieved ex-employees in Asia tend to be more interested in revenge than in the West.

Strategy 15

Localizing the Labor Force

WHAT'S IN THIS CHAPTER?

▷ Localize, Yes – But with What?
▷ Quantity
▷ And Quality
▷ The B-School Problem
▷ The China Syndrome
▷ Effects of the Shortages
  Poaching
  Sky-high Salaries
▷ Recruitment – Where?
▷ Training
▷ And Retention
▷ The Localization Irony

Localize, Yes – But with What?

Deloitte to hire 6,000 China staff

Dell to double India workforce

Wal-Mart to hire 150,000 Chinese

On the latest projections, the number of people working in IT and BPO in India will increase from 700,000 in 2005 to 2.3 million by 2010

Such headlines signal substantial new investment in India, China and other Asian economies – investment that will involve Western companies doubling, tripling, and quadrupling their Asia-based workforces. In October 2005, for example, Cisco Systems announced it would invest US\$1.1 billion in India. A month later Intel promised US\$1 billion over the next five years. Still in India, in December 2005, Microsoft announced plans to invest US\$1.7 billion over the next four years and the investment bank, J.P. Morgan Chase said that it wanted to double its 4,500 staff there.[1] Such plans were by no means confined to Western firms. At the same time, the leading Indian outsourcing companies, Tata Consultancy Services, Infosys and Wipro, were each recruiting over a thousand new employees a month. According to *India Today International:* "New investments and new capacities mean virtually every sector of the economy (barring agriculture) is creating jobs."[2]

But strangely, no mention is ever made of where the skilled workers to run these new or enlarged manufacturing facilities are to be found. Even more crucially, nobody seems to question where Cisco, Wal-Mart, Infosys and the rest will find the senior, middle and junior-level managers to run their ever expanding operations. No foreign company wants to pay the exorbitant costs associated with expatriate executives for long. Presumably they must be expecting to localize as quickly as possible. So how realistic are their expectations?

In fact, behind all the talk of billion-dollar investments, Western CEOs have been acknowledging that a desperate lack of skilled workers and managers could seriously impede their projected growth in Asia. More realistic headlines about expansion prospects in India, for example, would read: "A shortfall of project managers has boosted salaries by 30 percent to some \$23,000 a year, while attrition from lower level jobs approaches 50 percent."[3] In the retail sector, turnover is reported to be as high as 80 percent among sales staff, while according to a survey published in December 2005, India's IT industry faces a shortfall of 500,000 professionals by 2010.[4] Demand has become so intense that newly hired workers often simply don't show up to work because they find a better job between the interview and start day. The attitude is very much: "If you don't like a job, you can change it tomorrow and get three others."[5]

A similar situation exists in China. In 2005 turnover among engineers in Shanghai was running at 20–30 percent as new recruits moved quickly from one company to another in search of ever higher pay. Even highly profitable, high paying companies like Taiwan Semiconductor Manufacturing Co. (TSMC) have found it difficult to recruit the hundreds of technicians and engineers they need, again threatening expansion plans. In June 2006, the temp agency Manpower reported that wage inflation in the financial and professional services sector had pushed local employers to cut their hiring plans.[6] The situation is even more acute in areas such as marketing in China, where people with experience are few and far between. In 2005, turnover in the marketing department of the French cosmetics firm L'Oréal was running at almost 15 percent. Everywhere, job hopping is common among young staff, training costs are rising as firms take on less qualified candidates, only to then see their human capital investments walk out the door, and headhunting has emerged as a boom sector in its own right.

At the other end of the scale, manufacturing companies, who until now have relied on a seemingly inexhaustible supply of cheap, unskilled migrant workers eager to escape the hardships of life in the countryside to work in their factories, are also beginning to suffer shortages. As the Chinese government increases its efforts to improve conditions in the countryside, workers prefer to stay at home rather than travel far from home to work in factories. Consequently, turnover rates are increasing and it is costing firms more to train replacements. This in turn pushes up wages, which fuels inflation and raises the price of exports. Companies are trying to retain workers by providing quality housing and leisure activities, but this also raises costs.

Skilled labor is becoming even harder to find, as trained workers either defect to local competitors or move on to jobs higher up the value chain. For the moment, European and US firms are paying above the minimum wage and providing much better conditions than the sweatshops associated with some industries, but the problem will not go away.

Quantity

Most foreign companies that operate in Asia are stuck between a rock and a hard place. They might want to localize their staff but they cannot find the talent locally. The problem is more acute in Asia than in the West. A survey of medium-sized firms by the EIU released in early 2006 found that more than 40 percent of respondent Asia-Pacific executives said a shortage of talented staff was a major issue for them, compared with 36 percent in the US and 28 percent in Europe.[7] Ostensibly, India and China, for example, produce thousands of graduates each year. But the truth is that most of the local institutions from which they graduate are in no way comparable to many Western centers of higher education.

A further problem is that local staff do not sufficiently appreciate how lacking their skills and abilities often are. Many expatriate staff in Indonesia, for example, report substantial resentment on the part of local staff at what they see as "unfair" salaries given to expatriate staff without fully appreciating the differences in skills, abilities and hence productivity. Local staff might often feel ready for promotion and thus aggrieved at having been "overlooked," when in fact their current positions reflect their existing skills levels. These sorts of problem require careful management, lest they affect morale or even manifest themselves as expatriate versus local staff or even as a race issue within the workplace.

And Quality

But the problem in Asia is not so much quality of candidates as it is the quantity of quality candidates. There are too few. India produces around three million graduates a year, but they are of such uneven quality that many are unemployable. In February 2005, India's Supreme Court ordered the closure of almost 100 private universities because of quality concerns. Top of the class in India are the elite Indian institutes of technology, established in the 1950s by the country's first prime minister Jawaharlal Nehru to be world-class places of learning. Generally they are. They produce graduates of immense calibre who are able to and often do obtain jobs with big companies in America and Europe and go on to have successful careers. Foreign firms are all eager to replace expensive expatriate with Indian Institute of Management (IIM)-trained managers. The problem is there are just six IIMs awarding only 1,250 degrees a year. And competition for places in them is more intense than competition for the world's most prestigious universities such as Cambridge University or UCLA.

The gap between such elite institutions and the rest tends to be immense. Raw numbers are misleading. Gary Gereffi and Vivek Wadha at Duke University were intrigued by the commonly repeated assertion that only 70,000 engineers graduate from US universities each year but that China produced 600,000 engineering graduates and India 350,000.[8] When they took a closer look at the numbers and compared like with like, they found that the numbers of graduates from rigorous four-year engineering degree programs rose to 137,000 for the US but fell to 112,000 in respect of India and 351,000 for China. The Chinese figures probably still exaggerate its standing because it is likely that a large number are not engineering graduates as would be commonly understood in the West but more the caliber of car mechanics.

Another study by consultants McKinsey found that of the 2.5 million graduates in India each year, only around 25 percent of them were likely to have the standard of skills that a multinational company would want. The figure was 10 percent in respect of China.[9]

The B-School Problem

A similar problem exists in respect of business schools in India. Some are world class. But there are too few and so they are very choosy. Entrance exams for the top schools are the toughest in the world. The IIM Ahmadabad admits just 250 out of 140,000 applicants to its Postgraduate Program of Management.

Quantity and quality problems also overshadow the b-school boom in China. The Ministry of Education (MOE) first licensed schools to grant MBAs in 1991, beginning with nine universities with 100 students. By 2001, the MOE had approved 62 institutions enrolling 10,000 students while another 30 offered EMBAs (Executive MBAs). McKinsey has estimated that China will require 75,000 top-level executives with global experience by 2010 – about 70,000 more than the current number.[10] Unfortunately, after the top group of about 13 schools come a stream of inferior institutions offering low-quality MBA programs, taught in Mandarin by poorly trained faculty. Not surprisingly, they churn out graduates with no discernible skills. Others are little more than "diploma mills" that provide credentials for a fee but precious little education.

To improve their performance, Chinese universities have been forming partnerships with US, Australian, European and Hong Kong schools to offer state-approved MBA programs. The elite Chinese universities such as Peking and Tsinghua University in Beijing and Fudan University in Shanghai have both forged strong links with top US schools. MIT has an MBA program at Tsinghua and more than 40 of its faculty have each spent six months at the Sloan school and another 30 have been to Harvard for up to three months. Fudan has been sending faculty to MIT for the last ten years. Western companies are also becoming big donors to Chinese schools: ABN Amro, Bayer, Citigroup, Alcatel and Philips all fund courses or chairs at various b-schools, and John Browne, chief executive of BP, is chairman of the Tsinghua advisory board.[11] Senior managers can attend quality EMBA programs at schools like the China Europe International business school (CEIBS). Over 60 percent of the 550 students on the CEIBS' EMBA program are chief executives, chairpeople or presidents of their respective companies.

Through these partnerships, the Chinese aim to create a super league of universities that can produce graduates of the right calibre. But critics still find even these "top" graduates lack adequate English skills and problem-solving abilities. In part, this is a product of a system where plagiarism is commonplace, and academic rigor has been known to give way to government *force majeure*.[12] This was evident in the case of SARS where statistics that did not tally with the official line were suppressed.

In both India and China, the problem is linked to the poor system of elementary and secondary education. State schooling in India is often "appalling" at best, and many states are still debating whether or not to teach English (associated with colonialism) in primary schools. One study found that at any time, a quarter of Indian teachers are absent from their classrooms.[13] In China, where the government has pledged to make every Chinese literate by the 2008 Olympics, many children living in rural areas do not receive any education at all – the schools are closed due to lack of funds. A huge percentage do not finish secondary school.

However, at least foreign employers can take heart from the fact that India will continue to produce a pool of young workers until the middle of the twenty-first century. China, due to its one-child policy, has one of the most rapidly aging populations in the world. According to the McKinsey Global Institute, by 2008 India's pool of highly qualified graduates will be twice as large as China's.[14] And they will speak better English.

The China Syndrome

"The years under Communist rule have eliminated all management genes. You have people conditioned to obey not lead."[15]

In fact, China presents severe problems when it comes to localization. Foreign firms variously complain that the mainland Chinese management style is characterized by a lack of creativity, little aptitude for risk taking or strategic thinking and, above all, any ability to manage. To be sure, such comments are heard about many parts of Asia, but China is the one economy in Asia to which many Western multinationals are now exposed.

In part, such characteristics are due to a Confucian heritage that emphasized rote learning and hierarchy, so although many make good administrators, they lack initiative and will always defer to a superior. To this must be added the legacy of the Cultural Revolution (1965–68) – first a "lost generation" of uneducated people, and then the result of the one-child policy. Since most of their parents worked in SOEs, where markets were assured and production was tied to quotas, this generation has no role models when it comes to ambition or hard work, while the lack of siblings has reduced their ability to be good team players.

Managers who came up through the SOEs worked in a bureaucratic system in which they learned only to adhere to rules and regulations. These characteristics make localization easier for foreign manufacturing firms, where processes are well defined, documented by procedures and easy to follow. However, when it comes to HR, accounting, marketing, sales, distribution, branding and project management, all largely irrelevant in managing an SOE, such skills are in short supply.

Accordingly, expatriate managers still make up the majority of CEOs and top executives in multinationals operating in China. Indian managers are found in some of the higher levels, while local Chinese tend to occupy the middle and lower ranks. Analysts predict that it will be another decade before Chinese managers are ready to take the top spots, but can foreign firms wait that long? Good local managers at all levels are vital to bridge the linguistic and cultural gaps with factory employees, and to build contacts with local government to deliver the all-important *guanxi*. Moreover, firms that do localize are looked on more favorably by local and regional officials, as this is seen as a sign of commitment to the area. And as long as they are unable to localize, expatriate managers will continue to cut into their profits.

Effects of the Shortages

> If several hundred top quality engineers suddenly became available, we'd take all of them. (Hiroshi Matsuo, GM of Sharp operations in China)[16]

But China is not the only problem spot. Throughout Asia there is a huge shortage of workers with the right technical skills, and at every level of management a lack of people with experience in Western-style business. The most pressing skill shortage is among senior engineers with management experience in Western or Japanese companies.

Poaching

One result of all this is that poaching has become the most frequent way of hiring staff. In China and India, it has reached epidemic proportions. In February 2006, Morgan Stanley poached the head of Citigroup to head its China business, while earlier, Microsoft actually sued Google over the defection of a senior researcher to head its R&D center there. In November 2005, Indian airline companies were forced to cancel flights and adopt an anti-poaching pact to try and stop the flood of pilots moving jobs to take advantage of the boom in the sector. Business processing outsourcing (BPO) firms have also started to sign anti-poaching agreements.

Many Japanese and Western employers in China now write penalty clauses into the contracts of locally recruited engineers, stipulating that if they leave within a certain time of joining, they must repay a portion of their salary to cover training costs. However, this threat is often nullified by the fact that new employers are more than ready to pay the fee for them. Furthermore, provisions that seek to bind employees to particular employers might contravene International Labour Organization (ILO) conventions where they are relevant.

Sky-high Salaries

Not surprisingly, salaries for quality Asian managers are rising to football-star proportions. According to HR consultancy firms, India is currently seeing the sharpest salary hikes in the world. The chairman of India's construction and engineering firm Larsen & Toubro admitted in November 2005 that despite raising salaries for new engineers by 25 percent, he was still losing out to the software industry, multinationals entering India, or competitors in the Persian Gulf who were paying twice his current rate.[17]

When Siemens attempted to recruit a Chinese executive in his late thirties with experience in the US to a top management position, the attempt failed over salary negotiations. The executive wanted an annual salary of $500,000, three times the ceiling at Siemens. Even supervisors with engineering experience were asking – and getting – $15,000–25,000 a year. This was 10–15 times an ordinary worker's pay.[18] In 2005, the annual salary and bonus of a Chinese middle manager at a foreign firm in Beijing or Shanghai was between $27,000–32,000.[19] Bonuses, free housing and meals, a mobile phone and a company car are all becoming standard benefits, together with others such as longer holidays and maternity and paternity leave. These, plus the contributions that employers have to make to China's security fund system, make Chinese executives very expensive indeed.

Whatever happened to the notion of all those dollar-a-day Asian workers? Reality, that's what. Rapidly, Asia's labor market hot spots are becoming a case of "you get what you pay for" at the lower end of the market and you get something less than what you pay for at the upper end.

Recruitment – Where?

Companies are adopting a variety of ways to plug the shortage. In India, the outsourcing firm Genpact has opened recruiting outposts in six cities to look for less expensive liberal arts graduates. It is also linking up with local colleges to develop relevant courses. In China, Taiwanese firm TSMC has been advertising in local 7-Eleven stores. Other Taiwanese companies have been recruiting staff straight from university, or have joined forces with universities to pay tuition fees for engineers who commit themselves to joining the company after graduation.

Companies are also going further and further afield in the search for staff – to small towns and campuses that are beyond the main Chinese industrial centers, and offering placements to students and school leavers. However, they have found that many graduates who live long distances from the cities where the jobs exist are unwilling to relocate. Similarly, in Thailand, Katoen Natie (KTN), the Belgian logistics and high-tech services company, found that "Most people want to live and work in Bangkok, so it is hard to move skilled people from Bangkok out to the provinces, which is something of a problem for us."[20]

Hong Kong is another hunting ground for multinationals operating in mainland China. These recruits are well educated and many speak Mandarin, but the disadvantage is that two-thirds of those hired leave within 18 months or so as the entrepreneurial spirit takes over and they start up their own companies.

One solution, especially for companies in the manufacturing sector, has been to recruit Western "retirees" from North America, Europe and South Africa. Such managers have several advantages. First, they are cheaper as there are no school fees to be paid. Often their wives or partners have also retired so there is no friction over dual careers. Second, they are familiar with the low-tech processes and older machinery frequently found in Chinese factories. They usually know how to repair such machinery when it goes wrong and are not afraid to get their hands dirty. Finally, their age makes them automatically respected by Asian workforces. They are also generally more patient and have the paternal approach toward workers that fits with the Asian culture, so they make good mentors for younger local staff. Such people are often happy to take on a new challenge for a few years to get a project off the ground, or help turnaround troubled operations.

Another potentially rich source have been the so-called "returnees" – part of the 1980s' brain drain who left China but are now being tempted back. Like the Hong Kong recruits, they seem to provide the ideal mix of managers, China born but US bred. However, again like their Hong Kong counterparts, many return only to succumb to the urge to set up their own businesses once they have made the necessary contacts.

Recruiting the children of Chinese émigrés is another option. American by birth, culture and outlook, many of them now wish to have some experience of their ancestral home and work in the new China. But there are risks. One US firm hired a US Chinese, MBA-trained executive to run its operations in China, hoping that in this way they could finesse the problems associated with communications and managing local staff. Unfortunately, as the British expatriate manager sent to head the regional operation found when he visited the Chinese company, the American Chinese had in fact surrounded himself with newfound members of his family to help run the business, none of whom were remotely qualified for the job. Some were actually "managing" non-existent projects. An experienced Asia hand, he was not surprised on a later night visit to the office to find commercially sensitive documents left on the photocopier, and faxes showing that the information had been going to a competitor. Caveat emptor.

Training

Training is a big investment that foreign firms seeking to localize their Asian operations cannot avoid. The theory runs that those who have been trained and encouraged to plan their careers are more likely to remain loyal and, if they see promotion possibilities, remain with the company. Training can also make up for deficiencies in the educational system common to many Asian countries: concentration on memory, rote learning and following rules rather than developing the more creative, autonomous attitude favored by Western companies. Most important of all, it is the way for companies to build the competencies and capabilities that will enable them to achieve their production and profit targets. The problem of course is how to keep your staff once trained. No company wants to end up building up the skills base of its competitors.

Some multinationals are using psychological tools to identify and nurture talent early on. For example, Shell, the Anglo-Dutch oil company, spent US$60,000 on an internal psychological study profiling its existing Chinese managers and entry-level management trainees.[21] Competence profiling is another approach, used by Unilever in India. It's a process that involves employers listing the competence that recruits must have and then focusing on their behavioral responses to certain situations, rather than experience. The emphasis is on attitude and personality as much as on technical skills, developing the ability to deal with uncertainties in the workplace and cope with stressful situations.

However, such ambitious schemes need to be introduced slowly in the Asian context. Asian staff tend to prefer set routines, and situations that avoid the possibility of anyone losing face. The idea of moving around or being flexible is also disturbing to many. One Western MD found that his attempts to promote promising staff sometimes misfired badly. For example, he wanted to encourage one of the secretaries, whom he believed had the potential to become a top-level PA, to gain experience by working in different parts of the company. His suggestion that she might begin by applying for a vacant post with the deputy manager was interpreted as a sign that her work was unacceptable, and that she was being asked to leave.

Training to instil new hires with a sense of the company culture is another way of fostering loyalty. KTN tried to do this following its entry into Thailand, but found Chinese recruits reluctant learners. As the company's Vice President Dirk Lannoo observed:

> We find it difficult to attract well-educated Chinese for two reasons. First is that they don't find our business sexy enough – logistics is too down-to-earth for them. They prefer the computer industry. Second, they tend to be very ambitious and are not willing to wait and go through the KTN career process. In KTN this means that everybody – even high potential trainees like software engineers or a finance manager – has to spend their first three to six months at KTN working on the factory floor. The Chinese do not like doing this. If you force them they will do it, but they are not happy and see no point in such training. But we think that much of our success depends on knowing what happens on the shop floor so that if later you have to take important decisions, you know how KTN works from the shop floor upward. So we ask our people to be patient and go through this process to learn, but Singaporeans, for example, don't see any added value in it. If they do it, it is only because you are the boss.

Technical training remains a priority where operational standards need to be improved. The problem is how to do it. Do you send in technical staff from the home base to spend two or three months in the factory, or do you bring promising locals back to be trained on the spot and also, hopefully, absorb some different cultural notions? On their return, they can then act as mentors to their colleagues and spread ideas on production and safety standards. Either way is expensive and throws up problems of communication, and the possibility of homesick Asians or Westerners struggling in an alien work culture. But it must be done.

KTN believed in training people back at the home base, as Lannoo explained:

> Before any start up, local recruits are sent back to Belgium in groups of 10 for several months' training. In this way they learn how to do a job the KTN way in similar conditions, using similar machinery, procedures etc. Then, when they return for the real start-up they are already familiar with the task they have to do.

For KTN employees, training was ongoing: "We are always bringing people back to Belgium and, so far, there have been few problems." KTN also sent in a specialist team for every start-up: "Skilled people who are used to doing this and who stay for a month or two as needed, or until the operation is up and running."

Other companies have tried variations on this strategy. The Japanese auto makers Toyota and Honda both set up joint ventures with the Indonesian conglomerate PT Astra in the early 1970s. Both began by training engineers in Japan but later created their own in-house training facilities. For its new factory, the Indian textile maker Welspun paid a North Carolina consultancy US$2 million to train local workers. The price was double local costs, but the company believed the results were better. The chief executive of Wal-Mart Asia, on the other hand, has suggested that his company support a university degree program to train future employees for the expansion it anticipates in China. It has also started putting extra staff in its stores to learn on the job, so they can later move into newly opened stores. But perhaps the most interesting training method was that used by the Indian software firm Sierra Atlantic. In order to introduce the idea of teamwork to its middle managers, it took them to view team-oriented war movies such as *The Dirty Dozen*.[22]

These very different approaches reflect the findings of an analysis across the 21 APEC countries: "there are many ways of managing human resources for success ... but no evidence of 'one best way' being followed."[23] The important thing is that training is being done.

And Retention

Unfortunately, training is not always enough to ensure staff remain with a company. As one manager sadly noted: "It's difficult to get the right people in the first place. But what really hurts is when you give them the benefit of training and then they leave for a better salary."[24] Another described how:

> We have taken some of our young Chinese engineers and tried to accelerate their development by putting them in our overseas operations ... but either they don't want to return, or will do so only for a sky-high salary."[25]

Even high salaries are not always the solution to retaining people. In some India-based firms, salaries for senior managers nearly equalled those in Western multinationals yet there was still no certainty they would stay in place.

In fact, studies have found that the most frequent reason given for leaving is frustration with career advancement. To remedy this, companies need to offer Asian recruits the same incentives as they would in their home countries: management development programs, well-thought-out career structures that offer growth and promotion prospects and/or individual performance targets and bonuses. Larsen & Toubro (see above) has created an in-house IT solutions division to give employees who want to expand their skills an option to simply leaving. The car components manufacturing company Asimco overcame its problems by identifying 25 up-and-coming leaders every year, and giving them mentors and specific projects. After six years, 90–95 percent of the managers initially recruited were still with the company.[26]

Generally, again as in the West, Asian staff respond to bosses who encourage them, and enjoy working in a company with transparent HR policies – where they can see the possibility of both material reward and personal job satisfaction. Unfortunately, many foreign ventures have little idea of how to start developing training programs for local personnel, or put in place attractive career schemes. Simply transferring HR programs from the home country is unlikely to work in such a different culture, so adaptation is vital – which will add to costs. Blending the home culture and values with the local one will also take time and effort. Foreign companies also need to ensure they have good communications with people at all levels of the company to avoid the danger of grievances building up until they explode and suddenly a group of young hopefuls leave en masse to join your competitor – a common occurrence in Asia. To do all this, companies need to overcome the greatest hurdle of all – finding good local HRM staff – another rare Asian bird.

The Localization Irony

Companies go to low-cost countries for cheap labor and an abundant labor force, but today's reality in India, China and other parts of Asia does not, unfortunately, match the theory. The irony is that it is Western firms themselves, with their ambitious plans for expansion, that have caused the problem and caused the shortages and wage competition. Now they will have to put all their efforts into resolving the problems of quantity and quality in HR if their investment is to succeed, but they can only do so by pushing up costs. It's a vicious circle that will be difficult to break in the short term, or even the medium term.

The ABC of Localization

Adopt a Jesuit strategy to recruitment: get them young and instil loyalty to make them yours

By

- nurturing your own talent – think football club youth schemes

- sponsoring university courses

- funding your own courses or setting up training schools

Communicate with local staff – get feedback – be aware of grievances

Don't treat local and expatriate managers differently if they are doing the same job and performing equally well

Even if people leave, tell them they can always come back again, and they may return improved at another company's expense

Factor the costs of localization – salary + perks + charges into your overall budget. You may change your business plan

Guard against losing your own international managers – Chinese companies may soon start poaching your Western staff to head their subsidiaries in Europe and the US!

However –

If all else fails, exit China and perhaps consider Vietnam, where a new generation of young, skilled workers is waiting for opportunities. Or await the next economic downturn. Booms don't last forever and for those with the resources to stay for the long term, downturns present opportunities to localize as good local staff become cheaper in the face of diminishing opportunities.

Notes

1 *The Economist,* "The next wave," 17 December, 2005, p61.

2 *India Today International,* M. Goyal, "Good gets better," 28 November, 2005, pp28–9.

3 *Business Week,* "Desperately seeking talent," 7 November, 2005, pp24–6.

4 *Financial Times,* "IT skills," 26 January, 2006, p6.

5 *Business Week,* 7 November, 2005, pp24–6, op. cit.

6 *Financial Times,* "Higher wages drive Chinese employers to cut hiring plans," 13 June, 2006, p2.

7 *Business Times,* "Talent shortage in Asia-Pacific," 13 February, 2006.

8 *Wall Street Journal Asia,* "India's skill shortage," Tripathi, S., 5 January, 2006.

9 Ibid.

10 *Business Week,* "China's b-school boom," L. Lavelle, 9 January, 2006, pp54–9.

11 *Financial Times,* "China's lust for business learning," 1 August, 2005, p6.

12 *The Economist,* "A survey of higher education," 10 September, 2005, pp14–16.

13 *Financial Times,* "Colleges set to take on rivals," R. Marcelo, 22 March, 2005, p2.

14 *The Economist,* "The great Indian hope trick," 25 February, 2006 pp26–7.

15 *Business India,* "Management myopia," 10–23 October, 2005.

16 *Financial Times,* "World's manufacturers march into China," P. Marsh, 21 June, 2004, p6.

17 *Business Week,* 7 November, 2005, op. cit.

18 *Financial Times,* 21 June, 2004, p6, op. cit.

19 *The Economist,* "China's people problem," 16 April, 2005, pp57–8.

20 Taken from "Katoen Natie enters Asia," case study written by Charlotte Butler and Dirk Van den Berghe, INSEAD-EAC, 2005.

21 *EIU Business China,* "China on the couch," 28 September, 1998, pp2–3.

22 *Wall Street Journal,* "Shrinking Indian pool of talent leaves gap," J. Larkin, 4 January, 2006, p4.

23 Michael Zanko and Mat Ngui (eds) *The Handbook of Human Resource Management Policies and Practices in Asia-Pacific Economies,* vol 2, p608. Cheltenham: Edward Elgar, 2003.

24 *Financial Times,* June 21, 2004, p6, op. cit.

25 Ibid.

26 *Far Eastern Economic Review,* "Flight of quality," L. Wozniak, 1 January, 2004.

Strategy 16

Managing Change

WHAT'S IN THIS CHAPTER?

▷ Change!

▷ Resistance to Change

▷ A Different Business Culture

What Would You Do?

Insider or Outsider?

▷ Strategies for Change

The Need for Patience

The HR Labyrinth

Finance

Communications

▷ The Effects of Change

Leadership

▷ How to Measure Change

Change!

The raison d'être of Western multinationals making an acquisition or entering into a joint venture in the region is the opportunity it gives them to enter new markets and increase profits. Even before the deal is struck, the due diligence teams assessing the value of the targeted company will have signposted levers for change – ways to lower costs through efficiencies of scale, increase and expand production, improve quality, speed up distribution systems and so on. Where politically and socially acceptable, cutting down the workforce may also be on the agenda. Such moves will in turn be linked to the introduction of organizational, strategic and, the biggest challenge of all, cultural change.

Once the deal is done, therefore, Western multinationals will want to send in a general manager (plus possibly financial, technical or marketing experts) to look after their interests and introduce Western management concepts and operating methods. The endgame, of course, will be to integrate the Asian firm into their global organization, enabling them to benchmark and transfer best practices across national boundaries. Consequently, for most expatriates sent out to Asia, managing a local company will mean managing change.

Resistance to Change

Change management has become a specialized branch of management; as one expatriate whose experience covered both Asia and Africa observed: "Managing change is not an underrated skill, but it is an infrequent one." In the past, Western multinationals have discovered, to their cost, that not every manager has the skills to implement change and transform entrenched patterns of behavior in a firm. Even more difficult is ensuring that any changes made are permanent.

In the recent past, attempts to introduce Western management methods have not always been either welcome or successful in the region; there has long been a debate in the business media about the extent to which Asia is "different" when it comes to management. Many Asian observers have argued that Confucian values make uncomfortable bedfellows with "management by objectives" or the hire and fire culture of Western firms. In their view, such practices are not easily transferable and run counter to the customary Asian view of the paternal relationship between employer and employee. In any case, it was frequently said, since Asian companies were doing well without their influence, their introduction was unnecessary. The events of 1997 and its aftermath rather undermined this argument, but while Asian companies have since learned the mantras of focus and corporate governance and made statements about the need to change their ways and become more transparent, deep down there is still strong resistance to such concepts. As many Western companies have found, when looking more deeply into the finances and assets of a newly "restructured" Asian firm they might consider buying, any change is likely to be only skin-deep.

Change is never popular and in Asia can be a way of making enemies; Western managers run the risk of violence from disgruntled employees, and have occasionally been the target of death threats. Resistance –

passive or active – from those within a company to outsiders trying to change their ways is inevitable, and if well enough coordinated can effectively block or halt attempts at reform, even at the highest level.

Rana Talwar, for example, was appointed chief executive at Standard Chartered bank in a high-profile move to improve the bank's performance and revamp its old colonial image. Having targeted the usual suspects – strategy and culture – for change, he instituted a sweeping program of reform. Among measures he implemented was the promotion of local African, Indian and Hong Kong managers to positions traditionally reserved for British expatriates. These and other measures made Talwar many enemies within the higher ranks of Standard Chartered, where his modernizing efforts were not appreciated. Eventually he paid the price and, despite the support of the bank's executive directors, was ousted after only three years at the helm.

In truth, the challenge of operating in a radically different operating context, a society where both the work ethic and the cultural norms are completely different from those prevailing in the West, is enormous. That many expatriate managers have tried and failed to make any impact during their time in Asia is a matter of record, and in large part the fault of the Western firms themselves. Focused on the need for immediate productivity improvements rather than deep-seated structural or cultural change, they have tended to send in technical advisers rather than senior managers with experience of the change process. At sea in an alien culture and unable to exercise the influence that would result in any radical transformation, the poor technical managers not surprisingly chose to take the line of least resistance and concentrate on incremental productivity improvements. These delivered respectable results, but left the status quo unchanged.

For their part, the local managers took the cynical view that the expatriates would only last two to three years, and then return home. In the worst-case situation, if someone really made an effort to introduce serious change, they just battened down the hatches and waited for them to leave. They then resumed business as usual, their working practices remaining unaltered. As one veteran expatriate noted: "Local managers in Asia are no slouches at this game. They can stitch up any manager they wish. They control all the information flows."

In the future, this scenario will no longer be viable. Western firms wishing to be Big in Asia must send out people who can effect a deep transformation of the company, one that is measurable and that endures. This involves both structural innovation – the introduction of new systems and processes – and radical cultural change. But first know your enemy – what aspects of the Asian business culture are Western managers likely to find most difficult to deal with?

A Different Business Culture

Consider the following comments made by expatriate managers about the business culture prevailing in various countries in Southeast Asia.

"The loyalty of local employees," observed one, "is directed toward their classmates from school and university, rather than the company that employs them. This means that they have no idea of confidentiality or secrecy about the company's business." He was shocked to find that managers would "quite cheerfully tell their classmates all the company's plans, with no sense of betrayal." Working in Thailand during the booming economic climate of the mid-1990s, he quickly discovered that every worker carried a CEO's baton in his or her briefcase, and was busy building up another business of their own on the side, perhaps even at a tangent to the company that paid their wages. This might even involve rebranding materials and goods taken from your company stores, and then undercutting the price to sell them to your clients. Working for a Western firm might be a temporary expedient or a convenient way to get started. It also meant that "They would have a personal interest in whatever deal was going down ... Business life was a cosy environment of relationships based on long-standing arrangements and mutual friends."

Two months after his arrival to manage an acquisition in Bangkok, he was asked to sign a pre-prepared letter (in Thai) that set out the salary bonuses for that year because "You need to announce them soon." When he sought clarification, he was told that it was that year's performance. His objections that it was only November were brushed aside with "Well, we more or less know what it is." The bonus, he learned, was 2.5 months' salary. When he asked for the basis for this calculation, he was told: "Well, we budgeted for that." The criterion for this budget, he further learned, was "management discretion." His refusal to go along with the letter caused astonishment, even consternation. Finally, after a deal of bluster, it was reduced to less than two months.

Another commented on the "iron rice bowl" mentality that he found in Indonesia: "Life in the company was so easy that turnover was small. Nobody had a service record of less than five years – and all of them expected to be with the company for life." He too remarked on the cosy relationships between his staff. "The relatively small pool of skilled managers with the required technical background for the job meant that managers in the industry all knew each other. Most had graduated from the same university so it was a mafia, a very pleasant social club in which everyone knew everyone else." The company was overresourced and nobody worked a full day – "how could they run their private businesses if

I expected them to work for me for so many hours?" Staff making visits outside the company were invariably non-contactable.

There is general agreement that the operating style in Asian companies relies on historic practice. Nothing is written down, so there can be no accountability. Commercially, this means that there are no criteria laid down for setting commercial terms, giving discounts and so on. Rarely is there anything that Westerners would recognize as a marketing effort – all sales take place on the basis of price only. Also, not just managers, but suppliers and dealers all know each other from school; reciprocity is the name of the game, with information the prime trading commodity. In this situation, there is insufficient control for an audit to take place – so it is odds on that the company is leaking money.

Another expatriate manager recalled finding a grossly overstaffed finance department. However, as he quickly appreciated, "This was because the finance manager knew his countrymen, and their ways of fiddling money. So he had insisted on having all these pieces of paper that had to be signed in order to try and stop it happening. But this just ended up as a hopelessly inefficient and bureaucratic system."

Being wise to the scams going on, noted another long-time observer of Asian companies, and stopping them, is an almost impossible task when you are handicapped by a lack of language or inside knowledge. A colleague working on a mill site in Indonesia, he recalled, was puzzled by the disparity between the constant deliveries of cement, wood and lime and so on needed to keep the factory running and the actual amounts in stock.[1]

He decided to focus on deliveries of an estimated 20,000 tons of cement, needed to repair a water treatment lagoon. Ordered from a local supplier, 20,000 sacks had been duly delivered according to the log. The trucks entered the site at five-minute intervals, drove onto the weighbridge to register their load, continued round to the warehouse for unloading and then exited by the same gate, returning an hour later with another load. However, to his experienced eye, the amount of concrete delivered seemed inadequate for the repair job.

In fact, as he finally discovered from talking to his driver, instead of unloading at the warehouse, the trucks had exited with their loads intact, returning later with the same load. To disguise the shortfall, the proportion of cement used to mix the concrete had been cut by 50 percent – the implications for the repair job of this weak mixture were horrendous.

He then asked his civil engineering manager, a South American expatriate, to investigate collusion between the supplier, warehouse manager and batching plant supervisor responsible for overseeing the cement mix. His report said there was no evidence of fraud and that only about 800 out of 20,000 sacks had been lost – an insignificant percentage easily accounted for. Nobody was to blame but, "like flour when it was sifted for a cake mixture, the cement had simply blown away in the wind."

What Would You Do?

To make an impact on such an environment involves the exercise of highly sensitive political and managerial skills. Generally speaking, no MBA or executive training course will have prepared you for scenarios such as those that follow.

During your first week, you discover that your PA is a "minor wife" of one of the senior local managers in the company. Such a connection will clearly make confidentiality questionable, but can you risk alienating one of your senior managers by getting rid of her, and what message will that send through the company? What, if anything, should you do about the situation? Do you act quickly, or do you take your time?

Next take the organization you have inherited, which is your target for change. The organization is typical of the region, no better or worse than many other multinational Asian subsidiaries; all the senior managers have been with the firm since its foundation, and have developed a line management system involving about 80 more junior managers waiting around to be told what to do by them. When any Western manager is around, at least one or two senior managers – including the finance director – block the system, ensuring that no meaningful information goes up or down the organization.

The whole system needs to be cleaned up and made more transparent. But implementation of any change to this structure will be a problem, since the managers will say "yes" to your face and then go away and do nothing. What do you do about the blockers? How can you keep a discreet check on where people are and what they are doing, without acting like a heavy-handed policeman – even supposing you had the resources to do so? You must put in some means of control, and get the message over to your staff that change is definitely coming, you understand what they have been doing and it has to stop. The Chinese call this "killing the chicken to scare the tiger." But where do you begin to change the system without arousing strong resistance? And how do you find out who you can trust to carry out your wishes?

If you try to recruit new managers, you will probably find that they are related to those already in place. You will not be able to tell the difference. How can you avoid this situation and break the cycle of nepotism? How can you attract the more outward-looking, quality people you need? What key appointments do you need to make? Should they be locals or should you ask for backup from head office? And where in the organization should you put them?

Insider or Outsider?

To deal with such daunting situations, companies need to put in people who are strong enough to push change through in this inhospitable environment. For this there are two basic requirements; that the manager knows the business very well and is able to tread the fine line between cultural understanding and cultural acceptance.

The two extreme ends of the spectrum here are that either expatriates stick firmly to their own culture, make no concessions to local sensitivities and risk alienating the workforce, or they "go native" and try to understand and think like a local, with the risk of letting their standards be eroded by local customs. If you are too friendly with your local managers, if you socialize too much, then they may take advantage of this to probe your weaknesses, and then block you. It could also undermine your authority. Keeping them at arm's length, on the other hand, may prevent them from detecting any weakness but, then again, might stop you from being able to achieve anything.

So as a *farang*, a *mat salleh,* a *gweillo*, a *bulleh* or any other brand of foreigner, you must choose. Do you try to learn the language and respect the local customs? Do you accept all the invitations to attend weddings and funerals – and as the big boss and father figure in a hierarchical society this will be expected of you – or do you rigidly maintain your status as an outsider? Do you limit yourself to a beer on staff days and a chat to the reps, so nobody will be able to feel they have a handle on you or get too close? It's a personal decision. The strategy you adopt will depend on how you view your role, as a would-be insider or an unrepentant foreigner. Experience has shown, however, that it is no good pretending to be local. It is more important to be open and honest, "then at least they will say that he is consistent."

Moreover, remember that in some parts of the region, like it or not, you are a paternal figure expected to participate in the key events of your employees' lives. As the boss, you will have to get used to people crouching in front of you to ensure that they are never taller than you, or running ahead to open doors. It can be very insidious. One expatriate manager returned to the UK after three years in Thailand and was so used to doors opening like magic before him that on his first day back at headquarters, he walked into a plate glass door!

Strategies for Change

So what strategies for change have been found to work well in this environment? One veteran advised that the best method of attack was through a combination of expertise and getting key appointments in place as soon as possible. "You have to come in with the numbers ready and blow them away, and then recruit in people who owe nothing to the old organization, and are unhampered by owing favors."

The Need for Patience

However, this does not mean a rush to make wholesale changes as fast as possible but, instead, spending the first few months trying to understand the organization; who exercises influence and who is connected to whom. The language problem may make it difficult, but experience should help you to see who exercises influence, who is connected to whom, where the bells, buttons and levers are and where the proper processes and systems are missing. Then, when you are ready, begin with a non-contentious issue where you can justifiably bring in outside agencies to help to make changes, so avoiding accusations of partiality or unfairness.

One such area is the introduction of job descriptions. While in Asia, "everyone is a manager of some sort (including the tea lady) according to their business cards," full job descriptions of their responsibilities and accountabilities are neither common nor welcome. Inviting an independent and respected firm such as the Hay organization to devise and implement such descriptions can be the ideal way to gain a measure of control, without arousing strong resistance.

Along with this goes the recruitment of key staff through headhunting agencies, making sure to recruit and settle new staff in before taking people out. The bait of working in a multinational company that offers wider career opportunities is a powerful one in attracting high-caliber managers. They will be the basis of a team that is loyal to you alone and form the bedrock of the new culture. One key appointment here is a secretary who is discreet and loyal, and whom you can trust absolutely.

An alternative tactic is to establish your own network of loyal managers from the cadre already working in the company. This is a slower method, but can be equally effective. One experienced expatriate found that his weekly badminton sessions eventually resulted in a strong team spirit being built around him: "It took about six months before anyone dared to beat me but then hearing me swear at missing a point and showering and changing afterward changed their attitude toward me, and through these sessions strong bonds of loyalty were forged." This group became his own network, his personal *guanxi* through which he was able to get messages across and glean valuable gossip. Offered other jobs, a couple of managers even refused to leave out of loyalty.

Once you have a team in place that you can trust, you can afford to turn your back while you deal with other parts of the organization. Generally, the three most frequent flashpoints will be HR issues, finance and communications.

The HR Labyrinth

The HR function, covering issues such as working hours, bonuses, recruitment and promotion, can be quite undeveloped in most Asian companies. This is because, since people are promoted purely on the basis of relationships with senior managers, there is little need for a recognized organizational structure in terms of evaluation and the terms and conditions that go with it.

This especially applies to the issue of salaries. A look at the salary system will probably reveal a labyrinth, in which the lower grades are underpaid and the top managers overpaid, thanks to their big bonuses. They also benefit from a variety of fringe benefits – parking subsidies, lucky draws, football competitions, parties, gold necklaces and so on. Even where systems exist, they do not necessarily work in the accepted way. In one Indonesian company, for example, tables were published showing what people could expect to earn for each grade. In practice, no two people in the same grade ever earned the same amount; everyone knew that inequality existed, but everyone accepted it.

A key change, therefore, and one that multinational headquarters are increasingly demanding, is the implementation of a Western-style appraisal system. Unfortunately, the idea of a salary increment based on appraisal, and without an automatic cost of living rise, is completely alien to Asian managers. Previously, as they will point out to you: "We have always got 10–20 percent or even 30 percent, even those who have not performed well." So how do you even begin to introduce the concept of assessment and reward according to a performance matrix?

Introducing an appraisal system

In fact, introducing an appraisal system is usually achieved only after months or even years of patient negotiation. One expatriate first offered his managers the chance of being assessed according to a performance matrix, in which the top line represented the percentage of budget achieved, ranging from 80–120 percent and the other side the percentage of market share. A manager who maintained market share and achieved his budget got a one-month bonus. To get more, managers had to improve on both axes. However, the managers considered this far too difficult and rejected it. When the expatriate refused to give in, a compromise was finally reached whereby all the managers just settled for a thirteenth month's pay.

To roll out a clearly defined performance appraisal system that can form the basis of performance rewards can take months. One expatriate working for a Swiss multinational was under pressure from his head office to initiate such a system to conform with their global best practice.[2] He found it almost impossible, first, because the culture made it difficult to give negative feedback. His managers did not expect a frank discussion of their performance, but to be told how well they had done. He found himself giving a monologue at each evaluation meeting, and any attempt to provoke discussion was met with a polite, brief and non-controversial reply. Setting their own objectives was out of the question.

Second, and even more controversial, was the concept of a performance rating. The head office used a standard A–E rating in which, according to a normal distribution, an A grade would apply only to the top 3–4 percent of outstanding managers, and not necessarily the most senior. A C grade, into which 60–70 percent of managers usually fell, implied a good overall standard with all requirements fulfilled. The Western manager noted that his predecessors had clearly decided not to rock the boat by giving everyone an A grade, although there was some attempt at differentiation by giving an A+ or A−. This situation, he discovered, was a product of the country's school marking system, where a B grade meant "could try harder" and C meant disgrace. Psychologically, only an A grade was acceptable.

His attempts to award a C grade brought nothing but trouble. Hurt managers threatened to resign, and every attempt to explain the system foundered on total incomprehension. The first year, the Western manager gave up and created an "Asian exception," but the second year, having aired the problem at a regional conference and discovered others in the same boat, he introduced an adaptation that he first discussed with his staff. The A–E grades were replaced with more qualitative descriptors; C became a good performance, B very good and A exceptional. The D and E grades were replaced respectively by "satisfactory" and "unsatisfactory." Having been devised by the managers themselves, the new approach was deemed acceptable and they felt more committed to make it work.

Finance

There is unanimous agreement that a key move is to take control of the finance function, either by putting an expatriate finance director in place or by taking responsibility for signatory authority and visibility. This means insisting on having sole authority for signing any check or note involving money going out of the company, including credit notes, discounts or goods given free of charge and all checks over a certain threshold. One manager recalled how amazed he had been at the number of times that tires had to be replaced on company vehicles. After he insisted on signing every bill for tire replacements, he did not see a single one during the next 12 months. Many other credit notes also disappeared.

From this, he concluded: "You can manage these things politically if you let them know you have rumbled them in a particular area – but you leave the back door open for them. They know they must not do it again and this is OK. The thing not to do is to paint them into a corner … But you need to keep control." Eventually, the solution will probably lie in IT systems, in particular systems to interlink customer forecasts with orders and manufacturing.

Communications

Spreading the word about what you are trying to do and improving communications is one of the most difficult problems to crack because "information is power and so they keep it to themselves."

To succeed, you must find a way to get round this obstacle and directly reach the younger managers, who may be more receptive to new ideas. But, given the hierarchical nature of local society, bypassing the senior management to do this will be a major challenge. Leave your door open – but will anyone walk through it? After all, you will only be here a few years, and they have seen others come and go. Their seniors will still be here, bossing them around when you are back in your home base. So how to convince your junior managers that, this time, things will be different? One way is to hold regular meetings with as wide a group of managers as possible in order to tell them what you are doing and why, and what behaviors you expect from them, in the hope that they will then pass the message down the levels of the organization.

The Effects of Change

Predictably, the net effect of any move you make will be that morale plummets. For example, once they realize that you mean to reduce numbers, a stream of managers may come to see you and say something like "What you are doing is right. We know it should have been done a long while ago but we don't like change, and when it happens it is upsetting for us." How do you answer them? Insist on firing someone and they will probably reply, "OK, this person has got to go, but let's give them until the year end, give them time to get used to it." Incidentally, they will use the same technique with any price increase that you try to implement. They will tell the dealers in advance that the price increase will be in three months' time, "so they can get used to the idea," or, in reality, so that they can buy up the stock.

You will then have to decide who does the firing. Will it be the heads of departments, who have worked with that person for years and will feel extremely uncomfortable about doing it? Or you, as the hatchet man from the West? The consequences of you doing it may be twofold. Your managers will lose face if they do not do it (which may be a way of convincing them to act) and it could rebound negatively on the image of the company locally. So if you do start to reduce numbers, make sure that you also maintain the reputation of your firm as a fair international company, which people should be proud to work for and which can attract high-quality people.

One expatriate, reflecting on the consequences of firing people, noted that "Morale is always lower at the point of uncertainty. Once things become clear, morale recovers remarkably quickly." In his experience, "They didn't think they would get over the loss of their buddies, but three weeks out of the organization and they were almost forgotten."

Another, however, believed that, sometimes, firing people for the sake of reducing numbers could do more harm than good. In his experience, making junior staff redundant saved very little money, since they were paid so little, and any benefits were far outweighed by the resentment caused, since they would invariably turn out to be someone's friend or relation. Also, they performed all kinds of tasks and ran errands that more senior people would feel was beneath their dignity. Sometimes, perhaps, the most positive action could be to allow things to remain as they are.

Leadership

Finally, think about how you yourself can set an example by your personal behavior. Remember, any attempt to change an entrenched system is frustrating. It is not easy; no matter what personal energy you have, you can't do everything yourself. You can only lead by setting an example. And although you can dictate strategy, you cannot implement it. At the end of the day, it is the people in the organization who have to do the work.

Remember also that only so many ideas can be introduced at any one time. Therefore you must prioritize what you want to change. It may help to try and analyze the root causes of the situation. The problem may be not so much resistance, but ignorance. They have been doing things the same way for years and cannot imagine another way. Moreover, change is not only difficult in an Asian firm; the weight of inertia is just as solid in the West.

Once you have your list of priorities, think how to control the key points and make sure that the message is continually reinforced to keep the momentum going. You have to find a way to counteract the tendency for people to think that this will go away, it is not really happening and they should just keep a low profile for however long it takes.

How to Measure Change

Given that you are only going to be in place for a finite time, then from the beginning you should think about your successor. How far in the change process do you aim to be when you hand over? This in turn means you have to think of a way to find out whether or not you are having an effect. How do you measure change? How long do you need to make sure that things really are different, so that your successor can act more as a maintenance manager, with the task of fine-tuning the organization?

According to psychologists, people themselves do not change. What changes are their behavior patterns. Take away the pressure for this behavioral change, and they will revert to the old preferred ways. So it is important to keep the pressure on and drive through change to the extent where they cannot revert. This means that you have to have everything in place, the right terms and conditions. For example, systems such as swipe cards to check the hours people keep and logging telephone calls are effective tools in making people conform and keeping a check on them.

However, although you can bully people and force them to change outwardly, you won't get the inward commitment necessary to make it last any longer than your term of office, or the next business crisis. It is far better to set in motion that most powerful force for change, peer pressure. Experience has demonstrated that the best method is to convince a significant percentage of managers that this is the way forward, for once some managers buy into the new culture, others will follow. If the new working patterns result in greater profits and an enhanced reputation for the company they work for, nobody will want to leave, attracting good people will be relatively easy and they will automatically conform to the status quo.

After that, hopefully, momentum should take over. Once the ball is rolling, keep it rolling, so that the momentum becomes irresistible. And then, as soon as your people catch up with one new idea, move on to the next target. It is important to innovate and always keep one step ahead. This is classic business school theory, but, as with many things, it is a lot easier said than done.

Managing change is not something everyone can do and, often, it is too easy for expatriates to give up. You have got to have the confidence to drive it through, without leaving too much blood on the walls. But remember, given the fate of some who have tried to introduce changes in Asia such as restructuring or downsizing, that blood may well be yours!

Managing change in Asia

■ Have patience – don't make managers lose face by your actions

■ Begin with non-contentious issues and bring in neutral external agencies where possible

■ Build your own team

■ Try to involve local managers in devising and introducing new systems

■ Prioritize and control key points

■ Constantly reinforce key messages

■ Communicate as widely as possible

■ Think long term.

Notes

1 Taken from "Blowing in the Wind," case study by Charlotte Butler and Professor Henri-Claude de Bettignies, INSEAD-EAC, 1994.
2 Taken from "The Evaluation," case study written by Charlotte Butler and Professor Henri-Claude de Bettignies, INSEAD-EAC, 1996.

Strategy 17

Outsourcing: Where and Why?

WHAT'S IN THIS CHAPTER?	
▷	The Phenomenon Rolls On
▷	The Gap Closes on India
▷	China
▷	The Philippines
▷	Malaysia
▷	Still More Alternatives
▷	The Next Stage?
▷	Security Issues
▷	Consumer Backlash Potential
▷	Bad Politics
▷	Life Sciences Outsourcing in Asia
▷	Things to Consider

The Phenomenon Rolls On

Why outsource? The answer is easy: to save on costs. The savings can be enormous. Some industries are more amenable to outsourcing than others. Publishing is one. Consider Bloomsbury, the primary publishers of the Harry Potter books. The company's offices in Soho Square, central London, are small – they are little larger than any other three- or four-storey converted Georgian houses in London. But this small building in which a handful of staff work quietly at their computers is home to a company that now has a stock market capitalization of almost half a

BIG in Asia

billion dollars. How can this be? It is because almost everything that Bloomsbury does is contracted out and performed off site.

Outsourcing is a huge business now worth over a trillion dollars annually. Already about 20 percent of the world's IT services sector is carried out remotely, away from where the services are consumed. The huge investment in bandwidth in the 1990s by governments and big telecommunications companies and the consequent massive falls in telecommunications costs have made all this possible.

India has been a big beneficiary. Its IT and BPO sectors are booming. Hundreds of companies from the US, the UK, Canada, Australia and elsewhere have either established "captured" back-office processing centers there or they have contracted the work to companies based there. In 2002, Azim Premji, chairman of Wipro Technologies, one of India's leading IT companies, predicated that India would earn US$5 billion for software exports that year. The figure seemed incredible. It has now paled to insignificance.

By 2006, India was earning US$23 billion annually in software and IT-related exports. The industry's lobby, the National Association of Software and Services Companies (Nasscom) expected IT services to grow by 25–28 percent annually and BPO, albeit from a smaller base, by 35–40 percent. Oracle, the US software company, had 10,000 employees in India. Microsoft had 4,000 staff and was planning to take on another 3,000. And IBM had almost 40,000 staff in India. And of course the local stars such as Wipro, Infosys and TCS had tens of thousands more.

Software programming is big business in India but BPO has been the biggest source of growth in recent years. Much of the work is not sophisticated and rests largely on two factors: cost and English language ability. Indeed, around 70 percent of India's BPO sector's revenue comes from call centers. Around 20 percent comes from high-volume, low-value data work such as transcribing health insurance claims. Only 10 percent is from higher value work such as dealing with insurance claims.

India is also the home of BPO's distant relative, knowledge process outsourcing (KPO), a fast-growing business based on "data mining." Data is collated and subjected to complex analytical research to build forecasting models to predict future consumer behavior. It is project-based work "built round a demand for business expertise, such as legal services, the analysis that supports a merger, formulating patents and writing equity, industry and project reports."[1] In India, the sector is presently dominated by Gecis (former offshore arm of GE) and other big global players such as Merrill Lynch, while McKinsey also runs its own research units in the country. Inevitably, local companies, such as Evalueserve and

Office Tiger, are starting up fast and competing hard in this area. Many BPO companies are also looking to expand into this next lucrative business, which Nasscom believes will grow fifteenfold to US$17 billion globally by 2010.

The work that Indian companies receive from abroad is diversifying in many directions. Animation for children's cartoons and electronic games is now being outsourced to India, as is blood and urine diagnostic testing, and even the electronic pursuit of delinquent debtors in the US on behalf of companies such as American Express, Citigroup and GE. Financial wire service company Reuters has even established a team of editors and journalists based in Bangalore to cover and report on 2,000 American SMEs listed on the New York Stock Exchange. Each company's results and filings are received in Bangalore electronically, analyzed, written up and then sent out on Reuters' wire service.

But only one thing is certain about booms. They end. Wages are bid up, other costs rise and competitors are attracted into the marketplace. That is happening now in respect of India. Hundreds of outsourcing companies from Sri Lanka, Hungary, Russia, the Philippines, Malaysia, China, Egypt, Romania, Dubai, Argentina, South Africa, Brazil, Ghana, Mexico, Canada, Australia and South Africa to name a few are springing up to challenge the dominance of Indian outsourcing firms. Outsourcing conferences are yet to reflect fully that India is under challenge. Why? Because most are sponsored by the big names in Indian IT and BPO and they insist as part of their sponsorship arrangements that their own executives dominate conference programs as speakers. They continue to promote India and India remains hugely dominant. But India is not the whole story.

The Gap Closes on India

India's IT exports grew 30 percent in 2005 over the previous year and that was on top of a similar increase the year before. Not surprisingly, wage rates in the sector are rising at 10–15 percent annually, although Joseph Sigelman of Chennai-based Office Tiger says that wage inflation should be set against falling costs in other areas, notably telecommunications. Staff turnover is extremely high too, meaning that search and training costs are high. A 2004 KPMG study commissioned by Nasscom predicted that the industry will face an acute shortage of technical employees by 2009, falling short by 250,000 workers.

India produces 300,000 IT engineering graduates each year; the US produces just 50,000. But it is a mistake to assume that they are in any way comparable. Companies fight over India's top 30,000–40,000 graduates. The rest are not fought over. Another 90,000 business school graduates are produced each year and again it's really only the top 5,000 from the top six state-run institutes of management that are competed for. Clearly, quantity is one thing and quality quite another, and it is quality graduates that India is not producing in sufficient numbers. But even staff for call centers are becoming more difficult to find. All this means that India's cost competitiveness, while still great, is being eroded.

India's most often cited advantage other than cost is its English-speaking population. But it's easily overstated. English is not taught as widely in India as is commonly believed. There is a two-tier level of schooling in which only the elite are taught English. Often English language education does not extend to the village level. As it is, India is not the largest country of English speakers after the US. That honor goes to the Philippines, with its 90 million-plus population, almost all of whom are conversant in English.

For foreign firms looking to outsource to India, Bangalore has long been the first port of call. It accounts for about a third of India's software exports and nearly a third of those employed in IT services and BPO. In 2005, Wipro and Infosys were taking on 1,000 new staff each month. But Bangalore's growth has put a severe strain on the city's infrastructure, and the local government has been reluctant to allocate sufficient funds to update water, sewerage, power supplies, roads and so on. This has culminated in reports of "Bangalore crumbling." Such negative publicity is offset by the continuing lure of what has become known as Electronics City, a few kilometers outside Bangalore. With aspirations of rivaling Silicon Valley, its campuses have their own modern infrastructure, funded by the big IT firms.

Behind the leading IT cities come Gurgaon and Noida (just outside Delhi), Chennai (formerly Madras), Hyderabad (in the south), Pune (west) and, in north India, Kolkata (formerly Calcutta) – all of them eager to become the next Bangalore. In 1996, Salt Lake, just outside Kolkata, was "barren ... just a couple of firms."[2] By the end of 2005, it boasted 220 technology companies employing 24,000 staff, including IBM (4,000 software engineers) and HSBC.

Despite the growing competition from other countries, there is optimism that India will keep its lead in IT, BPO and now KPO. Even a temporary slowdown caused by new financial reporting regulations under the Sarbanes-Oxley legislation in the US was seen as just a temporary blip. There was confidence that since it would force US firms to adopt more technology-based processes to spot problems in their accounts, Indian firms would benefit in the end. Great potential for expansion was also anticipated in BPO activities, both in the call centers at the lower end but even more further up the value chain, including activities yet to be widely outsourced, in particular financial services: "We have barely scratched the surface yet," said Stefan Spohr of the consultancy A.T. Kearney.[3]

China

India might be a long way out in front, but the IT and BPO capabilities of China go from strength to strength. China's government has adopted a specific high-tech development policy and invested heavily in the country's communication networks. Telecommunications infrastructure in China's main cities is of a high standard. Starting fresh and from a low base means that they have the latest and best. Ironically, there are many Chinese cities that have telecommunications infrastructure that is now more advanced than many cities in Western Europe. The same cannot be said of India.

Literally millions of Chinese are learning English too. GE, Nokia and Siemens all have manufacturing-related R&D facilities there. China has another ingredient that has been important for India's success in the IT and BPO sectors: a focus on engineering in higher education. By 2005, it had around 200,000 IT workers compared with India's 850,000, but 50,000 software graduates are being added to China's pool each year. Nonetheless, the demand in China for any capable graduate with IT skills is high and so whereas an entry-level programmer in India might earn US$130 a month, the Chinese equivalent earns around US$150.

Chinese firms have leveraged their linguistic skills to set up customer support centers to service Chinese-speaking customers, notably in the Hong Kong market. PCCW, New World Telephone and other Hong Kong telecoms firms have moved most of their call centers and directory assistance operations to Guangdong Province.[4] Another small but lucrative segment is serving overseas Chinese clients of foreign firms from within China. HSBC, for example, uses mainland China centers to serve customers in North America and other markets. Even more niche markets served are in northwest China, where Japanese- and Korean-speaking locals provide back-office support to the Korean and Japanese clients of some US firms.

Some IT companies in China that provide outsourcing work to multinationals in China already look offshore for clients in the same way that Indian IT companies do. Beijing-based IT United Corporation is one such company. Its clients include Airbus (for which it developed promotional software in Chinese to promote its aircraft to Chinese airlines), British Airways, Cisco Systems, Siemens and Kraft Foods.

Several of India's top outsourcing companies, such as Tata Consultancy Services (TCS), Wipro and Infosys Technologies have picked outsourcing to China as a trend for the future and are now hiring Chinese staff and opening branches in China. TCS announced in October 2004 that it would double the number of staff from 180 at its Shenzhen office in China's Guangdong Province within the next 18 months. Initially, TCS focused on providing services to existing international clients that also had offices in China. By the start of 2005, Infosys had 200 staff at its office in Shanghai and four multinational offices. By 2007, Gartner forecasts that software and outsourcing services will be worth US$27 billion each to China and India, and that 40 percent of the work done in China will be owned by Indian companies.

There is a further twist in the outsourcing saga, in that some Chinese manufacturers, in a bid to avoid quota problems in their export markets, are themselves joining the outsource bandwagon. Chinese manufacturers (including foreign firms) in the garment, footwear and furniture industries are looking at Indonesia, Vietnam and Thailand as potential offshore locations.

The Philippines

That the US accounts for at least half the world's potential outsourcing business is good news for the Philippines. The Philippines, a former colony of the US, has a commercial code that is compatible with that of the US. Language is another advantage. Officially, Pilipino based on Tagalog is the first national language of the Philippines. But less than a quarter of Filipinos actually speak Pilipino. The true national language is English, which is spoken by 95 percent of the population.

A high literacy rate (92.6 percent, which is far higher than India's), a large pool of IT professionals as well as GAAP-trained accountants and a telecommunications infrastructure that might be patchy but is cheap to use all suggest the Philippines' competitiveness in the outsourcing arena. With almost 90 million, its population base is not small, but wages in the Philippines even at the level of back-office services are considerably higher than in India. But the Philippines remains attractive. It has a customer service culture that is lacking elsewhere in Asia, and Filipinos are familiar with American ways too, even jargon and slang.

Accordingly, US companies account for around 90 percent of all outsourcing deals in the Philippines and dozens more have opened call centers there, including America OnLine, the largest Internet service provider in the US.

Procter & Gamble (P&G), Delta Airlines, American International Group (AIG) and Citibank have all shifted back-office work to the Philippines. P&G centralized its back-office operations for Asia in the Philippines. US engineering giant Flour Daniel has much of its technical work undertaken there too by an almost thousand-strong team of local engineers, architects and draughtsmen. AIG's Philippines business processing unit now has more than 4,000 staff.

US call center operator Sykes Enterprises said in early 2005 that it would move half its business from India after complaints from its US-based customers that the accents of some Indian service representatives were difficult to understand. It was likely that Sykes would move the business to the Philippines where it already had facilities.

Medical transcription has become big business for outsourcing companies. Almost 7,000 US hospitals are now required by Federal regulations to convert medical records into data format. It's a US$15 billion market in the US. Some of the work has gone to the Philippines, which by 2006 was home to forty or more medical transcription companies up from just nine in 2001.

The Philippines' efforts in courting foreign outsourcing business has paid off dramatically. In 2001, local outsourcing firms had around US$350 million in revenues. By 2006, the figure was closer to US$4 billion. Collectively, they employed around 230,000 people, which means that, per capita, outsourcing is far more important to the Philippines than it is to India.

Malaysia

The Malaysian government has played an active role in promoting Malaysia as a technology and business processing hub. It established the Malaysian Multimedia Development Corporation (MDC) in 1996 to oversee the development of the multimedia super corridor (MSC), a 15 by 50 kilometer strip of land near Malaysia's new administrative center Putrajaya and its new international airport. (At 750 square kilometers, the MSC is about 100 bigger than all of Singapore.) At first the MSC looked like a white elephant and, at the outset, perhaps it was. But as its mission evolved and became more clearly defined, international companies were drawn to it, Shell, DHL, Intel, Motorola, Ericsson, HSBC, Standard Chartered, BMW,

EDS, IBM and Unisys among them. Today, the MSC promotes Malaysia as a regional and even a global hub for information and communications technology, BPO, call center operations and multimedia organizations. Consulting firm A.T. Kearney in its 2004 Offshore Location Attractive Index listed Malaysia as the third most attractive destination worldwide for IT-related outsourcing after India and China.

A benefit of Malaysia is its multicultural workforce and hence its competency in a wide range of international languages. And although staff costs are significantly higher than in, say, India, infrastructure is good and office rental is very competitive, even in central Kuala Lumpur. Malaysia also offers an attractive and safe lifestyle for expatriates and their families.

Still More Alternatives

Many other lower cost countries now are seeking to develop their own outsourcing sectors. Like India, the Philippines and Malaysia, many are former colonies of higher cost countries, a fact that they can turn to their advantage, given their language and cultural affinities.

Russia and the countries of Eastern Europe have also made a bid to attract outsourcing clients. However, although at first there was keen interest, political and market uncertainty has made global firms wary of rushing into Russia too quickly, and although many Eastern European countries offered a low wage and educated workforce, they also suffered from excessive bureaucracy. The entry of several into the EU also lessened their advantage in terms of cost.

By 2006, South Africa had an estimated 500 call centers operating within its shores that employed more than 30,000 people. Ghana and Kenya, with their English language abilities mixed with low employee costs, also had call centers and processing companies set up to service offshore clients. For example, at least 2,000 Ghanaians were employed by a US outsourcing company to work on health and insurance claim forms originating in the US.

Brazil announced measures in late 2005 to attract its share of the international outsourcing business, particularly from the US with which it shares roughly the same time zone. The country has excellent telecommunications infrastructure and competitive labor costs. Johnson & Johnson, Kimberley-Clark and Lucent Technologies were among those US companies to have contracted out BP work to companies based in São Paulo. The relative lack of English language proficiency is, however, a significant impediment to the sector's development.

Even tiny Mauritius is getting its share of the action. India's Infosys has established a disaster recovery and data backup center there to boost its share in the European market. Why Mauritius? Because of the French language skills of its population. The operations were targeted at French-speaking European clients.

The Next Stage?

The next in-house activity to significantly move East will be R&D. Already, many of the best IT researchers in the US and Europe are Asian expatriates, mainly from India and China. A lot of them eventually return home to set up their own companies offering foreign firms wanting to outsource some of their R&D activities a potent mix of design and managerial skills. This move is already evident in the electronics industry. Dell, Motorola and Philips are buying complete designs from Asian developers and merely adding their brand names (which is something of a turnaround). A trend that began with cell phones now includes everything from laptops and high-definition TVs to MP3 music players and digital cameras. India's Wipro already designs GPS systems for European sports cars, and HCL Technologies is working with Boeing to design software for navigation systems, landing gear and cockpit controls for its new 7E7 Dreamliner jet.

In the pharmaceuticals industry, GlaxoSmithKline and Eli Lilly are working with Asian biotech firms to cut the high cost of developing new drugs, while P&G has announced that, by 2010, it wants half its new product ideas to be generated from outside (presently it stands at 20 percent). Global networks between US firms, Taiwanese engineers, Indian software developers and Chinese factories to produce the ideal product at the cheapest cost are foreseen.[5]

Security Issues

The major reason why companies outsource offshore to places like India is because such places are competitively priced: wage and other employee costs are relatively low. But this also means that staff are more susceptible to inducements to hand over commercially sensitive information to competitors or even to organized criminal groups. Furthermore, cost cutting might mean that defenses are not as secure as they should be. This is a risk that must be accounted for. Contracts with subcontractors obviously need non-disclosure and security clauses but it remains the case that much offshore outsourcing is to countries where legal systems are poor and where judicial remedy is either not realistic or practical.

There have been instances, for example, when data and other private information held by outsourcing companies in India have been misused. There have been significant breaches of confidentiality and several cases of serious fraud when Indian call center staff have illegally acquired information and used it to defraud their companies' Europe- and US-based clients. Clients of Citibank, for example, were defrauded by Indian-based outsourcing staff in 2005, leading to several staff at the Indian outsourcing company MphasiS being jailed.

Care needs to be taken too that hard records are disposed of properly by subcontractors; they need to be shredded or burned and not simply dumped in landfill sites to which the public has access.

Consumer Backlash Potential

For customers based in the UK, the US and other mature economies, dealing with an Indian-based call center is often not as satisfactory as dealing with one based in their own countries. The voices at the other end often sound distant, accented and the service provided is often transparently the product of training and conditioning rather than what comes naturally. The question is how inadequate is it? Are these inconveniences minor or are they significant? Some companies will find that it is the latter. In late 2005, the UK's Abbey bank for one said that it was considering closing its call center operations in India. Abbey had certainly saved money by relocating call center work to India in 2003 but it found that its customers were less than satisfied. Many complained of poor call quality and language problems.

Another UK bank launched a television campaign based around the fact that it did not use foreign call centers. The campaign was in no way xenophobic, but rather played on the simple fact that customers generally prefer to talk with people from their own countries and cultures when discussing personal and financial matters. And as has been mentioned already, Sykes, the US communications company, relocated some of its outsourced call center operations from India to the Philippines after customer complaints about accents and call quality.

Bad Politics

The politics of shifting jobs from high-cost to low-cost centers are never good. It becomes a matter of managing and containing such news rather than dressing it up as positive. Political concern in higher cost countries at best has only slowed the shift. Several US states have considered introducing legislation to stop government contracts in IT from being outsourced to other countries, and critics in Congress are quick to react to complaints from disgruntled local workers. When Boeing moved some of its design work to Russia, an anonymous email claimed that this was "putting the safety and quality of Boeing airplanes at jeopardy."[6] The US also tightened visa conditions, which has made it more difficult for Indian IT professionals to work in the US.

In Britain, the head of HSBC caused an outcry in 2002 when he extolled the virtues of outsourcing UK back-office jobs to India. However, the outcry had little effect. The following year, HSBC announced that it would transfer another 4,000 back-office jobs from the UK to India, Malaysia and China. British insurers Aviva and Prudential along with British Telecom earned the ire of unions with their plans to open call centers in India, enabling them to shed jobs at home in 2002 and 2003.

The 850 jobs that Prudential announced in 2002 would be cut from its call center at Reading and transferred to Mumbai caused a public backlash from trade unions and the Reading community. The local media were vociferous in their attacks on the decision. The company agreed to stagger the cuts, which allowed Amicus, the relevant union, to claim victory, but from the company's point of view, it was a minor concession given to placate the opposition and allow the union to claim that it had won something for its members. The reality was that the jobs would still be transferred and the company would still achieve its costs savings, albeit over a longer time frame.

The industry in India has fought back. In the US, for example, Nasscom hired the US public relations firm Hill & Knowlton to lobby and put forward its case in Washington. The Indian government too has made representations to foreign governments via its embassies and high commissions abroad and also during trade and investment missions abroad by Indian ministers.

Life Sciences Outsourcing

Of course outsourcing is not restricted in Asia to IT-related services. Outsourcing of life sciences is another area that is beginning to grow. Rule changes in Japan in March 2004 allowed clinical studies for drugs to be sold in Japan to be undertaken in a handful of other countries. Diagnostic samples are sent from Japan to cheaper destinations for testing now too. Many shipments involve blood and urine samples, which deteriorate quickly. Consignments can reach Singapore within 24 hours, so making Singapore an ideal destination. Singapore has attracted American and European firms too that wish to get a slice of Asia's biomedical science outsourcing market. Albany Molecular Research Inc. of the US is one example. In January 2005, it announced plans to open its first overseas office in Singapore. The UK's NHS also sends diagnostic samples such as for blood and urine to lower cost destinations like India for analysis.

Animal testing is being outsourced to Asia. It has been estimated that 10–15 percent of the costs of drug discovery in the US and the UK goes toward animal testing, and that the total cost of bringing a new drug to the market is in excess of US$1 billion. Harassment by animal rights activists of animal testing laboratories, scientists associated with them and businesses that breed animals for research has significantly added to costs. How to get around this problem? Increasingly, outsourcing to Asia is one answer. Asia's more authoritarian governments, which clamp down on troublesome pressure groups and muzzle an inquisitive media, and Asia's cost competitiveness are proving an attraction.

Already, China supplies most of the world's primates used in animal testing. But a monkey used in China in preclinical testing costs about one-fifth of the US$5,000 that US researchers typically must pay for a monkey sourced from within the US.

So now animal testing outsourcing companies are setting up in China. US firm Bridge Pharmaceuticals (which was spun off from the Stanford Research Institute in 2004) opened an animal testing joint venture, Vital Bridge Zhongguancun Drug Development Laboratory, in late 2005 in Beijing's Zhongguancun Life Sciences Park. The facility is the first Food and Drugs Administration (FDA) and SFDA (China's FDA equivalent) compliant preclinical laboratory in China. The laboratory plans to act as a contract animal testing facility on behalf of client firms such as drug and cosmetic companies.

Locally owned, Shanghai-based WuXi PharmaTech also offers outsourced animal testing. It provides other biotechnology outsourcing services to 60 active customers, including 16 of the world's top 20 drugs and pharmaceutical companies and 8 of the world's top 10 biopharmaceutical companies.

Things to Consider

- When it comes to BPO, there are alternatives to India. Consider them as well as India. Other countries may offer a better overall deal, with tax and other incentives, lower office rents and better telecommunications infrastructure. Don't only look at relative labor costs.

- How secure will your and your customers' personal and commercial information be with the outsourcer? What legal remedies are available in the case of a transgression, on paper *and* in practice?

- Are there PR and customer satisfaction advantages to be had by NOT outsourcing customer contact services to offshore locations? Might these outweigh potential cost savings?

- Every company has its own culture – which can't be outsourced. In the excitement of slimming down the bottom line, don't lose sight of the need to develop your own workforce and to keep in close touch with your customers and their needs. Otherwise you may find your company has become a hollow shell with products nobody wants.

- Beware of cutting your own costs but at the same time indirectly financing new competitors. Asian firms are justly famed for their speed of learning (and know their own markets best).

Notes

1 The Financial Times, "Experts who mine nuggets of data," 29 April, 2005.
2 The Financial Times, "Cars edge out cars," 29 August, 2005.
3 The Economist, "The Bangalore paradox," 23 April, 2005.
4 Business China, "A small slice of IT," 2 February, 2004.
5 Business week, "Outsourcing innovation," 21 March, 2005.
6 The Economist, "Relocating the back office," 11 December, 2003.

Selling Consulting Services in Asia

WHAT'S IN THIS CHAPTER?

▷ Why Don't Services Sell Well in Asia?
  The Cultural Bias
  Getting Used to Low Fees
▷ Management Consulting in Asia
▷ Consumer and Industrial Market Research
▷ Media Management and Media Training
  The Blame Game: an Asian Spin on Blaming the Consultant
▷ Some Ideas on Selling Consulting Services in Asia
  What Sells?
  Managing Clients' Expectations
▷ Things to Keep in Mind when Consulting in Asia

Why Don't Services Sell Well in Asia?

Services do not sell well in Asia, and when they do, rarely are the fees comparable to what can be achieved elsewhere. Corporate Asia under-appreciates the value of services as a business input. Management consulting, IT, employee training, marketing, PR, legal advice and R&D are all underacquired by most Asian firms. Instead, there is a bias to tangibles – goods – as inputs. The reasons are twofold.

It is partly a matter of cultural bias and partly countries' levels of economic advancement. As a country's economy matures, the proportion of national output attributable to services grows. Rich countries have a high component of services in their GDP figures, while poor countries do not. Services are not capital intensive but people intensive, so it is difficult to get much productivity growth from the services sector. This is one of the reasons why economic growth rates of rich countries slow down the richer they get.

The low appreciation for services is apparent among Asian consumers too. One recent survey by managing consultants McKinsey, conducted in 10 Asian countries, concluded that, while 75 percent of consumers in the US are willing to pay for financial advice, in Asia the figure is less than a quarter.

All too often, when consultants and other outside professionals are used, they are brought in as window dressing to impress bankers or stock analysts; to lend an air of modernity when in fact family members are still very much in control. Sometimes, consultants must accept that they have done their job simply by being engaged.

The Cultural Bias

Traders at Heart

Many of Asia's entrepreneurs are ethnic Chinese. Like refugee and migrant minorities elsewhere, they are conservative and survive and prosper through trade. Trade is about buying and selling physical goods. It is not about services. Thus the most important group of entrepreneurs in Asia has little direct experience with the professional services sector, either as customers or providers.

Physical items are valued in corporate Asia, while intangibles are not. The Western manager might commission a consulting firm to review production processes and then marvel at the recommendations in the consultant's 100-page final report. The US$250,000 cost might even seem like a bargain to him. On the other hand, the ethnic Chinese founder/ entrepreneur is more likely to hold up the report and wonder how a "book" could possibly cost so much. As with payments for licensing and copyright, there is a mindset in Asia that militates against paying for ideas and other intangibles. Those of the old school simply cannot see the value in such things. If they spend money, they want something to show for it. And if it doesn't work or they decide they don't like it, they can cut their losses and sell it. Services, on the other hand, cannot be sold on once they are acquired. Once the money is spent, it is gone.

Loyalty vs. Productivity

As we have seen, the typical Asian firm, especially in Hong Kong and Southeast Asia, is family controlled and family members are trusted most. Outside professionals usually find that they are trusted far less than, say, in the West. When loyalty is valued above all else, the concept of hiring consultants, whose loyalty is at best only temporary and never really guaranteed, is something of an anathema. If a professional manager in Asia leaves his company to work for another, it is seen as treacherous. Yet consultants work for one company after another, so what standing can they have in such a cultural setting? At best they can expect to be regarded with suspicion.

Employees reach each rung on the corporate ladder in the typical Asian firm after having passed tests of loyalty. Productivity is often a distant second consideration. Consultants who breeze in and out of a firm in this setting stand little chance of being trusted, valued, taken seriously, or even having the necessary information for their work disclosed to them so that they can make sensible recommendations, let alone implement them. Sometimes consultants are invited in but then not given the access, information or freedom they need to do their work. Consultants need to learn about Asia but Asian companies also need to learn how to make use of consultants.

Getting Used to Low Fees

The cultural bias across Asia against services is reflected in the fees that can be achieved. Typically, they are way below those for comparable work performed in, say, the US or even Australia. This is not just a Southeast Asian problem. Even in Japan, the fees that can be achieved are substantially lower. Where the auditing fee charged to a major Japanese corporate might be US$600,000, the fee for a similarly sized company in the US might be around US$5 million.

The Asian dot-com boom saw huge numbers of locally owned service sector firms spring up. Usually they were owned and run by young Asian entrepreneurs trained in the US and other Western countries. Educated about the value of services, they took the philosophy back home, set up their new businesses and hoped for the best. Anecdotally, few have done well and when they have, they have not done so on the backs of local firms but by selling services to the local offices of Western firms or Western firms in the West. But the low-cost and high-grade skills of these small firms together with the speed of communications afforded by the Internet mean that tasks can now be divided up and parceled off to wherever good-value expertise resides.

A case in point is *Asian Eclipse*, a book previously published by one of the authors. Professional editors in Australia and Singapore edited it. A small firm of art designers based in the Philippines designed the cover. A small firm of Indians based in Mumbai did the index. Lawyers in Hong Kong did the legal work. The actual publishing and marketing was done in Singapore, as was the typesetting. Cost is the reason for such divisions of labor. In Asia, competition between service providers can be fierce. The potential market for their services is enormous, but the actual market is small.

So, if professional services in Asia are yet to be rewarded to the degree that they are elsewhere, which subsectors yield the highest returns? A survey published by international IT specialists Gartner Dataquest[1] concluded that of the consulting, education and training, development and integration, IT management, transaction processing and BPO subsectors in the Asia-Pacific region, consulting was the segment with the highest proportion of providers earning gross margins of 41 percent or higher. It also had the second lowest proportion in the low-margin range of 0–10 percent. Margins in the BPO segment were not as high as expected, which Gartner concluded was due to the immaturity of the segment in the Asia-Pacific region and the fact that many providers are still in the investment phase. But that is the problem for services generally in Asia. The market is still only in its infancy.

Five reasons why Asian firms don't like consultants

1. They are not trusted

2. They are likely to have worked and will work again for competitors

3. They charge a lot for apparently little

4. They lack legitimacy

5. They undermine the management's face and authority.

Management Consulting in Asia

The problems faced by management consultants in Asia are many. Management in Asia is via networks and relationships. Operational control is personalized rather than through systems. Asian managers typically like to rule through personal diktat and not with the aid of a transparent set of written rules. Nor are they good delegators, instead they tend to be autocratic. New management systems mean replacing personalized rule with something else, but it is personalized rule that is so ingrained in the Asian workplace. Asian entrepreneurs often see anything else as their loss of power, face and prestige. This is the cultural context in which management consultants in Asia must work.

Management consultants redesign companies' structures to enhance productivity. But most Asian firms are designed around job ladders based on loyalty rather than productivity. So there is a mismatch of aims that needs to be resolved before management consultants begin work.

Asia's entrepreneurs also tend to operate very closely to their markets. Many personally know their customers and sellers. They observe keenly and gather in all the information they need from their observations; they do not rely on outsiders to tell them what is going on. Their knowledge base is both highly detailed and built up over many years. Thus, when a management consultant comes along offering a management model that can be introduced to the firm in a matter of months, Asia's entrepreneurs might well react with skepticism. Each feels that their own market is unique and complex, and major changes cannot be sensibly proposed unless that same intimate market knowledge is first acquired. Consultants, especially management consultants who work with theories and models that are broadly applicable to whole classes of firms, simply lack legitimacy in the eyes of many Asian entrepreneurs.

Finally, the sort of services offered by management consultants are simply not wanted by many Asian entrepreneurs and their firms, no matter how much they would appear to be needed from the outside. Large, diversified conglomerates with dozens of subsidiaries that look as if they have over-reached themselves might well be structured that way to match large, complex Asian families – to ensure that each family member has a job. Structures that lack transparency might be that way so that taxation can be avoided and assets, costs and capital can be moved from one unit to another with ease. If Asia's entrepreneurs see virtues in tangled corporate structures – and from their point of view there might well be clear virtues, then management consultants who advise on how to enhance transparency when many clients have rational reasons for not wanting it face a hard sell.

Consumer and Industrial Market Research

Western companies tend to set up in a new country after first commissioning market research to demonstrate a market gap and the potential profits should they fill it. But Asian companies (apart from the Japanese, who are extraordinarily thorough in their market entry research) are more likely to invest in new markets simply on the basis of local connections. For example, a Thai businessman might choose to trade in Singapore because his son has moved there and he can act as the local agent. This is a cheap and efficient way of expanding to a new market but it is also rather limiting – entry to new markets is restricted not by demand but by the number of one's relatives. But while it works, there is little reason to change.

Companies that specialize in consumer and industrial market research in Asia have found that most of their clients are the local units of Western multinationals. Asian firms are reticent to commission outside market entry research and typically only do so if their bankers demand it, and then it becomes a piece of documentation to show outsiders and will be quickly forgotten internally.

Even consumer market research is still of most interest to Western multinationals in Asia, largely because they are most interested in brands and trademarks. Home-grown brands are emerging in Asia but they are still relatively minor compared with branded fast-moving consumer goods owned by Western giants such as Unilever and P&G. Trial and error remains the preferred mode of market entry by Asian firms.

The way in which such market research proceeds in Asia differs from the West. Typically, in mature markets such as the US, the UK and Australia, desk research comprises 80 percent or more of the work that might need to be undertaken. But in Asia, desk research typically comprises as little as 15 percent. The reason for the difference is because companies are required to file and disclose publicly much more information in mature economies than is generally the case in Asia. Also, companies in mature markets have more of a culture of disclosure and transparency and are less likely to hold back information when it is requested.

Media Management and Media Training

Professional media trainers have their work cut out for them in Asia. There ought to be a huge demand for their services, but the actual demand is small, as Asian entrepreneurs are notoriously media shy. They see their companies as theirs and theirs alone and, even if they are big employers and have outside shareholders, rarely do they feel the need or obligation to explain their intentions to the public. The media is not seen as a means for getting their message across – something to be used to their advantage. Instead, it is seen as something to be avoided at all costs. Western entrepreneurs typically spend a lot of time trying to get themselves media exposure, whereas Asian entrepreneurs probably spend as much time trying to avoid it.

Similarly, company directors could use training on how to handle themselves at shareholder meetings, but, Asia-wide, directors are notorious for not bothering to show up at AGMs.

Media outlets in Asia have enormous trouble securing interviews with locals, particularly if the outlet is television, and more so if it is not live and therefore subject to editing. Local entrepreneurs are enormously distrustful of the media. They dislike the lack of control they have if they agree to be interviewed. This is one of the reasons why stock analysts are quoted ad nauseam in the Asian business media rather than representatives from companies themselves, and also why, on Asian business television, a disproportionate number of the people interviewed tend to be Western expatriates rather than local entrepreneurs. When local businesspeople do agree to be interviewed, they typically demand to be given a list of all the interview questions beforehand, whereas Western expatriates and businesspeople almost never ask for this. Not surprisingly, researchers and assistant producers prefer to have Westerners on their shows because it means less work for them. The interview also has more spontaneity.

Regional business television such as Singapore-based CNBC Asia, which has sought to be more "Asian," has found its efforts largely rebuffed. The local audience might compain that they want to see more locals on television but few locals want to appear. The now largely defunct Hong Kong-based *Far Eastern Economic Review* had a spot for a guest columnist for its weekly "fifth column" but it too had trouble finding Asian faces to fill the spot.

The main Asian markets for media training are Hong Kong and Singapore, the two centers for regional media. But many Asian entrepreneurs largely see this as one service they don't need to spend money on, even if it actually occurred to them. Most have no intention of appearing in the media. Furthermore, very few Asian companies empower middle- or even top-level staff to appear in the media to speak on their company's behalf. There are some exceptions – professional companies such as Singapore Airlines and DBS Bank have used professional media trainers – but the number is small. It is still very much a case of "it's the tall bamboo that catches the wind"; the best profile is no profile.

The Blame Game: an Asian Spin on Blaming the Consultant

Consultants and after-hours office cleaners share an important attribute. They both offer convenient, face-saving targets for blame. Management can blame consultants for its own inadequacies, and after-hours office cleaners can be blamed for anything that goes missing. It is the same the world over.

Blaming consultants for mistakes is one of the reasons why they are engaged, be it in the US or Asia. But a nasty cycle of blame can evolve in Asia if it is mixed with nationalism, as in "the *American* consultants flew in, told us they could fix everything but instead knew nothing about local ways (read: Asian culture, Asian values) and have messed up."

Consultants face difficulties defending themselves publicly because of client confidentiality agreements. They might like to cite their client's chronic mismanagement, for example, and list a whole litany of errors and malpractice but are prevented from so doing.

Some Ideas on Selling Consulting Services in Asia

What Sells?

Many Western consultants come to Asia, see a vast, barely tapped market with obvious and huge needs and expect to make a lot of money. Inevitably, they are disappointed. Doing well in any type of consulting in Asia almost inevitably means accepting far lower margins and fees than those for comparable work undertaken in, say, the US, Western Europe or Australia. And very often, the main clients in Asia are not Asian firms but the local offices of Western multinationals.

The fastest growing market for consultants in Asia is China where restructuring and streamlining management is becoming big business. McKinsey[2] claims that its practice in China is growing by 20–30 percent a year, after having first set up there in 1994. Early on, its clients were multinationals but now almost 80 percent of its current clients in China are domestic companies. But then China's large companies are state rather than family owned and not run as they are in much of the rest of Asia. So the cultural context and management ethos differs in China compared with elsewhere.

So what sort of services are in demand in the rest of Asia? Try marketing. Ethnic Chinese traders dominate the regional economy outside Japan and Korea. Trading is about buying and selling, and marketing is about selling more. So, logically, marketing should be one of the first services that many Asian firms are likely to reach out for, and so it is. Most medium and large Asian firms that have something to sell now have a marketing department.

PR companies are also slowly gaining a foothold. Lobbying government is becoming more important in Asia as Asian governments become more sensitive to their electorates and pressure group activity. Companies' images are becoming more important in the media and with financial analysts and share and bond investors. Malaysian car assembler Proton found that it needed to engage outside PR consultants in 2005 when it came under attack for falling profits, management changes and competitive pressures. And the Indonesian conglomerate Gadjah Tunggal hired the PR firm Ogilvey in 2001 to help improve its image, for example, after huge financial and political problems. It did so on the advice of its overseas bankers. These are but two examples of a quickly growing trend in Asia.

Managing Clients' Expectations

One problem with consulting in Asia today is that the number of blue-chip companies that are comfortable with consultants and understand their role is so small that many consultants are forced to accept clients who lack the necessary sophistication to understand and implement the advice they have been given. This leads to disappointment and misunderstanding, with the consultants inevitably being blamed.

Western consultants and local clients may differ widely on what the advice from the consultants is supposed to accomplish. One of the key things consultants must do if they are to be Big in Asia is not just win new clients but also manage those clients' expectations. Sometimes getting Asian firms to use consultants is an enormous battle and when they finally decide to do so they expect that the process will lead to their recovery and prosperity. They might expect an immediate jump in revenue or profits and feel cheated when it does not happen. Management consultants cannot turn around all companies. Some have problems that are too deep-seated.

In Asia, it is extremely important for consultants to specify clearly and precisely what they will and will not do for their clients. This needs to be in writing and clients need to be talked through it and reminded of it as work progresses.

Things to Keep in Mind when Consulting in Asia

The *need* for consultants and their services in Asia is great. The *desire* for them is not. In this way, they are a bit like dentists – it is only through education that people visit dentists and almost never because of the pleasure of the experience. How can consultants go about tackling the Asian market? Here are some ideas:

- Many consultants and other service providers should establish a foothold in Asia first by chasing business from local offices of multinational firms and then later attracting work from local companies. This is the pattern followed by most new entrants in Asia, whether by design or default.

- Consultants who want to target a local Asian firm for business should first see if it employs any Western expatriates in influential positions. If so, they can be used as an entry point to the firm. Western expatriates (almost by definition) understand the importance of services as business inputs. They will understand their company's deficiencies and its needs. If the expatriates are trusted within the company, they can prove effective agents for change. Slowly, they can raise problems with management and then suggest the services of a consultant as a possible remedy. They can arrange for meetings and demonstrations for the management. Many big consulting assignments with local firms in Asia have been won because expatriates working in those firms convinced management of the virtues of seeking outside help.

- Local clients will tend to want to bargain hard on fees, be demanding on what physical deliverables they get, take a long time to decide whether they want to engage the consultant and, in the meantime, spend a lot of time calling for additional meetings, further details and fee reworkings. Winning business in Asia from local firms can be costly and then the rewards in terms of fees can be comparatively low.

- It is sensible in countries where legal systems are poor to require 40–50 percent of the agreed fee upfront and not to commence work until that first payment has been received. No or few exceptions should be made to this rule.

- Many Asian entrepreneurs are suspicious of slick marketing brochures, big names and high fees. The tried and tested method of gaining business knowledge in Asia – chitchat and gossip for want of better terms – will be an important way in which consultants will acquire new clients. Many will succeed or fail on the basis of word of mouth.

- Asian entrepreneurs tend to be very protective of their internal corporate information, even if this concern is not vocalized. Consultants must be prepared to sign strict confidentiality agreements. If such agreements are not presented, they can be offered to potential clients to give them a greater feeling of security.

- Trust and loyalty are important so confidence building is important. Consultants might need to be prepared to, or offer to, break up what would normally be one large project for a Western firm into four smaller modules, with progress (and payment) for each one being contingent upon client satisfaction with the previous one.

- Consultants need to work closely with staff and management and appear non-threatening, part of the team and observant of internal, informal structures of loyalty and respect. If this is not done, the clients' staff are likely to try quietly to undermine the consultant. Repeat business will certainly be unlikely.

- Asian clients are likely to want more oral briefings than Western clients. They are less receptive to research reports that must be read, compared with briefings that their staff and management can attend. Briefings tend to beget demands for further briefings. The client might even take the opportunity to use them as staff training sessions. Briefings also lead to questions and requests for more work to be undertaken, often with the expectation that the existing contract and fee cover the additional work. Consultants need to have clients agree beforehand the precise point at which the consulting work is to be considered completed by both parties and the final fee is to be paid.

"Act global, think local" applies even to management consultants. Names such as McKinsey and Boston Consulting Group mean less in Asia than they do in the West. It will be their staff – the personalities – that count most when it comes to winning projects. As always, personal connections are everything. It is important that some measure of trust can be established; that local consulting staff are sympathetic to local firms and conditions. When interviewed by the authors, a local consultant based in Pakistan explained:

> The challenge is to drop the functional business templates and vocabulary and work with the ethos of the client. Socially, this may mean sharing the same regional language rather than business school English, being equally comfortable eating from plastic plates while seated on the floor as one is with full china and cutlery with corporate regalia in a multinational's dining room and genuinely

sharing the personal experience of the client … It's hard work to develop such a working relationship but believe me, the payoffs for the business as well as for the consultant are great. If management consultants are prepared to use their emotional intelligence first, only then can their business competence and IQ get them and their clients anywhere. Establishing this trust and loyalty may take time and may initially seem fuzzy but I feel that it can be an extremely important driver of changing the way many businesses and their owners in Asia function.

A bonanza in consulting in Asia is not just around the corner. There is an enormous gap between what ought to be done and actual demand for management consulting and the like. The obstacles to closing that gap are largely cultural, and culture takes a long time to evolve. Consulting in Asia is still in its infancy. There will be solid business in the sector for those willing to lay the foundations now. But, in the meantime, consultants will need to learn more about Asia, and their clients will need to learn more about how to be a client.

Notes

1   Gartner Dataquest Research Brief, "Professional Services Gross Margins in Asia/Pacific," 21 August, 2000.
2   *Wall Street Journal*, "McKinsey and Chinese client spar over quality of services," 13 June, 2001.

Strategy 19   Tilt the Playing Field

| WHAT'S IN THIS CHAPTER? |

▷ An Eternal Obstacle Race
▷ Entering at a Tilt
     Applying Outside Pressure
     Take Advantage of the Down Times
▷ Play to your Strengths
     Choose your Weapons
▷ Brands
▷ Buy your Way In
▷ Keeping it Level
▷ Become an Insider
▷ Appeal Directly to the Consumer
▷ AIG: Tilting by *Guanxi*
▷ Future Prospects
▷ Key Lessons

An Eternal Obstacle Race

Few Asian markets are level playing fields, and, if they were, few local companies would be able to compete successfully with competitors from outside. During the past 30 years, the ethnic Chinese conglomerates in Southeast Asia, the *chaebol* in South Korea, the SOEs in China and the *keiretsu* companies in Japan operated behind protective barriers that foreign firms found almost impossible to breach. Those hardy or foolhardy firms that did succeed in entering markets in the region then found themselves up against every kind of obstacle from government monopolies, preferential tariffs, provincial and local interests, bureaucracy, local rules and controls, not to mention barriers linked with differing ethical standards.

Thus for most Western firms, the Asian experience became more of an unending game of snakes and ladders. Just as they had avoided one snake and had their foot on the ladder, another obstacle appeared to block their way – often aimed specifically to stop any foreign competitor who did seem to be succeeding despite the odds. However, since the economic crisis in 1997 forced Asian owners to sell off assets or allow foreign investors to take a stake in their firms, a swathe of foreign entrants has been able to set up and compete in the region. Some have built up strong positions in several markets and managed to tilt the playing field a little further their way. Some have succeeded despite the odds stacked against them. How they did it and what lessons there are for companies attempting to emulate them are the focus of this chapter.

Entering at a Tilt

Applying Outside Pressure

Some Western firms have mobilized international organizations to help them break into heavily protected industries. The WTO and the IMF have both played a major role in leveling playing fields in the region. The IMF has pushed Southeast Asian governments into liberalizing, albeit reluctantly and slowly, sectors such as banking and generally opening up previously closed markets, such as media, power and telecommunications. China's long-awaited entry into the WTO raised high expectations among foreign investors of the benefits – easier access to markets through cuts in import tariff rates, action on problems connected with IP and so on – they would reap from this move. Some of these expectations have since proved a little ambitious, yet despite China's snail-like progress on many trade issues (see Strategy 24), the recent successes (relative to earlier attempts to operate there) of multinationals in China are proof that WTO membership has indeed delivered a slightly more level playing field.

One of the best examples of the successful use of outside pressure in recent years was the use of the Office of the US Trade Representative (USTR) by the tobacco companies to prise open the potentially highly lucrative markets of the Asia-Pacific region. According to WHO (World Health Organization) figures, in 2000 Asia had the second highest annual per capita growth rate in tobacco consumption, thanks to 50–80 percent consumption levels among men in China, Cambodia, Vietnam, the Philippines and South Korea (where one in three of its 46 million population smokes an average of one packet a day).[1] Markets such as Japan, Taiwan,

South Korea and Thailand were potentially highly attractive markets, given their prosperity and a combined population of heavy smokers that is larger than the US. However, they remained closed to foreign manufacturers, protected by the high tariffs and punitive excise taxes imposed on imported cigarettes.

Not until the 1980s were these markets opened with assistance from the USTR. The US began to impose retaliatory tariffs on countries discriminating against US goods, using Section 301 of the 1974 Revision of US Trade Act. The first to cave in were Japan and Taiwan in 1987. Subsequently, imported brands grew from 1 percent to 20 percent in less than two years in Taiwan.

South Korea, traditionally a nationalistic and xenophobic market, was less easy – citizens caught smoking American cigarettes were subject to the equivalent of a US$1,000 fine. After prolonged negotiations, protests against the US invaders and a boycott, taxes and tariffs were finally lowered to enable foreign brands to compete there. BAT, which set up the first foreign-owned cigarette company there in 2001, announced that during the next decade it planned to spend over US$1 billion on expansion in Korea. For the tobacco industry, it was a victory for the leveling of the field.

Take Advantage of the Down Times

The years following the 1997 economic crisis saw an invasion en masse of Western hyperstores into the food retail markets of the region. In Thailand, Indonesia, Malaysia and later China, foreign retailers moved quickly to buy up assets sold off by indebted Asian firms and establish positions throughout the region.

New foreign entrants, for example, swamped Thailand. The UK food retailer Tesco, the French hypermarket chain Carrefour and Ahold of the Netherlands all entered the country within the same short period. In 1998, Tesco went into partnership with the Charoen Pokphand (CP) Group to operate the Lotus chain of supermarkets, eventually buying 93 percent of Ek-Chai Distribution System, which operates the Tesco-Lotus stores in Thailand. Its success can be gauged by the fact that in 2001 it had 27 stores but planned to have over 40 stores within the next two years. In South Korea, Tesco joined up with Samsung and by 2001 ran seven stores, and had one fully owned store in Taiwan. It also planned to open in Malaysia and was researching the feasibility of opening up in Japan and China.

Carrefour, which had been an early entrant in Taiwan in the early 1990s and China in 1995, seized the opportunity of the downturn to open its first hypermarket in Indonesia in October 1998, five months after President Soeharto resigned and despite frequent street riots and other political unrest. It also expanded its presence in China and went into Hong Kong. Makro entered a joint venture with local partners in Metro Manila in 1996, and evolved into a distribution giant, the fourth biggest retailer there, albeit in a sector with a host of small players.

Having successfully entered, the next task was to fortify their positions so that they would not be easily dislodged when the tide turned. The ways in which they did this should provide some heartening reminders that Western firms do possess some powerful strengths when it comes to competing, even on uneven playing fields.

Play to your Strengths

Marketing in the world's mature economies – the saturated markets of Western Europe and the US where companies scramble not for new markets but market share – has been honed to a fine art. Techniques have become sophisticated and complex and are light years ahead of the Asian approach, which amounts to little more than selling. Most Asian companies rely on their cost and speed advantages, and so have not developed strong marketing skills. Therefore, although in Asia foreign firms may be competing with similar products and targeting the same customer groups, their superior marketing approach can give them an enormous competitive edge when it comes to winning customers. Going one stage further and leveraging this know-how and technical superiority to the full, Western firms can revolutionize the market so that even when an attempt is made to tilt the field back in favor of local players, it is too late.

The truth of this has been demonstrated by the success of the Western hypermarkets. Few would have predicted that Thai consumers would desert their traditional wet markets that catered to their preference for fresh food, or their conveniently local "Mom and Pop" stores. But competitive pricing, a better range of goods and pleasant shopping conditions won the day. Hypermarkets have proved to be a success. Thai consumers voted with their feet.

Choose your Weapons

Good service and competitive prices are two elements that foreign firms can use to tilt the balance in their favor. Service, in particular, is often underestimated by Western firms. Customer service is still embryonic in much of Asia and thus one area in which new entrants can readily out-compete existing players. Simply by doing the basic things right, Western firms can transform the shopping experience of customers in China used to the eternal cry of "*méi you*" (No, I don't have it) usually accompanied by a "couldn't care less" shrug. Foreign firms put more emphasis on the availability of goods, consistent quality, money-back guarantees if customers are not satisfied, complaints procedures that really work and a general responsiveness to customer needs – elementary to Western retailers and consumers, but a surprise when you are used to a less welcoming shopping experience. Air conditioning, for example, was a winner in Western hypermarket stores, where shoppers were happy to find bikes, furniture and food all under one roof and to be able to browse in comfort. Comments such as "the prices seemed lower, the aisles roomier and the staff a lot more friendly," or "they have the best selection of products here, and they sell at good prices so I don't even bother going to the traditional market any more" show how easily firms can take for granted factors that Asian shoppers find irresistible, and how simple tilting can be.[2]

Price is an important weapon when it comes to tilting the balance. Their previous experience in low-margin, high-volume operations gave Western retailers a big advantage over local firms; goods sold in Tesco-Lotus stores in Thailand were on average 10 percent cheaper than in local stores. Western firms also have an armory of special offers, price promotions and loss leaders used at home in the frequent price wars that have shaken out the European and US markets. Western firms also have deeper pockets than most local players, many of whom face strict credit terms. And since they are in it for the long term and know the difficulties, Western firms are prepared, although not happy, to sustain losses for a time in order to build a long-term position.

Another great strength of Western firms is their superior IT systems. Supply chain management as an information-sharing exercise is a technique widely used by European and US firms such as P&G, Nestlé and Unilever, but its cost makes it an expensive luxury for Asian firms. Systems such as these allowed Western retailers to monitor inventory levels, turnovers, margins and the profitability of different product categories. In particular, this delivers great savings in cost and efficiencies in the supply chain, which can respond more quickly to consumer demand and forecast future needs. The system also leads to better inventory control and lower inventory overall. Consumers are guaranteed that products will be available on the shelves when and where they want them, another reason for remaining loyal.

Tesco, which has been at the forefront of technological innovation, played this card very well, using the combined strength of its superior supply chain management and greater purchasing power to revolutionize the food retail industry in Thailand. Tesco-Lotus installed Integrated Software Solutions' (ISS) NT Controller, a new point-of-sale back-office system. Being totally Web-based, this system can open or close stores from any location. It provides better service to customers by improving the processing time in the back office and at checkout lanes.[3]

The company also built up an excellent distribution network and developed close relations with the suppliers from whom it sourced cheap local produce. It was always ready to experiment with new products, always ready to innovate. Above all, it tried to understand its new set of customers and translate that understanding into new products and marketing ideas.

Western food retailers brought a whole new approach to the Thai food retail industry, and since nothing succeeds like success, once word got around that these companies were doing well, they began to attract the best and brightest of young local managers who wanted to work for them and learn the new techniques.

Brands

Brands can be another potent weapon. Asians have long been among the world's most conspicuous consumers: pre-crisis, Thailand was the second largest market for Mercedes-Benz cars. However, no Asian company has yet matched the allure of Western brands such as Cartier, the Louis Vuitton Moët Hennessy (LVMH) stable, Gucci and Prada, which have long had a playing field all to themselves. In Japan, where most have their Asian flagship stores, these brands continued to sell well despite the economic crisis. Post-recession, sales of luxury goods held up particularly in Japan. Consumers switched to buying their luxury goods at home rather than going abroad to buy the same goods. Brand equity built up over many years can provide excellent protection. Even the sharpest copycat product cannot compete with that, ensuring you a long lead time.

But, not every firm can have the branding of a Cartier, so it is worth building up your brand on other factors such as reliability, taste or value for money. In the past the most mundane product – such as Scottish biscuits or canned drinks – could bear a higher price, given the cachet of a Western brand name. Although this compulsion is less strong, it can still be a deciding purchasing factor. Carrefour charges premium prices for its French wines. Scottish brands of whisky and French brandy have long made great profits in markets that do not always have a tradition for drinking spirits, merely buying the brand as a status symbol. Once established, brand extensions are a way of keeping sales churning, as football clubs have learned only too well – change the strip and sit back as the customers roll in.

At the other end of the scale from the luxury brands are those with mass appeal. One of the most successful brands in Asia is Yum! Brands. However, few Asian consumers know it under that name. Rather, they know its three offspring, Kentucky Fried Chicken, Pizza Hut and Taco Bell, which cover different segments of the market. In China, its 1,378 KFC restaurants cater to the fast-food market, while its 201 Pizza Huts are positioned to attract casual diners. Since its entry into China in 1998, operating profits have risen from US$20 million to US$200 million by 2005. Yum! tilted the market its way by entering first and offering fast, affordable food cheap. Being first has continued to prove an effective tactic: in Shanghai, where Pizza Hut opened the first pizza home delivery outlet, sales grew by 23 percent year on year.

Quality can be another safeguard when local firms cannot match it – although consumers may take a little time to appreciate it. Some Asian countries have tried to use nationalist sentiment to tilt their markets. For example, since its entry in 1983, Malaysia's Proton car has been carefully nurtured by the government through the use of lower prices and protectionist tariffs and by encouraging its citizens to buy "Malaysian" rather than imported models. For two decades the strategy succeeded and the Proton was the number one bestselling car in the country. But in the long run, no amount of protectionism or even lower prices can make up for quality defects. By 2004, the Proton had a reputation as the worst quality car in the country, and was losing market share to Toyota and Honda. In the end, the most patriotic consumer will prefer a car that works to a cheap but poor quality one.

In fact, Japanese brands have long been the winners when it comes to quality positioning. This is particularly striking in China, which, in theory, should be a hostile environment for Japanese firms. History has long made relations between Japan and China difficult. Territorial disputes remain a cause of friction and propaganda in films and museums of wartime atrocities make anti-Japanese sentiment very strong in China. Yet despite this, when it comes to business, Japanese firms have managed to tilt the playing field their way.

Mainly they have done it through brands that exemplify Japan's reputation for high-quality goods such as electronics firms Panasonic and Sony, car makers like Toyota, Honda and Nissan, and the cosmetics company, Shisheido. This last company entered the Chinese market as early as 1981 and, over the years, has succeeded in creating an exclusive, glamorous image for its products. The effect has been to tilt a playing field composed of a female population discouraged from thinking about (or buying) products reeking of the decadence associated with cosmetics and beauty care to one that sees Shisheido products as the ultimate "must have." Similarly, Japanese car makers gained a 36 percent share of the Chinese auto market even while demonstrators were smashing up Japanese models in the streets. "I am not a great fan of Japan," explained one salesman, "but these cars are so well designed that I think it is worthwhile."[4]

Buy your Way In

For those companies unwilling to invest a decade in building up their market share, a shortcut to build a presence could be to buy your way in. All it takes is substantial resources – especially if it turns into a bidding war. Chinese firms have recently been doing this with some success in the US and Europe – Lenovo buying IBM's PC business and TCL the French group Thomson's television operations. The Japanese were quick to cotton on to this ploy. In 2002, the electronic firm NEC bought more than 40 local Chinese consumer electronic manufacturers.

Such a strategy is also a good way of consolidating fragmented markets. Western beer makers have been doing this in China with some success. Their first attempt to enter the China beer market with their own brews in the mid-1990s proved a disastrous failure. As they discovered to their cost, the China beer market is very regional, with over 500 brewers across the country. Consumers infinitely preferred their own cheap, local brands and were not prepared to pay premium prices for foreign beers. So on their second foray in 2004, the Western brewers went for acquisitions, buying up small local brands in order to sell a huge volume of cheap beer. In some cases, the battles between the foreign brewers became intense. Anheuser-Busch paid US$65 per hectolitre to outbid SABMiller for Harbin brewery, which had a mere 4 percent of the local market. Interbrew, Scottish & Newcastle, Carlsberg and Fosters all followed the same strategy, although by 2006, they were running out of breweries to buy. Some of the smaller targets were going for only US$10 per hectolitre. In this case, it was not so much a case of tilting the field as trying to take it over completely.

Keeping it Level

Using your marketing strengths and skills may help to build your position but playing fields in Asia rarely remain level for long. Once Western firms become successful, new obstacles are likely to appear. The nationalist card is one that is often played, regardless of the interests of consumers. In Thailand, foreign retail companies, welcomed as saviors of local firms initially, later found themselves under attack precisely because they were too successful. Under pressure from local retailers, the government planned new zoning laws and restrictions on opening hours, measures specifically aimed at stopping their further progress.

In another case, the Chinese authorities accused Carrefour, the most successful foreign retailer in China, of breaking central government regulations. In fact, in order to enter China in 1995, Carrefour had cleverly tilted the field by circumventing the State Economic and Trade Commission, from whom it should have obtained approval to open up stores. Instead, it had made individual joint venture agreements with local partners and authorities. This had proved a fast track for Carrefour, so that by the time the central authorities caught up with it at the end of 2000, it was well entrenched in the market, with 27 stores and 16,000 employees, and planned to open 10 more stores in the next year.

There was wide expectation that Carrefour would be heavily punished for its temerity. Either it would be forced to close down its stores or sell its stakes to its local partners but, in the event, it got off very lightly. The secret is that the bigger a local employer you become, the more reluctant central government will be to upset provincial authorities by adding to their unemployment statistics. In fact, Carrefour had created its own *guanxi*, one that proved a powerful talisman.

It was also lucky in its timing, as with entry into the WTO imminent, China was keen to polish its image. Consequently, after the usual round of lengthy negotiations, Carrefour was merely required to suspend the opening of its 10 new stores for six months, although Beijing did deliver a sideswipe by giving permission for the US retailer Wal-Mart to open five supermarkets in Beijing as a reward for playing by the rules.

Carrefour was lucky, but not every firm can rely on the WTO to save it from attack. However, there are some moves that Western companies can take to protect themselves from unfair recriminations and keep the playing field tilted in their favor.

Become an Insider

One way in which foreign firms can counter the argument that they are taking away the livelihoods of local traders is to become insiders themselves, by showing that they are benefiting the local economy with additional employment, technological expertise and exports.

Steps that might arouse local antagonism should be avoided. Don't get a reputation as a cost cutter or for laying off staff, instead respect local customs and be known as a good employer. For example, if existing dealers get rewards or have bonus systems, then work with it, rather than try to cut them out as soon as you take over. Invest in training schemes and make your company one that ambitious workers will want to join.

Again, Tesco proved itself a master at this.[5] It set up its head office in Bangkok, from where it supported logistics, IT, operational policy and the financial management of all its supercenters in the region. It also exported local food products for sale in its UK branches. In the first six months of 1999, these had a value of over Bt700 million. It also helped to source products for export to the EU, and to negotiate with EU officials when products were barred from the Thai market. Tesco worked with Thai farmers to introduce new technology to increase crop yields and set up a distribution center responsible for Bt1 billion in annual exports of locally raised chicken from CP to the UK and the EU. And its stores employed 3,000 people. In short, Tesco spread the message that it was a good citizen, bringing new technology, new markets and creating employment.

Taking your social responsibilities seriously is another worthwhile strategy; support local charities, fund educational scholarships and contribute to worthy causes that give good publicity and allay anti-foreign sentiment. The US petroleum firm ExxonMobil employed this strategy to try and appease anti-US hostility in Indonesia over its running of the Cepu oilfield. To integrate into the local community, the company used education, health and economic development, ensuring employment for locals before those coming from further afield, and providing Internet access and mobile libraries for parents and children.

Tesco, of course, has been another model citizen, having donated millions of baht to Thai charities. Each of its supercenters operates a collection box, from which it makes donations to selected community projects. When planning new stores, it is careful to meet local community officials and discuss their concerns, while laying emphasis on how its developments bring improvements to the local infrastructure. These include improved road, water, electricity and waste systems as well as bus stops, street lighting, green spaces and public seating. Who wouldn't want a Tesco-Lotus store near them?

Foreign firms often complain of receiving negative publicity in the press. One way to counter this is to cultivate reporters who work for the most popular press. In Asia, taking them to meals or tours of the factory or new site is a good way to get good publicity.

Appeal Directly to the Consumer

Companies, mainly those dealing in cosmetics, have found selling directly to the consumer another useful way to tilt the playing field. In India, the US-based Avon, Amway and Tupperware and the Swedish company Oriflame recruited an army of housewives working from home on a commission basis. Such was their success that Unilever copied the concept in parts of the country where it operated. Apart from selling cosmetic products, Unilever's representatives also gave makeup lessons and advice, which built up tremendous loyalty among the neglected rural population. Research showed that customers felt more comfortable buying relatively high-priced cosmetics when they could discuss and try the products first, a service that local stores did not offer.

In Vietnam, where direct selling was an unfamiliar practice, it proved an effective way of entering and developing the market. In 2003, the US-based Forever Living Products went into partnership there with a local firm that imported its products from the US, and recruited a local female sales force. As usual, the women networked through relatives and friends to sell or become sellers. Within a year, the venture had 3,200 active distributors who were selling US$470,000 worth of aloe vera products a month. A different way of reaching potential customers was followed by Oriflame, which got bank tellers to hand out their catalogues to customers as they served them. However, the firm's success led to a reaction from the government, prompted by department store owners. They sought to tilt the field back their way through regulations banning foreign firms from operating as direct sellers.

Finally, in any war of words with local competitors or governments, remember that your greatest allies are your employees and consumers. Appealing to them directly can be an effective defensive ploy, since no government will risk upsetting millions of shoppers. In Thailand, Tesco and the French groups Carrefour and Big C (run by Casino) account for over 30 percent of the nation's grocery sales, which makes for a lot of clout. In such cases, although government might slow your progress down, it won't be able to stop you. At the end of 2001, a Tesco-Lotus branch in Bangkok was the target of a rocket-launched grenade attack, the fourth such incident in a year. To counter this and attacks in the media, the company launched a massive PR campaign. In one newspaper advertisement, a store manager described how he was able to return from Bangkok to his home province, thanks to a job with Tesco-Lotus. All change creates winners and losers, and it's important to ensure that it is not only the noise from the losers that is heard.

AIG: Tilting by *Guanxi*

In 1992, the American International Group (AIG) reentered China.[6] The company was taking advantage of Deng Xiaoping's opening of some cities to foreign insurance companies. One of the largest insurance companies worldwide, AIG had actually been founded in Shanghai in 1921 and had sold insurance there from the 1920s until its expulsion from the country following the Communist takeover in 1949. Since then, AIG had waited for the day it could return to its roots.

In the meantime, it had built up a strong presence in the Asia-Pacific region. By 1975, it was the biggest foreign insurer in Hong Kong, Japan, Taiwan and Southeast Asia, and the only one with worldwide sales and support facilities. In 1987, it entered the South Korean market. However, its main target was always China.

As early as 1975, AIG's CEO Harold Greenberg began visiting China to begin the process of building up relations. In 1980, AIG opened a representative office and, to show its commitment, set up a joint venture with the People's Insurance Company of China (PICC). AIG began investing in Shanghai, which led to Greenberg forging a strong relationship with the city's then mayor, Zhu Rongji. Greenberg was also a founding member and chairman of the International Business Council, which played an important role in establishing Shanghai as a leading financial center. At the same time, Greenberg continued to keep up links with Beijing, lobbying successfully for China in the US so that the Clinton administration severed the links between its human rights record and renewal of most favored nation status.

In 1992, AIG was awarded the first license to sell insurance in China since 1949. By then, Zhu Rongji was the country's vice prime minister. In recognition, Greenberg traced 10 bronze windows that had disappeared from the emperor's summer palace in Beijing at the turn of century. Greenberg bought them and donated them to China. "No foreign corporation has ever returned missing relics to us. They only took things away," observed a Chinese official at the ceremony to mark their return.

Its long history and strong government links continued to give AIG a privileged position in China, the only foreign insurer allowed to offer life and non-life insurance. It was also the only company with wholly owned life insurance subsidiaries; every other foreign company had to be part of a joint venture.

In 1993, Greenberg was elected chairman of the US-China Business Council and, two years later, was appointed senior economic adviser to the Beijing city government. The next year, AIG began operating in Guangzhou

(Canton). Such was Greenberg's *guanxi* that the WTO negotiations were actually held up while he got an agreement that AIG could maintain its privileged position in China. At one point, his insistence on AIG maintaining the right to set up wholly owned branches even threatened to derail the talks. In the end a compromise was reached; AIG would be allowed to open two more wholly owned subsidiaries and would then have to enter 50/50 joint ventures like everyone else.

With such a start, success was virtually guaranteed, although profits remained "relatively small." In pursuit of greater returns, AIG announced in October 2003 that it was taking a 9.9 percent stake in PICC, China's largest property insurer. This move would enable AIG to expand by marketing accident and health insurance through PICC's 4,300 branch offices. In January 2004, it announced plans to launch a credit card in China in order to tap into the higher margin personal finance sector. The slogan chanted by the AIG sales force in China left no doubt as to the company's ambition: "Grow together, increase value together and create a new world for American International Insurance in 2004." In Shanghai, AIG owned the Shanghai Center, and visiting executives could stay in the Hank Greenberg Suite at the Ritz-Carlton. His *guanxi* remained strong: as one foreign rival remarked, "Every time he comes to Shanghai, he leaves with something new."[7]

Two of AIG's competitors, one Japanese and the other German, pulled out of the market, citing restrictive rules and the lack of likely profits in the short term in a market dominated by AIG. In a way it was the ultimate irony that Greenberg achieved this strong position by tilting the playing field his way, at the expense of his fellow foreign insurers.

In March 2005 at the age of 79, Greenberg was forced to step down as chief executive of AIG. He did not go voluntarily, his departure was connected to a wave of regulatory troubles besetting the company. After leaving AIG, his first port of call was China where he received the prestigious Marco Polo award. In the following months, while AIG's new management was immersed in sorting out problems at home, its China business was neglected. Greenberg, however, was a frequent visitor who stayed in close touch with his contacts. Thus, when the new AIG chief executive finally visited the country in October 2005 to attend a meeting of Chinese officials and a dozen heads of big multinationals, he found Greenberg already there – invited as a keynote speaker. By the end of the year, Greenberg was using his *guanxi* to try and outbid his old company to gain control of the Chinese operations. If he succeeded it would be a double tilt. According to one observer, "AIG will have to double its efforts without Mr Greenberg."[8]

Future Prospects

Competition in Asia will undoubtedly become keener as protection is slowly removed in the markets of the region. In this battle, Western firms should clearly have an edge, since they have, after all, been accustomed to playing in cutthroat markets for the past two decades, and possess both the techniques and the weapons. Asian firms, accustomed to having the playing field tilted for them, have not yet developed these powers. In this less protected environment, Western firms have a better chance of becoming Big in Asia.

However, do not expect miracles overnight. The WTO might have opened the gate a little for Western companies but certain sectors – telecoms, finance, media and oil exploration – are still heavily protected, and the legal maze is not likely to get significantly easier to navigate in the near future. State-owned companies may be disappearing, but you can still expect resistance from entrenched interests. There are still some uneven playing fields you just cannot tilt – for now. Even the all-conquering Carrefour eventually pulled out of both Korea – where it failed to tilt the field against local rivals – and Hong Kong, where it made little progress against two old Asia players in the local supermarket business, Jardine Matheson and Li Ka-Shing.

A few other straws in the wind show that, perhaps deep down, things have not changed so much after all. In 2002, the Bank of Central Asia, Indonesia's largest private retail bank, was finally sold after two years, not to the Standard Chartered consortium that had bid heavily for it but to Farindo Investments – which included the Hartono brothers, owners of Indonesia's largest cigarette manufacturer but with no apparent experience of running a bank. In South Korea, LG Telecom and its foreign partners won the auction for a 3G licence for mobile services in Korea. Speaking in June 2001, the country's information minister spoke of "the need for an unlevel playing field and asymmetrical regulation."[9]

Key Lessons

■ *Play to your strengths:* Use the many weapons in your competitive armory to fortify your position – build brands, innovate, change consumer tastes, change their habits. Customers will vote with their feet. Once you have captured them, leverage your IT systems to collect information on these tastes and preferences and build a database to monitor consumer tastes and spot unfulfilled needs. In fact, take a normal marketing approach.

■ *Be a good citizen:* Show you are benefiting the local economy, not taking away livelihoods.

■ *Don't tilt too much:* If you do, you may find yourself with a lot of powerful enemies. Remember, success breeds jealousy.

But remember, no firm can afford to rest on its laurels. Tilting is a never-ending process, so never relax your vigilance. The most dangerous time is when you think you have finally leveled out the playing field. That's when you will hit another obstacle.

Notes

1   Inter Press Service, "Health-Asia: Activists worry as more women puff away," M. Macan-Markar, Bangkok, 16 August, 2001.
2   *Asiaweek*, "Forget politics. Go shopping," 1–18 June, 2001, pp34–5.
3   *Business Wire*, "Asian supercenter completes rollout of ISS technology," 18 September, 2000.
4   *Financial Times*, "China ruled by pragmatism in choosing latest model," 13 September, 2005, p16.
5   "Tesco Lotus in Thailand," briefing paper, Tesco, April 2001.
6   Taken from "Back to the roots: AIG returns to China," case study by Guido Meyerhans and Professor Qiwen Lu, INSEAD-EAC, 1998.
7   *Financial Times*, "AIG reaps benefits of early arrival," 26 June, 2003, p18.
8   *Wall Street Journal*, "AIG's past, future meet in China," M. Langley, 5 December, 2005, pp16–17.
9   *EIU Business Asia*, "Auction or stitch-up?," 11 June, 2001.

Strategy 20

Think Global, Act Local – But How Far?

WHAT'S IN THIS CHAPTER?

▷ Going "Glocal"?
▷ Adaptation
   Those Who Do
   Unilever
▷ Media and Advertising
▷ Adaptation
   And Those Who Don't
▷ Trying to Look Less Western (and Moreover, Less American)
▷ Key Lessons

Going "Glocal"?

Most Western companies marketing their products in Asia have long recognized the need to adapt their products to local conditions and tastes. Some adaptations are straightforward and for obvious reasons. McDonald's, for example, does not sell burgers made from beef in India. The skin pigmentation and hair composition of Asian people differ from those of, say, European descent and, consequently, the formulae for personal products, cosmetics, shampoos and skin creams need to be changed. Different cultural habits are another reason for product adjustment. When L'Oréal decided to launch its cosmetics products in Indonesia, it had to take into account the customs of the mainly Muslim female population. For example, while the market for nail varnish was small for religious reasons, customers were heavy users of powder on their bodies and faces to protect their skin from the sun. Also, tampons do not sell well in Islamic countries but sanitary towels do.

By contrast, the need for some other adaptations has been less immediately obvious. The first cars marketed in Asia by European auto manufacturers were not adapted to the humidity and heat of Asia, and so rusted quickly. However, it took some time for Western manufacturers to appreciate the implications of this and adjust their product specification to make their cars salable.

Until recently, adaptation in Asia concentrated on this type of adjustment to match local customs and tastes – an approach characterized by the famous phrase "think global, act local." Even those who once believed that they possessed truly global products were eventually forced by poor sales in secondary markets to admit that perhaps the global village was yet to arrive, and that adaptation to local tastes was unavoidable. Coca-Cola, one of the greatest exponents of the global brand, was eventually forced to tinker with the formula of its most cherished product, the original Coca-Cola, and give it a sweeter taste. The company also had to adjust the product lines it sold in the region; about a quarter of the products it sells in Asia are not found elsewhere in the world – including oolong tea, bottled waters and a range of soft drinks. Likewise in 2005, McDonald's, another global brand, launched rice burgers – crispy chicken or sliced beef with lettuce served between two flavored rice patties – for consumers in Taiwan. Its success there led it to begin serving them in Hong Kong, Singapore, the Philippines and Malaysia.

Of course, adaptation did not stop at the product or product range, it also meant making adjustments to the rest of the marketing mix; price, promotion and place (distribution), all of which might need to be tuned to local purses, customs and market structures. Distribution in particular can be a difficult hurdle for Western companies in Asia. There is little point in having well-adapted products that are beautifully packaged if you cannot get them to the customers.

This vital part of the marketing mix often calls for a new approach since, in Asia, distribution networks may be tightly controlled, interwoven (as in Japan) and difficult to crack. Some firms try to build their own distribution networks, although this can be expensive in terms of time and financial resources. Others, such as the Western food retail giants, wait until they have grown to a critical mass and then use their size to bargain successfully with local distributors and suppliers. In India and to a lesser extent China, infrastructural defects also call for a rethink on the type of products – for example fresh versus long life – that can be sold, and sales methods. Direct selling methods have worked well in these countries where disparate rural markets make for poor and costly distribution systems.

However, apart from the more obvious situations such as those described earlier, when and how far foreign companies should adapt their products and marketing strategies to Asian markets remains an open question. Price has been the most important of the four marketing "Ps" in the region but, as markets become increasingly fragmented, it is anticipated that promotion and the way the product is positioned may move further up the list. This will have important implications for the way firms promote and package their products in Asia. In packaging and marketing, for example, should companies translate the ideograms conceptually or phonetically to avoid losing the intrinsic concept of their offering? (The now defunct Australian airline Ansett once launched a campaign built around its new fleet of passenger jets that it claimed were especially spacious inside. "The space-ships are coming" was the campaign slogan. The literal Chinese translation of this in Hong Kong was "Empty every day" – a slogan guaranteed to kill sales rather than generate them.) In Asia, brand management is still a fledg-ling subject but, in the near future, finer segmentation will require the use of more sophisticated marketing techniques, especially as more local brands emerge and compete more strongly.

Both markets and consumers are changing rapidly, and the right answer for "today" can only come out of a combination of thorough market research and experience. Many Western firms finally settle on a mix of global and adapted brands, while dividing the region between Japan and the rest of Asia. For them, the important thing is to convey the message that it wishes consumers to associate with their offerings; good value, luxury or reliability. The French group L'Oréal has global and adapted brands but, for both, the message remains the same; the emphasis is on quality and performance in every market it serves.

In the future, globalization may result in less need for a fully adapted local approach, but rather a halfway house between the two, an approach that has been christened "glocal." This will certainly be welcome in terms of cutting costs, but how will it go down in Asia? Are the markets there still so very different to the extent that intense adaptation is necessary, or are Asian consumers, increasingly exposed to Western products and adver-tising, more like their European and North American counterparts in their tastes and habits? Or are they growing more like each other, making a pan-Asian positioning possible? The next sections look at the experiences of some of the most successful companies in the region, to see how far they have been willing to go to satisfy their customers – the people who can make them Big in Asia.

Adaptation

Those Who Do

Retailing is a very localized concept, where companies need to be sensitive to local tastes and habits. Consequently, Western firms in the fast-moving consumer goods (FMCG) sector have been at the forefront of adaptation. For them, the necessity for some adjustment in order to operate successfully in the food retail or personal products sectors is not in dispute. Rather, their dilemma is the degree of difference in the Asian markets that should be considered when formulating their strategies. Are these differences of substance or context? Is Asia, or at least parts of it, so different that it merits a completely different approach, or are there sufficient similarities to allow for some coordination?

One set of reasons for acting locally that has remained constant in Asia is the existence of what are known as "structural inhibitors." These include factors such as the low purchasing power of households in many parts of the region, the lack of storage space in most homes and the small number of private vehicle owners. Taken together, these factors mean that consumers want low prices, they shop regularly (perhaps every other day), buy products in small sizes rather than in bulk and visit their local shops rather than a big store situated on the edge of town.

Cultural habits can also play their part. For example in China, there is a common belief that disposable nappies cause infertility or bow-leggedness. P&G had to get round this perception, as well as tailor products such as nappies, shampoo and toothpaste for low-income markets there and in other parts of Asia. It set up an experimental factory in Vietnam to find cheaper ways to manufacture goods and carried out a lot of research to find out exactly what consumers wanted. In China it discovered that poorer consumers were prepared to do extra hand washing to compensate for water hardness, so it produced a cheaper version of its Tide detergent without water softener. At its headquarters in Cincinnati, it even set up rooms that replicated the heat and humidity of Asia to test the resilience of its products before they went on sale. Now it is even offering adapted products to different segments of the market. For example, for toothpaste products, it has found that "The premium tier dentifrice consumer in China likes multiple health benefits ... The mid tier consumer just wants basic cleaning and caries prevention."[1] Adapting products based on such findings ensures that it does not spend too much on unnecessary differentiation, and reaches all segments of the market.

Different buying habits obviously had particular implications for the foreign hypermarkets when they moved into Southeast Asia. Those that did not take these factors into account made some expensive false starts, such as opening poorly sited stores in areas not served by public transport. Sometimes the errors can seem astonishingly basic, particularly with hindsight. The US-based Wal-Mart realized rather too late that trying to sell clothes to the Chinese in US sizes was a mistake.

Generally, the most successful Western companies in the FMCG sector have taken their basic business model and adapted it to take account of local tastes when entering the region, while retaining key home strengths, either because they appealed to Asian consumers or they gave them a competitive advantage over local rivals. One of the best operators to have used this formula in the food retail sector is the French hypermarket group Carrefour. Known in its home markets for offering low prices and value for money – a positioning ideal for Asia – it also possessed strong IT capabilities that put it way ahead of the domestic competition in Asia.

Carrefour, the first hypermarket to move into the region, undertook a careful study of local conditions before opening its first store in Taiwan in 1989.[2] As a result, it adapted the Carrefour concept to take into account the particularities of the local environment. This meant adapting both the physical layout of the stores and the products it offered to suit local tastes, besides managing its relationship with suppliers very differently. However, onto these changes Carrefour grafted its home competitive strengths; one-stop shopping, free parking and low prices. The result was the successful launch of a store in Taiwan; 10 years later, it had 18 stores in the country.

By the time Carrefour opened up in Indonesia in 1998 (despite the economic crisis), it had 44 stores operating in the region and an "Asian recipe" ready to roll. In Indonesia, Carrefour focused on sites in central business areas and shopping malls – which were also much cheaper to rent in the aftermath of the crisis. The stores stocked more Indonesian than French goods, fresh prawns and leafy vegetables at low prices that customers could afford. In Malaysia, where more widespread car ownership allowed people to shop in bulk two or three times a month, Carrefour's hypermarkets completely changed the habits of consumers, offering them shelves stocked not just with all their favorite local noodles and herbs, but French wines and Carrefour brands exactly like those sold in France.

As this example illustrates, the tradition of local adaptation is fairly well entrenched in the retailing sector. However, even players in newer industry sectors, such as telecoms, have discovered that it pays to research local tastes and adapt your product accordingly. The Finnish company Nokia gained a commanding lead over its rivals in the Indonesian mobile handset market by adopting a classic segmentation strategy toward the developing market. It segmented the market into four types, premium, business, fashion and entry-level users, and then introduced a range of handsets to match the tastes of each segment. To sell these offerings, Nokia built its own distribution network with four major handset distributors and an accessories firm. While Nokia provided the branding for the mobiles, the locals provided the tactical promotion.[3]

But a word of warning; going local does not automatically guarantee success. Carrefour, perhaps surprisingly, failed in Japan due to overadaptation. Its strategy of being local meant that there was no incentive for consumers to shop at Carrefour rather than a Japanese supermarket. So they didn't. Therefore, it had to go into reverse and emphasize its French heritage.

Carrefour's great rival Tesco also successfully localized its operations, notably in the difficult Korean market where it went into partnership with Samsung. By 2006, it was the second largest player behind the local leader. Apart from the actual shopping area, its hypermarkets housed fast-food bars, coffee shops and restaurants and even an art gallery, plus an Internet café, a financial services center and a car repair shop. Tesco also made the interior of the stores brighter and lowered the height of shelves. The company's success was such that it was one of the favorites to win the bid for Carrefour's Korean assets – to be sold off as Carrefour withdrew from the market after poor results.

Boots, another UK retailer, first entered Thailand very successfully. A spokesman for the company noted:

> Clean shops and good service have gone down a treat, but we did have to make some adjustments. Customers were uncomfortable that the shops were so quiet – so we had to install banks of video screens broadcasting pop music and videos.[4]

Boots' key ranges underwent some adaptation, for example in Thailand it found a high demand for tights because of air conditioning.

Unilever

> Successful brands can only grow out of a deep understanding of Asian consumer attitudes and behaviours. Transferring Western mixes is by no means a certain recipe for success. (a Unilever manager)

Undoubtedly, the grandfather of local adaptation is the Anglo-Dutch consumer giant Unilever.[5] Many of its portfolio of 400 brands – known throughout the world – began as local brands that were acquired by Unilever and turned into international brands. The famous Pond's range, for example, was originally a US brand, bought and adapted by Unilever and a bestseller in China. It is a skill that the company has honed to perfection.

Unilever's heritage of strong local autonomy meant that the degree to which products were adapted to suit local markets was the decision of Unilever country managers throughout its global empire. In Asia, its hair products ranges – shampoos and conditioners – were designed and crafted for each market in the region and tested to the liking of, say, Indonesians and Thais before going on sale.

In Southeast Asia, where markets had a high proportion of poor rural customers, Unilever sold its hair care products in small quantities, one-shot sachets that consumers could buy two or three times a week, rather than the big bottles of shampoo sold in the West. This was backed up by a highly efficient sales and logistics system, since the company was producing millions of these sachets, often selling three a week to the same consumer. Where necessary, the company built up a distribution system from scratch, training local salesmen who traveled by whatever form of transport was best suited to the local terrain – tricycle, boat or motorcycle – in order to reach retailers in remote areas of the country. This is a consideration that has broader application across Asia. Roads, particularly in rural areas, are poor or often too narrow to allow for conventional delivery trucks.

In these markets, Unilever rolled out its product range according to a tried and tested pattern that the company had identified as most appropriate for developing markets. It began with the cheapest products, and then slowly introduced more expensive ranges to develop consumer tastes, increase market share and forge brand loyalty. In India, it reinforced its presence by also providing a local film show for villages that would otherwise never have had such entertainment. Unilever's approach to local markets has been to capture customers while they are poor and grow with them, then they will hopefully be yours for life. It was also a long-term approach, since it can take 10–15 years to get a return. Consequently, it is only a strategy for companies with strong financial resources and shareholders prepared to wait for a return.

The Unilever strategy proved highly successful in India and, more recently, Vietnam. There, Unilever put all its experience to work to steal a march on its rivals to build a strong position in soaps, detergents and personal products (especially hair), virtually gaining a 100 percent share of the markets in the poor rural parts of the country. In these areas, where consumers typically bought just enough for their daily needs, Unilever expanded aggressively via its one-shot shampoo, toothpaste and detergent packets that could be found in every village.

Its sales managers visited remote retailers in the country regularly – often by boat in the Mekong Delta area – to push them to expand and offer the full range of Unilever products, from soaps and shampoos to tea and skin-whitening products. From time to time, Unilever would flood the local market with a new product at a slightly higher price, to push consumers up the value chain. Retailers were offered incentives such as refrigerators to display Unilever brands, while a big advertising campaign reinforced the brand identity.

One Unilever move to appear local in Vietnam was particularly audacious. It began selling the salty fish sauce, *nuoc nam*, which is eaten daily in Vietnam, under its Knorr brand. The launch was backed up by a marketing campaign and television adverts that asked Vietnam customers to "taste the legend." This was a reference to the fact that Unilever's sauce was actually Phu Quoc fish sauce, made by local producers in the traditional way and prized as the most authentic of all sauces. As the managing director of Unilever's food division explained: "By starting to look at fish sauce and to connect ourselves with fish sauce, we will be seen more as a Vietnamese company and brand than as an international brand coming from Europe."[6]

However, although Unilever remained the strongest exponent of local adaptation, in the early 1990s it concluded that its emphasis on strong local autonomy meant that its products were often adapted unnecessarily, leading to losses in economies of scale. Increasingly, given the trend toward large-scale economies, rapid innovation and flexible response times, such an approach was proving a handicap. So, Unilever opted for a more regional or "glocal" approach, whereby it would take a Southeast Asian idea and adapt it marginally for Thailand, the Philippines, Malaysia and so on. Instead of expensive and time-consuming total adaptation, the basic product would merely be fine-tuned.

One of its biggest successes using this approach was in its Wall's ice cream business.[7] Unilever was quick to identify the huge potential that existed for a regional ice cream created specifically for Asians, whose tastes differed markedly from the rest of the world. When its red bean ice cream failed to make any impression due to poor marketing and inadequate research into the choice of ingredients, the company's Bangkok innovation center (one of 11 set up by Unilever in Asia) was asked to completely redesign the product, its packaging and promotion.

When Asian Delight was launched, it used Thai and English on its packaging in Thailand, and English only in Malaysia, Singapore and Indonesia. It was targeted at the segment located between products that Unilever sold worldwide, such as its Magnum range, and local brands acquired by other multinationals. The basis of the recipe was coconut ice cream, mixed with a variety of fruits and vegetables traditionally used in sweets throughout the region. It was a runaway success. Within three years, varieties of Asian Delight were being sold in supermarkets, and available on sticks, in cups and pint containers. In Thailand, a television advert showed Asian women teasing each other into doing a native dance in order to get a taste of Asian Delight, and Wall's dominated the market with 41 percent, followed by Nestlé with just 15 percent.

Media and Advertising

The cultural diversity and strong national pride that characterize many countries in the region mean that anything other than a local positioning is difficult to sustain in the media industry. A big story on Thailand, for example, does not pull in readers in Malaysia or the Philippines. The experience of the weekly *Asiaweek*, which tried to position itself as a pan-Asian journal, appears to confirm this view. *Asiaweek*, which became part of the US Time Warner media empire, tried to straddle the diversity of the region by aiming at Asia's emerging middle class – English speakers interested in Asian affairs. Unfortunately, the journal found itself caught in a no man's land between global players, such as *Time* and *Newsweek*, and local competitors. In the end it folded, defeated by the struggle to find the right audience among so many local ones.[8]

Advertising is another area where it still pays to be local. As the head of Leo Burnett Worldwide observed: "The key to making money in the Asian advertising business is to recognize that it is not one region but many."[9] The evidence supports his contention that those who understand, and have some insight into, the various markets in Asia are more likely to succeed than those who "arbitrarily globalize or generalize Asian Pacific." Take the flagship brand of the US-based tobacco group Philip Morris, Marlboro, incarnated in the world-famous image of "Marlboro Man," the free-ranging cowboy roving Marlboro country. It was the most successful and longest running campaign in history – until it got to Asia. There, the image of a hired hand was not one locals aspired to and so when the brand was launched in Hong Kong, Marlboro Man became a boss.

In some countries, censorship and cultural norms shape what can and cannot be shown in television advertisements. In 2004, the Chinese government banned ads for "offensive" products such as feminine hygiene pads, hemorrhoid medication and athlete's foot ointment during three daily meal times. Beer ads were limited to two between 7pm and 9pm. Western advertising companies also discovered the hard way that, in China, using sexily dressed women to advertise products was unacceptable. L'Oréal tried using the Chinese film star Gong Li, now famous in the West, to sell its products there, but the glamorous image did not prove as attractive as the company anticipated, suggesting that Western notions of beauty differ from those of average Chinese viewers.

In Beijing, local scenes and historical characters as a background to television advertisements were long the preferred choice of local viewers. However, this is not always an infallible method of pleasing viewers: in December 2004 the authorities banned a Nike advertisement because it roused "indignant feelings." The ad showed a black US basketball star defeating a pair of dragons and a kung fu master. Viewers were allegedly upset that the Chinese culture was tarnished by seeing all the Chinese images defeated.[10]

However, foreign advertisers have noted that tastes are changing and that more creative ads for rice cookers, sports shoes and even hamburgers are succeeding. McDonald's announced that its next global ad would come from a Chinese firm, although this level of sophistication is as yet limited to urban audiences. Otherwise, advertisers must continue to respect certain no-go areas, for example "We can't undermine the position of authority figures, primarily teachers and parents, in Chinese society."[11]

Adverts must be further tuned to take account of the differences between north and south China. Food adverts, for example, emphasize different ingredients according to regional tastes; in Sichuan, where the locals like spicy food, the type of noodle advertised is chosen accordingly. In Xinjiang, which has a largely Muslim population, pork noodles are not advertised. Only a few established brands, such as Unilever's Lux and Pond's cold cream, use the same advertisements throughout China.

In multiracial Malaysia, different audiences require different messages: Chinese consumers prefer a rational message – how much does the product cost, how does it work, while Malays prefer a more emotional appeal. In Thailand, dark humor goes down well but is not appreciated in other countries. Adverts made for Thai audiences often win awards at international festivals.

However, one of the biggest mistakes was made by that old Asia hand, Unilever. The company roused the anger of women's groups in Malaysia following the running of an advert to illustrate the efficacy of its Pond's skin-lightening moisturizer.[12] The implication that the girl in the advertisement was more attractive after using it caused great offence, since it seemed to send the message that only fair people were beautiful. This again raised old prejudices, since historically a fair skin was associated with wealth and status and a dark skin with those who worked out of doors. The modern version of this is that "white" means "Western." Even the most experienced can get it wrong.

Adaptation

And Those Who Don't

Western producers of luxury and designer goods have had a field day in Asia in the last few years. Although volatile economic conditions in Europe and North America have an effect on sales in Asia, and most notably in Japan, demand has remained fairly constant. Japanese shoppers buy about 40 percent of the world's high-quality leather goods, and account for more than half the sales of luxury goods groups such as Gucci, LVMH and Christian Dior. Then there is the purchasing of luxury goods outside Asia by Asians. The long queue that forms daily outside the LVMH concession within the Galeries Lafayette department store in Paris almost exclusively comprises visiting Japanese. All this reflects the Asian perception of Western luxury brands as status symbols. Buying them to keep up appearances is the main motivating factor in their purchase.

These are companies for whom brand adaptation clearly makes no sense. The chairman of the Vendôme Group, which houses brands such as Chloé, Jaeger, Cartier and Karl Lagerfeld, noted that "We represent tradition. We don't want to dilute that tradition by over-adaptation to the Asian market," while the chief executive of Cartier has said that "Culturally, Asia is not a luxury market. It is only a consumer market. Luxury was born in Europe. Here it is just a status symbol."[13] These companies' struggle in Asia is not with adaptation but with counterfeiting, thus prompting the need to protect the value of their brands from being diluted by fakes.

Other brands that trade on the cachet of being expensive Western products include Scotch whisky, BMW cars and French cognac Hennessy XO. For some of its premium perfume and cosmetics products, L'Oréal has insisted on keeping their positioning as international brands, while making some cultural adaptation in its advertisements. Thus, Christy Turlington, the then top US model, was replaced by a famous Asian model for certain cosmetic products.

Trying to Look Less Western (and Moreover, Less American)

It's not commonly realized that most of the world's Muslims do not live in the Middle East but in Asia, 70 percent of them in fact. This means that issues to which Muslims are sensitive, such as US policy on Israel and the war in Iraq, play out quite loudly in Asia, particularly in Asian countries where Muslims form an absolute majority, such as Pakistan, Bangladesh, Malaysia and Indonesia, and also in regions of Asia that are largely Muslim, such as southern Thailand and the southern Philippines.

In these countries and regions, foreign companies may want to appear as local as possible. And to put it bluntly, many might want to underplay their associations with the US.

The Iraq War of 2003 was the first occasion on which significant Muslim consumer boycotts of US products and brand names was initiated in Southeast Asia.[14] There was some targeting of obvious US brand names in Asia by protesters. McDonald's fast-food restaurants in Indonesia were the scenes of anti-war and anti-US protests. Members of Indonesia's small Islamic Youth Movement approached the main McDonald's in central Jakarta to look for Americans to force into signing promises that they would leave Indonesia. The protesters were arrested before entering the restaurant. The group then announced that Americans had two days to leave Indonesia or be forced out. The irony was that the McDonald's franchise holder for Indonesia is a local Muslim, Bambang Rachmadi, a son-in-law of former Indonesian Vice President Soedharmono. Essentially, McDonald's in Indonesia has Muslim owners. The problem was then how to demonstrate that. The media was briefed, and Rachmadi's ownership was emphasized, as were his Islamic credentials. An effort was made to quickly demonstrate to the public the local nature of McDonald's in Indonesia and to show that it was not an entirely American concern.

Muslims in Thailand's five most southern provinces called for a boycott of US brands of goods and services. A list was drawn up of 100 US and British brands and products and distributed in the form of leaflets at an anti-war rally of more than 20,000 local Muslims in the southern seaside town of Songkla. Among the companies and brands on the list were Coca-Cola, P&G (Olay, Vicks, Pringles), Colgate-Palmolive (Fab, Colgate, Palmolive), Unilever (Rexona, Pond's, Omo) and Johnson & Johnson (Johnson talcum powders, Carefree). Fast-food chains listed to be boycotted included KFC, McDonald's, Pizza Hut, Starbucks and Burger King.

Nestlé was also on the list despite it being Swiss-based. Nestlé executives in Bangkok responded by sending teams to the south to explain to consumers that Nestlé was not in fact American.

Another risk to companies, particularly food companies, is the spreading of malicious rumors that halal food is in fact not halal. This is not infrequent in Indonesia particularly but also in Malaysia. Such rumors may be spread by competitors or by those with a grudge against the targeted companies. Typically, the companies are locally owned but owned by local Chinese interests. But foreign-owned companies can also be targets. The rumors now spread at astonishing speed via mobile phone text messages and chain emails that can lead to almost instantaneous consumer boycotts. Such instances can be particularly costly to companies because of the speed with which they can eventuate, the decentralized nature of the passing on of the misinformation and the difficulty in locating the source of such rumors. Gardenia Bakeries, a major manufacturer and distributor of bread and bread-like products, faced such a campaign in mid-2004. Messages were spread across Malaysia via SMS texts and poison-pen letters that Gardenia products contained non-halal products. The company had to respond with prominent and costly media advertisements in which it explained that it had been manufacturing bread and similar products in Malaysia for almost 20 years, that the rumors of non-halal ingredients were "blatant and malicious lies designed to injure and undermine Gardenia" and that it had allowed its factories to be inspected by representatives from the Muslim Consumers Association of Malaysia.[15] Hitting back loudly, quickly and directly, emphasizing the company's longevity in the country and other local credentials are all part of what must happen to contain the damage. Once more, there are benefits in appearing "local."

Key Lessons

■ Remember the importance of research: never enter a market without undertaking thorough market research into local spending habits, purchasing power, customs and so on.

■ Don't automatically jettison your home business model; think how you can combine your own well-tested strengths to give you a competitive advantage in Asian markets.

■ Adaptation does not end with the product or the product range; set it in the context of the whole marketing strategy – the price, how it will be packaged and how it will be promoted and distributed.

■ Try out your products first in chosen points of sale. Try to collect customer feedback and use it to make final adjustments.

- Use IT to gather information about the market that can feed into developing new follow-up products.
- There is no such thing as an Asian market. There is not even a singular Chinese market. The degree of adaptation will depend on your product and where in Asia you hope to sell it.

Notes

1 *Financial Times*, "Check the depth of the pocket," J. Grant, 16 November, 2005, p8.
2 Taken from "Carrefour in Asia" (A) and (B), case studies by Pierre Courbon and Professor Philippe Lasserre, INSEAD-EAC, 1994.
3 *EIU Business Asia*, "Lifestyle in a phone," 29 May, 2000.
4 *Marketing*, "Tesco braves the dangers of taking brands abroad," C. Murphy, 22 April, 1999.
5 Taken from "Unilever in Asia," case study by Charlotte Butler and Professor Philippe Lasserre, INSEAD-EAC, 1994.
6 *Financial Times*, "Unilever has a taste of succccess in Vietnam," A. Kazmin, 2 December, 2003, p11.
7 Taken from "Wall's ice cream in Thailand," case study by Deborah Clyde-Smith and Professor Peter Williamson, INSEAD-EAC, 1998.
8 Taken from "*Asiaweek*: Positioning a regional magazine," case study by Jocelyn Probert and Hellmut Schutte, INSEAD-EAC, 1999.
9 *Wall Street Journal Europe*, "Interview with Leo Burnett," J. Saranow, 29 November, 2001.
10 *Wall Street Journal Europe*, "China bans Nike ad," 8 December, 2004, pA7.
11 *Wall Street Journal Europe*, "China proves unexpectedly rich in ad talent," 23 October, 2003, pA9.
12 *Wall Street Journal Europe*, "Unilever ads are called racist," C. Prystay, 30 April, 2002.
13 *Asian Wall Street Journal*, "Vendôme expects strong growth in Asia," 5 October, 1994, and "Upscale firms weigh strength of Asian sales," 7 May, 1992.
14 See Backman, M., *The Asian Insider: Unconventional Wisdom for Asian Business*, revised edition, Palgrave Macmillan, Basingstoke, 2006.
15 The quote is from one such advertisement which appeared in the *New Straits Times*, 28 July, 2004.

Strategy 21

Building a Profile in Asia

WHAT'S IN THIS CHAPTER?

▷ Are Asians Good at Branding?

▷ The "Starbucksization" of Asia

▷ China: Asia's Big New Advertising Market

▷ Sponsorship

▷ Never Misjudge the Consumer

▷ The Internet for Profile Building in Asia: the Case of China

▷ The White Envelope Issue

▷ Local Branding

▷ Understand the Message

▷ Things to Consider

Are Asians Good at Branding?

It's often said that Asian companies are not good at building brands and that there are few truly Asian brands. This isn't strictly true.

Among the brands indigenous to Asia are: Giordano, Pacific Coffee, Café de Coral (Hong Kong); Banyan Tree, The Hour Glass, Raffles (Singapore); Padini, Renoma, G2000, Sugar Bun, Boh Tea, Selangor Pewter (Malaysia); Indofoods, Mustika Ratu, Bintang Beer (Indonesia); Jolly Bee (the Philippines); Alibaba, Harnn Soaps, Chiang Beer, Singha Beer, Black Canyon Coffee (Thailand); Lenovo, Tsingtao Beer, Haier, Hongtashan cigarettes (China); Acer, Evergreen (Taiwan); Trung Nguyen

Coffee (Vietnam); Tata, Barista Coffee (India); plus many prominent
Korean firms such as LG, Samsung and Hyundai and Japanese firms like
Sony, Toyota and Mitsubishi.

Still, it is true that businesspeople in Asia generally are prepared to
spend less on brand development than is the case in the West. This is partly
because the region's most successful businesspeople have tended to be
ethnic Chinese who focused on trading in commodities that are difficult to
brand. Furthermore, commodities tend to be high volume, small margin.
This also makes the economics of branding less feasible. Culturally too,
the region's ethnic Chinese businesspeople have been loath to spend on
intangibles and services such as branding, viewing such expenditure as
paying a lot for nothing much, and certainly something for which there is
little physical evidence. They are well disposed to goods and goods'
trading, not to services.

The geographic and cultural gap between Asia and Western markets
allows for a degree of brand segmentation. For example, Rockport Shoes,
a successful shoe brand in the US, is associated with older consumers in
that market. But in Asia, the brand is targeted at younger buyers with
associations of outdoor activities like walking and hiking. Horlicks, a
distinctly unfashionable English brand of hot drink powder in its home
market, is seen in Malaysia as a slightly upmarket drink that attracts a
premium in small cafés and food stalls, something to be drunk for a
slightly special occasion. Similarly, Debenhams, a lower to mid-level
clothing and appliance retailer in the UK, is seen in Southeast Asia as
expensive and upmarket. Fast-food chains such as KFC and Burger King
are seen as venues for family nights out, perhaps to celebrate a special
occasion, and even venues for office lunches in much of Asia, be it China
or Malaysia. This has a lot to do with incomes in most of Asia compared
with the West and also education. A whopper with no cheese (picture
provided) is an easier concept to grasp than foie gras served with roundels
of char-grilled bread, onion and raisin marmalade and a Sauternes.

The "Starbucksization" of Asia

Starbucks' success in Asia has been rapid and extraordinary. It doesn't
use paid advertising to build its brand, and as most of Asia comprises
societies that are traditionally tea drinking, its success is even more
extraordinary.

The Seattle-based company is the world's largest coffee chain. By 2005,
it had more than 6,100 outlets in the US and almost 8,500 worldwide.

In the absence of formal advertising, its stores are its advertising. Enormous research goes into determining the location of each store. They must be visible and they must be accessible to the right demographic. Emphasis is also put on "lifestyle." In Asia for example, the stores are not so much a place to buy coffee as a good place to sit, meet friends and generally hang out. The price of a coffee is effectively the price of renting a table; the price paid to imbibe the atmosphere.

Starbucks' first overseas outlet opened in Tokyo in 1996. Its expansion since has been phenomenal. By 2005 there were 1,169 Starbucks stores in East Asia, 544 of these were in Japan. Sazaby Inc. is its local partner in Japan. Sazaby too is a retailer. The licensing agreement with Sazaby became the prototype for its expansion elsewhere in the region: choose a good local concessionaire, license them and let them do the rest (Table 21.1).

Taiwan was next. Starbucks opened 138 stores in Taiwan between 1998 and 2005 in conjunction with President Enterprises, its local partner.

The first Starbucks opened in Shanghai in May 2000. In Shanghai 50 stores were planned in partnership with President Enterprises.

In southern China, more Starbucks stores were planned, this time in conjunction with its 50/50 partner, Maxim's, a Hong Kong cake shop company that's 50 percent owned by Dairy Farm International. By 2005, 111 Starbucks stores had opened across mainland China (including 44 in Beijing and 43 in Shanghai) plus another 34 in Hong Kong and one in Macau.

Starbucks opened in South Korea in May 2000. Its partner in South Korea is the local Shinsege Group and together they planned to open at least 45 stores there in the following five years. But they did far better than that. By 2005, 106 Starbucks stores had opened in South Korea. And in 2002, it opened its first store in Indonesia with local partner PT Mitra Adiperkasa, a part of the Gadjah Tunggal Group. By 2005 there were 27 Starbucks stores open in Indonesia.

Table 21.1 Not going it alone: Starbucks' initial partners in Asia

Country or region	Partner
Malaysia	Berjaya Group
Southern China and Hong Kong	Dairy Farm International
Shanghai and Taiwan	President Enterprises
Beijing	Mei Da Coffee Co.
Singapore	Bonvests Holdings
The Philippines	Rustan Coffee Corp.
Japan	Sazaby Inc.
Indonesia	Gadjah Tunggal Group
South Korea	Shinsege Group

Few Asian countries have been left untouched by the Starbucks' phenomenon. There are now dozens of outlets in Thailand, Malaysia, the Philippines and Singapore. Again local partners were used to facilitate the roll-out. The diversified Berjaya Group controlled by local entrepreneur Vincent Tan is its Malaysian partner. And in Singapore, its partner initially was Bonstar, a subsidiary of Bonvests Holdings, the owner of the local Burger King franchise.

Local partners have helped Starbucks to add local touches. In Malaysia for example, where it is partnered with Berjaya, it has added curry puffs to its selection of snack choices. In Hong Kong, its local partner Maxim's advised it to add mooncakes to the available bakery items when it is Chinese New Year, while Starbucks in Beijing offers a green tea-flavored frappuccino. The model of using local partners has been key to Starbucks' rapid roll-out and its localization and acceptance. Young, fresh-faced local staff serving coffee behind the counter also help to localize the brand and make it more aspirational. Serving coffee at Starbucks in China or Malaysia is seen as "hip" in those countries, but in the US and the UK for example, it's a job that's typically reserved for students and temporary migrant workers, a job to have while waiting for something better to turn up.

China: Asia's Big New Advertising Market

Unlike Starbucks, most companies cannot afford the luxury of not advertising to build their brands. China is Asia's biggest emerging consumer market and is quickly emerging as Asia's biggest advertising market. International agencies such as Ogilvy & Mather and J. Walter Thomson have been quick to enter and at first concentrated their efforts on helping foreign companies build their brands there. However, aware of the greater marketing experience of the foreign firms they are competing against, local companies have also been eager to take advantage of their services, and are now beginning to incorporate Western selling points such as "quality," "reliability" and "innovative technology" into their advertising. But local competition remains keen. There are approximately 47,000 advertising agencies in China, all of them are eager to prove that they are as good as (and much cheaper than) their foreign rivals when it comes to helping firms to push their products.

The boom in advertising has come with the growth in shopping and shopping facilities, which no doubt will reach a crescendo as the 2008 Beijing Olympics approach. The advertising spend on Chinese television alone was US$24 billion in 2004, with annual growth rates of 20–30 percent. The opportunities for such advertising have never been greater. The number of television stations in China has expanded rapidly from a few dozen to almost 300 by 2005. The number of households with a television set has grown too: most Chinese homes now have one. And by 2005, around 110 million homes also had cable television access.[1]

Newspapers and magazines are another route for advertisers as is outdoor advertising such as billboards. In 2004, a total of 2.58 trillion copies of national and provincial newspapers were produced and 2.69 billion copies of magazines were printed.[2]

Outdoor advertising opportunities are growing exponentially as toll roads and other highways are built, thus providing more places to place billboards. The construction of thousands of high-rise office towers around China affords another opportunity in the form of the naming rights of prominent buildings.

Another advertising outlet that has been quick to emerge is the use of flat screen televisions in lift lobbies, train station platforms and other places where the public congregates. This business was started in 2002 by locally owned Focus Media Holdings. The company, listed on Nasdaq, has grown through acquisitions. In early 2006, it paid US$325 million in cash and stock to buy its rival Target Media Holdings. The purchase gave Focus Media a massive network of 60,000 display sites in 75 Chinese cities.

Both domestic and foreign brands are taking full advantage of all these outlets to build their brands within China. Other techniques such as direct marketing, database building and loyalty programs are also being adopted. However, the biggest expansion has come in the field of sponsorship.

Sponsorship

Sponsorship has long been an important tool for Western companies seeking to put their brand names in the public eye. Where advertising regulations, tax conditions and other factors proved unfavorable, sponsorship became crucial in the long-term image building of a brand, providing national media publicity, access to influential people and promoting a positive image. When it first entered Asia, Cartier had an edge through sponsoring major cultural promotions. In Hong Kong, for example, it used highly prized concerts and ballet performances to get across the message of Cartier as an exclusive product, available only to the elite.

The television boom in China and relaxation of rules has allowed local and foreign companies to introduce their brands to Chinese consumers via program sponsorship. Ford, Nestlé and even Lycra have sponsored programs that feature or are even built around their products. Ford, for example, produced a program in which 12 contestants on a tropical island tackled various challenges while driving a Ford Maverick sports utility vehicle, wearing Nike clothing and sipping Nestlé drinks.[3] Heinz sponsored a program called "Mommy & Baby – Healthy World" that featured Heinz baby foods.

Television sponsorship can also be a good way to create a market for an unknown brand. Home buying, for example, is a new concept to the Chinese but one that is catching on fast. B&Q, the British do-it-yourself chain, was quick to see the possibilities of reaching a mass audience quickly and cheaply via television and building sales in its chain of 18 stores across the country. It sponsored its own TV show, "Home Show," which ran on nine networks and featured home renovation tips. As B&Q's managing director explained: "In China, people are purchasing homes for the very first time. We want to be considered the top name so it's all about being an authority."[4]

Even small Chinese companies are using these same brand-building tools. Skyworth is a television manufacturer based in Shenzhen. It has sponsored a program to benefit blind people in order to show what a good citizen it was and build awareness of its products. "Branding tells the customer to buy Skyworth and gets us a good price," said Zhou Tong, the company's vice president.[5]

For companies whose products could not be advertised on television, event sponsorship has provided an effective alternative. This has applied particularly to the tobacco companies. Following the prohibition of cigarette advertising on TV and radio, sponsorship, first of major sporting events and later of the arts and social foundations, became a major tool in promoting their brands. The US tobacco companies largely built their brands through sponsoring events; a Marlboro Soccer League, a Marlboro Music Hour, a Kent Billiards contest and a Salem tennis tournament. Cross-border media such as the Internet and satellite TV opened up further opportunities. For example, Star TV, which by 2000 had 300 million viewers in Asia, aired 1,237 hours of tobacco-sponsored commercials in a one-year period. Chinese companies have been quick to see the possibilities here. Lenovo was a sponsor of the 2006 Winter Olympic Games in Turin, and along with other well-known foreign brands such as Samsung, Swatch, Coca-Cola and Kodak has already signed up as a sponsor for what promises to be the biggest sponsorship opportunity in Asia this decade, the 2008 Beijing Olympics. Elsewhere, Singapore's Tiger Beer sponsors Arsenal Football Club in the UK and Thailand's Chiang Beer sponsors Everton Football Club.

An offshoot of event sponsorship is celebrity endorsement, and spending on this has greatly increased among local and Western firms. Apart from famous film stars, sports stars have increasingly been used to boost brands by celebrity association. Yao Ming, the Shanghai star who plays in the US National Basketball League and is the Chinese equivalent of the Beckham phenomenon, has become a brand all by himself. US firms have been queuing up to be associated with him. Pepsi, Reebok, Gatorade and McDonald's already have deals with him and, in the run-up to the 2008 Olympics, a host of others hope to join in. According to Pepsi, sales were up almost 30 percent in China after a year of Yao as its spokesman, and McDonald's has appointed him its first ever "worldwide brand ambassador." "It usually takes five or six years to build a brand. Yao has obviously accelerated that for himself and can do that for others," said a Columbia University marketing professor. The global director of Interbrand Corp. put it concisely: "If you are teamed up with Yao, you have an instant leg up in a marketplace of a billion people."[6]

Never Misjudge the Consumer

Chinese consumers are very brand conscious. When it comes to attracting consumers in a relatively poor country, one would expect price to be paramount. But, counterintuitively, branding is at least as important and probably more important to Chinese consumers than price. This doesn't mean that luxury goods necessarily do well in China. Rather, when shoppers buy goods in a supermarket, quality and brand recognition – as a proxy for quality – matter. So it is not so much a matter of Gucci versus Prada as Palmolive versus Lux. Prices need to be competitive but not necessarily the cheapest. Chee and West provide an example of the power of brands over price in their *Myths about Doing Business in China:* Kodak and Fuji films both charge "about 50 percent more than their local competitor, but less than they do in developed countries. Between them they have 90 percent of the Chinese market."[7] The message is: don't be cheap so much as give value for money.

A survey by Kurt Salmon Associates of middle-class consumers in China found that characteristics such as brand, impact on health and customer care were all regarded above price when it came to the decision to buy. Among those surveyed, 78 percent said they buy toiletry products based on brand and that if their preferred brand was unavailable, they would be unlikely to switch.[8]

The survey also found that consumers' preference for foreign or local brands differs according to the type of product they are buying. When it comes to home improvement products and electronics, the consumers surveyed showed a strong preference for foreign over local brands. When it comes to food and personal care products, they prefer local brands. And in the case of clothing and footwear, no strong preference is shown. Accordingly, Kurt Salmon advises that home improvement products and electronics entrants should retain their foreign identity in their marketing, but food and personal care products entrants should try to appear more Chinese, more localized.

Indian consumers have also been giving foreign companies similar lessons when it comes to judging their preferences. Like China, India is a difficult market as it is divided into a small but important group of wealthy urban consumers, beneficiaries of the IT boom, and the millions of poor countryside consumers who nevertheless represent an important segment. Then, as with China, there are many significant regional differences.

Some global brands have successfully adopted a dual approach to building sales in the Indian market. To consumers in the countryside, they offer a small, cheaper range that comes in one-shot sachets or bottles appropriate to the lack of space in village homes. To the cities they offer a wider premium brand. In this way the brand is reaching consumers country-wide and building up recognition, so that when consumers graduate to more expensive products, they will stick to the brand name. This is what Unilever has done so successfully with everything from soap to washing powders, and Pepsi-Cola with its soft drinks. Besides selling small reusable bottles at about 20 cents each, it also sells juices, bottled water and Diet Pepsi in small and thus affordable bottles.

In India, as in China, many foreign firms assumed that price would be the determining factor and so offered cheaper products, from televisions to fridges to mobile phones. They were wrong, as the Chinese consumer electronics firms TCL Corp. and Konka Group discovered. In the late 1990s, both failed to make an impact in India due mainly to misjudging their potential customers. Indian consumers associated their low priced products with poor quality, and consequently both were forced to withdraw from the market. When Haier, their home competitor, moved into India in 2004, it learned from their experience and entered with a range of higher end quality products, priced similarly or higher than those of the well-known Korean brands, LG Electronics and Samsung.

Mobile phone brands have also found that, in India, consumers are just as brand conscious as their richer counterparts in the developed world. Nokia, for example, has benefited richly from brand recognition and, by the end of 2005, had a 58 percent share of the market, despite the existence of slightly cheaper Motorola models – people want the brand they know. Hence in early 2006, Motorola, lagging in fourth place at 6 percent, embarked on a big marketing and advertising campaign to promote the brand and close the gap with Nokia. "Lowering the price of a phone will help to drive some demand in the short term, but creating brand value is the way to succeed in the long term," observed a telecoms analyst.[9]

The Internet for Profile Building in Asia: the Case of China

In early 2006, Internet search engine Google announced its top search words or phrases, and the top 10 gainers, for the previous year. Top of the list was Janet Jackson, no doubt because users were keen to relive her costume "malfunction" during the previous year's Superbowl. But it's the top gainers that suggest the true dynamics of the Internet. First was Myspace, a blog hosting site. Second was Ares, a music downloading site. And at number three was Baidu, a Chinese language search engine in which Google happens to own a small stake.

Baidu's prominence in Google's overall results is testament to its popularity in China. Around 80 percent of Internet users use it as their primary search engine. Like Google it offers a sophisticated and popular search tool that's ahead of the rest. It allows for searches in Chinese using Chinese characters but also via phonetic or Pinyin renderings of Chinese words. This is useful when users know how to say a word but not how to write it in Chinese.

Google been successful because it has a clever search engine. That's important to attract users. The other clever part is its advertising. If you do a search on Google, advertising related to your search usually appears along with the results. Put in "China hotels," for example, and apart from the list of websites mentioning this topic, a series of sponsored links for hotels and travel companies related to China appears to the right of the screen. Click on these and Google earns money whether you make a reservation or not. In this way, Google makes direct use of the intentions of people who are looking for things. Its advertising thus has the character of well-targeted direct mail.

This means that advertisers on Google do not spend money advertising to people who are not interested in their products. (Yahoo!, on the other hand, has been more dependent on banner advertising, which is less targeted.) Baidu also uses the search-plus-targeted-advertisements model, except that whereas Google makes it clear those links that are sponsored and those that are not, Baidu makes it less clear. Indeed, for some searches on Baidu, the first few pages of search results comprise nothing but sponsored links. This might annoy some users but it's good for shareholders, and Baidu is a business after all. It also shows the degree to which sellers believe that Baidu is a good way to reach Chinese consumers, at least those who are young and relatively affluent.

The White Envelope Issue

Brand building requires media advertising (although there are exceptions, as Starbucks has shown). This requires a lot of paid advertisements. But in many parts of Asia, including China, Indonesia and Thailand, journalists often improperly accept money to place brands, products and personalities in straight news pieces. Companies in Asia need to determine their policy on whether such payments should be made. It's all very well to decide that such payments to journalists are improper and will not be made, but the problem is that the practice is so widespread that your competitors almost certainly will be engaging in it and getting the media coverage to match. Correspondingly, companies may be approached by journalists who threaten to run negative news pieces, with a view to being offered payment not to do so. This is far more pernicious and amounts to extortion. The practice is becoming increasingly common in China. Companies need to determine ahead of time what their policy will be when such an approach is made.

Local Branding

One way that foreign companies may achieve an edge in advertising is to change the name of their product for something with local meaning. This can have more impact than keeping a Western brand name that is meaningless to locals. Names are very important to the Chinese and in Asia generally. Before deciding on a name for a baby or a business, people might well consult a fortune teller to determine a propitious name. Asian consumers often prefer names with clear and positive meanings such as "good health" or "good fortune."

Some of the best-known Western companies have been quick to appreciate this. For example, the Chinese name for Coca-Cola is pronounced *Ke-ko-ke-le* and means "palatable and enjoyable to your mouth." BMW

(Bao-ma) means "treasured horse" and Pepsi-Cola *(Bai-shi-ke-le)* means "hundreds of enjoyable things."[10] When the Swedish brand Absolut vodka launched its advertising campaign to coincide with Chinese New Year in February 2005, its bottles bore the Chinese character "fu," which means "blessing" or "fortune." When turned upside down, the character changed its meaning and became "welcome."[11] The US investment bank Goldman Sachs is known as "height blossoming," a name it registered early on but only decided to use together with a visual brand to illustrate it in 2004. Registering a name as soon as possible is important if you don't want to find that a local Chinese firm already has. Copying brand names is rife in China, as Starbucks discovered. In 2004, it started litigation against a Chinese coffee shop company that used the same set of characters, but put "Shanghai" in front.

Ironically, some Chinese companies have reversed this process in order to build their brand outside their home country. The computer manufacturer Lenovo began life as "Legend." However, in 2004 it changed its name "in order to improve its brand recognition."

Another advantageous move can be to localize your website by adding foreign language versions. By communicating with customers in their own language, you can both inform them about you and ask them questions to gather important information on their likes and dislikes, or use it to explain how your product works. Absolut's 2005 integrated advertising and marketing campaign, for example, included a new website. Since vodka was a little known drink to the Chinese (imported spirits then accounted for just 1 percent of the Chinese spirits market), the website featured hints on mixing and drinking vodka. Absolut also set up an outside billboard in Shanghai featuring a giant-sized bottle that passers-by could rotate using a street-level button.

Finally, be on the lookout for brands that can be reverse-engineered from Asia into Western markets. One famous example is the French magazine *Elle*'s range of bags, T-shirts and shoes. This range began life in Japan in the 1980s as special gift items to be given away to new *Elle* subscribers.[12] However, they became so sought after that the company began to produce the range of products, at first just for the Japanese market, where it became the fourth largest foreign brand, and, after 1991, for the rest of the region and later the West. Another is Red Bull, the caffeinated soft drink that originated as Krating Daeng in Thailand. This drink, used in Thailand by truck drivers to keep themselves awake, is now used by London nightclubbers for the same purpose, making a billionaire of the Austrian entrepreneur who thought to take the drink global.

Understand the Message

Although Asian consumers are familiar with the notion of the brand as image – hence the obsession with luxury designer goods – this does not yet extend to a widespread understanding of the message behind the brand (or brand identity) that companies wish to convey. This can mislead foreign firms, especially if sales of their products are strong, into believing that their Asian consumers are susceptible to the same message as in the West. The realization that they are not can mean a rethink of their strategy for promoting their product in Asia.

This can happen to even the best-known names. When the Walt Disney Co. opened its latest Disneyland in Hong Kong at the end of 2005, it was confident of success. However, after six months, executives were dismayed to find attendances well below expectations. The reason, they learned from travel industry representatives, was that "people knew the Disney name but didn't feel compelled to visit the park" since they didn't understand what the experience meant.[13] As the president of Disney's parks and resorts observed, "People from the mainland didn't show up with the embedded Disney software [in their heads] like at other parks." The result was that Chinese visitors were more bemused than amused.

Disney countered with a major marketing campaign, launched in June 2006, that highlighted the individual experience and specified what a Disneyland visit offered. The park's dining area was enlarged to accommodate slower Chinese eating habits, and extra warning signs were posted at the Space Mountain attraction to warn that it was a rollercoaster ride (previously unsuspecting visitors have left the ride feeling sick). Said one travel agent, "Initially they were the kind of Americans that were not willing to learn about the local market and Chinese culture. Then they learned some lessons and started listening to us." However, since many of the ads featured a family of two parents and two children, there were still some doubts about whether Disney had really got the message about key facets of the Chinese family and China's one child policy.

The South African diamond group De Beers had a similar experience when it first entered Asia in the 1980s. Until then, it had successfully promoted its diamond rings as a "gift of love," since the custom of the diamond engagement ring is culturally embedded in all its Western markets.[14] It entered the Japanese market with the same "symbol of love" message, and its first cinema advertisement showed a Hollywood rather than a typically Japanese romantic scene. Despite this, the concept of a diamond engagement ring was readily accepted, partly because its value was associated with status by Japanese families, and also because it fitted in with the traditional engagement ceremony or *yuino*. By the late 1980s, Japan had become the second largest market in the world for diamond jewelry.

However, by 1996 engagement ring purchases had started to decline. This was due partly to several years of economic recession but, more importantly, it reflected a trend among the younger generation away from the formal traditions of the *yuino* with which De Beers had successfully associated ring buying. De Beers discovered that, in fact, the "gift of love" message had not really been accepted in Japan; the motivation for buying a ring had not been emotional, but rather a desire to conform socially.

It further concluded, as it researched other markets in the region, that there was no such person as an "Asian consumer." The company had first thought of opting for a "glocal," pan-regional positioning but, in fact, in the face of the different historical and cultural influences that drove jewelry sales, this proved impossible to sustain. In countries such as Korea, Taiwan and Hong Kong, the insecurity of life meant that jewelry was viewed as a store of wealth. Love and romance were not so freely discussed – there was not even an equivalent word for "romance" in the Chinese, Thai, Malay or Korean languages. In Southeast Asia, some women "did not feel dressed" unless they were wearing jewelry.

Through its research, De Beers eventually uncovered a whole new segment of diamond purchasers in Asia that it had never targeted before; women who bought jewelry for themselves, just for the joy of wearing it. The Western "gift of love" message actually risked alienating this powerful segment. And in some quarters, the gift of expensive jewelry is associated with keeping a mistress. In light of all this, De Beers decided to create a special "women's desire" advertising campaign to appeal specifically to the Asian self-purchase market. By 1997, this segment accounted for up to 60 percent of the company's total sales in every Asian country except Korea. It existed nowhere else in the world.

Again De Beers sought to use the wedding ring as the sales vehicle. Unfortunately, "love" in the Chinese context proved a difficult concept to pin down, since attitudes to marriage were highly materialistic. A survey of 18–28-year-olds, commissioned by De Beers and a consortium of Western firms, showed that this generation used wealth as the key criterion for judging success. Marriage was a partnership toward achieving future success, and husbands were chosen on the basis of their financial status and prospects. Consequently, positioning diamond rings in the context of the romantic wedding day image made little sense.

After a great deal of research, one of the final advertisements chosen by De Beers followed the life and times of a young Chinese couple. The advert began with the husband giving his wife a wedding ring. The next frames followed through the subsequent years of happy marriage, so associating the diamond with a future together. The positioning was expressed as "The symbol of our enduring commitment, to build a future of harmony, brightness, success and marriage." And so the diamond ring in China has come to symbolize not so much love as a successful joint venture.

Things to Consider

- Localizing your brand can be a good idea – but going completely native might prove counterproductive. You might lose the "foreign" cachet that made the brand attractive in the first place, or make it too easy to copy!

- Brand extension: in Asia, as in the rest of the world, new segments develop very fast, so don't miss out – have the right product ready.

- Remember – a brand's image can quickly turn to negative if customers associate it with a bad experience.

- Coming to a store near you: for local companies, building the brand in their domestic market is the first step before they go international. Be warned.

Notes

1 *International Herald Tribune*, "China's answer to Larry King?," 7 February, 2005.
2 From www.chinaguide.org/guide/china-statistics.
3 *Far Eastern Economic Review*, "Switched on for a hard sell," G. Fowler, 3 June, 2004.
4 Ibid.
5 *Financial Times*, "China offers new brand opportunities," A. Harney, 22 April, 2004.
6 *Business Week*, "Yao," T. Lowry, 25 October, 2004.
7 Chee H. and C. West, *Myths about Doing Business in China*, Palgrave Macmillan, Basingstoke, 2004, p31.
8 Kurt Salmon Associates, *Consumer Outlook Survey for China*, October, 2004.
9 *Wall Street Journal*, "Brand not price is king in India," C. Prystay, 3 January, 2006, p6.
10 *Journal of Asia-Pacific Business*, "Naming products in China: local or foreign branding," Zhan G. Li and L. William Murray, 2001, pp53–70.
11 *Wall Street Journal*, "Absolut ads begin," C. Lawton, 14 February, 2005.
12 *Far Eastern Economic Review*, "Elle is for label, in Asia," S. Yoon, 28 February, 2002.
13 *Wall Street Journal*, "Disney targets a China gap," 12 June, 2006, p4.
14 Taken from "De Beers: Diamonds are for Asia," case study by Jocelyn Probert and Professor Hellmut Schutte, INSEAD-EAC, 1999.

Caveat Emptor: Beware the Banks of Asia

WHAT'S IN THIS CHAPTER?

▷ Financing in Asia

▷ The Sins of Asia's Banks

    Beware Spiders at the Center of the Web

    Beware Chinese Whispers and Chinese Walls

    Of Relatives and Related Parties

    What Protection the Central Bank?

▷ Avoiding Corporate Suicide

Financing in Asia

You have spotted a window of opportunity, you have done your research, devised a business plan and now you need some financing. Most large companies will have an existing global arrangement with a bank or group of banks, but smaller investors may not. One possibility then is a local bank in Asia, but very few Asian banks are involved in banking alone and most are still controlled by a majority shareholder. This makes them very different from banks in the US, Australia and Europe. It also makes them potentially quite dangerous. Table 22.1 gives a brief view of the main local banks in Asia.

Table 22.1 Local banks in Asia (the top three in selected Asian countries, ranked by assets)

China	Industrial & Commercial Bank of China Bank of China China Construction Bank
India	State Bank of India Bank of India Bank of Baroda
Japan	Mitsubishi UFJ Mizuho Financial Sumitomo-Mitsui
Taiwan	Land Bank of Taiwan Taiwan Cooperative Bank Bank of Taiwan
South Korea	Kookmin Bank Woori Bank Shinhan Bank
Thailand	Bangkok Bank Krung Thai Bank Thai Farmers Bank
Hong Kong	HSBC Hang Seng Bank Bank of East Asia
Malaysia	Maybank Bumiputera Commerce Bank RHB Bank
Singapore	DBS United Overseas Bank Overseas-Chinese Banking Corporation
Indonesia	Bank Central Asia (BCA) Bank Nasional Indonesia (BNI) Bank Dagang Nasional Indonesia (BDNI)
Philippines	Philippine National Bank Metropolitan Bank & Trust (Metrobank) Equitable PCI Bank
Sri Lanka	Bank of Ceylon People's Bank Hatton National Bank

Asia's 1997–98 economic crisis hit the region's banks hard and they have not all recovered at the same rate. Banking in Asia today is perhaps healthiest in Singapore, Hong Kong and Malaysia. Malaysian banks suffered much in the crisis but made a quick recovery. Non-performing loans were cut out of the system quickly and efficiently by Danaharta, the vehicle established by the Malaysian government for the purpose. Overseeing Malaysia's banking sector is Bank Negara, Malaysia's central bank, which, although not above making mistakes, is now widely regarded as highly professional and free of corruption. Malaysia's rapid moves to restore confidence in its banking system in the wake of the crisis won wide praise. Lim Say Boon of Crosby Corporate Advisory said at the time:

> [Malaysia] has followed the textbook prescriptions – setting up a bad debt agency, a bank recapitalization agency, and a corporate restructuring committee. Run by thorough professionals, the processes have been transparent and unrelenting.[1]

Banking problems appear almost intractable in China. Some progress has been made, but the state-owned banks are moribund with bad debt. Routinely the bad debts are excised, the banks are recapitalized and then they take on new bad debts. There are definition problems too. The China Banking Regulatory Commission admitted in 2003, for example, that 24.1 percent of the loans at the big four are non-performing. But analysts thought the true figure to be at least 40 percent.

Part of the problem is that most of the bad debtors are other SOEs, and they and their owners, usually local authorities, combine and simply refuse to pay back their loans. They also make for a strong coalition against effective reform. In any event, loans are often handed out to this or that sector as a matter of government policy, rather than from any tenets of sound banking practice. The reality is that China's formal banking system has become another arm of the central government's welfare delivery program.

There are around 20 local banks in South Korea. Laws prevent Korea's conglomerates – the *chaebol* – from owning more than 8 percent of the equity in any given bank, so banks are relatively independent of the non-banking business groups in the country in terms of equity. But the past practice has been for the Korean government to direct the bank's lending. This meant that lending decisions were not based on due diligence and credit assessments but on government orders. There was US$130 billion worth of bad debt on the books of South Korea's banks by mid-2000. There has long been a culture in Korea that private corporate interests are subverted to national goals, which has caused banks and other Korean companies to invest in sectors for reasons other than the expectation of maximizing returns.

The Japanese banking system is also beset by problem loans, largely because banks tend to reschedule loans endlessly and ease their conditions rather than declare them in default. In this way, loans worth hundreds of billions of dollars that are inadequately serviced and in technical default have been hidden. One problem in cleaning up bad debt in Japan's banking system is that banks have been reluctant to admit to them.

Banks, like so much else in Asia, may not be all they seem – sometimes literally. Central Jakarta is full of banks with obscure names but they're housed in office blocks with modern, reflective glass windows. Prominent signage announces their existence, the foyers might be marbled and the staff have their corporate uniforms. But look again. Many of these banks, with their shining, mirrored, high-rise offices, are a fiction. The "windows" are in fact cladding on billboards several storeys high to make customers feel as though they are banking with a solid bank. The actual building is often little more than a converted bungalow or a shop-house.

Many banks like this aren't really interested in lending to outsiders anyway. Their owners have set them up to accept deposits from the public. These are then lent to the owners' other interests. The benefit to the owners is that they then pay deposit rates of interest on large loans that they would otherwise have to pay far higher interest on. Nor do they need to go through due diligence and loan approval processes – which they may not pass. They simply lend the money to themselves, regardless of their creditworthiness. Beyond some point, the practice is illegal and highly imprudent.

The Sins of Asia's Banks

The ownership structures and behavior of Asia's banks differ from the way banks tend to operate in the more mature markets of the West. This can mean some traps for the unwary. What can happen in Asia, and why?

Beware Spiders at the Center of the Web

Asia's big banks are moving away from majority family ownership but that does not mean that their founding families no longer control them. Bangkok Bank, which prior to Asia's economic crisis was Southeast Asia's largest private bank (Singapore's DBS Bank now has that honor), is controlled by the founding Sophonpanich family even though it only owns around 15 percent of the bank's stock and not much more in the way of guaranteed support from other shareholders. The family retains control because other shareholders are so dispersed and own such small parcels of shares. Similarly, Wee Cho Yaw and his family control Singapore's United Overseas Bank and do so even though they now own little more than 10 percent of its stock.

One problem with a single entity such as a family controlling a bank is that rarely does it want to give up that control. That can mean that it will be loath to hold a new share issue to help to recapitalize the bank if one is needed. A new share issue might see the family's equity diluted, pushing it closer to losing its control.

The most likely local bank that a foreign firm might borrow from in Southeast Asia is a Singaporean bank. Singapore is the regional supplier of financial services to Southeast Asia. It is to Indonesia what Hong Kong is to Guangdong, for example. Its banks are well managed, accessible, professional and, most importantly, have the cash. Contracts and other loan documents can also be drawn up under Singapore law, which is important. However, Singapore's banks are not without some problems – problems shared with banks elsewhere in the region but less likely to be encountered in Western economies.

Consider for example, Singapore's United Overseas Bank (UOB). It is controlled by its founder Wee Cho Yaw. Wee is a banker but he is more than that and therein lies a potential danger. He also controls United Overseas Land (he serves as its chairman) and many other companies outside banking. He is also the chairman and part owner of United Industrial Corporation. This company manufactures household detergents, is involved in printing and packaging, running shipping and travel agencies and trading in computers. In turn, it controls Singapore Land, an important commercial real estate owner in Singapore. Wee is in the hotel business as well, with stakes in Singapore's Plaza Parkroyal, New Park Centra and Grand Plaza Parkroyal Hotels. Some of Wee's interests are privately held, others are not. It all leads to many potential conflicts of interest.

Henny Sender wrote about this in an article in *Institutional Investor* back in 1991:[2]

As the principal family asset of Singapore's Wee Cho Yaw, United Overseas Bank is subject to an inherent conflict of interest – the Wee family's temptation to use UOB to build their personal wealth rather than that of their shareholders. This concern arises at least partially from the fact that there is a string of private investment companies that compete with the public investment companies in which UOB has a stake. Stories are told of the bank's foreclosing on choice properties (Gold Hill Square in Singapore being the *most* recent example) at the first hint of difficulties – only to have ownership pass to UOB's property arm.

UOB's control over Singapore and its banking system was strengthened in 2001 when it acquired its rival Overseas Union Bank, which had been controlled by its founder Lien Ying Chow and his family. They are now shareholders in UOB. They too have vast real estate interests. "Buildings are my hobby," Lien said in 1992, which must have been cold comfort to borrowers with desirable real estate mortgaged to OUB.

Overseas-Chinese Banking Corporation (OCBC) Bank is Singapore's second largest private bank. In 1999 it disclosed for the first time that it had a massive landbank of some 187 properties and pieces of land around Singapore, of which only about a quarter was actually used for banking purposes. It turned out that OCBC Bank was probably Singapore's biggest holder of land among Singapore's non-property companies. It also owned stakes in many listed companies, including 8.3 percent of soft drinks bottler Fraser & Neave. OCBC said that it would sell off its non-financial assets, but in 2001 announced that the sell-off would be delayed and then staggered. OCBC's revelations showed that it too was not just a bank but a web of potential conflicts of interest. Its declaration that it intended at some point to sell its non-core assets seemed to be an admission of that.

Finally, Singapore's DBS Bank, the city-state's largest, is controlled by Temasek Holdings, an investment arm of the Singapore government. Temasek also has large stakes in Southeast Asia's biggest property company Capitaland, Singapore Airlines, ST Engineering and Chartered Semiconductor Engineering. Possibly the same conflict of interest argument made above could be made in respect of DBS Bank.

Yet corporate and banking supervision is better in Singapore than anywhere in Asia. But then who could feel comfortable mortgaging real estate to a bank that is also a significant player in the local real estate market?

Beware Chinese Whispers and Chinese Walls

Borrowing from a bank involves giving information to it that companies give to few others. Their financials, their business plans and other commercial in-confidence information are handed over. How safe that information is in Asia, even if it's with a bank, often depends on who the bank is and who are its business partners.

An ideal banking system is one in which banks are not compromised in their lending decisions by their other business activities or the other business interests of their principal shareholders. But the number of banks in Asia like that are in the minority.

If a bank belongs to a group of companies that all have a common controlling shareholder, and there are board meetings at the group level and the companies all routinely trade with and help one another, would it be so surprising in Asia, where in many countries the legal system is patchy, for the bank to tip off its sister companies as to what its clients are up to? If you were the founder of the group, from the old school and a strong believer in winning at all costs, you might even expect your bank to do that.

One reason why so many business families in Asia have owned a bank of their own is simply that they didn't trust anyone but themselves when it came to borrowing money. Take Indonesia for example. It is a "low trust" society. Laws are weak and often the only protection available is that which you provide yourself. It is one reason why almost every one of Indonesia's top 200 conglomerates founded a bank. Few of them dared to borrow from anyone else. It left Indonesia with a banking system populated by more than 200 banks. The system was said to be overbanked but underbranched. The government did close down 67 banks in the wake of the region-wide economic crisis of 1997–98 and took over 13 others. But the industry remains absurdly fractured, with many small banks that do not generate sufficient economies of scale.

Of Relatives and Related Parties

Banks work because they pool risks. This is fundamental to banking. Loans are given to a range of borrowers, and the more the loan portfolio is spread across as many borrowers as possible, the less likelihood there is that the default of one or several borrowers will destabilize the bank. And then there is Asia.

Most banks in Singapore and Hong Kong are thought to be prudent lenders. Banks in Malaysia are less prudent but not dangerously so. Elsewhere, banking is a mess. Banks in Korea, Japan, Thailand and Indonesia have tended to lend far too much to too few and very often to borrowers linked to the owners of the bank. Their behavior endangers the funds of their depositors and their other borrowers.

Banks in Indonesia were permitted to lend 20 percent of their total capital to any single non-affiliated party and no more than 10 percent of their capital to related parties. These restrictions were comprehensively ignored. The banking supervisory unit of Indonesia's central bank was either incompetent in administering these provisions, corrupt or both. In the Asian economic crisis, some banks were found to have lent more than 60 percent of their total loan portfolios to companies that were all related to each other and in turn often related to the owners of the banks.

"Circular" loans are often used to get around rules designed to restrict lending to affiliates. Bank owners might organize back-to-back loans to each other's non-banking subsidiaries. The owner of Bank Y might organize for Bank X to lend US$50 million to his property business and, in return, Bank Y lends US$50 million to Bank X.

What Protection the Central Bank?

Asia's central banks have faced difficulties in carving out a role that is both independent and accountable. Independence is fine if bank officials conduct themselves in a professional manner. But less accountability can spell corruption, nepotism and other ills. Indonesia passed a new central bank law in 2001 that guaranteed its central bank more autonomy. It was meant to prevent government interference in the bank's monetary policy decisions but instead was misused to protect criminal activity in the bank.

This is not a particularly Asian phenomenon. All countries face difficulties in managing their central banks but none so keenly than developing countries. A study in 2001[3] found that at the Peruvian Central Bank of Reserve, almost half the employees were related to other employees at the bank. Among the 1,300 staff were 77 brothers, 52 married couples, 52 uncles and aunts and their nephews or nieces, 54 brothers-in-law and sisters-in-law, 40 cousins and 7 fathers and sons. The recent past records of some central banks in Asia are similarly less than honorable.

In early 1998, almost 100 senior staff at Japan's central bank, the Bank of Japan, were disciplined for accepting lavish entertainment from banks and other financial institutions. One official was arrested for providing sensitive information to private banks in return for entertainment. The bank's then governor and his deputy both took responsibility and resigned.

In late 2000, five of the seven directors of Indonesia's central bank attempted to resign. They claimed that the bank's "loss of legitimacy" made it difficult for them to continue in their posts. A dispute between the government and the IMF over changes to the central bank law made it impossible to appoint replacements and so the directors remained in their posts.

And in 2006, the China Banking Regulatory Commission admitted that in the previous year, no less than 1,228 of its employees were involved in irregular funds such illegal loans, starting businesses without authorization and holding stakes in rural credit cooperatives.

There are some highly professional central reserves around Asia. The Monetary Authority of Singapore, the Hong Kong Monetary Authority and Malaysia's Bank Negara immediately come to mind. The rest, such as Thailand's, have some work to do.

Avoiding Corporate Suicide

Banks have grown stronger in Asia since the 1997–98 economic crisis. There have been banking mergers particularly in Singapore and Malaysia. Banks there are now bigger and better capitalized than perhaps they have ever been. Progress has been slower elsewhere and so a few precautions are advisable when dealing with them.

If depositing in Asia's banks, split the funds between several banks and preferably in a range of currencies. The last Asian economic crisis saw many banks close and their depositors' funds frozen. Also, in the midst of the Asian economic crisis, many banks simply ran out of foreign exchange and were unable to buy any. Transfers of even relatively small amounts of US dollars between banks even within Indonesia took days to be completed, and international transfers that previously had occurred overnight took weeks, with the funds simply unaccounted for during the intermediate period. Diversifying your holdings of deposits makes sense in Asia, particularly in those countries with weaker banking systems.

For borrowers wanting to borrow from an Asian bank, some new options have appeared since the economic crisis. Foreign banks and Singaporean banks have acquired strategic stakes in some banks in Hong Kong, Thailand, the Philippines and Indonesia. This has seen these banks become more professional and able to draw on the capital of their new and well-capitalized shareholders. Singapore's DBS Bank, for example, acquired contolling interests in Manila's Bank of Southeast Asia and Hong Kong's Dao Heng Bank Group. It now has banking units in Hong Kong, China, Indonesia, India, the Philippines and Thailand as well as Singapore. The UK's Standard Chartered bought Thailand's Nakornthon Bank in 1999. And so on.

One final thing to remember when dealing with banks in Asia, whether you are a big or small customer, is that practically all aspects of their activities can be negotiated upon. Published rates and fees need not be fixed. Consider negotiating on not just the interest rates on loans but also on deposits, particularly term deposits. Negotiate on exchange rates for foreign exchange conversions, as well as all fees and charges.

Strategy checklist

If you wish to borrow from a local bank in Asia, here are some points to consider when choosing a bank:

1. Does the bank have a controlling shareholder? If so, research the controller's other interests. Do they compete with yours? Are there any obvious incentives for the bank to foreclose on your loan and seize your collateral that are suggested by these other interests?

2. Get hold of the bank's annual report if one is available and learn about its directors and their other corporate interests. Look at the related-party transactions, if any. They will provide an indication as to what sorts of company are related to the bank.

3. What guarantees does the bank offer about the security of your information? Where is the information sent, how is it stored, who is authorized to see it and who can access it? Are loan approvals made at the branch level or centralized with a commercial loans unit?

4. Does the bank itself have a property arm?

5. Does the bank have a reputation for foreclosing too early? Does its controlling shareholder have a reputation for buying up the assets that have been foreclosed on? Are there local rules to prevent this and how well are they enforced?

6. Is the bank prudent or likely to be a significant lender to related parties?

7. Does a broad cross-section of local companies choose to borrow from the bank?

8. Is there a banking ombudsman or equivalent to whom improper banking practices can be reported?

Notes

1   *Far Eastern Economic Review*, "Real change in Asia," Rethinking Asia column, Lim, S.B., 22 June, 1999.
2   *Institutional Investor*, "Inside the overseas Chinese network," Sender, H., August, 1991.
3   *International Herald Tribune*, "A family affair at bank," 9 May, 2001.

Avoid Blood Loss as a Minority Shareholder

WHAT'S IN THIS CHAPTER?

▷ Majorities, Minorities and Families

▷ The 12 Biggest Sins Committed Against Asia's Minority Shareholders

Sin 1: Ownership is Spread Too Thinly

Sin 2: Listing as a Form of Dumping

Sin 3: Too Many Rights Issues

Sin 4: Unfair Related-party Transactions

Sin 5: Refusal to Return Excess Funds

Sin 6: Bizarre Morphing

Sin 7: Too Many AGMs on the Same Day

Sin 8: Stock Price Manipulation

Sin 9: Insider Trading

Sin 10: Poor Disclosure

Sin 11: Boards are Often Too Small or Too Big

Sin 12: "Independent" Directors Not So Independent

Majorities, Minorities and Families

Question: What's the best way to avoid losing out as a minority share-holder in Asia?

Answer: Don't be one.

That's what CalPERS, one of the largest pension funds in the world and the largest public fund in the US with US$151 billion under management, decided in February 2002. It announced that it would pull out of Indonesia, Malaysia, the Philippines and Thailand because those countries did not meet its new standards on "political stability, labor standards and transparency, including a free press and good accounting."[1] (The Philippines was later reinstated.) The more likely reason, however, was that it was simply tired of being ripped off.

Western companies tend to list on the stock market so that they can raise funds to expand. But the situation is often quite different in Asia. Listings all too frequently are little more than exit strategies, as founding families seek to offload assets that no longer perform well and they no longer want. "What is profitable is mine, but what is not is yours" is the guiding principle of many a majority shareholder in Asia. The result is that Asia's stock markets are not so much home to Asia's great companies but often home to companies that nobody really wants.

Families control most listed companies outside Japan and China. And typically these families list not their holding company but just one or two of its subsidiaries. This means that most listed companies are not stand-alone entities but parts of webs of mostly privately held companies. So not only are Asia's stock markets full of second-rate companies but the companies are parts of wider groups, with all the potential conflicts of interest which that might entail.

Ratings agencies have a hard time in Asia assessing credit ratings for the business groups of Japan, Korea, Indonesia and elsewhere. Should companies be assessed as stand-alone entities or is it the group as a whole that should be rated? But some groups are more integrated than others. And when the group comprises a mixture of privately owned and publicly listed companies with cross-shareholdings, cross-borrowings, loan guarantees and plenty of related-party transactions, the ratings process becomes very complex – and more imprecise. How to rate a member of a *chaebol* in Korea, when loan and other guarantees are given but not often declared? Many Asian companies traditionally have borrowed only locally and on a secured basis, but now many borrow internationally, usually by issuing securities. These borrowings are subordinated debt, which introduces more complications for outside investors trying to get a window on the risks of investing in Asia.

The risks for investors who wish to buy stakes in unlisted firms can be more perilous. The general rule of thumb is do not buy into an unlisted firm in which you cannot take the major stake and control the board of directors and management. Even then, it must be asked why the company is up for sale. Good companies are rarely sold in Asia, particularly to outsiders; if they are sold, it is to insiders. Any company in Asia that comes onto the open market can be assumed to be in trouble. In that case, it might be best to consider buying the company's assets rather than the company. Buying the legal structure as well as the assets can mean inheriting huge but undeclared tax liabilities and other hidden contingencies. It might also mean inheriting large numbers of employees that you may not want and local labor laws might make it difficult and costly to shed. Buy the assets alone and then hopefully they will come free of the legal, tax and labor problems that the previous owners have accumulated, which presumably are part of the reason why they are selling out.

Sin, sin, sin and not much repentance
The 12 biggest sins committed against
minority shareholders

Sin 1   Ownership is spread too thinly

Sin 2   Listing as a form of dumping

Sin 3   Too many rights issues

Sin 4   Unfair related-party transactions

Sin 5   Refusal to return excess funds

Sin 6   Bizarre morphing

Sin 7   Too many AGMs on the same day

Sin 8   Stock price manipulation

Sin 9   Insider trading

Sin 10   Poor disclosure

Sin 11   Boards are often too small or too big

Sin 12   "Independent" directors not so independent

The 12 Biggest Sins Committed Against Asia's Minority Shareholders

Sin 1: Ownership is Spread Too Thinly

The vast majority of Asia's listed companies have less than 30 percent of their equity traded publicly (compared with the US where most companies have at least 95 percent of their stock traded freely). Most stock exchanges in the region have rules on the minimum number of shareholders a company must have to be and remain listed. This can be manipulated with the use of lots of nominees, each taking out small numbers of shares, especially among small capitalized (cap) stocks that are of little interest to most investors.

Sin 2: Listing as a Form of Dumping

Asia's truly profitable companies generally are not those that are listed. If they are very profitable, they usually remain in private hands. Often companies are listed when their owners want to get rid of them. (Significantly, China has decided that one remedy for moribund, poorly capitalized SOEs is partly to list them.) Similarly, listed companies that become highly profitable are quickly delisted and made private.

Sin 3: Too Many Rights Issues

A rights issue is an invitation only to existing shareholders to acquire additional shares in the company. The benefit of a rights issue to the company is that it is an easy way to raise money; such issues impose on it few additional statutory obligations. The benefit to the controlling shareholder is that its control of the company is not lost or weakened if it takes up its quota of new shares. Minority shareholders, however, find that they must either buy the new shares or their minority stakes are made even smaller and so too their returns. In Asia, the complaint has been that companies raise too much cash too frequently from their shareholders and are not sufficiently focused on returns. Minority shareholders might find that no dividends are paid, instead it is they who are always handing over cash to the company rather than the other way round.

A practice that is more insidious than too many rights issues is when there are too many share placings. These are shares issued by the company and then "placed" with certain parties – normally associates of the controlling shareholder. Minority shareholders are not given the option of taking up any of the shares so placed. Again, the effect is to dilute their equity and their returns.

Sin 4: Unfair Related-party Transactions

Related-party transactions among listed and unlisted companies are rife across Asia and many are not on the commercial basis that they should be. This has the effect of moving inventory, costs, revenues and profits around groups of companies, usually to the detriment of minority shareholders.

Controlling families in Asia habitually sell assets that they no longer want to their listed companies. These might be old plant and equipment or even entire companies, which end up as subsidiaries of the listed company. There is nothing wrong with the practice if the sale price is fair. But often it isn't and the controlling family has the incentive to ensure that it is not. Transactions such as these are used by controlling shareholders to strip listed companies – and thus their minority shareholders – of their capital and their profits.

Receivables – which are contracted payments for goods and services for which cash is yet to be received – are something to watch out for in a company's accounts, particularly if they appear high and especially if they are to related companies. Receivables are a common way for companies to boost profits and revenues but without cash actually having to change hands. Profits might grow year after year but if receivables are growing at the same rate, then the company might actually have no more funds flowing through than in the initial year.

Another way in which listed companies can be milked by a controlling shareholder is when a private company owned by the shareholder provides services to the listed company. These might be for "management" and general consulting. Such vague services are hard to quantify, which makes it difficult to determine whether the payments are fair or not.

One final aspect of unfair related-party transactions is when the books of companies do not all close on the same day. Some companies, including banks in Indonesia, for example, end their financial year at the end of the calendar year but others end theirs on 30 June. This means that there is a six-month window of opportunity during which funds can be transacted between banks and non-banks within the one group to boost the revenues and profits of each artificially. One guide to fictitious profits is when companies announce large profits but then don't declare a dividend.

Minority shareholders do have rights. Related-party acquisitions and sell-offs usually must be voted upon by the minorities in most stock exchanges in the region, but related-party transactions involving goods and services often do not. However, votes are not always as they should be. Shareholders who pose as independent of the controlling shareholder but are in reality nominees and will vote for whatever the controlling shareholder proposes are common at AGMs and EGMs around Asia.

Sin 5: Refusal to Return Excess Funds

Listed Asian companies tend to do anything with surplus funds other than return them to shareholders. The safest thing for shareholders would be to get their cash back. Instead they find that the management wants to sit on it and wait for the next big acquisition, lend it to related parties or use it to play the stock market themselves. Rarely is excess cash returned to shareholders.

Sin 6: Bizarre Morphing

It is not uncommon for a listed company suddenly to change its core business or have another added to it that has little to do with the first. This comes about largely because many listed Asian firms are controlled by a single majority shareholder and many of these have other businesses that can be sold into the company.

Perhaps an investor wants to invest only in cement stocks and so buys shares in an Asian cement producer. However, the controlling shareholder might happen to own a textile factory that he no longer really wants so sells it to the cement company. Minority shareholders who wanted to invest in cement now find that they are also investors in textiles; the synergies between the two are not exactly obvious.

Sin 7: Too Many AGMs on the Same Day

AGMs frequently clash in Asia, sometimes excessively so. This is common in Japan and also in Singapore, although to a lesser degree. Most listed companies in Singapore have a 31 December financial year end. The Singapore Stock Exchange requires listed companies to hold their AGMs within six months of their financial year end, so in the last week or so of June, many companies rush to hold their AGMs. Individual shareholders who hold stock in more than one of these companies can find it difficult getting to all the meetings, as some inevitably clash. Not all AGMs are held in city hotels, some are held at distant factory sites and industrial parks, further hampering ordinary shareholders' access to them.

The situation has been far worse in Japan. In 1996, out of 1,864 listed Japanese companies that closed their books at the end of March, 1,766 or 94.2 percent of them held their AGM on just one day, 27 June of that year. Investors with a well-diversified portfolio stood little chance of attending more than a few of the AGMs of companies in which they held stock. Not surprisingly, the average Japanese AGM is very brief. The average duration of all those held on that one day in June was just 26 minutes.[2] The tradition in Japan has been that directors enter and leave an AGM accompanied by the applause of shareholders, hearing little or nothing from them in between. The situation has improved but there is still a long way to go.

The docility of local minority investors in Asia means that company managers rarely face direct criticism. Local investors prefer simply to sell out. Typically, Asian minority investors do not use "voice"; they just use "exit." Things are changing in the wake of the Asian economic crisis but only in so far as there are now some examples of local minority shareholder activism when before there was none. There is still a long way to go.

Sin 8: Stock Price Manipulation

The prices of small cap stocks are routinely manipulated all over Asia, from Malaysia to Indonesia to Hong Kong. Stocks that have thin markets tend to be highly volatile. They may not trade at all one day and then rise the next day by 30 percent, fall the following by 20 percent and then barely trade for the next two days, a not uncommon week for a small cap stock on an Asian bourse.

Not surprisingly, they are prone to price manipulation by buying syndicates. Stocks can "ramped", whereby companies trade in their own shares to force the price up and then sell out at a profit. They might be "pooled", whereby investors collude to buy and sell shares rapidly in a company to each other, so that turnover increases, the stock looks "hot", thereby attracting other investors, which forces the price up and then the members of the pool sell out at a profit. Stocks might be "cornered" too. Cornering is relatively easy in Asia's stock markets because in most firms so little equity is publicly traded. It involves a syndicate quietly acquiring a large proportion of the publicly traded shares and then contracting with brokers to buy even more shares at a later date and at a given price, knowing that the order is unlikely to be filled because they already have most of the available shares. When the contract falls due, brokers have little choice but to pay an exorbitant price for the shares to fulfil the contracts, usually from the syndicate itself via nominees.

Sin 9: Insider Trading

Insider trading is rife in Asia. Company announcements are frequently preceded by movements in the share price suggesting that those with inside knowledge are trading on that basis. Trading by public auditors in the stock in the companies they audit is not uncommon in Asia.

Singapore Hong Kong Properties Investment (SHKPI) announced on 27 March, 1999 that it was in discussions with another company about its possible takeover by that company. Astute followers of the Hong Kong Stock Exchange might have noticed that something was in the wind. SHKPI's shares had rocketed up by 97 percent in the three days before the announcement was made.[3]

Similarly, the share price of Shin Corp. the then family holding company of Thailand's Prime Minister Thaksin Shinawtra, rose dramatically in early 2006 ahead of the announcement that it was to be acquired by Singapore's Temasek Holdings. An insider trading investigation was launched but members of the prime minister's family were exonerated.

But generally, stock market and other corporate misdemeanors rarely lead to successful prosecutions. Even in Hong Kong, despite millions of dollars having been spent on investigations and the preparation of cases, there have been few convictions. Prosecutors face heavy burdens of proof and cases can be so complex that about the only thing which can guarantee a conviction is an open confession.

Sin 10: Poor Disclosure

Listed Asian firms tend to be remarkably poor at disclosing information. It is as if their controlling shareholders refuse to accept that, once listed, the companies are no longer totally theirs. Minority shareholders are expected to hand over their cash but then are denied the right to have a full explanation about what happens to it. Annual reports might be glossy and full of fine photographs but not much else. Stock exchange filings can provide more information but are often provided late. Sometimes requests for further information from minority shareholders are simply ignored.

Sin 11: Boards are Often Too Small or Too Big

Being appointed to a board is often seen in Asia as an honor. It is not viewed as an obligation charged with fiduciary duty but as a reward, a title to be collected and displayed. This is especially so in Japan where boards with more than 20 directors have been the norm and some have had as many as 60. The Nissan Motor Company cut its board from 37 to 10 after France's Renault acquired a 37 percent stake. But Nissan remains an exception to the rule. Being elevated to the board is seen as a sinecure for retired executives in Japan, the local equivalent of the gold watch retirement gift.

The small, family-run listed companies of Hong Kong have the opposite problem. Many have boards that are too small. Hung Fung Group Holdings listed on the main board of the Hong Kong Stock Exchange in 1998 with a board of just three executive directors. Two of the three were married to each other. One of the two "independent" non-executive directors was a consultant to one of the co-sponsors of Hung Fung's IPO.[4]

Almost all Asia's stock exchanges now require listed companies to have an audit committee. Few imposed this requirement prior to Asia's economic crisis. It has been a move in the right direction, although many companies in Asia, particularly those that have a relatively thin professional class, have found it difficult to find enough directors sufficiently knowledgeable about auditing processes and willing to accept the additional personal liability that being on an audit committee involves. Consequently, most companies now have an audit committee but they may not be as diligent or as skilled as needed.

Sin 12: "Independent" Directors Not So Independent

About 40 percent of listed companies in Japan now have one or more directors who have been recruited from outside the firm – but that means that about 60 percent do not. Elsewhere, listed companies continue to indulge in all sorts of questionable actions to benefit their majority shareholders, begging the question of where are the independent directors?

The Hong Kong Stock Exchange now requires that all listed companies appoint two independent non-executive directors, which sounds fine in principle but has been a flop in practice. Most listed Hong Kong companies are controlled by a single shareholder. Independent non-executive directors are appointed by the board of directors and then re-elected by the shareholders at the next AGM. But with the majority shareholder typically controlling the board and most of the votes at the AGM, only independent non-executive directors who are "friendly" to the majority shareholder tend to get appointed. Independent non-executive directors must comprise a majority of the audit committees, but with these directors being sanctioned by the majority shareholder, the audit committees lack the independence that they should have.

Look first, buy later
Some things to consider before buying
into a listed company in Asia

1. Prudent and cautious investors in Asia would do well to buy stock only in those companies that either have no controlling shareholder, are not part of a wider group, or both. Do your research on companies in which you might invest. Are they part of a group of companies?

2. Who controls the company? Is there a single majority or controlling shareholder? Assessing a stock in Asia involves more than just looking at the company's "fundamentals." The appropriate way to value a company must also include consideration of who is the majority shareholder and what else they own.

3. What is the company's policy on transactions with related parties and does it engage in them?

4. Does the company pay fees in relation to management services, IP, secretarial or other administrative services to any private companies and if so, what are the relationships between those companies and the controlling shareholder?

5. Does the company have any inter-company loans? Are they high and have they been increasing year on year? Are they on a fully commercial basis?

6. Do the company's accounts contain a lot of receivables and how has this changed in the last three or more years? Have the receivables arisen from transactions with related companies?

7. Is the market for the company's stock deep and wide? Does it trade each day? Is there a good spread of shareholders? Are there any Western institutional shareholders who are likely to give voice to minority shareholder concerns?

8. Does the company have a substantial core business or is it an amalgam of assets with few complementarities pushed together for the convenience of the majority shareholder?

9. Is the board of directors an optimal working size, say about seven directors? What are their qualifications? Do at least some of the directors have recognized accounting or legal qualifications?

10. Are there independent non-executive directors? How independent are they? How are they elected and by whom? How many other boards do they serve on? Do they have the time to exercise sufficient vigilance over the company? Is there an active and well-qualified audit committee?

11. What is the company's record on rights issues and share placings?

12. Does the company have an investor relations officer or office and is the company responsive to requests for information?

13. Is the company related to other listed companies with differing financial year ends?

14. Asset-backed securities are still a comparative rarity in Asia, but they do offer more transparency and less risk to investors. They differ from conventionally collateralized loans or bonds in that the assets to be securitized are separated out from the other assets of the issuer and are normally held by a special holding vehicle. The Wisma Atria shopping mall on Singapore's Orchard Road, for example, was used to back the issue of S$451 million in bonds by the mall's owner in mid-2002. Are asset-backed securities available as an alternative investment option?

Finally, minority shareholders can consider taking class action suits against majority shareholders or companies themselves. But the expense of this in those Asian countries where legal systems operate inadequately often prevents this course of action. Elsewhere, legal systems are too abysmal or may not recognize class actions. Shareholder lawsuits have become more common in Japan. They were once taboo but minority shareholders have been emboldened by a decision by the Osaka District Court in September 2000 in a case brought by shareholders against 11 former and current directors of Daiwa Bank to pay the bank US$775 million in compensation for having insufficient safeguards to protect against unauthorized bond trading in the US.

Notes

1   *Asian Wall Street Journal*, "Big US pension fund says it will leave markets," 22 February, 2002.
2   Backman, M., *Asian Eclipse: Exposing the Dark Side of Business in Asia*, Wiley & Sons, 1999, 2001.
3   Webb, D., "Singapore Hong Kong Properties," Webb-site.com, 7 July, 1999.
4   Webb, D., "Money for nothing," Webb-site.com, 8 August, 2001.

Strategy 24

China!
The Frenzy
Continues

WHAT'S IN THIS CHAPTER?

▷ A Challenging Process
▷ Take Your Partners
   Moving Goalposts
   Despite Everything
   How to Succeed
   Success Stories?
   SOEs: Mission Impossible?
   Future Investment Prospects
   Go West
   On the Other Hand
▷ A Chinese Riddle
   The Chinese Consumer
▷ Navigating the Market
   A Few Hints
   The Case for Caution
▷ What Next?
▷ Key Lessons

A Challenging Process

Entering the Chinese market as a foreign company is generally described as a "challenging process," a phrase most businesspeople (whether Asian or Western) with any experience of China would regard as a massive understatement. The first Western companies entered China as early as 1979 when Deng Xiaoping announced the famous "Open Door" policy, and those brave pioneers were followed by successive waves of optimistic investors. Mesmerized by the sheer size of the market and the increasing wealth of China's urban middle class, they have made major commitments in anticipation of reaping massive gains. Unfortunately, for most, these expectations have since given way to disillusion and red ink.

Take Your Partners

For early investors into China, a joint venture (usually with an SOE, chosen for them) was the only way to enter the market. Their experience was invariably an unhappy one. If setting up the venture proved complicated enough, running the operation in partnership with local Chinese managers then proved even tougher, given the strictly limited opportunities for foreign firms to exercise any influence. Controls on hiring, firing and recruitment protected an inflated and, by Western standards, uncommitted and unproductive workforce, and left employers with high labor costs. To add to their frustration, Western managers found themselves forced to seek further permissions to sell in markets that were undeveloped, never as large as the optimistic forecasts on which entry had been based, and where the lack of infrastructure made building distribution and marketing capabilities a nightmare. There was also the piracy problem: any product that could be copied would be, in the shortest possible time.

As if all this was not enough to contend with, after the first few years, foreign investors frequently had to bear the financial burden alone, as the Chinese contribution tailed off, sometimes to less than 10 percent. Many also discovered an unbridgeable gulf between their aims – to build a market for their goods – and those of their local partners who, guided by the current five-year government plan, had little motivation to expand or increase productivity.

Too late, Western firms found that they had grossly underestimated the difficulty of entering this most frustrating of business environments. As they struggled to turn around the abysmally run SOEs, and tried in vain to find good local managers, they were hit by keen competition from local players who benefited from the favors of local officials. Some hardy survivors stayed in and gritted their teeth for the long haul (the average time for turning a profit was 10 years) but the majority of Western investors eventually withdrew to count the cost. The French car maker PSA Peugeot Citroen, for example, entered China early in 1985 with a 22 percent stake in a joint venture to produce the Peugeot 505. The story was downhill all the way as losses piled up, until finally, 12 years later, it sold its stake to the Japanese automotive group Honda. Many of the foreign companies that entered the power market in the

1990s with the promise or expectation of guaranteed returns as China expanded were similarly disillusioned. Almost all of them later exited a market that never materialized.

To add insult to injury, the collapse of their joint ventures left foreign companies with little hope of recovering any of their investment, since the bankruptcy laws put them well down the queue for compensation, behind the claims of employees and the tax authorities. And although joint venture rules later became more flexible, those on management control remain weak, making it still the biggest potential point of conflict. Many of the other obstacles – non-existent markets, workforces neither as productive nor hardworking as is commonly believed, a dearth of skilled managers, poor infrastructure, broken contracts and little or no profit – all remain in place, a quarter of a century after the Chinese market was officially thrown "open."

Some things have changed. Following a revision of investment rules in 1998 and 2001, foreign investors have been allowed to set up wholly foreign-owned enterprises (WFOEs). Their eagerness to avoid taking a local partner was witnessed by the fact that according to the Ministry of Commerce, in the first half of 2005, WFOEs constituted almost 74 percent of new FDI projects. However, both these and other types of investment vehicles such as the foreign-invested enterprises (FIEs) are still tightly controlled. Any corporate restructuring or change in business subject requires permission from the all-powerful Ministry of Foreign Trade and Economic Cooperation and other authorities.

Another reform has allowed some early entrants to restructure their agreements and take control of their operations, either by grouping their joint ventures together under a Chinese holding company, acquiring the partner or increasing their equity share, so enabling them to to introduce new systems and reduce headcount. In 2002, for example, Alcatel raised its 31 percent share in its joint venture firm, Shanghai Bell, to take a majority holding. Its 10 joint ventures were merged into a new company, ASB, which would have full access to Alcatel's patents and technology. The company has since gone from strength to strength.

Amendments and reforms to the rules governing foreign investment continue to be issued; in 2006, the rules were eased again to authorize provincial and local governments to approve new overseas investments, especially in the retail sector. The government has also announced that from January 2007, accounting and auditing practices will be brought in line with international standards, so there should then be more data available on the real value of a company. However, old observers of the China business scene will wait and see what this actually means in practice.

With every change or recodification of investment rules, and especially following China's entry into the WTO in December 2001, foreign firms have pinned their hopes on obtaining a more even playing field and a more predictable business environment. Further deregulation, they anticipated, would to open up new opportunities. Unfortunately, the opportunities have seldom turned out to be golden and, as the chief executive of Volkswagen commented in August 2003, "WTO is spelt very differently in Chinese."[1]

In January 2006, new rules made it easier for foreign firms to buy shares in listed Chinese companies, a move the government hoped would encourage greater M&A activity to pump in new investment. However, institutional investors have noted that in China, corporate governance remains a contradiction in terms. Chinese listed companies continue to be characterized by "a lack of independent directors, Byzantine share ownership structures, poor regulations and disclosure," while the Shanghai stock market, targeted by the government to become Asia's leading financial center, rests in "a mire of scandal and regulatory peculiarities."[2] Has this discouraged foreign investment? Not entirely. China seems to make even the most sober investors lose their heads.

Another recent move has allowed private equity companies and foreign investors to take controlling shares in state companies in non-sensitive sectors; so in October 2005 the US Carlyle Group paid $375 million for an 85 percent stake in the Xugong Group Construction Machinery Co. But other sectors such as energy, media and defense remain firmly under state control, and any concessions always come at a price. Frequently, companies have to agree to pay more, take on loss-making subsidiaries and/or keep the existing management in place.

Entry barriers to other key sectors remain high. In January 2006, *The Economist* wrote of many services from telecoms to media being "strangled by onerous regulations and inconsistent policies."[3] AT&T, the biggest US telecoms group, was one of the first multinationals to set up a Sino-foreign telecoms service joint venture in 2000. But it has only a 25 percent stake compared to the 60 percent held by a subsidiary of China Telecom, and the 15 percent held by the Shanghai municipal government. Moreover, since the venture has been restricted to Shanghai, it has achieved little. Likewise, the frustration of early investors in the media sector such as Rupert Murdoch has been well documented (see Strategy 30), while in the banking sector, investors face limits on the types of business they can conduct. Finally, legal services remain off limits to foreign lawyers, who cannot practice, comment on Chinese laws or appear in a Chinese court.

Moving Goalposts

Even after promising to open sectors, the Chinese government is notorious for changing its mind if it fears that foreign competition will be too strong, or it comes under pressure from local interests that feel threatened. Another frequent occurrence has been for foreign firms negotiating with one arm of government to reach a deal only to find another arm tearing it up and restarting negotiations. In the early days, this frequently happened to telecoms companies, who found themselves "lost" between several ministries, not knowing which really had the power to give them operating licenses. Many examples of this bureaucratic maze can still be found. In the tobacco sector, the UK tobacco company BAT thought that it had permission to build a US$1.5 billion cigarette factory for domestic consumption. In January 2005, however, the government confirmed a ban on new cigarette ventures that were not domestically funded. After three years of negotiation, Shell, ExxonMobil and Gazprom all believed they had an agreement to build an US$18 billion gas pipeline across mainland China jointly with PetroChina, the country's biggest oil firm. In August 2004, the deal fell apart and the companies withdrew, leaving behind field development plans, designs and technology. In 2005, Thames Water pulled out of a $73 million advanced waste water treatment plant it had built and was running in Shanghai because Beijing suddenly changed the rules and declared that the fixed annual 15 percent return was now illegal.[4]

Some firms have hoped to gain an advantage by arriving late in the market, so profiting from reforms to the rules governing investment in China. Unfortunately, whatever revisions are made, past form indicates that the government will continue to interfere as and when it seems necessary, and that the rules will remain liable to arbitrary change. So in the summer of 2006, Carlyle found its deal threatened by a rival bid from a Chinese manufacturer – albeit one far smaller than Xugong – which for some reasons of "national sovereignty" sought to keep a company under Chinese ownership. A piece of paper really is worthless in China, and any foreign investor who believes otherwise is simply naive.

Despite Everything

Despite this complex business environment and the dismal history of failure by Western firms trying to operate in it, the rush of foreign investors eager to enter China has not diminished. By the end of 2005, 450 of the world's top 500 multinationals had invested in China, the hottest targets being the high-tech and service sectors. M&A activity has broken records every year since 2002: in 2005, US$46 billion worth of inbound and domestic deals were recorded – up 34 percent from the previous year.

In 2002, China overtook the US to become the biggest recipient of FDI with $52.74 billion – a billion each week. Two years later, the figure stood at $61 billion (although by then China had fallen behind the UK). The first nine months of 2005 saw a steady $43.25 billion worth of investment, but economists expected that for the first time since 1999, Chinese FDI would begin to decline. However, this did not necessarily signal a reluctance on the part of foreign firms to invest in factories and other facilities in China, merely that some sectors were becoming saturated. Further regulatory adjustments, including new rules limiting management buyouts to small SOEs only, have also caused a slowdown.

The US has been especially faithful to the Chinese dream. US-based multinationals have entered partnerships with Chinese companies in every sector open to them despite the fact that the combination – or perhaps clash – of American "can do" entrepreneurism with the well-documented shortcomings of local managers and SOE workforces, set in the context of the bureaucratic political maze, was hardly the most promising recipe for success. On the whole, US firms have not had great success in China. Among many expensive failures, Whirlpool lost over US$50 million in a series of joint ventures, defeated by a price war with local competitors and a "Buy Chinese" campaign, Wal-Mart has made little impact, failing in its first foray on the east coast but trying again by moving west, Kraft withdrew in 2001, after eight years of loss and car makers GM and Ford have both had chequered careers despite heavy investment. Yet in November 2005, a majority of senior executives in large US manufacturing companies said they were optimistic about opportunities overseas, especially in China, where 42 percent had already begun or planned to invest.

Meanwhile, their European, Japanese, South Korean and Taiwanese counterparts have proved just as eager to gain a foothold there. South Korean investment reached $5.2 billion in 2005, while Taiwan's premier was moved to call for local businessmen to explore markets other than China, which was taking over 71 percent of the country's FDI. Japan's record US$6.5 billion investment, mostly driven by auto manufacturers and electronics companies, was especially surprising, given the boycotts, demonstrations, political tensions and historic territorial disputes and so on that have long dogged the Sino-Japanese relationship. But late entrants like Toyota and Nissan have flourished in recent years. The picture shows that foreign companies in every industry – from machinery, automotive, computer, communications, energy, infrastructure and finance, to insurance, oil and petrochemicals and so on – all see China as their savior in a world of saturated markets.

Where once the auto industry inspired a lemming-like rush to invest, China's banking sector, destined (in theory) to be fully open by the end of 2006, seems to be the new Eldorado. The sector is widely acknowledged to be technically insolvent and riven with corruption and fraud but, of course, the Chinese authorities claim to be committed to overhauling it. Consequently, the flood of investment by bankers – uncharacteristically throwing all caution to the wind – is well under way. By October 2005, 22 foreign banks had spent US$16.5 billion on stakes in 17 mainland lenders. Two US financial institutions, Goldman Sachs and American Express, together with the German insurance firm Allianz announced a US$3 billion investment in the state-owned Industrial and Commercial Bank of China. Bank of America bought a 9 percent stake in China Construction Bank, one of the country's biggest lenders, for US$2.5 billion. Even the traditionally sober Swiss were getting into the act, taking a US$500 million stake in Bank of China in September 2005.

The pièce de résistance came in January 2006, when Citigroup thought it had outbid Société Générale and ABN Amro to become the first foreign bank, and only the second foreign investor, to gain control of a Chinese bank, when it paid US$3 billion for an 85 percent stake in Guangdong Development Bank (GDB). To get it, Citigroup paid 2.3 times the book value for a bank whose liabilities exceed its assets by Rmb35 billion and – among other conditions – agreed not to set up a joint venture with GDB in credit cards, the most promising financial business in China and one where GDB had done well. However, in May 2006, the bid had still not won approval, and looked likely to fail as the government pulled back.

Given that their stakes only represented between 5–10 percent, investors will obtain little in the way of influence or control in return for their money. Prospects for a future increase in their share appeared to deteriorate in December 2005, when the bank regulator warned that if any foreign investor was granted more than a 25 percent share, that bank would be considered foreign and subject to restrictions. Moreover, despite claims that the banks have been restructured, modernized and have sold off their vast burden of NPLs, none of the new backers are in a position to know the true state of their books. More than anyone, bankers should know that due diligence in Asia often means little.

So once more, the China lure is causing a group of foreign investors to take a huge leap in the dark – despite strong warning signs that their gamble may not pay off. In this case, Western bankers are gambling on continued reform and the success of coming IPOs but, realistically, it seems more likely that the banks will actually accumulate a new mountain of bad debt. The Chinese government has a long list of ambitious infrastructure projects for the future, and the finance for new roads and railways, or new steel and energy plants, will come from these same banks. SOE lending, still protected by officials at many levels, will be another drain: in 2005 they accounted for 25 percent of output but got 65 percent of lending. All these demands will quickly swallow up the new cash infusions from foreign partners, leaving the banks once again drowning in a sea of bad loans. To add to the depressing picture, corruption continues to be rife – in March 2006, it emerged that five officials in a remote branch of the Bank of China embezzled Rmb430 million. And since net new household borrowing is said to be in decline, bankers cannot look to consumer spending for relief. The outlook is not rosy.

But it seems that whatever disasters befall them, and however capricious government policy, China remains an irresistible magnet for foreign firms eager to leverage its low wage levels, build an export base or tap into the potentially huge domestic market to sell their products. Operating in China, Western companies believe, can make them Big in Asia. Certainly, it can make them big investors. A UN Conference on Trade and Development survey, conducted in September 2005, found that 87 percent of multinationals ranked China an attractive place to invest. Are they deluded? Or is the continuing frenzy justified? And where can they look for help in avoiding all the potential dangers that have ruined so many hopes, not to mention careers?

How to Succeed

Not surprisingly, how to do business in China has become one of the hottest topics for business writers and an overcrowded field in academic research. Much has been written about the pitfalls and how to avoid them. Negotiating in China is a well-plowed field, and any company not sufficiently clued up on the importance of preparation and post-negotiation periods, and the tactics used by Chinese negotiating teams to pressurize would-be investors (changing the personnel or location, or imposing false deadlines), would be wiser to hold back until it has obtained and digested the information.

Similarly, companies should be aware of the different values that Chinese negotiators might have when assessing the potential benefits of your investment. For example, given the central government's high anxiety about unemployment and the threat of civil disorder, especially in rural areas, it would be wiser to emphasize how your involvement will help to create jobs, increase skills through training and, of course, transfer technology. The more usual Western emphasis on partnerships as vehicles for delivering cuts in costs or manpower would clearly be a mistake.

When assessing the projected profitability of any venture, the need for thorough market research by the investor, rather than relying on figures supplied by the local partner, should by now also be obvious. Equally, the importance of concentrating not just on production issues, but on how the products are going to reach their markets (distribution is one of the top three difficulties faced by foreign firms) has been well researched and recorded.

All this information is easily available and so is not repeated here. Instead, in the spirit of optimism that characterizes all foreign investment in China, what follows focuses on some successful partnerships, and recent changes that may help future foreign investors have a happier experience there.

Success Stories?

Partnerships with one of the few excellent Chinese companies where both sides have something to offer have, by and large, prospered. Amstrad, for example, entered the mobile phone market via a joint venture with the successful, formerly state-owned, consumer electronics group Haier and Hong Kong CCT Telecom. Haier has a proven marketing and manufacturing record and is one of the most lauded of Chinese companies. Hence, this particular joint venture, Haier CCT, was one of only a handful of companies granted the necessary license to manufacture and distribute phones in China.

As always in Asia, those with a long history in the country have had the most successful partnerships, albeit with both ups and downs. The German group Siemens set up its first Chinese joint venture in 1989. Since then, it has gradually expanded its stakes to obtain a majority, and bought out other ventures including its successful Beijing International Switching Corp. Although in January 2005, Siemens sold its stake in a Chinese power station bought in 1997 due to falling profitability, for the year overall it exceeded profit expectations for China. Unilever, the Anglo-Dutch consumer products manufacturer, likewise has had a long and relatively profitable presence in China, although not without serious problems with its partners at times.

Those companies that have stayed in the market are beginning to reap the benefits. They have localized staff, established relationships and their affiliates are developing knowledge and capabilities that can be transferred back to the parent company. Technology transfer is no longer a one-way street, and the R&D capability in China is evolving rapidly. The French telecoms company Alcatel, for example, which entered China in 1984 and established a dominant position early on, has 80 percent of its R&D based in Shanghai. A key component of its broadband equipment was largely conceptualized and developed in China, and in 2006 the company employed almost 3,000 engineers there.

In fact, over 700 foreign R&D labs have been set up in China since the first was established by Motorola in 1993, with US, UK, Japanese and German firms well to the fore. GE has one of only four R&D centers world-wide in Shanghai, while Microsoft and Minitel have both opened fully fledged R&D labs in the country and are integrating local staff into their research networks in the US and Europe. In September 2005, Ericsson said it would invest US$1 billion in manufacturing and research over the next five years. Tsinghua University has many collaborations with foreign companies, and research deals with GE, Lucent, P&G and BP. By 2008, China could be the most attractive R&D destination in the world (see Strategy 17).

However, much of the R&D work is still said to be more development than higher level research, and is concerned with customizing products for local markets. Even worse, and proving once more that in China everything is not always as it seems, 2006 has seen admissions by top universities of widespread plagiarism and faked research results that have called the credibility of the research establishment into question.

In truth, all success stories should be tempered by a word of caution, since almost every company will have been scarred by the experience of working with a local partner. The German auto manufacturer VW has long been regarded as a great survivor, leading the market in 2004 with a 50 percent share, However, over its two decades in a joint venture with Shanghai Automotive Industry (SAIC), it has learned to cope with inefficient distribution systems, pirated parts and the problems of achieving economies of scale to justify the costs of building a plant. Probably the nadir of the relationship was in June 2002, when it was revealed that SAIC had been using VW's original parts in a bestselling car made by a rival company that was 20 percent owned by SAIC. The price of joint venture success in China is eternal vigilance. You never know when you might get an unpleasant surprise.

Unfortunately, most routes into the Chinese market will involve a relationship with a local partner. In some sectors, a joint venture is unavoidable – car makers, for example, are limited to a 50 percent stake. Invariably your partner will be an SOE. Few companies have successfully managed such relationships in the past, so what makes them so difficult and is it possible to avoid disaster when paired with one?

SOEs: Mission Impossible?

SOEs have long had a poor press. Generally characterized as corrupt and poorly managed conglomerates conducting obscure business transactions between listed and non-listed entities, SOE managers have pulled some appalling scams on their joint venture partners. One US firm discovered that, over a long period, one of its managers had been transferring equipment from the pipe threading shop to his father. Over the next year, the father sold US$150,000 worth of pipes back to the company.

Since SOEs still dominate most sectors, they are the most likely partners or acquisition choices available. The few private firms emerging are often offshoots of SOEs restructured by local entrepreneurs, who are unwilling to sell. Reform of the sector began in 1983 and over the next two decades, over a third of the worst, mainly small and medium SOEs were sold off or closed, laying off millions of workers. But still, in 2004, non-incorporated SOEs numbered 150,000, with 17,000 run by provincial or subprovincial governments. In 2006, the state held a majority share in many, including larger ones operating in areas seen as vital such as national defense, utilities and so on. The top 190 or so were directly controlled by the State Assets Supervision and Administration Commission. A few of the large ones are available to foreign investors and said to be profitable. However, this is questionable and, in any case, without being able to take control, investors have little hope of reforming them.

For foreign investors, acquisition of an SOE is often the best way to acquire low-cost manufacturing capacity and market share, although the latter often turns out to be more myth than reality. Buying up parts of fragmented industries, as occurred in the beer or consumer electronics sectors (where NEC bought over 40 local electronic manufacturers) can also be a way to achieve economies of scale. Sectors such as retail and logistics have also undergone consolidation by this route. However, the acquisition process is by no means easy, and about 75 percent of potential deals fall through during the negotiating stage due to arguments about price and employment issues – often SOE workers cannot be laid off for a set number of years. Hidden liabilities can be another pitfall. Many have been accused of falsifying their financial statements with the help of accountants, underwriters and local government officials. Some were investigated by the Chinese Securities Regulatory Commission, although few actually went bankrupt.

The failure rate of those partnerships that do get off the ground is high. Trying to restructure an SOE can be a nightmare, with huge cultural, linguistic and operational barriers to overcome. The lack of a strong work ethic, sufficient commitment and discipline among SOE workers is well known, as are the obstacles to imposing any control or introducing notions of a performance-oriented approach. Having for years worked to set targets, these companies lack any formal planning processes for sales, resource or project management, since the long-term survival of the firm has never been their problem. To make them profitable is a considerable task, especially since few foreign firms are probably prepared to act as ruthlessly as Haier. Assembly-line workers who failed to meet Haier standards were required to stand on a pair of yellow feet painted at the end of each production line to confess their failings to their colleagues and promise to do better.[5]

One SOE that was successfully restructured was the Anqing TP Goetze Piston Ring Co. Ltd. (ATG), a three-way auto components joint venture between a UK firm, a Japanese one and a Chinese SOE. Located in Anqing in faraway Anhui Province, ATG got fast and favored treatment from local officials in order to set up its venture and build a new factory and, within five years, was number one in its market. The key to its success was said to be "tight budgeting policy at the beginning, the effort to cultivate name brands and independent development." In 2005, ATG was named a pillar enterprise of the province. So it can be done.[6]

Recently, changes in the attitudes of local workers and managers seem to indicate brighter prospects for the success of SOE joint ventures. Since the end of the 1990s when the state sector began cutting jobs, attitudes among SOE workers have begun to change, and many see foreign investors as the only way of saving their companies and jobs.

At the same time, another set of potential partners is emerging, as China reorganizes its industries to conform with WTO membership, splitting up large former state monopolies to create new companies. These companies are being run by a new generation of managers with a different approach to business. These younger managers (below the age of 40) are the "little emperors" born after the introduction of the single-child policy. Frequently described as more entrepreneurial and better educated than their predecessors, they are said to be more attuned to foreign ways and easier to deal with. But they are gaining a reputation for greater venality than previous generations.

Future Investment Prospects

Although many sectors – notably automobiles, telecoms and electrical goods – have become saturated, others offer solid prospects for would-be investors. The most attractive ones are likely to be tied up with the service sector, currently representing 20 percent of FDI and widely expected to overtake manufacturing as the favorite investment vehicle. So for example:

- The opening of the finance and insurance sectors by the end of 2006 is expected to provide a new magnet for accountants, lawyers and bankers. Already the US buyout firm Carlyle has paid US$409 million for a 24.975 percent stake in the number three life insurer China Pacific Life Insurance Co. at the end of 2005. Alternatively, the increase in tourism means new opportunities in hotels, restaurants and transport – not forgetting the construction industry that will be building the necessary roads, hotels and so on. Caterpillar Corp. has already been moving strongly here, hoping to cash in on construction throughout the country via both direct investment and joint ventures. However, its China profits in 2005 still represented less than 2 percent of its global sales.

- As the population becomes better off, the beauty and leisure sectors (clothing, home entertainment, hobbies, education) could also offer good growth possibilities. It is estimated that the leisurewear sector will almost double to US$58 billion by 2010, but with over 2,000 brands competing in the sector and new arrivals entering all the time now that foreign companies are allowed to set up wholly owned operations, competition is fierce. The strongest foreign player is Hong Kong's Giordano International, an early entrant in 1992. By 2006 it had 680 outlets in the country, accounting for 45 percent of its total operations. Giordano targets different brands for different segments – lower priced trendy basics for teenagers, Giordano Ladies for affluent working women in Shanghai and Beijing, and the BlueStar Exchange for the less well off.[7] Spain's Zara is also growing fast. But beware, to succeed you will need a strong local sourcing base and a good manufacturing partner – and in this sector, copycat brands are rife!

- Any business connected with the Olympics is also likely to offer potential and can count on government support, since making the Olympics a success is tied up with the need to demonstrate China's triumphant progress to the rest of the world. So, for example, the government wants to see more credit card use to prepare for the expected rush of visitors to the Olympics, and to encourage Chinese consumers to buy more. It has told larger Beijing merchants that it expects 90 percent of them to accept credit cards by 2008. After the Olympics, the World Expo to be held in Shanghai in 2010 will offer similar opportunities.

- Education – especially in management and English language speaking – is another strong growth area. Colleges offering English language courses, business schools offering management training and offshoots such as bookshops and magazines, are all likely to expand rapidly. And with education beginning early, educational toys could be another good bet. However, the toy sector is very crowded, with over 6,000 companies operating there in 2005.

■ The market for luxury, premium priced goods used to be associated with products or services used by party officials or factory bosses. However, according to Merrill Lynch, over 300,000 Chinese now have a net worth of over US$1 million, excluding property, and are more openly splashing out on luxury brands.[8] Forecasts indicate that within a decade, China will become a top luxury market. The top end of the auto industry has been benefiting – the Rolls-Royce outlet in Beijing is one of its top selling dealerships and Bentley Beijing has sold half a dozen stretch limos at US$1.2 million each. They are now targeting second- and third-tier cities. Luxury goods makers such as Cartier, Piaget, Gucci and LVMH also report growing demand for designer goods jewelry, lighters and perfume, and are opening new stores in all the main cities. In October 2003, Lacoste said it expected China to be its top market within the decade, although it warned that there were over 100 brand counterfeiters operating in China.

And of course, behind all the new ventures will be openings for specialists in marketing, advertising and public relations to help the market along.

Go West

Finally, foreign firms are also looking to the hinterland for investment prospects, encouraged by a central government concerned to avoid rural unrest (87,000 riots in 2005). The government's "Great Western Development Policy," announced in its tenth five-year plan (2001–05), offered tax breaks and other incentives such as cheap land and bank loans to firms investing in the poorer inland regions of the northeast and west of China, and many, including Whirlpool, Intel and, perhaps most surprisingly, Gucci, have taken up the challenge. A popular destination is the western province of Sichuan, whose capital Chengdu calls itself "the Shanghai of western China."

The move makes good sense in view of the labor shortages and rising wage and land prices beginning to push up costs in the urbanized Guandong Pearl River Delta, Fujian and Zhejiang Provinces and Shanghai. Other companies moving there include BP, Ford Auto, Alcatel, Intel,

Corning, Ericsson, Microsoft, Motorola and Nokia, plus Korea's SK Teletech. However, despite FDI there is still only a trickle – a mere US$2 billion between 1999 and 2004 – with half that amount going into Shanghai alone. Note also that heading west can mean high start-up costs if you have to put expatriate managers into hotels for long periods, and training local workers will be tough. It will also mean longer supply chains and dealing with the biggest barrier of all, huge infrastructure problems.

Logistics costs in China represent over 20 percent of GDP, compared with 10 percent in Europe. With no national trucking license available, hauliers must get permission from each province to move goods across the country and unload them onto different trucks at each border. Local governments often maintain inefficient supply chains to protect local jobs. B&Q has 1,800 suppliers for 48 stores, compared with 600 suppliers for 300 stores in UK.[9]

Although the road network is reasonably efficient, the rail network is undeveloped and river transport slow. In the west, the Yangtse River is the main transport link to Chongqing, the major inland port. However, it is notorious for its dangerous currents. Not surprisingly, Western logistics providers such as APL Logistics, UPS, DHL, Maersk and TNT have been quick to seize the opportunity and move into a market currently estimated at only about US$1–1.5 billion but growing fast. UPS, which paid $100 million to take full control of its joint venture in 2005, and TNT, already present in 600 Chinese cities, are both on the acquisition trail. DHL has a joint venture with Sinotrans, the state-owned giant. All have also been setting up wholly owned operations in major ports along the Yangtse. FedEx has also entered strongly and, by 2006, had more flights into China than any other express delivery company. In March 2006, it relocated its regional hub to Guangzhou.

On the Other Hand

On the other hand, foreign firms that do move west risk finding a rerun of all the problems that dogged early entrants into eastern China and the coastal regions – red tape, unhelpful local officials, bureaucracy and corruption. When it comes to repatriating profits, piracy, counterfeiting and administrative delays there are always problems.

Corruption and piracy are still endemic and any redress in the local courts is difficult if not impossible since they are controlled by local governments that protect their own. The auto industry has especially suffered from piracy: Honda, Toyota and GM have all accused partners of copying their designs. Consequently, their components suppliers have long been reluctant to enter China, despite its growth, since car parts from fluids and brakes to fuel filters, spark plugs and batteries are all swiftly copied and on the market. Computer software, tennis shoes, DVDs and every kind of luxury good also continue to be reproduced with impunity. The slow growth of franchising is put down to fear of copycats – companies such as Starbucks and McDonald's are understandably reluctant to train locals to run a business, only to find them leaving and setting up their own operation next door.

However, there are signs that foreign firms are beginning to win redress. In 2004 the Swiss agrichemicals group Syngenta won an apology and damages and 2006 saw Starbucks and the confectionery company Ferrero Rocher win court rulings. The latter has spent US$800,00 to defend rights in China against counterfeiting. In April 2006, LVMH even sued Carrefour over claims that fake copies of handbags were being sold in its stores.

Government interference also remains an ever present threat. Although there is official recognition that the government should change its style and be "a good football referee or a good investor or manager of the court, but not a player or boss of the team," it is not a lesson that has yet been taken to heart.[10] In February 2003, fears of the dominance of foreign retailers such as Carrefour, Makro and Wal-Mart led the State Economic and Trade Commission to announce new rules to curb the expansion of these stores. There are signs that similar fears of M&A activity leading to foreigners dominating certain sectors could provoke a backlash: acquisitions in the beer, skin care and soft drinks sectors have all been described as "malicious." There are also calls to halt foreign involvement in sectors that could threaten China's economic security or national sovereignty.

Realistically, foreign companies can only expect the competition to get tougher and the markets even more difficult to call. In many industries – automotive, consumer electronics, telecoms, beer – foreign companies were forced to withdraw after their first foray into the market, sadder and poorer, having been defeated by brutal competition from local firms who were already entrenched and had local conditions in their favor. Since then, Chinese companies that were medium sized a decade ago have learned fast and today consider themselves the equal of any foreign multinational. However, many of them are also keen to spread beyond the domestic market and go global, following in the footsteps of TCL (telecoms), Haier (consumer electrics) and Lenovo (PCs – formerly Legend). This ambition may give an opening for foreign companies that can offer export opportunities to enter more equal partnerships with their Chinese partners. However, when it comes to operating on their home ground, the strategy of local companies will remain as it always has been: cooperate with foreign partners for their technology; learn from them how to gain market share; improve distribution and service – then leave them defeated at their own game. So how to survive in these perilous markets?

A Chinese Riddle

The China markets have long presented a riddle to foreign firms. In theory, they present a target of over a billion consumers but in practice, few foreign firms have been able to boast of the high returns they have made, and many have retired after suffering years of loss. In 2003, the estimated profits of US companies in China were just US$4.4 billion, similar to what US companies made in Australia. No country has attracted more hyperbole about market size than China, and nowhere has the gap between potential and actual returns been greater, as foreign companies entered to find the gloss was just that, and market forecasts were designed more to please.

Unfortunately, what too many failed to notice was the fact that China's per capita GDP still ranked lower than 100th in the world and that of the 1.3 billion Chinese, only 400 million were the urban consumers of their dreams, mainly found in the rapidly growing and urbanized east. Shanghai, for example, is an urban conglomeration as big as Los Angeles, with 18 million inhabitants. According to Gallup surveys, incomes in China's top 10 urban regions are more than five times those in its vast rural interior – and the gap is getting wider every day. Over three-quarters of a billion Chinese exist in poverty (almost half China's population lives on less than $2 a day), without the means or desire to buy expensive Western goods. The majority of the population still use bicycles and buses for transport. So it is not surprising that Western firms found the bottomless markets of their dreams singularly elusive.

Of course, their calculations were not completely based on a myth. Since 1979, the Chinese economy has been expanding steadily, growing at an average annual rate of 9.6 percent. Revised data released in December 2005, which included activity in the services sector for the first time, put China's GDP for 2004 at US$1.983 billion, making it the world's sixth biggest economy. But one of the first rules about China is never trust government statistics, since, as the country's chief statistician acknowledged, there are "widespread flaws in the system used to compile economic data."[11] One economist described the original official 2004 statistics as a "fantasy world."[12] Another observer noted that "One cannot help but feel exasperated by the opacity of the National Bureau of Statistics' operations, and the frivolity with which the NBS seems to treat its numbers."[13] Lies, damned lies and statistics, but in China it is mostly the first two.

So what is the truth about China's markets and that much sought after bird, the Chinese consumer? Who are they and what goods and services are likely to interest them?

The Chinese Consumer

According to a Credit Suisse First Boston report, one of the largest surveys of consumer attitudes in China ever attempted, household consumption spending in 2005 was 3.8 percent of the global total. China was expected to overtake Italy in 2006 and probably France the following year.[14]

Findings indicate that middle-class households – public servants, academics, teachers, doctors, engineers, white-collar workers of all kinds – have incomes of at least US$10,000 per annum, the lowest income at which people can afford both an apartment and a small car and the expansion of glossy car magazines demonstrates that car ownership is a priority for them. With increasing wealth, they will also seek to upgrade home appliances and buy more expensive goods such as LCD screens, PCs and telephones. Also highly ranked is education. However, savings rates in China remain high.

The youth market, a product of the one-child policy, is identified as the most brand conscious and receptive to new foreign products. Many young people live with their parents and so – like the tide of single Japanese girls that has regularly invaded Europe to buy up luxury brands – they have been targeted by producers of upmarket goods, mobile phones and electric gadgets, designer clothing (especially the sports sector) and cosmetics (L'Oréal is targeting the 20–30 age group for skin care), along with those involved in the tourist and restaurant trades. When Sony, for example, discovered that its products were seen as appealing more to older people, it designed its MP3 specifically for the youth segment. It is predicted that the young will remain the largest consumer segment until 2014, after which growth is expected to slow as demographic trends kick in. The total population is forecast to hit around 1.31 billion in 2019 and rapidly decline thereafter.

Research suggests that the number of people under the age of 40 may already have peaked at 800 million and will decline by a third over the next 20 years. By 2024, the "oldies" will make up 58 percent of the population and by then, 75 percent of Chinese households may be childless.[15] Increasingly, the 40–60-year-olds will have the most purchasing power, which they are expected to spend on travel, eating out and financial services.

Looking ahead, it is the older, retired generation that will take over as the largest segment. Their history – having lived through the last years of Maoist Socialism and the Cultural Revolution – means they are much more abstemious and likely to take a more practical approach to buying decisions. Their tastes being more dictated by what is practical rather than luxury, they are more likely to be concerned with health and environment issues. This will be a significant market in the future and some firms are already appealing to such concerns. Nestlé, for example, is selling fortified milk powders, while P&G Safeguard soap is thought to be selling well mainly due to its promise to shield families from germs. More research will undoubtedly emerge as companies try to anticipate how they can appeal to these two extremes of consumers in the short and very long term. And while studying these data, don't forget the future generation; China adds the equivalent of Australia (20 million) to its population every year. Maybe your key market hasn't even been born yet.

Navigating the Market

Unfortunately, even identifying a viable consumer group does not automatically guarantee success, since in China, perhaps more than in other parts of the world, markets are hard to control and difficult to predict. Under the force of the competition they attract, they can go from opportunity and rapid growth to overcapacity, bitter price wars and collapse in a short time, so flexibility and vigilance are vital. In many of them, the easy money has already been made and with profit margins declining, things can only get harder. So how to find a market in which you might stand a chance of making some money – at least for a while?

A Few Hints

1. Despite the very real difficulties described earlier, do at least consider moving into the more remote areas. Being further from Beijing and less favored, these provinces are more likely to offer you a better deal and give you support, as they are keen to attract foreign investment. Also,

the local competition may be less fierce so as long as you do your research thoroughly, and get a good logistics partner, the market may turn out to be a winner.

2. Clear your mind of all the hype about a billion consumers. Instead, go back to basics and do a classic marketing strategy exercise. Look at the external and internal environments, list the threats and opportunities, your strengths and weaknesses. Ask every question you can think of. Can we be competitive? Can the product be competitive? Will it make money? Is anyone making any money? Study the local competition. Who are they? Would any of them make a good partner? Remember, it might be easier to sell a service than a product, since services are more difficult to copy.

Remember, emerging markets are just that, and in China, as in every other country, new segments are developing all the time as industries expand, salaries rise and spending power increases. It is important for companies to have the right product ready to match each segment as it emerges, as Giordano has done in the retail clothing sector.

3. Based on this, don't go for a blanket market approach; try to identify a segment with unfulfilled needs. The more tightly defined the segment, the better your chance of success. Try segmenting by age, gender, household income and size, education or occupation, or by the three Rs – religion, race and region. Remember, over two-thirds of the population live in the countryside, and still have a "collective" mentality.

4. Remember your four Ps – China is no different from any other market so you need to understand your customers, tailor your product and make sure it is efficiently distributed and promoted. Although price is still important, there has been a growing trend among middle-income shoppers to put quality before price. A recent survey also found that brand awareness was growing and would be the next most important factor for the richer segments, followed by price, packaging, advertising and promotion. For the moment, huge outside billboards are still one of the main advertising avenues in China (see Strategy 21) but do check that your advert is visible. Chongqing boasted the world's biggest advertising billboard but, unfortunately, it turned out to be surrounded by fog all the year round and not easily seen.

5. If you missed out on a market the first time around, how about considering the replacement market? When many consumers bought their TVs, washing machines, refrigerators and so on, it was a novelty actually to own one. But next time round there may be particular pluses that could be attractive, such as flat screens, power consumption or noise on which you might compete.

6. Invest in sectors where you have world-class capabilities, or where the government wants to push growth, for example the energy and infrastructure sectors. Taiwanese chip manufacturers, not normally the most welcome entrants to mainland markets, have found their expertise greatly in demand to feed the growth of China's semiconductor industry. They have traded their technology for access to a fast-growing market, fueled by demand for mobile phone, computing and communications equipment manufacturers. However, in order to guard their advantage, they are only transferring mature technology. Similarly, the retail firm Carrefour used its logistics and back-office superiority to build up a lead and become the only profitable foreign supermarket chain in China, while the French American oil services company, Schlumberger, which had its first technical contracts in the 1970s and opened an office in Beijing in 1980, is benefiting from China's emphasis on the need for energy security. It works on high-tech projects, its major customers being PetroChina, Sinopec and CNOOC.

7. Start small and build according to demand (not the hockey stick forecasts supplied by local managers) to avoid being left with a warehouse full of unwanted products.

8. Finally, remember you don't have to rush in just to be "in China." If conditions are not yet right, then wait. In 2005, the owner of Harvey Nichols, the upmarket British department store, said that China would not be ready for entry for another two to three years as the rich were only buying major brands, and were not yet the sophisticated luxury goods shoppers his stores would attract.

The Case for Caution

The Belgian logistics and high-tech services supplier, KTN[16] also took a cautious approach to China, although for other reasons. Although many of KTN's biggest customers were already operating there and it was being hyped as an unstoppable business bonanza, KTN's vice president's pragmatic view was that:

> I am here to make money for the company. A lot of people try to make me crazy about investing in China – they say you must do it now or lose the opportunity of a lifetime. Maybe in 1995–96 I believed it, but now I am older I'm not so nervous about not being there.

His reasoning was straightforward:

KTN must go into businesses where it can have profitable growth. In China, the infrastructure is not yet there and there is a huge corruption problem – and if we feel it's impossible to do business there then we don't go. We won't go for the sake of saying "We are in China." We want a framework in place that guarantees we will be successful before we move there … Today you cannot operate in the field of logistics as a wholly foreign-owned company in China unless you operate in a free trade zone and these are very, very expensive. The minimum investment for me is 15 million euros, depreciated over 30 years. Therefore location is an essential consideration. So I am not going there if I know that if in a few years the markets will open, and the trade zones will lose part of their privileged status – I will have done a very stupid thing and invested in the wrong location.

What Next?

So what does the future hold? Will China be the Shangri La of multinationals' dreams or the grave of investors' hopes when, as some analysts predict, spectacular growth ends in an overheated economy and boom gives way to bust? Could the doomsday scenario, in which politics dictate a complete volte-face and government abruptly turns off the tap leaving foreign investors stranded, ever come true? Less dramatically, can the "workshop of the world" continue to grow apace and still maintain harmonious relations with the US, the EU and other trading partners? And for foreign firms, will the attraction again prove fatal, or will they be successful the second time around and actually begin to make profits in China?

Whatever happens, you can bet that companies will continue to be pulled into its markets, however many times they read about treacherous partners who see alliances solely in terms of expediency, about poor corporate governance, accounts that bear little relation to reality, the pitfalls of operating in diverse markets where local competitors indulge in savage price wars, opaque bureaucracy, delays and interference from local and central government, the difficulties of repatriating profits and where, whatever problems arise, turning to the judicial system for help or redress is not an option. Despite all this, the frenzy seems set to continue. Many claim to be cheered by the fact that foreign earnings are increasing – but this is from a very low base. And while foreign firms are busy trying to find ways to crack the China markets, they shouldn't forget to watch what the big Chinese firms are doing in overseas markets. Companies such as

Haier, Legend and TCL, and car makers like Geely and Chery are moving fast, and could soon be taking your domestic market share.

Perhaps a fitting last word should go to the chairman of the Italian tyre maker Pirelli. A late entrant into the market, Pirelli has just taken a 60 percent controlling share of a joint venture with a private industrial group. Despite this promising start, the keynote of the chairman's approach was caution: "I think no-one knows enough about China," he said.[17] Just hold on to that thought.

Key Lessons

■ Remember that the Chinese are expert at extracting the maximum from foreign firms in terms of technology, know-how or capital – and giving the minimum in return.

■ Remember that there is no such thing as "the Chinese market." China is a series of regions and potential markets, each deserving of its own market strategy.

■ All procedures in China take time, patience and money, so the two main requirements are deep pockets and good connections.

■ Start small, target your segment and adapt your offering to its needs. Never underestimate the power of local competitors. Remember, an effective distribution and sales network is critical to success, but also very, very difficult to build.

■ Try to be master of your own destiny. Go for a WFOE if possible and play to your strengths. When the market gets tougher, make sure you have the skills and management in place to cope.

■ If you discover that you have the wrong partner, if management clashes make the relationship one long battle or if the partner turns out to be useless, it is better to abandon ship than try to make it work.

■ Moderate your expectations. Don't be hypnotized by the hype, but concentrate on the reality.

■ Remove the word "consistency" from your vocabulary. The Chinese have.

Notes

1 *Financial Times*, Comment and Analysis, 25 August, 2003, p11.
2 *Financial Times*, "Cosmopolis dreams large," 12 April, 2006.
3 *The Economist*, "Are you being served?," 14 January, 2006, pp61–2.
4 *The Economist*, "Fools rush in," 7 August, 2005, p50.

5 Taken from "China's Haier Group: Growth through Acquisitions," case study by Robert Crawford, Ming Zeng and Hellmut Schutte, 2000, INSEAD-EAC.

6 See "ATG: A Chinese Miracle?," case study by Charlotte Butler, Anne-Marie Cagna and Henri-Claude de Bettignies, INSEAD, 2001.

7 *Wall Street Journal*, "G could offer lessons in China," Mei Fong, 24–26 February, 2006.

8 *Business Week*, "To get rich is glorious," 6 February, 2006, pp46–7.

9 Op cit., *The Economist*, 14 January, 2006.

10 *China's Foreign Trade*, no 320, "How far can China's motors drive in the international market?," September 2003, pp16–18.

11 *Financial Times*, "China's data chief 'confident' about statistics," 1 March 2002, p7.

12 *Financial Times*, "Economists cast doubt on China's GDP data," R Mcgregor, 24 October, 2005, p6.

13 *Far Eastern Economic Review*, "Why China's New GDP matters," C.A. Holz, January/February, 2006.

14 *Financial Times*, "Young seen as leading Chinese consumer drive," G. Dyer, 13 October, 2005.

15 *The Economist*, "China's golden oldies," 26 February, 2005.

16 Taken from "KTN enters Asia," case study by Charlotte Butler and Dirk Van den Berghe, INSEAD, 2005.

17 *Financial Times*, "Pirelli treads carefully in China," 23 December, 2005, p8.

Strategy 25

Negotiate the Law in Asia: Bankruptcy, Contracts and Defamation

WHAT'S IN THIS CHAPTER?

▷ The State of Play
▷ Bankruptcy
▷ The Value of Contracts when the Law is Poor
▷ A Note on Defamation in Asia

The State of Play

There are crooks in business all over the world. The reason why there are fewer in the West than in Asia is not because of culture or tradition but simply because they can be taken to court in the West. The legal system also works well in Singapore and so its citizens are generally law-abiding. The threat of punishment has the same effect the world over.

A basic prerequisite for any developed country is an effective rule of law and that means an enforceable judicial regime to which every individual and every institution is subject. Political leaders, hereditary leaders and anyone else in a high position must be subject to the same constraints of the law as anyone else. The law should not exist merely to allow rulers to impose their whims on everyone else, no matter how benevolent. Rule *by* law is not the same thing as the rule *of* law, although in Asia the two are commonly confused.

One essential aspect of an effective rule of law is that legal codes should be written in plain language. They should also be clear as to their intent and thus minimize the opportunity for interpretation and discretion. If they do not do this, they invite corruption and favoritism. They also allow people to operate "within the law" but nonetheless in a manner that is clearly "wrong."

The agencies charged with administering the law should also be as streamlined as possible. Approvals processes are best centralized within one arm of government for consistency, timeliness and to reduce the opportunities for discretion among far-flung and diverse bureaucrats. On this measure, Vietnam followed by India, then China, Thailand, Indonesia and the Philippines routinely top surveys of businessmen as the worst economies in which to operate when it comes to red tape. Hong Kong, Singapore and Australia rate as the best.

Good laws are essential for establishing and enforcing property rights and property rights are essential for good and transparent markets. Peruvian economist and writer Hernando de Soto writes:

> Imagine a country where nobody can identify who owns what ... addresses cannot be easily verified, people cannot be made to pay their debts, resources cannot conveniently be turned into money, ownership cannot be divided into shares, descriptions of assets are not standardized and cannot be easily compared and the rules that govern property vary from neighborhood to neighborhood or even from street to street. You have just put yourself into the life of a developing country or former communist nation.[1]

In Asia, de Soto's excellent description applies in varying degrees to Indonesia, China, Vietnam, Myanmar, the Philippines, Thailand, Cambodia, Laos, Bangladesh, Pakistan, Nepal and even India. De Soto points out that one reason why the poor stay poor in the developing world is that while they might often have assets, particularly land, they cannot adequately demonstrate title to the point where they can sell them. Most businesses are started with borrowed money, but how can you mortgage an asset that you cannot prove you own? Houses and shops with no titles, crops with no deeds and businesses with no statutes of incorporation inhibit individuals' abilities to borrow against these assets and sell them. And when they do, they or the buyers risk attracting claims from others who also claim ownership.

Problems with property rights are not restricted to the poor. Asia's governments were advised by the IMF to privatize state-owned assets in the wake of the 1997–98 economic crisis. But how do you privatize an asset over which even the state's title is unclear? This is just the problem that the Indonesian government faced when it wanted to ready parts of Jakarta's international airport for privatization in 2000. It was not clear that the government had title to all the land on which the airport had been built. Months were lost while consultants and lawyers sought to determine who owned the land on which the hangars and cargo sheds stood.

Arbitration is the most common form of commercial and labor dispute resolution in China. The China International Economic and Trade Arbitration Commission (CIETAC) is the usual body that mediates in disputes over commercial contracts involving foreign parties. If the local party refuses to go to the CIETAC, the dispute must go to a local arbitration commission. Arbitration in commercial cases in China is usually a last resort and signals an irretrievable breakdown between the parties.

As rich as Japan is, it still has an inadequate legal system. It is understaffed and underresourced, judges are given skimpy budgets, and too little is spent on training lawyers and the judiciary. Most importantly, there are too few lawyers. There are about 17,000 lawyers in all Japan, most of whom do not practice commercial law. But there are more than 60,000 lawyers listed at the New York bar alone and as many as 150,000 law graduates in China. There is only one state-sanctioned law school, the Legal Training and Research Institute. Undergraduate law students face one of the toughest bar exams in the world. It takes the average student five attempts to succeed and only one attempt a year is allowed. Lawyers' fees are outrageously high owing to the shortage of lawyers.

The problem with the law in Asia is not only enforcement. The laws themselves are often poorly drafted. Sometimes they are vague to the point where it is unclear what is within the law and what is not. Consumer protection laws are weak in most of Asia and so too are competition laws. Companies can merge with their competitors to dominate a market, or use predatory pricing to force competitors out of the market, often with little legal repercussion.

Bankruptcy

High numbers of bankruptcies are a sign of a well-functioning economy and not a sick one. Too few bankruptcies are not a sign of a healthy economy, but rather of a poorly functioning legal environment. A World Bank report published in 2001 found that among 37 countries surveyed, the countries with a greater than average ratio of bankruptcies to total firms throughout the 1990s were all OECD countries, bar two, South Africa and Singapore.[2]

In Asia, bankruptcy law as it is written and applied works relatively well in Taiwan, Hong Kong, Singapore, South Korea and Japan. The main criticism, though, particularly in respect of Korea and Japan, is that procedures are too rigid and slow. Part of the problem in Japan is the insufficient number of lawyers. Elsewhere in Asia, forcing debtors into bankruptcy can be more trouble than it is worth.

Enforcement is the main issue but the laws themselves require fine-tuning. Indonesia's new bankruptcy laws, introduced in 1998, allow single creditors to petition for the involuntary bankruptcy of apparent bad debtors. This means that the existence of one unpaid debt could bring about a bankruptcy even though the debt might well be the subject of a bona fide dispute between the debtor and the petitioning creditor. Bankruptcy in such circumstances is not warranted. The condition of bankruptcy requires that the debtor is generally unable to pay its debts to several or more of its creditors. Bankruptcy laws need to reflect this.

In Thailand, Indonesia and the Philippines, creditors still prefer to go through voluntary debt work-outs rather than risk costly and unpredictable court proceedings. Thailand's new Central Bankruptcy Court was established in 1999 and it did not attract the rush of applications that might be expected. Indonesia's new bankruptcy court, established in 1998, attracted only 38 applications in its first five months. By way of comparison, there were approximately 1,000 similar applications in Australia for the same period, and Australia had not just been through an economic crisis and has about 10 percent of Indonesia's population. Many of the applications in Thailand and Indonesia were in relation to small debts and then fewer than half led to bankruptcies. Meanwhile, huge segments of the local business scene were obviously technically bankrupt. Furthermore, many mischievous wind-up applications have been submitted by disgruntled ex-partners, ex-employees and even customers, rather than from serious creditors, and in some cases, the courts have found otherwise solvent companies bankrupt after having presumably been provided with the right inducements.

China has bankruptcy procedures but they date from 1988 and are out of date. In any event, enforcement is a huge problem. At the beginning of 2006, a new bankruptcy code that had been prepared almost two years ago still had not been passed. In any event, even SOEs have trouble with getting bankruptcy decisions enforced. The head of China's state-owned China Construction Bank has said that between 1998 and 2000, his bank took 1,300 of its corporate bad debtors, many of which are other SOEs, to court. It won judgments against 98 percent of them but the bank was still unable to get much of its money back because China's courts are so ineffective at enforcing civil judgments, especially against SOEs.[3] If this is so for an important state-owned bank, then what hope do foreigners have in China? How the new codes will solve this problem if and when they are enacted remains to be seen.

The Value of Contracts when the Law is Poor

If the law and its enforcement are poor, of what value are contracts? The answer is that they are essential, particularly if large sums of money are at stake. While contracts may not always be enforced, sometimes they are. The best approach to Asia's more difficult markets is to have a range of measures to cover all contingencies, and a contract is one of them. In more developed markets, a contract might be a necessary and sufficient requirement but in others, contracts are merely necessary. Many companies opt to have contracts drawn up in jurisdictions with sound legal systems such as Singapore and Hong Kong, although the value of such documents in third countries such as Indonesia or Vietnam is questionable.

The value of contracts in Asia can be enhanced according to how they are presented. Contracts and other legal documents should be written as simply as possible using plain English and then translated into the local language. They should be explained clause by clause to the local party and each clause should be agreed on separately before discussion moves on to the next clause. If the local side is not given the opportunity to fully understand it, they might sign it anyway to save face. This will only lead to problems later on. If the local party does not understand the contract but signs anyway, they will be tempted to renegotiate it later on. Indeed, as any sort of serious negotiations progress in Asia, confirmation of whatever is agreed should always be sought in writing. Verbal confirmation might often mean confirmation that the matter will be considered rather than has been agreed to.

Contracts dwelling on penalties and dealing with relationship problems and exit clauses might prove detrimental to your relationship with your partner if presented at an early stage in the relationship-building process. "We're still getting to know one another and already you're thinking about what to do if we bust up?" might be the surprised response.

Getting a local partner to sign a contract might prove difficult. Signing contracts might be routine in the West, but for some in Asia, the practice might be unusual and thus cause uncertainty. One Western businessman interviewed by the authors commented that in India:

> often contracts are not worth the paper they're written on. Often they won't sign any formal agreement before business begins. They want to see how business

goes first and then they'll commit to signing a contract. It's as if a contract is not the precursor to business but rather a signal that it can continue to proceed.

It is a sentiment that applies throughout Asia.

Who draws up the contracts, joint venture agreements, articles of association and whatever else local laws dictate as being necessary is important. The foreign company might find it useful to offer to pay all the legal costs itself, if this means it can choose the law firm to do this. Otherwise, the local side might be tempted to choose a law firm on the basis that someone's cousin works there and so on. Law firms need to be chosen for the quality of their expertise and not because of personal connections. There are limits to the useful application of personal connections.

Often contracts are not seen in Asia as fixed for all time as they are in the West. They are viewed as a statement of principles that reflects current conditions. Should these shift unexpectedly, don't be surprised if the local side wants to repudiate the contract, pleading that it is no longer "fair" that it should be enforced. It needs to be emphasized at the negotiating stage that the contract is fixed. When Asia's currencies plummeted in 1997, borrowers saw this as an excuse unilaterally to ignore their loan agreements, even if they still had the capability to service their loans. This was most evident in Thailand, where many large corporate borrowers felt that they should no longer have to meet their loan obligations. The "fairness" of transferring their losses onto their creditors did not come into it.

Asia is home to some spectacular cases of contract repudiations caused because things did not work out as planned. The debacle that was Enron Corporation's US$3 billion Dabhol Power development in the Indian state of Maharashta is one example. The plant was the largest single foreign investment in India ever and when the demand for electricity in the state did not rise as forecast, the state government refused to buy all the power it had contracted to buy. It then stopped buying power from the project altogether. These difficulties contributed to Enron's collapse in late 2001.

A similar problem arose in Indonesia in 2000 between Indonesia's state-owned power company PLN and foreign investors who had been invited in to build power plants. Economic conditions had changed and so PLN felt this should allow it to repudiate its contracts. That same year disputes arose between the state-owned telephone company PT Telekomunikasi Indonesia (PT Telkom) and five foreign operating partners, including NTT of Japan, Telstra of Australia, Cable & Wireless of the UK and AT&T of the US. The five partners accused the state company of breaching its contracts with them when it failed to lift telephone tariffs in accordance with a contracted formula and to cede management control to the five.

Arbitration can be sought in such circumstances but even this may not lead to the desired results for the outside party. If the local party will not meet its obligations under a contract, why would it comply with an unfavorable arbitration award? US energy company Karaha Bodas sought compensation from the Indonesian state-owned oil company Pertamina after the Indonesian government suspended the company's geothermal power generation project in west Java in 1997. Pertamina had been the contractee. The dispute went to a Swiss arbitration panel in 2000, which awarded Karaha Bodas US$261 million. Pertamina refused to pay and so Karaha Bodas then applied to seize Pertamina's assets in the US. Payments for oil and gas produced by Pertamina and its partners are often made to trustee and escrow accounts in the US and Karaha Bodas sought judicial access in the US to these accounts so that it could collect the arbitration award.

One of the five international partners of PT Telkom, the AriaWest consortium in which AT&T had a 35 percent stake, signalled its desire to sell its business in Indonesia in September 2000 after PT Telkom ignored its contractual obligations. It demanded that PT Telkom pay US$735 million for the fixed line network that it had already laid down. Telekom refused, saying it was worth only US$280 million. AriaWest then filed a US$1.3 billion arbitration claim against PT Telkom in Geneva in May 2001. Perhaps mindful of Karaha Bodas's troubles in obtaining its arbitrated settlement in Indonesia, AriaWest's owners agreed to sell it to PT Telkom in March 2002 for between US$320 million and US$350 million.

The main centers in the world for arbitration are London, Hong Kong, Paris, Kuala Lumpur and Sydney. Singapore is attempting to position itself as an international arbitration center too. In 2002, more than 60 international arbitration cases were registered in Singapore. The actual number probably was higher as not all cases are registered. The Singapore International Arbitration Center cut its fees for case management and appointment fees by almost half in mid-2003 to further position Singapore as an international arbitration center.

A Note on Defamation in Asia

Businesspeople in Asia typically do not sue for defamation or libel. This is partly due to the insufficient appreciation for intangibles. Paying service providers such as lawyers is almost an anathema for many in Asia. To pay them to protect something as intangible as one's reputation compounds the apparent folly. The smart ones are more likely to respond to an article or book about them that they don't like by simply claiming that "not everything is correct." Precisely what is not correct is left unsaid, so that the entire article or book is held in question – a clever tactic.

Having said that, the use of defamation action is growing in some Asian countries. Nowhere is this more so than in Malaysia, where sums sought for alleged damages have escalated dramatically. The 1994 award of M$10 million (currently about US$2.6 million) to Vincent Tan, the founder of Malaysia's Berjaya conglomerate, against a local freelance business journalist was a turning point.

Tan has since sued others for defamation, including a Malaysian academic for remarks printed in the *Asian Wall Street Journal*, the journal itself and a Malaysian journalist now based in Sydney for comments circulated by email.

In 2000, then Prime Minister Mahathir's son Mirzan sued the Malaysian printer of the *Asian Wall Street Journal* for remarks carried in the journal about his business interests. He sought M$150 million from the printer, notwithstanding the fact that the printer had no editorial control whatsoever over what was published. The matter was settled out of court. Separately, Mirzan had also settled out of court the previous January with two Malaysian dailies in relation to allegedly defamatory comments they had published.

Later that year, the CEO of a listed Malaysian company claimed that he was defamed by his own company and two of its other managers when they proposed, without giving reasons, that he should be removed from his position. He claimed that the inference was that he had done something wrong. He claimed he had not and sought M$60 million for the alleged damage to his reputation.

Two Malaysian companies commenced proceedings against an *Asian Wall Street Journal* reporter in Malaysia around the same time for comments attributed to him but which he claimed he never made. The damages sought were M$40 million. In February 2001, Malaysia's largest private television station was ordered by a judge to pay M$100 million in damages to a little heard of local businessman. And later that year another Malaysian businessman filed suits against nine local newspapers claiming a total of M$1.3 billion in damages for their remarks about his business methods.

Outside Malaysia, Asia's businesspeople might be quick to threaten litigation for defamation or libel but rarely do they follow through, even in Singapore. The intention is more to threaten and discourage further exposure of their affairs. Many in Asian business do not appreciate that with defamation proceedings comes the process of discovery, whereby the court can compel the plaintiff to table all sorts of documents relating to their private business affairs, thus exposing them to even more scrutiny. The threat of discovery is one means of heading off defamation threats from proceeding to court.

Some reminders on entering markets where the law is poor

- Insist on a contract or similar document regardless of where in Asia you intend to operate. Contracts are necessary but not sufficient in markets where the law is poor. They become one of the modes of self-defence rather than the only mode in such countries.

- Make sure that contracts are written in plain language. English is the second, not the first, language for most people in Asia, so if they are to be presented with contracts in English, it is far better that they are not loaded with archaic terms such as "herewith" and "thereupon."

- The parties need to sit down and discuss proposed contracts clause by clause so that each clause is fully understood and individually agreed upon.

- Contracts in Asia are likely to be better received if they are not heavy on penalties for this or that breach.

- Offer to pay the legal bill to ensure that you can choose the legal team that will draw up contracts and other legal documents.

- Arbitration is the most usual and preferred means of solving commercial disputes in Asia. Outside parties need to understand local arbitration mechanisms before they enter into contracts of any substance in Asia.

- Bankruptcy is still not a viable option in much of Asia for creditors attempting to recover debts. Creditors need to prepare for often drawn out, negotiated debt work-outs.

Notes

1   *International Herald Tribune*, "Why capitalism works in the West but not elsewhere," De Soto, H., 5 January, 2001.
2   World Bank, "Bankruptcy around the world: Explanations of its relative use," background paper, 2001.
3   *Asian Wall Street Journal*, "Asia banking-reform efforts losing steam, bankers warn," 11 September, 2001.

Strategy 26

Intellectual Property Abuse: Contain the Risks

WHAT'S IN THIS CHAPTER?

▷ The Problems you will Face
▷ What is TRIPS?
▷ Which Countries are the Worst Offenders?
▷ What to Do?
  Legal
  Lobbying
  Help the Agencies and Pay for Investigators
  Reduce the Incentive Gap
  Staff
  Technical Solutions
▷ Some Things to Consider before Setting up in Asia

The Problems you will Face

A visit to Beijing's Bar Street, the city's famous nightlife area, demonstrates clearly what copyright enforcement officials are up against. Pirated CDs and DVDs are widely available in the area but not from shops or even from street stalls. Instead, passers-by are invited to step inside bars where hawkers carry bags full of pirated music and movies. It's discreet and the vendors are highly mobile. Walk along The Bund in Shanghai and the problem is the same, only this time, every vendor seems to sell not pirated movies but fake Rolex watches.

Pirated music and movies are a massive problem across Asia. Another big offender has been Malaysia. Hundreds of copies of the British group Coldplay's latest album were selling in Malaysia less than a week after its late 2005 release in London. The only problem was that it hadn't yet been released in Asia. Malaysia's copyright pirates had been at it again. Well resourced and highly technically proficient, they are among the best in the world when it comes to illegally replicating CDs, VCDs and DVDs, whether for films, music or software. Stalls in Kuala Lumpur's Chinatown night market routinely displayed copies of the week's US Billboard Top Ten, and the films – all illegal copies on VCD priced at only US$1.50 each – were available for purchase.

Films were sometimes available in Malaysia before they had even been released – anywhere. Preview screenings might be held in the US and someone might go along with a concealed digital camera and film the movie as it was screened. The recording was then emailed to Malaysia and replicated over and over for sale the next day. Sometimes the Malaysian versions even showed people's heads popping up as they head out to the toilets or to buy popcorn during the illegally filmed screening!

Occasionally there's a police crackdown, such as in 2003. Suddenly, the supply of pirated movies and music dried up in Malaysia's night markets. At last, enforcement officials were serious about enforcing their own laws. But the enforcement was selective. Louis Vuitton and Gucci handbag rip-offs still abound in Kuala Lumpur's Chinatown as do fake designer perfumes, sunglasses, T-shirts and wallets. The situation returned more or less to normal after several months, but instead of being cased in hard plastic, pirated CDs and DVDs are now sold in cellophane wraps so that they take up less bulk and are more easily concealed should the police come.

One little-realized driver of the demand for pirated movies in countries like Malaysia, is government censorship. Scenes that feature intimacy or bad language, and subjects that touch on religious matters in a way deemed to be socially detrimental are doctored or cut before being aired or formally distributed in Malaysia. Watching pirated movies is one way to circumvent this. The movie *Babe,* for example, was banned outright in Malaysia. But many Malaysians have seen it because pirated versions were sold freely in the country's night markets. Mel Gibson's *The Passion of the Christ* too was banned from general release on account of Jesus being a prophet in Islam and the depiction of prophets is contrary to Islam (Jesus is known to Muslims as Isa). But again thanks to Malaysia's night markets, many Malaysians saw the movie before many Americans did.

Movies like *Kill Bill*, with heavy language and violence, are similarly censored and occasionally banned. What this means is that the film industry's claims that viewers of pirated movies are watching an inferior product are wrong. Often, the pirated version is the complete product and so, in this regard, is superior.

But IPR abuse is not restricted to manufactured and audio-visual goods. Services too are targeted. Around 1997, a "Dome" coffee shop first opened in Jakarta's upmarket Pasa Raya shopping complex. The concept, the name and the interior all looked like a Dome coffee shop, the Australian-based chain that now has dozens of outlets in Singapore, Malaysia, the Middle East and Australia. But the first official Dome coffee shop did not open in Jakarta until 2000, at least three years after the first "Dome" appeared. In the meantime, Dome's management found there was little it could do about the copycat Dome.

Patents, copyrights and trademarks are all at risk in Asia. Patents are legal, scientific documents that disclose the technology associated with an invention and award exclusive rights over a period of time to the inventor or registrar of the invention in order to exploit the technology or license others to exploit it.[1] They are granted to the first to invent in the US and to the first to file for the patent in much of the rest of the world, subject to tests of utility, non-obviousness and novelty. Patents expire after a specified period and they confer monopoly rights on the holders for that period. Copyrights are similar but apply in respect of certain creative endeavors such as film making, music and writing.

Trademarks differ in that they endure indefinitely, subject to recurrent registration. They offer the developers of brand names, logos and geographic indications protection against infringements by others.

Violations of IPR are not unique to Asia. Counterfeit Calvin Klein underwear can be bought in many street markets in London. Nigerian migrants selling fake designer handbags beset Europe from Italy to France. Full IPR have not always been recognized even in the US. Alexander Hamilton, the first treasury secretary of the US, established a copyright system for authors but only if they were American. The intended consequence was that foreign authors – largely British authors – could have their works copied endlessly in the US without them receiving any royalty payments whatsoever.

What makes Asia unique today is perhaps the degree to which IPR are disregarded generally. The idea that intangibles such as ideas and designs should be paid for is a very new concept in Asia, particularly in China. "Why should I pay for something if I can get it for free?" is a common question and one that is difficult to answer in the Asian cultural context. Traditional Asian entrepreneurship is about trading – which means low margins and high volumes. Voluntarily lining up to make payments that will go to a faceless creator somewhere and will chip away at margins that might already be wafer-thin simply beggars belief among the old school. Paying for services comes unnaturally but to pay for something as intangible as an idea is beyond comprehension. So in Asia, IPR violation comes from a mixture of wilful intent and simple bewilderment at the laws. Legislators have trouble getting compliance to laws anywhere if those laws are seen to be ill-founded and illegitimate. So the size of the challenge is clear, given the cultural context and Asia's variable legal systems.

Estimated levels of software piracy are higher in Asia than anywhere. One survey found that Vietnam was the worst offender in 2000 in terms of pirated software in use as a proportion of the total. An estimated 97 percent of all software in use was believed to be pirated. The figure for China was 94 percent, in Indonesia 89 percent, in Pakistan 83 percent and in Thailand 79 percent. Even in rule-bound Singapore, half of all software in use was believed to be pirated, placing Singapore considerably above the estimated world average of 37 percent. The figure for Japan was 37 percent, right on the estimated world average. But given the size of Japan's economy, this means that, in dollar terms, the loss to software manufacturers from software piracy in Asia is highest in Japan – about US$1.7 billion annually, according to industry estimates.[2] Figures such as these suggest not only that laws for the protection of software are practically unenforceable but that there is a general consensus that breaking them is quite acceptable.

Microsoft did win a rare victory in 2001 in a Jakarta court when a local computer vendor, who had installed pirated versions of Windows and other software, was ordered to pay US$4.4 million in compensation and take out newspaper advertisements apologizing to the company. The company had argued that Indonesians were "too poor" to pay Microsoft's full retail price. No doubt it was a pyrrhic victory for Microsoft, as enforcing such decisions is another battle.

Books too are copied mercilessly around Asia. High-margin trade and technical books are routinely copied in Korea and Taiwan to the point that the copies sometimes look better than the originals. Even governments are not immune. In 1995, Australia's embassy in Hanoi found that photocopies of the *Vietnam Country Economic Brief*, a summary of Vietnam's economy produced by the Australian Department of Foreign Affairs and Trade and supposed to be available only to Australian businesses, were being sold on street corners in Hanoi to anyone prepared to pay. Similarly, pirated versions of the Chinese government's own anti-corruption propaganda film *Life and Death Choice* were widely available around China throughout 2000.

Harry Potter or *Ha-li Bo-te* as he's known in China is hugely popular there as elsewhere. Cheap, authorized local editions sell in their millions. J.K. Rawling's *Harry Potter and the Half Blood Prince* was released worldwide in July 2005. How long did it take for China's copyright infringers to translate the enormous work into Chinese, print it, bind it and have it for sale on China's streets? Less than two weeks after the English language version of the book was published in the West.

Manufacturers sometimes circumvent copyright laws, rather than breaking them outright, by slightly modifying existing brands. And it is not only American and European brand names that are targeted for such mimicry. Executives from Hitachi of Japan once traveled to Jakarta to find that their local competition included electronic goods branded "Hitachin" and "Mitachi." There's the Crocodile brand of polo shirts sold across Asia with a crocodile logo embroidered over the left breast, which look suspiciously like Lacoste polo shirts from France. A book called *Malaysian Eclipse* was published by several Malaysian academics in 2001. Not only was the name remarkably similar to the book, *Asian Eclipse*, published two years earlier by one of the authors of *Big in Asia*, but so too was its cover, which featured a darkened visage of the world on a black background with yellow and white writing. Mimicry as opposed to outright copying makes the application of IP laws just that little bit more difficult.

Industrialized countries account for about 97 percent of patents worldwide. Around half of all royalty payments made in the world for patents are channeled to patent holders in the US. It is therefore not surprising that there is a huge domestic lobby in the US urging protection for IPR. Japanese manufacturers of course are a big target for IPR abuses in Asia. The Japanese Patents Office is an important source of funding for the APEC-sponsored Asia-Pacific Industrial Property Center, which trains delegates from APEC member countries on IP protection. But as Asia outside Japan develops its own brands, the problem of counterfeiting and other IPR abuses will be felt more there too and slowly lobbies in Asia will arise that will themselves demand better protection. In China, perhaps 40 percent of all tobacco products sold are counterfeit, but the crime hurts not so much Western brands as the makers of China's most popular local brand, Hongtashan (Red Pagoda) cigarettes.

What is TRIPS?

Western countries and particularly the US have invested huge resources into pressuring other countries to better protect intellectual property. The means for doing this now is TRIPS, the Agreement on Trade-Related Aspects of Intellectual Property Rights. It is administered by the WTO and was an outcome of the Uruguay Round of trade negotiations concluded in 1994, the same round that led to the WTO being established. Developed countries were required to comply with TRIPS by 1996, developing countries by the beginning of 2000, and those with least developed status by 2005.

Under TRIPS, all countries must commit themselves to a uniform set of intellectual property protection rules or face retribution from other countries, most particularly the US and the EU for non-cooperation and non-compliance. Retribution is largely in the form of trade sanctions.

WTO member countries must establish judicial channels to protect IPR and enforce effective deterrent penalties against violators. TRIPS also creates a harmonized global system under which inventors are granted patents for a minimum of 20 years. The logic of establishing property rights in this area is clear but the 20-year figure is arbitrary, other than it was the period in use in the US, the prime mover of TRIPS.

Regimes for intellectual property protection were enormously diverse across Asia 10 or 20 years ago due to differing histories and legal systems, but international pressure for better laws has seen a flurry of legal reform in the area so that intellectual property protection laws across Asia are now more consistent than ever before. Many are now signatories to TRIPS. This means that now more than ever a uniform approach can be taken by companies to protect their patents, trademarks and copyrights in Asia.

Which Countries are the Worst Offenders?

What are the most typical abuses of intellectual property in Asia? And in which countries? The following list has been developed from information supplied by the Office of the US Trade Representative.

- *China*
  Intellectual property protection laws commenced in 1982 with the passing of the Trademark Law. Other similar laws have been passed since. In combination they are sufficient to protect IP. Also, there is

genuine concern at the top levels in China for greater IP protection and China's courts have issued some significant decisions in the area. But the problem is enforcement, which varies across China's regions and is hampered by a lack of transparency in procedures, poor coordination between police and government agencies, penalties that are too low and the all too rare filing of criminal actions.

Trademark counterfeiting and the large-scale manufacture of fake goods from designer sunglasses to shampoos to pharmaceuticals is widespread, as is the unauthorized production and sale of copyrighted products. Foreign books are commonly pirated. Pirated movies have become so common that it has become almost impossible to sell legitimate versions in many parts of China. The film *Titanic* did sell 300,000 legitimate copies in China, although it is estimated that another 20–25 million pirated copies were also sold.

China is also an important manufacturer of clothing and footwear for leading US and European fashion houses, but factories licensed to make the goods sometimes overproduce and secretly sell the overruns in the same markets in which the licensed goods themselves are sold. In this case the goods are not counterfeit, making detection even more difficult.

China is a major exporter of pirated goods, particularly to Hong Kong but also to lesser markets in the region such as Myanmar. Smugglers use large, custom-made, fully submersible containers that they pack with pirated goods. These are then dragged by ships along the bottom of Hong Kong harbor to avoid detection. The containers are landed at night, emptied and usually dumped where they are landed.

- *India*
  Copyright legislation is a good standard in India but inadequately enforced and so piracy of films, music, software, books and video games is rampant. India's patent system is not compliant with its TRIPS' obligations. Patents are difficult to obtain because of a large backlog of applications (30,000 patent applications were pending in mid-2001), too few patent examiners and opposition procedures to the granting of patents (usually launched by competitors) are overly generous. All this can conspire to delay patent registration until the patent period has actually expired. The term for patent protection for pharmaceutical processes is seven years, compared with the 20 years demanded by TRIPS. Patent protection is not available for pharmaceuticals and agricultural chemical products. Fake goods abound – it is

said that more Johnny Walker Black Label whisky is sold in India alone each year than is ever produced in Scotland.

■ *Indonesia*

Copyrighted and trademarked goods are pirated across Indonesia with more vigor than perhaps anywhere else. Everything from blue jeans to TVs to cigarettes is pirated, and done so with such brazenness that it would appear that, from manufacturers to distributors to retailers, some of the operators in the chain do not even realize that laws are being broken.

Industry estimates that piracy levels for music and business software are 87 percent, 90 percent for all forms of motion pictures sold and 99 percent for games software.[3] These are among the highest figures in the world.

■ *Korea*

There is widespread piracy of trade and educational books in Korea. IP laws are not fully TRIPS consistent, and some are so vaguely worded as to make it difficult to determine if they are TRIPS consistent. The quality of pirated goods is sometimes superior to the originals.

■ *Macau*

Convictions for IP infringements have been few and when they do happen, the penalties levied have been light. Many of the counterfeit goods sold in Macau come from China.

■ *Malaysia*

Copyright infringements in Malaysia are substantial, particularly with regard to films, music and software. Although a crackdown in 2003 was temporarily effective, pirated DVDs soon returned to the streets. Trademark violations in respect of clothing, footwear, watches and perfumes remain common. Numerous raids have been launched by police and copying equipment confiscated but there have been few prosecutions. The growing intensity of raids in recent years is pushing some of the piracy industry offshore, particularly to neighboring Indonesia. Not only have pirate DCDs been available widely in Malaysia but films are frequently screened without authorization in public, such as on long-distance public buses. To add insult to injury, the versions screened are themselves usually pirated. Malaysia is also a regional center for credit card cloning and fraud – not because its residents are any more devious than those elsewhere in the region but once again because of the degree of technical sophistication in that country.

- *Pakistan*
  All manner of goods are pirated in Pakistan from books to CDs and these flood the domestic market and are exported to neighboring countries such as Afghanistan and India. Court proceedings are delayed and non-deterrent fines hamper the effectiveness of IP protection.

- *Philippines*
  Copyright enforcement is weak and piracy of textbooks and other trade books is rampant in the Philippines. The production of pirated films has increased in recent years. Judicial procedures for IP violations, like judicial procedures generally, are slow to the point of being glacial, and cases can drag on for years.

- *Taiwan*
  Taiwan is one of the largest pirated optical media producers in the world and production capacity is thought to outstrip local demand, suggesting that Taiwan is an important exporter of pirated films. Enforcement is sporadic, prosecutions rare and legislation patchy. Taiwan's manufacturing sector largely comprises tens of thousands of small, dynamic, family-owned and managed companies, which makes monitoring and enforcement difficult.

- *Thailand*
  IP violations, although common, are not as great as might be expected in Thailand. Trademark abuses are common as are pirated films and software. Legislation is relatively good and has improved considerably in recent years but as usual it is enforcement that is the problem. Pirated goods are visible on the streets in important commercial centers such as Bangkok and Hat Yai but in lesser quantities than in Kuala Lumpur, Jakarta and Guangzhou. Foreign business representatives enjoy a good working relationship with Thai IP enforcement agencies, although the degree to which property rights are enforced varies with whichever government minister is in charge of anti-piracy policy. Frequent ministerial reshuffles have meant frequent changes in policy emphasis.

  Pantip Plaza is the most notorious location in Bangkok for obtaining pirated VCDs, DVDs and CDs. Buyers choose from empty CD jackets from any of the Plaza's dozens of fixed shops. A runner returns 10 minutes later from a hidden location bearing the ordered goods.

- *Vietnam*
  Both protective laws and enforcement are weak in Vietnam when it comes to IPR. Trademark abuse is rampant and the country abounds with pirated goods of all types.

What to Do?

Violations against IPR can be combatted in the following ways:

- Effective laws must be in place and they must contain sufficient deterrent provisions
- The laws must be enforced – enforcing agencies must be well resourced
- Courts must be prepared to impose deterrent sentencing
- There must be the political will to protect IPR
- Police and judicial corruption needs to be minimal
- The system of protecting IPR must also have legitimacy. Patents and copyright protection that can be portrayed as "unfair," for example the registering of patents for Asian food crops such as strains of jasmine rice have elicited government protests from Thailand. They serve to undermine the whole IPR system and legitimize violations.

But what can companies do to protect themselves against IPR violations? The London-based BAT now says that its real competitor in the world marketplace is not America's Philip Morris but counterfeit cigarettes and other tobacco products. It estimates that around 30 percent of all tobacco products sold in the world today are counterfeit. And what is BAT doing to combat this onslaught and protect its many trademarks? It is urging governments to enforce penalties against counterfeiters and passing on information about counterfeiters to the relevant agencies. Beyond that, it is at a loss as to what to do. Most other multinationals are in the same position.

The powerlessness of even big companies effectively to combat IP infringements was summed up by a "Leaders' Meeting" of senior officers of some of the world's biggest companies in February 2002 in New York. Present were the CEOs, chairmen or similar of BAT, Gillette, GSK, Henkel, Nestlé, Pentland, P&G, Richemont, SC Johnson and Unilever. Johnson & Johnson, Microsoft, AOL Time Warner, Diageo and Compaq sent observers. The group met again in London a few months later. To

date, little has come from the meetings apart from general agreement that
no one has yet come up with an adequate solution to the problem of IP
theft. One of the resolutions of the initial meeting was that those present
needed to "embrace the interests of brand-owning companies from
developing countries" to help build coalitions against IP theft in those
countries. A decision to establish a task force to look at the problem
served to highlight just how impotent companies are when it comes to
this problem.

The intangible nature of IPR makes violations difficult to combat,
especially in countries where legal systems – both the laws and their
enforcement – is poor. This calls for a multi-pronged approach.
Companies should also devise a plan to combat IP violations of their products from the time they set up in Asia. What avenues for redress are there?

Legal

Legal remedies are an obvious measure, particularly in Singapore, Hong
Kong, Japan and Malaysia. But in many parts of Asia, while seeking
legal recourse should still be attempted, if for no other reason than to
signal a determination to assert IPR, little real benefit might eventuate.
Also, legal action can drag on for years, especially in the Philippines,
India and Pakistan. Interim orders to cease and desist may not be given
or enforced. So, while the legal processes are worked through, the trademark, copyright or patent violations might continue unabated. Nonetheless, laws in this area have improved greatly in Asia with the advent of
the WTO and TRIPS, and violators have been brought before the courts
in many countries.

Lobbying

US companies can complain to the local US chamber of commerce, which
will make representations on their behalf to the host government and the
relevant IP enforcement agency. Representations can also be made by
companies directly to politicians and the relevant local commerce
ministry. Written and oral briefings can also be made to the commercial
section of the relevant embassy or high commission, if the aggrieved
company is foreign. Such companies should also enlist government
support at home to have serious IP breaches brought via TRIPS mechanisms to the WTO, if combative measures prove ineffective locally.

Help the Agencies and Pay for Investigators

Perhaps the biggest problem in the area of IPR enforcement in Asia is that those agencies charged with enforcement are not unwilling to act but are underresourced. When provided with evidence of violations and information on where and when violators can be apprehended, they will act. Accordingly, some larger American and European companies have banded together to hire local investigators to assemble the necessary information. Production facilities have been identified and evidence collected. The authorities are then tipped off and representatives of the US and European companies have accompanied them on their raids to ensure that the desired arrests are made and the replicating equipment is confiscated. It is an expensive business, but it has led to police raids in China, Thailand, Malaysia and the Philippines.

Reduce the Incentive Gap

A new release music CD that goes on sale at London's HMV Records in Oxford Street for £16.49 (US$29.00) sells for the equivalent of RM8 (US$2.16) in the night markets of Kuala Lumpur (the prices of pirated CDs and VCDs at Kuala Lumpur's street markets are surprisingly uniform). A similar legal copy in Malaysia sells for around RM46 (US$12.40).

One way to reduce IPR violations is to reduce the incentive for it. Prices for legitimate products could be reduced so that the difference between the price of legitimate and pirated copies is reduced. Such action should reduce but will not eliminate the incentive for counterfeiting. International record companies tried this in Malaysia in 2001. It was accompanied by a police crackdown on vendors selling pirated CDs and the taking effect of the Optical Disc Act 2000, which allowed for greater penalties, including jail terms, for producers and exporters of pirated films. Two things happened. The number of street vendors selling pirated CDs and VCDs fell noticeably, and the price of a pirated CD fell from RM10 (US$2.70) to RM8 (US$2.16). The pirates dropped their prices to maintain their competitiveness. Producing pirated CDs in Malaysia was no longer as profitable as it had been.

Another incentive gap relates to time. For example, films released in January in North America might not be officially released in China and elsewhere in Asia until the following September, yet the media hype for the US release spills over to Asia where consumers might well purchase pirated versions simply to see what all the fuss is about overseas. Timing the release of new products in Asia with releases elsewhere is one obvious measure to help to make the pirated products less attractive.

One final consideration is that the quality of pirated goods may be superior to the licensed product. This means that if consumers are to stick with buying the licensed good, not only must they pay more but also buy an inferior product. This is asking a lot of consumers. Pirated textbooks in Korea, for example, are sometimes printed on better quality paper than the originals (which can lead potential buyers to believe that it is the legitimate copies that are pirated), or Malaysian pirates will add maybe six bonus tracks to a new release CD from the artist's previous recordings that are not present on the original new release.

Staff

Commercial in-confidence information is often lost in Asia, as elsewhere, via companies' own employees. Disgruntled staff are a prime cause of sensitive information leaking from a company. But so too are lowly paid staff who may be susceptible to monetary overtures from competitors to leak confidential information. Here are some things to consider:

- Where are the loyalties of the local staff – to the company, the state, or friends and relatives who work with competitors?
- How would local staff react to offers of bribes to copy documents and pass them on? (Keep in mind that many companies which undertake due diligence work in countries such as China actually source information about companies by bribing their staff to hand over copies of documents.)
- Have non-disclosure agreements been signed with local joint venture partners?
- Is it possible to limit the circulation of proprietary information to local employees on a need-to-know basis?
- Local vendors and subcontractors can be another problem. Have due diligence checks been carried out on them? Do they also work for or supply competitors? Have they signed confidentiality agreements?
- Should data be encrypted when it is transmitted between factories and between factories and the country head office?
- What procedures are in place for staff terminations to ensure that data security is not compromised?

- Is it worth having offices, executive residences and boardrooms swept regularly for bugging devices? Most Western embassies in Asia have at least one room that is routinely swept and is isolated from local staff and cleaning contractors to render it "safe" for confidential discussions. Is it worth establishing a similar "safe room" on the company's premises?

Technical Solutions

Some manufacturers have taken to adding technically difficult design features to their products such as holograms and watermarks. These are useful in some circumstances but might be ineffective when consumers are indifferent to the problems of pirated and legitimate goods – consumers after all, often know that they are buying counterfeit goods. Hitachi of Japan has created what it calls flexible mu-chips – small microchips which can be embedded in items such as clothing labels to help with tracking and anti-counterfeiting measures. But again, innovations such as these are ineffectual in the context of a poorly enforced legal environment.

Some Things to Consider Before Setting up in Asia

- Do you have industrial processes or products that are at risk of IP violations?
- If your industrial processes are at risk, might it be better to manufacture elsewhere – in environments where there are more guarantees for IP safety?
- Are there technical processes that can be used to make your products more difficult to copy?
- How are your competitors dealing with violations of their IP?
- What legal protection is offered in the countries of your choice and are they TRIPS consistent?
- What judicial protection is there and can judicial decisions be enforced?
- What is the most relevant IP protection agency for your particular products? Are its officers amenable to cooperation? Are they aware of the nature of the potential violations of your particular intellectual property rights?

Notes

1   These definitions follow those used by Cheah, H.B., "Monopoly rights and wrongs: Two forms of intellectual property rights violations in Asia" in Kidd, J.B. and Richter, F.J. (eds) *Corruption in Asia*, World Scientific Press, Singapore, 2002.
2   Ibid.
3   Office of the United States Trade Representative, "USTR Special 301 Report," 2001: and *Asian Wall Street Journal*, "Asian-Pacific region takes lead in purchases of pirated software," 23 May, 2001.

Strategy 27

Ethical Traps on the Road to Being Big in Asia

WHAT'S IN THIS CHAPTER?

▷ A Rock and a Hard Place
▷ Environmental Enemies
   New Rules?
▷ Ethics at Work
   Gambling
   Safety First?
   Gas Leaks
▷ Sweated Labor
▷ Socially Responsible Investment (SRI)

A Rock and a Hard Place

Asia has generally had a bad press when it comes to ethical issues; corruption, counterfeiting, IPR and so on have all been well publicized. In these cases, Western firms generally class themselves as the victims. But there is another set of ethical issues where they themselves run the risk of being seen as the guilty parties, and these concern their responsibility for the damage to the natural and human resources of the region.

In recent years, many foreign firms have faced unwelcome publicity brought by Western or local pressure groups and NGOs (non-governmental organizations) over issues including the use of "sweated" labor, environmental damage from mining or logging activities, or from investing in other projects considered environmentally unsound. Schemes such as China's massive Three Gorges project faced scrutiny and several Western firms have been forced to pull out by pressure groups protesting at the displacement of up to two million people that it will cause. Investment in Myanmar with its poor human and labor rights record is another perennial target for criticism.

The senior management of Western companies involved in scandals have often claimed to be unaware that the factories producing their goods were in effect sweatshops, or that illegal logging was taking place in their forest concessions, unaware, that is, until they opened their local newspaper or saw a headline in *Business Week* pillorying them for unethical behavior. More recently, Western companies have tried to protect themselves by contributing to organizations investigating working conditions, only to find that this too has failed to save them from attack, not just in their home countries but in Asia as well. Frequently, they are caught between powerful Western lobbies and increasingly vocal local critics and organizations in the countries where they are operating. Doomsday forecasts have increased awareness in the region about the scale of the problem. An Asian Development Bank report has warned that Asia is on the "brink of environmental catastrophe" and that "environmental degradation in the region is pervasive, accelerating and unabated."[1]

For any company accused of unethical behavior, the consequences can be highly damaging, not only financially but, more crucially, in terms of the company's reputation. The growth of the Internet means that allegations and evidence can be made available the world over cheaply and quickly. Protestations of innocence can appear flimsy against the power of emotive statements and petitions. And such accusations tend to linger in the collective memory for a long time, as Nestlé and Shell have discovered to their cost.

This chapter examines some of the most frequent ethical traps which companies risk falling into in Asia, and the choices open to them if the worst happens and they wake up to find themselves public enemy number one.

Environmental Enemies

Using the region's natural resources, whether it is prospecting for oil, mining coal or metals, or logging timber, can be a very risky business. Western firms dealing in certain industries – timber, paper, or furniture making – are open to accusations of environmental abuse, even in countries where, until recently, the emphasis on sustainable resources was not a government priority. But forewarned is forearmed, and the only real weapon for such companies is to prepare carefully for any attack that might come and have all the necessary evidence ready to refute any charge of poor practice or damage to the environment as soon as it occurs. After that, the only remaining alternative is withdrawal.

This worked in the case of the UK group, Inchcape plc, which was in the middle of a media exercise to reposition the company as a focused, international marketing and services company, when it woke up to a huge spread in the UK's *Sunday Times* taking it to task for poor management of its logging activities in Borneo.[2] The newspaper's "Insight" investigative team had produced an emotive article entitled "Log 'em and leave 'em." It was potentially highly damaging to Inchcape's prospects for a successful relaunch. However, its corporate affairs department was very quick off the mark and able to refute fully all the accusations. This worked as a short-term measure but the company knew that this particular business, although profitable, would always be a potential source of trouble, and so finally took the decision to sell it off.

Companies in other environmentally sensitive businesses have come to the same conclusion, faced with the unrelenting attacks of pressure groups. For example, the energy firm Cogentrix set up in Mangalore, a region of India deemed of environmental concern. After eight years of negotiation, three revisions of its power purchase agreement and an investment of US$27 million, its power project had still not got off the ground, but remained blocked in the courts by environmentalist suits. Cogentrix decided to withdraw.

One company that is perennially accused of various transgressions in its operations in Asia is the US company, Freeport-McMoRan Copper & Gold Inc. Since it began mining operations in Indonesia's Irian Jaya Province in 1973, it has been accused of causing massive destruction to one of the world's richest and least explored environments. In May 2000, not for the first time, the government threatened to suspend its operations after a rock-waste storage facility collapsed, causing flooding and leaving four workers dead. Under intense pressure, Freeport has spent US$40 million annually on environmental monitoring and funded a comprehensive survey of the region's biological diversity and richness. In 2005, it joined a corporate monitoring program overseen by the Indonesian environment ministry.

None of these actions lessened the pressure on Freeport. In February 2006, the Indonesian environment minister threatened to take legal action against the company if it did not improve practices at its Grasberg mine in Irian Jaya.[3] A report indicated that mining waste from Freeport was causing pollution there, allegations the company has always denied. Freeport was also under intense pressure from campaigners, shareholders and politicians in both Indonesia and the US over allegations that it made millions of dollars worth of payments to the Indonesian military guarding the mine.

The company is likely to remain a target for environmental activists and NGOs for the foreseeable future and, if Indonesia continues to take a tougher line, could find itself caught up in a long drawn out legal and environmental battle. This what happened to the US gold-mining firm Newmont, accused by the Indonesian government of causing pollution near its mines in Sulawesi. In 2004, the government filed a civil suit against the company, and the case dragged on through the courts until a partial resolution was reached in February 2006. In a "goodwill agreement," Newmont agreed to pay Indonesia US$30 million over the next 10 years to fund community development projects and scientific monitoring around the site of the mine, now shut.[4]

New Rules?

Under pressure, Asian governments are slowly tightening the rules relating to forest management and downstream emissions. Indonesia, for example, has trialled open tendering for forestry concessions that in the past were handed out on the basis of cronyism, corruption and nepotism. Many concession holders were responsible for driving out indigenous people and using slash and burn techniques, which destroyed valuable forests and eventually led to the forest fires that engulfed much of Southeast Asia in choking smog during 1997. Theoretically, there will be more rigorous checks on the expertise of companies granted the concessions, who will also be required to share profits with the local community and grant part of the land to a local village cooperative. There are also proposals for a certification process such as the one operated by the Forest Stewardship Council, an international environmental organization that certifies wood products.

Such moves may give Western companies, with their better developed environmental systems, more of a chance to enter these industries. However, despite the growing awareness, enforcement will probably continue to be lax and left to local governments, making it easy for local companies to flout the rules. A January 2003 report on Indonesia by the Anglo-American environmental group, the Environmental Investigation Agency (EIA) concluded that "the processes under way to tackle illegal logging" had "very little chance of success," hampered as they were by rampant corruption.[5] In 2005, another EIA report alleged that US$600 million worth of timber was being smuggled from Indonesia into China each month – with the active help of the army and the police.[6] The EIA also monitored the laundering of timber from Indonesia to China via Malaysia, which led the Malaysian government to try and stop the export loopholes and prompted another campaign, Operational Sustainable Forest.

Some Indonesian firms are trying to act responsibly by using barcodes stapled to either end of the logs they sell, to show that they are legally and sustainably harvested. But as long as the Indonesian army, police and officials are implicated in illegal logging and the courts remain weak, there is little hope of stopping a practice that leaves Indonesia losing an area of forest the size of Switzerland every year. Another huge obstacle to progress is China, the biggest importer of illegal logs. Its appetite for ever increasing quantities of timber from the region looks like remaining undiminished, and is drawing in not just Indonesia but also Myanmar, which is plundering its own forests with the connivance of the Burmese military.

Western firms such as IKEA, Carrefour, Axel Springer Verlag and trade associations such as the UK Timber Trade Association and the American Forest and Paper Association all have policies stating that they will not purchase illegally cut wood. But given the context described above, any Western firm entering this arena should remain extremely vigilant – if their own lobbies don't catch them, the locals probably will. And there will be a high price to pay.

Ethics at Work

Gambling

One little-reported issue that Western managers often face in the betting-mad Chinese environment is that of gambling on work sites: do they try to stop it or turn a blind eye? One expatriate in Thailand was informed by one of his supervisors that an illegal lottery was being run on the factory site. He decided to ignore it after further investigation revealed that the supervisor was only motivated to complain because the lottery was affecting the takings from his own gambling activities. Companies can choose either to ignore or prohibit it – either way, it is worth having a policy on gambling before it becomes an issue, so that when a response is required, it is not ad hoc and made on the run.

Safety First?

A more serious issue is that of safety standards, which are rudimentary in many parts of Asia. Most Western managers are appalled by their first experience of safety practices in many parts of Asia, and the total lack of precautions taken by workers clambering up swaying scaffolding or working with electric equipment. One veteran construction manager, sent out from Europe to head a team building a factory in Indonesia, was shocked on his first day on the site to see workers hanging upside down from bamboo scaffolding, wielding blow torches with no sign of goggles, safety hats or shoes. Further on, he saw his foreman hammering in rivets using a home-made hammer, his bare toes curled over the scaffolding as he hung down, hardly able to see where the blows were going. On the ground, barefoot workers – male and female – in jeans and T-shirts worked in deep muddy trenches pulling cables, surrounded by moving machinery and unstable scaffolding.

However, within a few weeks the same manager had become inured to the risks, having realized that when he insisted on safety clothing, it caused more accidents than it prevented. Few of the local workers, for example, wore shoes habitually and so were used to clinging on barefoot. They found the heavy safety boots a hindrance that made them clumsy and more likely to fall, apart from the fact that finding the right size to fit their slender feet was a big problem. The same was true of the hard hats he gave out, which they usually left at home, along with the shoes, for their children to play with. They found the masks uncomfortable in the hot and humid weather but the goggles were accepted, although, again, size was often a problem and workers complained that they caused headaches. "It's amazing," he concluded, "every second guy is doing something wrong but considering the risks, they don't often hurt themselves."

Another manager working in Thailand, spent months organizing safety lectures for his employees, and was gratified one day to see a worker wearing a safety harness as he worked high up on a gantry. His pleasure did not last long, however, as a second later he realized that the harness was not actually attached to anything. He also noted how, when he toured the site, workers would disappear into doorways and then ostentatiously reappear carrying pieces of safety equipment. But rarely did he see them put them on. The Western manager of a chemical plant received a safety report that noted happily how "Nobody was smoking on site, and almost all personnel were wearing hard hats." Fire drills, he discovered, were a novelty that caused much merriment.

In fact, most Western firms try to put safety rules and procedures into practice in the plants they run in Asia, aiming to have the same standards throughout their global operations. A key post in any post-merger plan is usually that of safety officer. However, finding a qualified person to fill it can be difficult, if not impossible. One multinational attracted many applicants when it advertised for a safety officer, but none of them actually had any experience or formal qualifications for the job. Usually, the only way to find one is to poach them from another company. Choosing a likely candidate and sending them for training is another option, but it is odds-on that they in turn will soon be poached. One multinational found the ideal safety officer, then lost him two days later when he accepted the same job at another company. The difference was in the job title, the second firm called him the safety manager – albeit on a lower salary.

Currently, safety and labor rights are receiving a great deal of attention in the Western press, and these concerns are spilling over into the Asia-Pacific region. Consumer movements, the media and NGOs are investigating safety standards around the world, and it also tends to be one of the subjects CEOs enjoying writing about in annual reports – statistics about the excellent safety record are always non-controversial and an occasion for self-congratulation. Consequently, many expatriate managers find themselves under greater pressure to impose Western safety standards in their Asian operations. Some companies issue safety charters as part of a corporate-wide drive for better health, safety and environmental standards. These standards are often reinforced by guidelines and local workplace procedures based on best practices. Special pleading on the grounds of different cultural attitudes is no longer accepted. But should safety standards be universal? How far should Westerners impose their standards on other cultures, especially if the result is to cause more accidents, not fewer?

In reality, most experienced managers working in the region concentrate on what is possible, and take a step-by-step approach to inculcate new safety habits. "Safety," observed one, "is a way of life. It's a long-term process of education and training. You can't expect it from people who have never been taught it." Therefore companies might begin by concentrating on maintaining a clean environment on the factory site – no spilt oil, no empty drums rolling round loose, machinery kept clean – these are all important tasks that managers can focus on, leading to an improved safety record. Following up after accidents and putting up notices around the factory with large illustrations showing the effect of bad practices can further reinforce the message. By setting an example and getting their managers to follow them, company heads are more likely to succeed. Once the managers are committed and begin to enforce the rules, then safe behavior may spread to other areas such as the use of safety equipment. Acting in this way and setting aside time to drill and teach basic behaviors is usually far more effective than trying – and failing – to impose strict Western standards.

Gas Leaks

Another perennial threat for those operating in industries involving chemicals is the danger of leaks – gas, chlorine or other toxic substances. The chemicals industry has a high profile in Europe, where pressure groups are quick to demonize any company thought to be neglecting safety issues. Equally, in Asia, leaks are a safety hazard that Western managers must treat seriously on two fronts, the operational and the emotional. Dealing with the source of the problem is likely to be a matter of automatically activated systems but what they must deal with equally promptly is the local media in order to avoid bad publicity. Nobody wants the tag "Another Bhopal" attached to their company name.

One manager found how damaging this issue can be when he received a call from one of his supervisors at the factory site in an industrial park outside Jakarta.[7] He learned that during his absence on a one-day training course in Jakarta, there had been a chlorine leak from one of the chemical storage tanks. The leak was not due to any breakdown, but had been caused by an operator, who had only been with the company a few months, taking a short cut when carrying out a maneuver instead of following procedures. Luckily, the technology installed in the plant had triggered an immediate shutdown and of the 15 tons of chlorine stored on site, only one kilo escaped. According to the supervisor, this low concentration meant that there was no danger to any personnel on site, and everyone present had been accounted for.

His next decision turned out to be vital; should he return to the site at once, or rely on his professional, qualified staff as he would in, for example, Europe? In the end, the manager stayed put, but he had forgotten one vital cultural trait that might have made him change his mind. In Indonesia, as elsewhere in Southeast Asia, nobody likes to make their superior feel uncomfortable by reporting bad news. How bad was the spill really? Had all the bad news been reported and had it been reported accurately? It turned out that the real problem was not the leak itself but the perception of it by the local media. As is often forgotten in Asia, the crisis had two elements – the physical one and the PR element. The former was adequately dealt with, whereas the local media greatly exaggerated the leak and its effects, in what had been, in reality, a minor episode. The lesson is clear; whatever the incident, however apparently innocuous the emission, be on the spot to give your interpretation and, above all, to show concern for the community as a responsible investor.

Sweated Labor

Perhaps one of the greatest public relations disasters that can befall a Western company in Asia is to be accused of breaking a country's labor laws, using sweated labor or, worst of all, employing child labor via the contractors and suppliers that work for you. On the eve of the World Cup in May 2006, Oxfam reported that top sportswear manufacturers making boots for famous players were failing to respect human rights in developing countries. An Indonesian company making boots for David Beckham was said to have fired 30 workers who had gone on strike for better pay.[8] In China, the past decade has seen a stream of damning reports come out concerning conditions in the manufacturing facilities operated by foreign firms there. The effect has been bad publicity for the firms involved, followed by attempts to ameliorate the problem and then, a short while later, the emergence of new reports demonstrating that the changes were only cosmetic, and easily circumvented.

In 1999, for example, the Asian Monitor Resource Center, which monitors working conditions in China, reported that workers making Disney products were being forced to work up to 16 hours a day, seven days a week with almost no overtime pay. A second report on toys named four factories, which were subcontractors to Mattel, the world's largest toy maker, with similar sweatshop conditions.[9] Yet both companies had done a great deal to improve working conditions in their Asian factories and both had codes of conduct; Disney carried out 10,000 inspections. Some observers believed that the allegations were false, either based on unchecked allegations or maybe made by people with a grudge. But this is irrelevant – once the allegation is made, companies know they are in trouble.

IKEA, the Swedish retailing group, was caught out by accusations of using child labor in India, where it sources its carpets. To improve its credentials as a socially responsible citizen, in 2004 the company launched a child labor initiative there in partnership with Unicef. The scheme helps lower caste women get out of debt – usually the main motive for sending their children to work. IKEA also set up "bridge schools" to help children catch up before joining mainstream schools. In the short term, the scheme has proved a more successful tactic than merely setting up a school that remains empty – as many other multinationals have done.

Another approach to changing poor working conditions has been made via the Social Accountability International (SAI), which designs and oversees the SA8000 factory conditions standard. Launched in 1998 by a coalition of US activists and multinationals including Toys R Us, Avon and the food company Dole, the SAI sets standards and appoints inspectors to fight the sweatshop war, especially in China. It limited workers to 48 hours of regular shifts a week, with 12 hours' overtime. Wages had to be adequate to meet basic needs, and the factories were scheduled for inspection twice a year.

Some companies, such as Levi's, have made an ethical stance the core of their company. The company pulled out of China in protest at human rights abuses in the late 1980s and long before other companies, Levi's global sourcing task force created guidelines designed to hold its overseas contractors to the highest possible standards of labor practices. Wal-Mart has been asking its suppliers to sign a code of basic labor standards since 1992, and hired outside auditing firms to inspect supplier factories. Nike, Reebok and Gap have set up similar procedures.

Perhaps the company that has suffered the worst publicity in this context has been Nike, which has subcontractors in 700 factories in 50 countries. There was global coverage of the notorious email asking for "sweatshop" to be printed on the side of one of its running shoes, and a BBC documentary on child labor in Cambodia that showed children hand stitching footballs for Nike. In response, Nike plus Gap and other vulnerable companies set up the Global Alliance for Workers and Communities to report on sweatshop conditions in Indonesia, Vietnam and Thailand. Nike is also a member of a US-based group, the Fair Labor Association, a coalition of clothing and footwear companies such as Levi-Strauss, Adidas-Salomon, Phillips-Van Heusen, Reebok and Liz Claiborne. Founded in 2001, it sends in external monitors to audit factories around the world and publishes detailed tracking charts of progress in improving working conditions. Such transparency is designed to encourage brands to take corrective action when abuses are uncovered. Although much of the emphasis on sweatshops and labor abuses has so far been on the garment and footwear industries, campaigners are now turning their attention to conditions in the IT and electronic industries, which are similarly vulnerable.

Yet despite all these efforts, still the horror stories come out. In China, surveys describe guards beating up workers, illegal deposits to cover food and lodging in the factory dormitory, workers handling toxic glues and solvents without gloves, and factories burning to the ground after an explosion, with the workers still inside. Many suppliers and contractors to Western firms either fail to implement promised reforms, or simply close their factories down, then open them up under new names and go on producing the same goods with the same people.

Almost a decade after the first reports on sweated labor in China, a 2006 study based on a three-year investigation into 100 Chinese export factories producing goods for UK retailers found conditions unimproved, despite inspections and other ploys to enforce change. It described "an army of powerless rural immigrants toiling up to 14 hours a day, almost every day. Many were allowed only one day off, and paid less than £50 a month for shifts that breached international law and International Labor Organization rules." The clothing, toys and electronic goods produced were all on sale in the UK stores, including some with ethical buying policies. Some of the factories had actually passed so-called ethical audits, although this was no surprise, given that factory managers usually knew when they would take place and drilled staff in what to say, at the risk of being fired. One long-time campaigner noted that:

> What has surprised and depressed us since 1998 when we started working in China is that all the efforts of the companies have made little difference to working standards. The response by the Chinese factories is to work out how better to cook the books.[10]

The Chinese authorities themselves acknowledged that 80 percent of private companies frequently violated workers rights.

Perhaps the only sustainable signs of improvement are those linked to labor shortages, which force firms to treat workers better and improve conditions. In April 2006, Shenzen announced plans for a raise of up to 23 percent in the minimum wage, a move that would be copied throughout south China. FIEs in this region are already paying above the minimum wage in order to keep workers.

In most of China, however, the problem will remain unresolved as long as companies can take advantage of a cheap workforce. So Western consumer groups and labor organizations will continue to keep up the pressure and foreign companies will remain vulnerable to accusations of using sweated labor and all the attendant negative effects on their reputation. It is not easy to alter attitudes and practices unless people genuinely want to change, or are convinced that the alternative is more profitable. But, if you are going to continue to earn the high profit margins commensurate with having your products made in low-wage countries, you cannot expect to get away unscathed. Those who play with fire are liable at least to feel some heat.

Socially Responsible Investment (SRI)

The fact that ethical issues are becoming more prominent is demonstrated by the emergence of SRI funds in Asia, which follows the rapid growth of this industry in Europe and North America. In the US, the total size of these funds doubled to US$2.2 trillion in two years, showing that it has become an important issue. Increasingly, companies in the West have begun to realize that they cannot afford to ignore these funds, and this pressure has increased the impetus for maintaining high environmental and safety standards throughout their global operations.

In February 2001, the Association for Sustainable and Responsible Investment in Asia was set up with the backing of a group of mainly Western-based fund management companies. Its aim was to build a regional research base to allow socially responsible funds to be set up. Companies will increasingly be asked questions about their safety records, how they treat potentially dangerous emissions from their plants, how environmentally friendly their products are, where they are made and by whom.

Early in 2002, CalPERS, the Californian pension fund, announced it was pulling out of three Asian markets on mainly ethical grounds. Such moves send a powerful signal.

The same year saw a different but equally strong warning delivered via a landmark case in the US, where a judge ordered the oil giant, Unocal Corp. to stand trial for alleged human rights abuses committed by the Myanmar government, Unocal's partner in the development of a gas field. Exxon-Mobil found itself under similar attack over abuses by Indonesian security forces protecting its natural gas fields in Aceh. Such developments threaten US multinationals with a new and potentially very expensive risk in their foreign operations, and one that may be picked up in other countries.

Myanmar has, of course, long been on the blacklist of countries that ethical investors avoid and the focus of much lobbying over its human rights record. Heineken withdrew as early as 1996 in response to international pressure over human rights, followed by the Danish brewer Carlsberg and Pepsi-Cola. In March 2002, Triumph, the German-owned lingerie firm, joined a long queue of firms pulling out, partly in response to the "Clean Clothes Campaign."

Between 2000 and 2003, over 40 US firms joined a boycott of products from Myanmar, prompted by the US government, which, in September 2003, banned all imports from the country. The last two British firms to withdraw were Premier Oil and BAT, the latter in November 2003 at the request of the British government. However, in June 2004, it was reported that the number of firms doing business in Myanmar was once more on the rise and numbered over 400 companies. The ILO recommended sanctions but with little visible effect on either Myanmar or foreign investors. In February 2005, a global campaign of over 50 human rights groups was launched to target the French oil group Total, the biggest Western supporter of the military dictatorship. The group also faced lawsuits in

France and Belgium, filed by villagers abused by Burmese soldiers. A boycott of tourism has been organized by several US groups.

However, the downside of such actions is that they invariably do more harm than good to the workers involved. One European executive described how the government took over the factory after his firm's departure and, he assumed, the plant was now operating without the safeguards for the workers or the environment that it had insisted on. Similarly, the boycott by US clothing retailers such as Saks Inc. and others led to the collapse of the garment industry, one of the country's main sources of employment. ASEAN has adopted a policy of engagement with Myanmar, but this has not had any noticeable effect either. While East and West continue to cancel each other out, the generals will continue to ignore and continue its isolationist road to the country's ruin.

The Kingsway Group, which launched an Asian SRI program in 2000, believes that companies will come to see that a focus on ethics can reduce the risk of being named and shamed in the press, with the resultant negative consequences on share prices. Increasingly, being seen to behave in a principled and ethical manner has real, tangible payoffs.

Whatever you do, in the long term you probably cannot win – at least not totally. Adverse situations can be moderated but rarely eliminated. The poor working conditions of subcontractors can be influenced only so much, for example. Outside companies may have to accept that they will be in a permanent state of issues management and damage limitation in this area – to the extent that they are held hostage by circumstances beyond their control. Operating in Asia means being exposed to a whole range of ethical traps. As always, the key is to develop policies that anticipate problems before they arise, rather than rushing to develop responses as they occur. It is not the ethical traps that are the problem – they are unavoidable – but how companies respond to them.

Notes

1 *Financial Times*, "Asia propelled to "brink of environmental catastrophe," 19 June, 2001, p8.
2 *Managers and Mantras: One Company's Search for Simplicity*, by Charlotte Butler and John Keary, Wiley & Sons (Asia) Pte Ltd. 2000, p103.
3 *Financial Times*, "Indonesia orders Freeport to clean up mine," 14 February, 2006, p21.
4 *Financial Times*, "Newmont agrees pollution deal," Shawn Donnan, 16 February, 2006, p16.
5 *Financial Times*, "Graft mars crackdown on illegal logging," 14 January, 2003, p4.
6 *The Economist*, "Tackling wood-nappers," 7 May, 2005, p53.
7 Taken from "A Difficult Start," case study by Charlotte Butler and Professor Henri-Claude de Bettignies, 1997 INSEAD-EAC.
8 BBC News, 5 May, 2006.
9 *The Economist*, "Sweatshop wars," 27 February, 1999, p66.
10 *The Independent*, "Shop Until They Drop," M. Hickman, 14 January, 2006, pp1–2.

Corruption: The Business Practice that Dare Not Speak its Name

WHAT'S IN THIS CHAPTER?

▷ Why Must There Be Corruption in Asia?

▷ Forms of Corruption

  Petty Corruption

  Serious Corruption

▷ Which Asian Countries are Most Corrupt?

▷ Moves against Corruption in Asia

▷ Moves against Corruption Internationally: US and OECD Laws

▷ Strategies for Dealing with Corruption

  What Should You Do When You Are Asked for a Bribe?

  Are "Carried Interests" a Good Idea?

  Integrity Pacts

  Purchasing and Supply

Why Must There Be Corruption in Asia?

An African infrastructure minister calls on one of his Asian counterparts. The African asks the Asian infrastructure minister, "Your house is magnificent! How can you afford to have such a large house?" The Asian minister takes his visitor over to the window and points to a newly built bridge that crosses a nearby river.

"See that bridge. 50 percent went to me."

A few months later, it is the Asian minister who calls on his African counterpart and it is his turn to be impressed.

"This house is fantastic. How can you afford it?"

The African minister takes his visitor over to a window and points to a river.

"See that bridge?"

The Asian minister shakes his head. "No, I don't see a bridge."

"I know," says the African. "100 percent of it went to me."

Not all of Asia is corrupt and nor is corruption unique to Asia. There is a genuine desire on the part of most officials in Asia to get things done despite corrupt practices. There does seem to be a sense even among the corrupt that corruption does need to be balanced with the national interest. So things in Asia are not hopeless when it comes to corruption; those with a genuine desire to fight it do have something to work with.

Corruption is bad. It is unfair at best and severely damaging to an economy at worst. Corruption is not an acceptable practice in Asia, neither is it an intrinsic part of any of Asia's cultures. The sanctions – legal and social – that apply in respect of it might differ but there is not a single culture in Asia that sees corruption as a "good" thing or even as acceptable. It causes embarrassment to the perpetrators whenever it is exposed. Everyone who engages in it in Asia is aware that they are doing something wrong.

China increasingly influences perceptions of corruption in Asia as its economy grows and becomes important and more open, relative to the rest of Asia. Corruption statistics show an alarming increase in recorded corruption in China, although that need not mean that actual corruption has increased. Nonetheless, anecdotal evidence from foreign business-people who do business there is that China's new generation of businesspeople is ruthless, intensely driven to succeed and prepared to do almost anything to reach its goals. Elsewhere, if rules and laws are lacking as a means of constraint on private actions, social and religious constraints can help to fill the gap. But not in China. The current generation is, after all, the product of Communist ideology during its formative years and the Cultural Revolution, with its repudiation of religion and parental authority.

Confucianism is often blamed in part for the prevalence of corruption in Asia, particularly in Korea and China. Confucian principles dictate that honesty is a relative concept and can be traded away for the sake of loyalty. Officials who use their positions to help friends and relatives are seen as corrupt but also loyal, and loyalty in Confucian eyes is a mitigating factor. But it is more of an excuse than a sensible explanation. Confucian but corruption-free Singapore provides an excellent counter-example. Indeed, Singapore is something of an embarrassment to the rest of Asia. It shows that when it comes to corruption, culture is no excuse. At the end of the day, the real victims of corruption in Asia are not outsiders but Asians.

Forms of Corruption

Petty Corruption

Civil servants in countries such as Indonesia, China, the Philippines, Thailand and Myanmar routinely ask for small payments to do their jobs – to hand over forms, process them, provide statistics and undertake the minutiae of bureaucracy. Payments such as these help to speed up bureaucratic processes. They are a form of user pays, even a form of tax that is used to top up bureaucrats' meagre salaries. The amounts paid are typically trivial – a few dollars – and amount to paying civil servants to do their jobs rather than influencing them to do something that they otherwise would not do.

Examples of such payments are the "fees" that might need to be paid to staff at the Central Bureau of Statistics in Jakarta to get hold of publicly available data on imports, or payments made to immigration officials in the Philippines to get visas processed in a timely fashion. Depositors at state banks in Myanmar have found that they need to pay small processing fees even to withdraw their *own* money from their bank accounts, otherwise a five-minute transaction can take half a day. In Vietnam, the relevant agency or ministry might even collect all the unofficial payments together, pool them and then divide them among all the staff on a regular basis.

Other ways in which small payments might be extracted are from the sale of items such as stickers, pens and calendars for employees' welfare funds and the like. Contributions are usually "voluntary" in the same way that civil servants can choose to handle your requirements either slowly or quickly.

Such payments are small compared with the hassle and costs that can be imposed by not making them and foreign businessmen should not be too bothered when asked to pay them. They are an irritant and in their own small way do little for transparency but payments such as these are not properly considered bribery and rarely are they treated as such.

Some aid agencies have even formalized the process whereby part of their project budgets are allocated to topping up the salaries of local officials. This ensures that the local officials actually implement the aid programs rather than pilfer from them. It has been estimated that foreign donors pay as much as 53 percent of all government wages in Cambodia, often through this means.[1] Western aid agencies that have chosen not to go down this route have found that their programs may be completely obstructed, leading to money being spent but no aid being delivered. Their choice is stark – either be pragmatic or stay away.

Serious Corruption

Serious corruption – payments in cash or in kind – to secure significant advantage that cannot be guaranteed using fair and regular methods is reported to be widespread across Asia. Sometimes the payments are so regularized that negotiations are not necessary. They might even be non-negotiable. It is widely believed that the current flat "fee" for getting a project approved in Manila is US$50,000. Perhaps almost all such projects would be approved anyway. But that does not make such payments any less corrupt. Their size, for one, ensures that they are. Cutting senior officials and their families in on a deal to ensure approval is another means of overt corruption. Sometimes this can be disguised as a "carried interest," which is discussed later.

Kickbacks to ensure that supply tenders are won are another form of corruption. Famous instances of this type of corruption abound. The Lockheed scandal in Japan is perhaps the most famous but is only the tip of the iceberg. Also in Japan, the Tanaka faction of the Liberal Democrat Party always ensured that one of its members was appointed construction minister. This wasn't out of the faction's abiding interest in national development, but rather to ensure that it took a mandatory 3 percent on all major infrastructure projects and thereby earned itself tens of millions of dollars. The Bofors corruption scandal in India is another example. But more mundane purchases by government almost inevitably seem to require a kickback to someone somewhere in most of Asia, be they the provision of new computers for schools or cleaning contracts for government offices.

Kickbacks and commissions are hardly unique to the government sector. One businessman from a Western country interviewed by the authors tells the story of how he lost the business that he was doing in India because he refused to pay "commissions" to the new purchasing manager of a large company that had been buying his products. He describes how he was "character assassinated" by the purchasing manager, causing him to lose the business that he had so carefully cultivated, and how the senior managers in the company were unwilling to properly investigate the matter – he suspected because they too were to be cut in on the "commissions."

Taxation revenues are way down on what they could be in much of Asia due to corruption. Probably most local and many foreign companies in Indonesia "negotiate" their tax obligations with the Ministry of Finance. Partly they do this because ministry officials expect it. Pay them a bribe and they will come up with a sensible assessment. Don't and they might hit you with something extraordinary. But corruption is not restricted to income tax collection. One more example comes from tax and excise stamps and labels that are overprinted from Indonesia to Vietnam and Myanmar. They are sold to alcohol and tobacco producers at discount prices; the proceeds being pocketed by the officials.

Asia needs fewer civil servants who are paid more, rather than more who are paid less. But, in the wake of Asia's economic crisis of 1997–98, countries in the region following the IMF's remedies of cutting government spending opted for cutting civil servants' salaries. South Korea, for example, announced pay cuts for its almost one million civil servants in early 1998 of 20 percent for those at vice-ministerial level and above and 10 percent for the rest.

Another difficulty is in defining corruption. Freeport-McMoRan Copper & Gold Inc., a US company, has as its main asset a massive open pit copper and gold mine in Irian Jaya, eastern Indonesia (see also Strategy 27). In early 2006 it was revealed that the company gave officers in the police and military nearly US$20 million in direct payments and had also spent tens of millions more for military infrastructure such as roads and barracks. Essentially, the company had been renting the local police and military for its private purposes. Is this improper? Is it corrupt? Certainly Freeport-McMoRan was criticized around the world for its actions.

Which Asian Countries are Most Corrupt?

Corruption by its nature is impossible to measure. But it is well known in which countries it is greatest and where it is least. Similarly, it is hard to know the costs of corruption, although as a rule of thumb about a third of all government procurement budgets in Indonesia, the Philippines, Vietnam, Cambodia and Thailand are thought to be lost through misappropriation, fraud and other forms of corruption. A similar proportion is probably lost in India, Pakistan, Bangladesh and Nepal.

Perceptions are the best way we have to measure corruption. But perceptions come through a mixture of reality and myth. It also depends on whom you ask. Malaysia is seen by many Westerners as corrupt. But the perception might come more from Westerners being uncomfortable with past policies in Malaysia, which called for the selection of indigenous businessmen for contracts and privatizations rather than from any real corruption. Ask a Filipino or a Thai if Malaysia is corrupt and the response is often one of genuine surprise. "Our country is corrupt, but not Malaysia. That is why Malaysia is rich," is a typical response.

Indonesia is the clear and persistent winner in Asia in the perceived corruption stakes. Corruption is not seen as "right" in Indonesia as it is not anywhere else, but it is widely accepted and tolerated. There are few social sanctions against it. Those who become rich through corruption are actually accorded respect on account of their wealth even though it might be widely known how the riches were accrued.

Susilo Bambang Yudhoyono, who was elected Indonesia's president in 2004, has sought to grapple with the problem. He set up an anti-corruption court that year as part of his efforts to stamp out high-level corruption. But by January 2005 only three of the nine positions on it had been filled. There was a shortage of judges willing to serve on it. No doubt some were shy of hearing cases that involved powerful people. Others perhaps didn't feel that it would be a good place to be to make money. Judges in an anti-corruption court after all would be expected above all the others to be free of corruption. Still, several lawmakers were arrested for corruption and some senior government bureaucrats. Some were jailed. Yudhoyono's actions have been important in sending a message, but the problem of corruption has become ingrained in Indonesian culture. Furthermore, generally, corruption in Indonesia is only considered as such under law if it causes damage to the finances of the economy or the state. Thus, stealing state funds is corrupt by law, but receiving a bribe may not be. Each of the recent high-profile arrests have related to missing state funds – quite a narrow subset of the universe of sins inflicted upon the Indonesian people by government officials.

That Indonesia is seen as Asia's most corrupt country and one of the most corrupt in the world is not a judgment that comes only from outside. One of its finance ministers admitted in 1999 that a full crackdown on corruption would not be possible because economic activity would "grind to a halt" and "most businesspeople" would end up in jail. The defense minister had only just explained that it would be "impossible" to end corruption in the Indonesian military because its needs far exceed its official budget allocation.[2] At a conference at around the same time, the then attorney general referred to the "massive commercial fraud that took place [in Indonesia] in the last 10–15 years."[3] His replacement entered office claiming that corruption in Indonesia's courts was so deeply ingrained that it might take "more than two decades" to clean up. There is much corruption in Indonesia and it will stay that way for a long time. It is an issue that all companies must face if they wish to operate there – as they will if they want to operate in China, India, the Philippines, Korea and Thailand. The key is to have a strategy to deal with this eventuality before it arises rather than rushing to deal with the issue at the time that it does.

Moves against Corruption in Asia

All governments in Asia recognize that corruption is a problem, but not all are serious in tackling it. China today has the most onerous sanctions against corruption. Large numbers of officials found to be corrupt have been executed. The first comprehensive statutes on criminal law were adopted in 1979, which included allowing for officials who took advantage of their office to be jailed or, in serious cases, executed. Revised regulations were issued in 1997, which set out in more detail the types of instance that could be considered corruption. Included was a more detailed scale of punishments. Cases of corruption involving Rmb5,000–50,000 now lead to jail terms of 1–5 years. Cases involving Rmb50,000–100,000 earn 5–10 years in jail, and those involving more than Rmb100,000 earn 10 years to life imprisonment. Finally, there is the death penalty and the confiscation of property for especially serious cases. And yet corruption remains a huge problem in China. The highest number of convictions not surprisingly are in economic hotspots such as Shenzhen, Guangzhou and Shanghai.

Some Asian countries have established national anti-corruption bodies. These differ widely in their powers. Asia's two most powerful corruption fighting agencies are Hong Kong's Independent Commission Against Corruption (ICAC) and Singapore's Corrupt Practices Investigation Bureau (CPIB). These are also the two countries in Asia that happen to score the best in Transparency International's perceptions of corruption index.

Hong Kong in the early 1970s was a hotbed of corruption. Today, instances of overt corruption are infrequent and the civil service and the police are regarded as highly professional. This is partly due to the rise in civil service and police salaries, but the setting up of the ICAC in 1974 was especially important. It was given the powers of investigation, arrest and detention. It was also empowered to embark on a community education program about the evils of corruption. It used radio, television and print media advertisements to publicize its work and tell the public how to report instances of officials' corruption. It even sponsored television dramas with anti-corruption themes. The ICAC is well resourced and has a massive staff of 1,400.

Hong Kong's Law on Bribery Prohibition and the rules that govern the conduct of civil servants have also been important. Together, they mean that civil servants are not allowed to receive cash, gifts and entertainment of any substantial nature without the permission of the chief executive. Loans from friends must not be more than HK$2,000 and must be repaid within two weeks. Measures such as these are strictly enforced.

Singapore has had its Prevention of Corruption Act for many decades. The CPIB operates under the Act. The prime minister appoints the head of the bureau although the bureau itself is independent. It can arrest any suspects without a warrant. It comprises 49 officials, including 41 special investigators, which is relatively small but it cooperates closely with other government agencies.

Thailand introduced a new constitution in 1997 and with it came the National Counter Corruption Commission. The commission has shown itself to have teeth, although to date it has largely concerned itself with determining the eligibility of politicians to remain in parliament. It comprises nine commissioners who are appointed for nine-year terms. One of its biggest "successes" involved Sanan Kajornprasart, a deputy prime minister and minister who was convicted in 2000 of concealing his assets and forced to relinquish his government positions. "I love Petrus," he was quoted as saying two years later, referring to a Bordeaux wine that sells for US$1,000 a bottle or more for a good vintage, "I drink about a bottle a week."[4] Sanan might not have been all that repentant but at least he was no longer in office.

South Korea has the Board of Audit and Inspection as its corruption watchdog. The board does not have powers of investigation though and must refer cases to the public prosecutor. It has 800 staff, although this number might still be insufficient. The board is not as powerful as Hong Kong's ICAC or Singapore's CPIB but it still has some teeth. For example, it referred the cases of 100 people to the Prosecutor General's Office in December 2001 pending further investigation. All were banned from going overseas in the meantime.

The government of President Kim Dae Jung introduced a Citizen Ombudsman System in 1999, whereby citizens can force an investigation into corruption of a particular government agency or body if they request one in sufficient numbers. One thousand requests must be received with regard to a central ministry and 500 for a provincial body. No doubt it was a move designed to appeal to the electorate but surely a single citizen's well-founded allegation of government corruption is worthy of investigation.

In 2006, the administration of Thailand's Prime Minister Thaksin Shinawatra set up a website on which members of the public could leave allegations of corruption against government officials. It was a useful gesture but somewhat blunted at the time by allegations of his own massive conflicts of interest in selling his family's billion dollar telecommunications interests to Temasek Holdings after his government had passed legislation to ease the tax treatment of such a sale.

Moves against Corruption Internationally: US and OECD Laws

Investigations by the US SEC in the mid-1970s found that more than 400 US companies admitted making questionable or illegal payments worth in excess of US$300 million to foreign government officials, politicians and political parties. The US Congress passed the Foreign Corrupt Practices Act (FCPA) in 1977 in response to these findings. The Act makes it illegal for US citizens and companies to bribe foreign officials to obtain or maintain business or to have third parties do so on their behalf.

An amendment to the Act in 1988 removed the illegality on making "facilitating payments" for "routine governmental action" such as payments to obtain permits, licenses or other official documents; processing official documents, such as visas and work orders; providing police protection, mail pick-up and delivery; providing phone service, power and water supply, loading and unloading cargo, or protecting perishable products; and scheduling inspections associated with contract performance or transit of goods across a country. Thus these types of petty corruption would no longer be caught by the Act.

Other countries followed the US's anti-bribery stance via the OECD's Convention on Combating Bribery of Foreign Public Officials in International Business Transactions. It was unveiled on 21 November 1997 and was modeled on the principles of the FCPA. Thirty OECD members and four non-members were signatories. Almost all signatories have since ratified the Convention and introduced legislation into their national parliaments to make it a criminal offence for their companies and their citizens to bribe foreign public officials to obtain or retain international business. Among the signatories who have brought in such laws are the US, Canada, Sweden, Australia, Italy, the Netherlands, New Zealand, Spain, France, Germany, the UK, Ireland and Japan.

The Convention obliges its members to make it an offence for its citizens, companies and other legal entities to offer, promise or give "any undue pecuniary or other advantage." It is also an offence to use intermediaries to do the same, nor does the form of the bribe matter, be it cash or gifts – "or other advantage" is a very broad, catch-all caveat. Authorizing bribes is also an offence.

Companies and employees will be charged if they pay or offer bribes, not only to procure contracts but to obtain permits or influence taxation, customs, judicial or legislative proceedings. The Convention also calls for bribery to be an extraditable offence.

The legislation introduced by the Australian government subsequent to its ratification of the Convention is typical. It allows for jail terms of 10 years and a fine for bribing foreign officials. It specifies that in determining whether a pecuniary advantage or benefit was "undue," regard must be given to the following:

- the fact that the benefit may be customary, or perceived to be customary, in the situation
- the value of the benefit
- any official tolerance of the benefit.

The Australian legislation includes within the definition of "foreign public official" employees of international organizations and individuals who perform work for such organizations under contract. Thus a bribe paid to a UN official or even to a consultant to the UN would be caught by the legislation.

Thus, laws on bribing foreign officials are now uniform across much of the West and even beyond it. No longer can American companies complain that they are at a disadvantage in foreign markets compared with their competitors because laws at home prevent them from offering bribes to officials. If companies believe that their competitors have won contracts overseas through bribery, they should report it to the winning company's home government.

Strategies for Dealing with Corruption

Companies once believed that, rather than pay a bribe in cash, they could not be found to be behaving corruptly if they entertained an official and his wife on foreign shopping trips and so on. However, the OECD Convention and the resultant national laws now catch inducements such as these.

Some foreign companies now offer trips back to the head office for "research and training" for officials, ostensibly so that they can achieve a better understanding of the company's capabilities and thus make a more informed decision when it comes to allocating contracts and tenders. Inducements such as these are in more of a gray area and may still be caught under the terms of the OECD Convention, depending on how local legislatures have interpreted their obligations under the Convention. Any sort of travel or similar benefits for officials paid for by companies is open to question.

Gift giving and entertainment are a part of many Asian cultures. But at what point does this become corrupt? It all depends on whether it is "excessive." Companies doing business in Asia need comprehensive and clearly worded policies on bribery and corruption, which detail the limits and the consequences if they are not followed. Some Western companies now do not allow their employees to have meals bought for them. What is your company's policy on giving and receiving entertainment?

What Should You Do When You Are Asked for a Bribe?

- If you are an employee of a foreign company, explain that laws at home prevent you and the company from offering such payments in any form. Explain that it is a criminal offence and that the company could receive a massive fine, your government could jail and fine you and you would almost certainly lose your job.

- Alternatively, explain that you are not authorized to make such a payment. If you were to seek authorization from your superiors and they agreed, they would be putting themselves at risk of possible extradition and criminal penalties, including fines and jail. You too could face prosecution for conspiracy to corrupt.

- Offer an alternative. Are there any good works projects the officials are interested in that could be funded by your company instead? Perhaps your company could show its commitment locally by offering to fund scholarships for local schools or contributing to the cost of local playgrounds. Mining giant BHP-Billiton agreed in late 2005 to be a major sponsor for the Beijing 2008 Olympics at a time when there was friction between the company and China over soaring iron ore prices. No one at the time seemed to think that the sponsorship deal was actually about sport.

- Remember that projects come and go but once a bribe is given, it is always there to be unearthed – by investigators, competitors and the media.

- Should companies pay to secure meetings in Asia with senior officials and politicians? Preferably not, but then access is everything. Professional lobbyists in the US and elsewhere are well paid for the access they have. The important thing is that companies should adopt clear guidelines on this, whether they decide that this practice is acceptable or not.

Are "Carried Interests" a Good Idea?

Another way to acquire influence in some Asian countries has been to cut local officials, politicians and their families into projects by allocating them equity in the project under consideration. The equity is not given to them, as that would run foul of the OECD Convention and the US FCPA, but instead is provided in the form of a loan, which is paid back from earnings from the project. The maneuver is known as providing a "carried interest." The effect is the same as a bribe even if technically such equity transfers cannot be deemed as such.

Carried interests are not without their problems. One large US company gave 15 percent of its Indonesian venture to a company owned by a relative of the then President Soeharto. That company contributed no cash for its stake – the deal was structured whereby the American company "lent" the Indonesian side the sum for its stake. After Soeharto was removed from office, the deal fell apart and questions were asked about its efficacy. The American company conducted an "internal inquiry" in 1999, which found that everything was above board. But the media fallout didn't look good. The conduct of the American company was criticized in a number of newspaper columns, articles and editorials. Carried interests have their dangers.

Integrity Pacts

Transparency International has developed what it calls Integrity Pacts for Transparency in Public Procurement Procedures, processes that interested companies might consider suggesting to agencies for consideration when they call for tenders for projects. These pacts involve a commitment on the part of all bidders, and the agency overseeing the bidding process, not to give or accept bribes, or collude with other bidders, to disclose all payments, and to report any violation of the integrity pact by other bidders during the bidding or the execution of the service. In the event of a breach of the pact, sanctions come into force against bidders and officials, including liability for damages and blacklisting from future tenders.

Transparency International monitored such a pact used in combination with a least cost selection method tender in Pakistan in February 2002 to select a consultant to design the Greater Karachi Water Supply Scheme. It did this in cooperation with the Karachi Water and Sewerage Board. The board had set aside the equivalent of US$4.2 million for the tender, but the process led to a winning bid of just US$1.04 million, leading to a saving of 75 percent on what the board expected it would have to spend. Transparency International believes that the bulk of the savings was due to the openness of the process brought about by the integrity pact. It recommends the use of such pacts elsewhere and to date has overseen around 100 similar integrity pacts worldwide.

Purchasing and Supply

Purchasing and supply are huge areas for potential corruption in Asia. Kickbacks are so commonplace in many countries as to be practically routine. Companies doing business in Asia must protect themselves against corrupt practices when they buy their own supplies. They must scrutinize all purchasing officers in Asia carefully. They need to be on the lookout for:

- Unnecessary purchases
- Family connections between purchasing staff and suppliers
- Unexplained wealth of purchasing staff which might suggest significant kickbacks have been received
- A lack of preparedness on the part of purchasing staff to be active in seeking out new and cheaper suppliers
- Stationery and stores cupboards that are filled to the point of lavishness
- Purchases from suppliers that seem inconvenient when more convenient options are available, for example meeting rooms are booked in hotels on the other side of town when more convenient venues are nearby
- Monogramed gifts from suppliers – purchasing staff on low salaries can attach great importance even to gifts as minor as cheap wristwatches, mugs and shoulder bags. Monitor the importance that staff attach to such things
- Just as it is wise practice to change internal accounting staff occasionally, it may be prudent occasionally to change staff who are responsible for purchasing, in order to guard against long-term cosy relationships between the staff and suppliers.

Notes

1   *Wall Street Journal*, "Aid agencies often spend money on paying civil servants' salaries," 8 February, 2002.
2   *Asian Wall Street Journal*, "Kwik cites dangers of Indonesian cleanup," 9 December, 1999.
3   Backman, M., "The new order conglomerates" in *Perspectives on Chinese Indonesians*, Godfrey, M. and Lloyd, G. (eds) 2001, Crawford House, Belair (Australia).
4   *Asian Wall Street Journal*, "Label-obsessed Asians flaunt big-name wine," 22 March, 2002.

Strategy 29

Dancing with the Devil: Doing Business with Asia's Politicians and their Families

WHAT'S IN THIS CHAPTER?

▷ Can "Good" Connections be Carried Too Far?

▷ Asia's Politician-businessmen

▷ Be Sure to Know your Local Partner
  Falling from Grace
  Dealing with Unwanted Politically Connected Partners

▷ Potential Problems with Politically Connected Local Partners

Can "Good" Connections be Carried Too Far?

Relationships and connections matter a great deal in Asia, and the weaker the local legal system, the more they matter. But how far do you go? A good local partner is one who can open doors and keep them open, smooth things over with the authorities and help to get approvals in a timely matter. But does this mean that the local authorities themselves make even better local partners? What about senior bureaucrats, the military or even senior politicians and their families? Instead of trying to win approvals from senior politicians, might it not be better simply to make them or their families your local partner, so that the approvals will be guaranteed?

The answer is fairly simple. The ideal local partner can do a range of things, including managing the relationship with government. If you choose the family of a local politician as a local partner, typically, handling the relationship with the government is about all the local partner will manage, unless they are already successful in business and can bring some genuine local business attributes to the relationship. Partners who already are in business and have a good understanding of dealing with the local bureaucracy and the government typically make the better partner, if indeed one is needed.

Politically connected partners might bring connections to the table but they might also bring unwanted intrusion, stigma and, ultimately, risk, if they fall from grace. Rarely will they bring capital. "The mountains are high and the emperor is far away" is one maxim that's commonly heard to explain why China's southeastern provinces have done so well compared with the rest of the country. Proximity to power is not always a good thing.

Asia's Politician-businessmen

Politicians all over Asia have shown a tendency to want to get into business. Very often, they use their political positions to enrich themselves and their families. Foreign investors with cash are one source of funds for such politician-businessmen. Sometimes, the families of political leaders simply want a passive stake in new enterprises, perhaps in a nominee arrangement. This was the preferred mode of the Marcos family of the Philippines. They wanted riches without the responsibility. Other politicians and their families want to be directly involved in business themselves. They see themselves as entrepreneurs and have a genuine and active commitment to their enterprises.

It is not just Asia's politicians who seek corporate advancement from their official positions, but also civil servants and the military. Among civil servants, it is senior officials of SOEs who are most likely to have a personal involvement in business. Many set up private companies which become suppliers to the SOE.

The military's involvement in business in Asia generally comes from its need for off-budget financing. Governments in many Asian countries give the military less funding than required and, in any event, many generals want to develop a separate source of funds to ensure some measure of financial independence from government and politicians. Thus, the defense forces of Indonesia, Thailand, Myanmar, China and the Philippines have direct involvement in running and managing businesses. These are among the most opaque of all businesses in Asia. It is difficult to appreciate the importance of the military's involvement in business. Little is published, military-backed companies rarely list on stock exchanges and rarely file corporate records or results.

Sons and daughters of government officials who use their parents' positions or names to go into business are another variation on the theme. In China, they are called the princelings or *taizi*, and they include the sons and daughters of senior Communist Party officials or senior officials with China's many SOEs. Some foreign investors in China seek out the *taizi* as partners on the assumption that they can open doors and help to protect their investments. This might prove to be true, but since the mid-1990s, senior officials and their families have fallen in and out of favor in China with increasing regularity, often in the wake of embezzlement and corruption scandals. Officials in China have been known to be very senior one day and executed or imprisoned for life the next. Silent partners are one thing, dead partners are quite another.

Using one's official position to financially benefit oneself and one's family is expected in Indonesia. There is a story – possibly true – that one of former President Soeharto's ministers came to him and said he could no longer live on his ministerial salary and would it be possible for a pay rise? Soeharto was incredulous. "You have been a minister in charge of a large department all these years. What on earth have you been doing?" said Soeharto or words to that effect. Soeharto used his position to enrich his family and he expected all other officials to do the same.

When Soeharto stepped down as president, his family had interests in at least 1,251 separate companies in Indonesia alone.[1] Many ventures were with foreign investors who saw linking up with the family of the president as one way to have investment approvals fast-tracked and potentially obstructive bureaucrats frightened out of the way. But Soeharto was not alone in the practice. Many of his ministers arrived in office with little but left with a conglomerate. Soeharto expected this of his ministers and other senior officials – indeed he wanted them to behave like this. It saved the need to remunerate senior officials properly and provided a better context for the nepotism of his own family.

Be Sure to Know your Local Partner

The flip side of selecting a well-connected local partner is that occasionally they present themselves but do so without fully disclosing who they are or with whom they are connected. This can lead to later embarrassment for the foreign investor.

Business development managers of one Western firm eager to sign up a local partner in Indonesia in the mid-1990s did so with what they believed to be a company backed by several former senior military figures. In their haste they did insufficient due diligence and, some months later, found out that their new partner was in fact one of the more odious members of the Soeharto family.

One American producer appointed a local company in Myanmar as the distributor for its products. It ended the relationship in 1998 as part of an informal international boycott against Myanmar for human rights abuses. But the end also came after it was disclosed that the local company was the private investment vehicle of one of Asia's most infamous drug lords.

Mistakes like these can be averted with more thorough research. It is obviously far better to determine as much about a prospective partner before, rather than after, a deal is signed. One problem with signing up politically influential partners is that unsigning them can prove difficult. What was supposed to be a business development move might end up closing doors rather than opening them. Signing up the prime minister's younger brother might seem like a good idea, but firing him as a partner could prove devastating.

Falling from Grace

Choosing a local partner because of his current high political connections is a dangerous thing if for no reason other than that power and influence are rarely permanent. The family of President Soeharto is a case in point. Since Soeharto left office, most of his close relatives have been investigated for corruption and related matters and several have been arrested and imprisoned, including his youngest son Tommy Suharto who was jailed for fifteen years in 2002. Soeharto's cousin Probosutedjo was sentenced to jail in late 2005 for corruption, although he was expected to appeal. Foreign investors find that local partners who people once queued to see are now *persona non grata*. On top of that, they are left with the public stigma of being linked to a partner who might now be openly acknowledged to have been corrupt and nepotistic, or worse.

Dealing with Unwanted Politically Connected Partners

Sometimes, foreign or outside investors do not choose to go into business with politically connected parties. Instead, the politically connected choose them. When Soeharto was president, he personally approved almost all foreign investment projects in Indonesia. Thus he had close knowledge of who wanted to invest in what and where. From this it is thought that various members of his family were tipped off about promising projects and they would then present themselves as "partners." Foreign investors found themselves in a position in which they had to choose between having the Soehartos as their partner or not proceeding with the project at all.

The best advice for outsiders in such situations in whatever country is that they should resist such entreaties as far as they possibly can. If they can stall for as long as possible, hopefully the local party that is attempting to inject itself into the new venture will give up. But if it does not and it becomes clear that the project will not proceed unless the local "partner" is taken on board, the investor must decide whether to proceed at all, or how the unwanted party can best be accommodated, keeping in mind the future risk that political circumstances might change and the local partner might suddenly fall from grace.

Potential Problems with Politically Connected Local Partners

- Politically connected partners are subject to sharp reversals of fortune either due to politics or policy. Well-connected partners might one day be an anathema and a liability the next.

- Getting information on prospective politically connected local partners can prove difficult. Their proximity to power might mean that they can avoid all the corporate filings and declarations that lesser connected parties are obliged to make. Many Soeharto-backed companies in Indonesia simply never bothered to lodge articles of association, for example. A powerful local partner might mean having one that is opaque, even by Asian standards.

- The military is short of cash everywhere, and this is often why it goes into business. The military will bring almost no business expertise, no capital and will be more interested in what it can take out of a venture compared with what it can put in. Other local businesspeople may be loath to do business with your venture because of its military links.

- Business is not the main attribute of politically connected partners and rarely is business their main occupation or skill. In such circumstances, rarely will such local parties be in a position to contribute their ascribed share of capital to the venture.

■ Linking up with the powerful so that their power can be utilized is a risky business. If there's a falling out, that power can be turned against you. James Peng, an Australian businessman of Chinese descent, discovered this in the early 1990s. He formed a business relationship with Deng's niece, Ding Peng. The two fell out and, as a consequence, he lost control of Shenzhen Fountain, the company he founded. It was seized by Ding Peng, and James was kidnapped from a Macau hotel room, spirited across the border to mainland China, put on trial for embezzlement and jailed for 18 years. He was released in November 1999 after six years' imprisonment, following the intervention of the Australian government.

Some things to consider when linking up with politically connected local partners

1. Will the form of the partnership have any implications under the US Foreign Corrupt Practices Act or similar legislation?

2. Can the prospective partner genuinely bring anything to the venture other than political connections?

3. What arrangements are there for either party to exit the relationship?

4. How secure are the prospective partners' links to power?

5. Should opposition forces come to power, how will that affect your business?

6. Will your prospective partner be in a position to threaten your business or your staff should the relationship flounder?

7. What other partnerships does your prospective partner have with outside business interests and how have they been treated?

Note

1   Backman, M., *Asian Eclipse: Exposing the Dark Side of Business in Asia*, John Wiley & Sons, 1999, 2001.

When Things Go Wrong

WHAT'S IN THIS CHAPTER?

▷ History Repeats Itself
▷ Chinese Takeaway
▷ Indian Soap Opera
▷ The Thais That (Don't) Bind
▷ Rising Sum
▷ Star Wars Part I
▷ Star Wars Part II
▷ A Learning Process

History Repeats Itself

Disappointment and even disasters are more frequent than success for most foreign firms investing in Asia. These are often associated with the breakup of joint venture relationships and the consequent deterioration of the company's investment. Sometimes the breakup is reasonably amicable, sometimes it can end in a protracted court case. An acquisition, too, is more likely to disappoint than prosper, and can be even more expensive if a firm paid a premium for what it thought was a rising star, only to discover it was a black hole. In many cases, Western companies decide to cut their losses and withdraw, but those who do often return to the region later, unable to resist the lure of those untapped markets, only to make similar mistakes. History repeats itself because few people listen sufficiently the first time around, and rarely are mistakes dissected. People are normally too busy ducking for cover.

The following true stories illustrate some of the most common reasons why attempts to be Big in Asia all too often lead to a retreat from Asia.

Chinese Takeaway

A typical disaster was that experienced by Asimco, a Beijing-based investment company set up in 1993 with three US majority shareholders; TCW Capital Investment Co., Dean Witter Capital and GE.[1] By 1999, it was one of the biggest investors in China, having put US$450 million into 15 auto-related joint ventures and two breweries.

In the auto industry, its strategy was to take majority stakes in promising Chinese component makers and provide them with management expertise and new technology. In 1996, it paid US$7.5 million for a 60 percent stake in a Chinese company, CAC Brake Ltd, run by a Guangdong entrepreneur. The company produced auto brake components and clutch disks, and appeared to have a healthy order book, so the investors simply put in a financial manager and left the entrepreneur (who was vice chairman of the board) and his team of deputy general managers to run the company.

Subsequent events would have come as no surprise to those with experience in China. The entrepreneur proceeded to strip the company of as much money as possible via a series of simple but effective frauds. For example, employee housing that remained under CAC's control was rented to the joint venture, with the proceeds going to the entrepreneur. Another ruse was to raise mortgages from a local bank for two new buildings, supposedly for additional factory space even though the existing space was ample. Although they were actually built, the shoddy workmanship and low ceilings made them unsuitable for use as factories but the entrepreneur was able to take his cut anyway. As a grand finale, the entrepreneur opened up letters of credit (LCs) to pay for non-existent equipment and, in the last few months before he left town, stopped paying vendors and took the cash himself. In December 1996, he disappeared during a business trip to the US, having looted the company of over US$6 million.

Moral: Don't run your joint venture at arm's length. Make sure that you keep a firm eye on what is happening, put in your own senior finance people and check the books.

The rescue: Asimco finally sent in an experienced auto man to run CAC, and recruited a financial manager. It also sued the local bank, arguing that there must have been some collusion and the bank should have realized that the LCs were fraudulent. Not surprisingly, the local city court ruled against Asimco, which then took its appeal to the provincial court in Guangzhou. From there the case went to the national court in Beijing where nothing happened for two years, despite pressure from the US embassy.

In the meantime, the two new managers turned the company around by improving production and introducing stricter controls. Wastage was cut and quality standards raised, enabling CAC to win an ISO9002 qualification. A key move was to cut the number of products from 400 to 100. More units of lesser variety allowed for greater economies of scale and this led to greater productivity. Taking advantage of being in a buyer's market, the US manager negotiated discounts and an extension of payment terms from 30 to 60 or 90 days, and to cut fraud instituted a strict purchase control system.

Salesmen were paid on a commission-only basis, and travel expenses were phased out. Distribution was improved by using CAC's own trucks to take stock to a warehouse, from where it went by rail to three distribution points and then on to customers by truck. Export sales were increased to account for 45 percent of revenues, the rest coming from OEM auto makers and the after-sales market.

As a result, CAC stayed in business and, despite a setback in 1998 due to the economic downturn, broke even. Financing remained a problem. In the short term, CAC employees were given a bond, which was redeemable at the end of the year for a month's salary plus 8 percent, in lieu of a month's salary. In the longer term, the plan was to cut the labor force and win more OEM contracts.

Indian Soap Opera

The Indian subsidiary of Unilever, Hindustan Lever (HLL), one of the largest private sector firms in the country, fell victim to a different sort of disaster – the rise of a new local competitor, who proceeded to revolutionize the market for detergents that HLL had dominated for years.[2]

HLL had a long and highly respected presence in India; the first crates of soap were unloaded in Kolkata in 1888 and HLL soon emerged as the market leader in soaps, detergents and personal products, as well as food and beverages. Unilever gave its subsidiaries great autonomy, and in India this was reinforced by HLL's reputation for successful innovation and effective local management. For ambitious young Indians, joining HLL was the first step in a successful career as a professional manager – the right to wear an HLL tie spoke for itself. They were an elite corps serving an elite company.

India was one of the largest fabric wash markets in the world and HLL had played a great part in developing it, as customers graduated from using laundry soaps to detergent powders. Its leading product, Surf, led both in terms of value and volume and, with a 67 percent market share, was unbeatable. By the late 1970s, the industry was marked by an almost feudal structure, with HLL presiding majestically over what was known as the organized sector for detergents, as opposed to the vast unorganized sector that still used cheaper laundry soap. HLL felt secure in the knowledge that, given the range of international brands it could call on from the parent company, it had nothing to fear in the future. HLL managers had made the rules of the game; they took it for granted they would continue to win.

This complacency was rudely shattered in the late 1970s by the eruption into the industry of one small cottage firm, armed with little packets of yellow soap powder labeled Nirma. It was the creation of an ambitious entrepreneur Karsanbhai Patel, who set up a business in 1969 with the firm intention of making his brand the biggest in the world. His belief in the principle of "develop a good product and there will be a market for it" was absolute.

Production of the brand, that within a decade would become one of the largest in the world, began in a small shed in a suburb of Ahmedabad. The detergent powder, made from materials bought locally and dumped on the shed floor, was hand-mixed in batches by Patel and packed into polythene bags that he stapled together. He then loaded the packets in gunny sacks onto his bike, and sold them through house-to-house rounds of the city.

During the next decade, Patel barely diverged from this simple approach to the four Ps – product, price, packaging and promotion. Although refined and enlarged according to market circumstances, the formula remained essentially the same, enabling him to run an efficient operation at a fraction of the cost incurred by HLL and other big firms. The simple Nirma chain of distribution, for example, contrasted starkly with the complex HLL machine and won him great loyalty from the distributors. They discovered that lower trade margins were compensated for by larger volumes and quick rotation, and refused to desert him even under pressure from rivals. His greatest extravagance was in advertising.

At first young women were hired to visit shops asking for Nirma. Later, he offered prize draws, and Nirma was the only Indian advertiser at the 1980 Moscow Olympics, apart from the state bank. Hoardings blazoned the Nirma message, and its catchy jingle, "Nirma washes whiter than white," punctuated every radio program.

As sales grew, Patel took his relatives into partnership and methodically extended his operation to adjoining districts, provinces and then the whole of western and northern India. By 1977, HLL wrote to a branch manager in Ahmedabad asking for information on this brand called Nirma. The reply was dismissive: "You can't expect me to know about every junk product coming out of Ahmedabad."

But between 1977 and 1985, Nirma sales grew at a compound rate of 45 percent, and by 1980, Nirma was outselling Surf by 3 to 1. It had also spread into southern and eastern India and, with a market share of 58 percent to Surf's 8.4 percent, was one of the largest selling detergent powder brands in the world. HLL finally woke up to the fact that it was losing a war it didn't even know it was fighting.

Moral: Never underestimate an Asian entrepreneur.

The rescue: Nirma's greatest success had been to convert the unorganized soap market in urban areas and, more importantly, in rural India to detergent powders, all under HLL's nose. The realization forced HLL to alter its strategy and mindset in order to regain its market position. Its response came in stages: it began selling Surf in polybags instead of the more expensive cartons; changed its advertising message to show that Surf represented value for money; and launched another soap powder to match Nirma directly on price. These were successful in shoring up Surf's market share. By then Patel was moving into the toothpaste and toilet soap markets to offer a full range of Nirma products.

In the longer term, HLL implemented a "stop Nirma" campaign code-named STING (Strategy To Inhibit Nirma Growth). This campaign led HLL to rethink its attitudes to quality, financial management and production methods. The whole episode had a traumatic effect on HLL's management; in the future their watchword would be "edge" – competitive edge through marketing, distribution and technology. But a decade later, Nirma dominated the low-end market for detergents, and had a 35 percent share of the overall detergent market to HLL's 30 percent. Patel was planning an attack on the premium detergent market, and said to be contemplating the Chinese market.

The Thais That (Don't) Bind

Ferodo Thailand Ltd (FTL) was another company which fell into many of the well-documented traps associated with a joint venture relationship.[3] What made this particular failure all the more interesting was the fact that the three partners were all well known to each other, and had successfully cooperated for many years. Yet within a few years of forming a joint venture, the relationship between two of the partners had irretrievably broken down. The three-way split was between Ferodo Ltd (the friction materials subsidiary of the UK-based auto components group T&N), its long-time associate, the Japanese brake manufacturer Japan Brake International (JBI) and the Thai Boonpong Group.

Like most Thai trading companies, Thai Boonpong Co. Ltd was a family firm, founded in 1949, initially as a bus company and maintenance operation, specializing in brake and clutch systems. The son of the founding entrepreneur, who took over in 1977, decided to concentrate on distributing brake and other automobile parts, mainly for passenger cars, and from its early days Boonpong sold imported Ferodo products, which had a worldwide reputation for quality. These were marketed under the Boonpong name, since the Ferodo brand was not well known in the Thai market.

In 1985 Veeravej Subhawat, grandson of Boonpong's founder, succeeded as managing director of Boonpong. Within two years, he came to the conclusion that Boonpong should stop importing and instead produce brake pads in Thailand. Following a visit to the Ferodo headquarters in the UK, he decided to build the Ferodo brand name in Thailand and, on his return, invested between Bt40–50 million in advertising on buses and radio announcements, sponsored racing events, and even offered clients a Ferodo discount card.

In 1992, Subhawat decided that Boonpong should begin manufacturing brake pads in Thailand. He therefore invested in a factory and new machinery and approached Ferodo Ltd for a manufacturing license. Since Ferodo was then setting up several joint ventures in Southeast Asia, it readily agreed. Boonpong paid Ferodo Ltd Bt5 million for the transfer of the necessary technology to start up the factory, and agreed to pay Ferodo UK an annual 4 percent royalty on sales volume. After 18 months of successful production, Ferodo Ltd and Boonpong began discussions to turn the license into a joint venture.

The move came at a time of rapid growth in the Southeast Asian automobile industry in general, and in Thailand particularly. For Ferodo Ltd, which supplied brake parts to all the main auto manufacturers, expansion into the region was of major strategic importance. This opening in Thailand seemed a golden opportunity to manufacture brake pads cheaply, since Boonpong's factory was already producing a variety of Ferodo models. It would be relatively simple to increase production there, and in time use Thailand as a hub to supply the rest of the region at lower cost. The prospects for success seemed dazzling, given that, in 1996, the Thai automotive industry was valued at US$12 billion, accounting for 6 percent of GDP and 2 percent of the country's exports (valued at almost US$1.3 billion).

However, T&N, the holding company to which Ferodo Ltd belonged, required that if technology was being transferred to a joint venture, then T&N must remain the majority shareholder. For Subhawat, this meant giving up the independence of his family-run firm, but he was loath to miss this opportunity and more importantly, given the long relationship with the UK team, he believed that Ferodo Ltd's management respected him. As he recalled: "When I went to the UK, it seemed we were all one family." Ferodo Thailand Ltd (FTL), the new company, was capitalized at Bt80 million. T&N's shareholding was 51 percent, Boonpong's 49 percent. Later, the shareholding was revised with the entry of JBI, which took a 9 percent stake at the expense of Boonpong.

Unusually for Ferodo, the terms of the joint venture agreement applied only to the manufacturing side of the business and excluded sales, marketing and distribution. Sales and marketing for the domestic market were exclusively Boonpong's preserve, leaving the export market to Ferodo Ltd. It was also agreed that brake pads manufactured by FTL would be sold to the joint venture partner at cost plus 15 percent, to ensure that the company would be profitable, again an unusually high margin. Because the majority shareholder was British, the Thai Board of Investment (BOI) regarded FTL as a foreign company. This meant it was required to export at least 60 percent of the product during the first five years, for which Ferodo Ltd took responsibility. At the time Ferodo Ltd was confident that its sister company, Ferodo Australia, would pick up the 60 percent export quota for the export market.

However, within a year of the joint venture being signed, things began to go downhill as the relationship between Subhawat and Lambert, the new Ferodo managing director for joint ventures, deteriorated. On his first visit to Thailand in 1996, Lambert identified a number of problems; quality defects, low production volumes and, most disturbing, huge stockpiles of unsold products. A series of complaints from Ferodo Australia, FTL's chief export customer, confirmed the production defects. To make matters worse, he realized that the terms of the joint venture agreement gave him little latitude to change the way things were being done. His views were clearly communicated to both the factory management and Subhawat, who had not begun to repay the huge debt owed to Ferodo for equipment supplied or kept up with royalty payments.

Lambert did not make a good impression on Subhawat, who was not prepared for what he considered to be the tougher and more aggressive way of working adopted by Lambert and his boss Sam Thomas. He believed that:

> They didn't have any respect for me ... Ken had his ideas, and was going to put them into place. I have six companies in my group, and would never be disrespectful to middle management. But Lambert interfered with middle management ... He brought in new people from the UK. Some of them had a bad attitude to the Thai people.

Lambert introduced weekly reporting systems. He kept in close contact and asked for reports more often than before. He also complained about the relationship between Boonpong and its dealer network, which typically in Thailand meant giving presents of gold bars as a bonus, winning rich raffle prizes or being sent on luxury weekend holidays with their families. To Lambert, this was a waste of scarce financial resources that could have been put to much better use.

Another issue concerned the potentially profitable motorcycle after-sales market, which was larger than the automobile market. Lambert wanted Boonpong to go after this but, due to the terms of the contract, was unable to exert the influence he wished. He also suggested to Subhawat that the 15 percent margin should be lowered to be more competitive. Subhawat refused and tensions rose.

Because FTL was having difficulty in filling the orders from Ferodo Australia, a backlog was developing. There were also problems with the quality of the exported parts that needed sorting out urgently. Again and again, Lambert pointed out all these problems to Subhawat, underlining how FTL had to increase market share so that it would be ahead of the game when the competition arrived. His blunt way of explaining these and other facts did not go down well with Subhawat. The rows finally culminated in December 1996 in the dramatic resignation of Subhawat, not only as chairman of the board but also as director of FTL. Announcing that he had "better things to do than sit in boardrooms with high-ego people," Subhawat swept out of the room. Subhawat's resignation took Lambert by surprise. He had realized he was not popular with the Boonpong team but thought that, given the discoveries he had made on his arrival, he had been very gentle with them.

All these tussles were having their effect on Worawut, the Thai deputy director of the factory and an old school friend of Subhawat. He felt more and more unhappy as the situation deteriorated: "Ken Lambert quarreled with Mr Subhawat about the non-payment. They were both wrong. I felt like I was in the middle. There was no trust between anyone." When FTL's managing director moved to Ferodo South Africa, Lambert appointed Worawut in his place. But this put him under great pressure, made worse when the technical and control manager also resigned. For Worawut, it was all too much. The next day he sent a fax to Ken Lambert, resigning.

This was the last straw for Ken Lambert. It left him with a factory that was not running to capacity, quality complaints, stockpiles of goods destined for the domestic market, on the one hand, and unfulfilled export orders on the other, and a huge gap in the management structure. This was before taking into consideration the failure to meet the BOI 60 percent export quota. Morale had already been low before Worawut's resignation – now it would reach rock bottom. In addition, Thailand was about to be hit by a major currency crisis, whose effect on business was unknown at the time. How on earth was he going to put the joint venture back on track?

Moral: The story illustrates many of the points covered in previous chapters. A relationship can still go badly wrong, even when it is founded on a long-term knowledge of each other and a good record of cooperation. Having formed a closer partnership, it turned out that they were in the same bed but dreaming different dreams. The way the agreement was drawn up built in difficulties that could not be overcome, given that their strategic goals were not aligned, there was not enough technical standardization and the final exacerbating factors of cultural clashes and different management styles.

The rescue: The story had a happy ending. Lambert sent in two veteran managers from Ferodo's South African subsidiary to be managing director and marketing manager respectively. Together, they turned the company around, despite the Asian crisis, sorting out the backlog and extracting payment from Subhawat. The key move was finding a new market in the after-sales market for older cars. This was identified by the marketing manager who, after studying the statistics, realized that as cars in Bangkok braked about every 70 metres on average, new brake pads were going to be a regular must. By 2000, FTL had the potential to expand, its workforce was highly skilled and motivated and it was working toward an ISO/QS9000 award. Its problems were not over, but it was on the right path. Ken Lambert oversaw the changes and then retired.

Rising Sum

In 1998, the US-based Merrill Lynch International[4] entered the Japanese market for the second time with high hopes. The memory of the 1980s' disaster, when it had set up a small retail operation of six retail branches, which, on closure in 1993, boasted only five or six customers apiece, had dimmed. This time it moved in via the 33 rented branch offices and 2,000 salespeople it had bought from Yamaichi Securities Co. for $300 million. Yamaichi, Japan's fourth largest brokerage, had collapsed to the tune of ¥3.2 trillion (US$25 billion), the biggest bankruptcy in Japanese history. The chairman of Merrill Lynch had spotted an opportunity to be first into the market and moved quickly so that, almost overnight, the company had become the first Western concern with an independent brokerage network in Japan, staffed by experienced locals.

Its nearest rivals were Japan's big three, Nomura, Daiwa and Nikko, but Merrill Lynch believed that its US business model could not fail to attract customers. Japanese customers are conservative savers, preferring to put 94 percent of their savings in the post office, despite earning less than 1 percent in annual interest. The lure of these ¥242 trillion in savings, together with the 1998 deregulation of the broking industry, was an irresistible target that Merrill Lynch felt it could crack. It aimed to transform the Yamaichi brokers into US-style financial advisers, where commitment to clients and integrity would be paramount. What could possibly go wrong this time?

Merrill Lynch Japan Securities opened for business on 1 July 1998. The market was not favorable, given an economy that, by then, had been flat for years. Ominously, from the beginning revenue failed to meet expectations, with a loss of ¥25 billion in the first nine months. A forecast revision pushed the venture's breakeven point out by another two years to 2002.

Perhaps even more unfortunately, the US-style business approach unsettled both employees and customers. The former did not take to the new merit-based reward system, while the retraining program foundered on the branch managers' dislike of being required to read instructions in English. Dress-down Friday was another cultural hurdle few Japanese could cross: many arrived in suits and changed in the office washrooms. As one explained: "If I left home in casual clothes, my wife would think I was having an affair."

The US business approach also upset customers, for whom trust in a relationship was an important element. Merrill's request for customers to fill in forms asking for family and financial details was deemed intrusive in Japan. It also offered unfamiliar products and stressed long-term buy and hold investing, which was not common in Japan. Merrill also broke a local custom whereby Japanese brokerages frequently covered the losses of favored clients. Understandably, Merrill refused to do this but it didn't endear it to the big end of town.

Its advertising campaign, costing tens of millions of dollars, also backfired. The ads and Merrill's shop fronts featured the company's trademark bull. One possibly apocryphal story had it that a Japanese mistook a Merrill branch for a Korean barbecue restaurant. Such instances of the lack of awareness and understanding of the Merrill brand took the US management by surprise. It finally realized that "Our market research was too simple."

Nevertheless, the chairman persisted in his belief that it was just taking a while for the Japanese to adjust to the cultural change and, in the first year, brokers were told not to worry about missing asset targets. However, when results failed to improve in the second year, hundreds were dismissed and more followed in succeeding years. Merrill reorganized its business, closed branches, cut staff and concentrated on big account holders. Still the retail venture lost about US$600 million in three years.

Moral: As Merrill's chief financial officer reportedly observed: "What works in one place won't necessarily work in another. It sometimes looks easier than it is when you get into someone else's backyard."

The rescue: There was none. In November 2001, the operation became part of major, worldwide cutbacks at Merrill. Most of the 28 retail branches left were closed by early 2002, and about 700 financial consultants, three-quarters of the sales force, were dismissed. Merrill took a US$2.2 billion fourth quarter charge in 2001 to cover the cost of the job cuts and other measures. Still, third time lucky?

Star Wars Part I

In 1993, Rupert Murdoch, chairman and chief executive of News Corp., acquired the pan-Asian broadcaster Star TV for US$950 million. With it, he hoped to achieve his aim of breaking into the Chinese market. However, over the next nine years, it failed to live up to its profit potential, despite continued investment. In April 2002, it finally came out of the red, announcing an operating profit of US$2.4 million in the third quarter of its fiscal year ending June 2002. That year also saw it opening in China, where it launched a 24-hour Mandarin language channel offering light entertainment. The channel was aimed at the growing young *nouveau riche* segment in Guangdong.

For Murdoch, this represented the fruits of nine years' hard labor to correct the effects of a disastrous after-dinner speech in London, when he noted how modern telecommunications had "proved an unambiguous threat to totalitarian regimes everywhere." Satellite television in particular, he observed, made it possible for "information-hungry residents of many closed societies to bypass state-controlled television channels."[5] In response, Beijing enforced a ban on the reception of foreign satellite television in China.

In the intervening years, Murdoch slowly inched back into favor with the Beijing government. Star TV stopped showing BBC news. Control of Hong Kong's *South China Morning Post* was sold to an ethnic Chinese tycoon perceived as sympathetic to Beijing. He also pulled out of a book contract with Chris Patten, the last governor of Hong Kong. As he said at the time: "We're trying to set up in China, why should we upset them?"

The first signs of rehabilitation dawned in 1999, when News Corp., Murdoch's media group, was allowed to open a representative office in Beijing, the only major foreign media company granted that privilege. President Jiang Zemin praised Murdoch for "presenting China objectively and cooperating with the Chinese press." Murdoch single-mindedly continued his campaign. There was a venture to archive the Chinese newspaper, the *People's Daily*, and a documentary about Tibet made under Beijing's direction, which cost $450,000 but made only $175,000 in its first year of release. Murdoch's new wife, a mainland Chinese, also contributed – she was reported to be working on "special projects" for the company in China.

The payoff came in March 2002 when Xing Kong Wei Shi (Starry Sky Satellite TV) began broadcasting for the first time. One of the programs, "Wanted," was produced in collaboration with the Chinese Ministry of Security.

Moral: You can probably work it out for yourself.

Star Wars Part II

In the next few years, Star seemed to go from strength to strength. In 2004, it set up a joint venture, Phoenix (Qinghai) Satellite TV with Liu Changle, an ex-army officer in charge of military broadcasts, and gave CCTV, the national broadcaster, a stake in the venture. Phoenix became popular all over

China, especially its game shows, including one in particular. Called "Women in Control," its novelty was that the contestants were men and the judges women. It also featured scantily dressed models. Chinese leaders were said to particularly appreciate Phoenix's smooth, professional coverage of state affairs, in which they appeared far less gray and dreary than in the official media. Perhaps for this reason, they conveniently overlooked the fact that Phoenix was on air thanks to black market satellite dishes.

Meanwhile, Star TV itself gained approval to launch China's first wholly foreign-owned advertising company in July 2004. Announced with some fanfare, the new venture, to be based in Shanghai, was to handle Star's advertising for its TV channels. "For us this was a chance to expand our commitment to the China market," said Star China's president, Jamie Davies. "We are excited about the speed with which we were able to go through all the approval processes."[6] Once again, it seemed, Star was ahead of rival broadcasters.

Mr and Mrs Murdoch also seemed to bask in the sun of government approval. They were said to have acquired a residence near the Forbidden City in Beijing, and Murdoch himself became a privileged insider, sharing a viewing of the film *Titanic* (made by his own Fox film studio) with Jiang Zemin, who apparently praised its depiction of the "class struggle."[7] Murdoch even gave a lecture at the Central Party School that trained future leaders and was named "trusted mentor" of the China TV industry. What *guanxi*.

However, beneath the veneer, Star was not making the headway Murdoch had anticipated. Far from proving to be the gateway into the world's largest untapped media market, his Shanghai venture still remained subject to strict limits, only allowed to broadcast to parts of the southern province of Guandong and to approved residential compounds and upmarket hotels. Moreover, the new Chinese President Hu Jintao appeared less taken by the Murdoch charm and instead of leading the long expected opening up of the sector, initiated a crackdown on foreign media. Promises of a limited opening of the TV production business disappeared in a flurry of concerns over "national cultural security" but this was not the worst. In August 2005, Star's Phoenix Satellite joint venture, in which it was said to have invested $40 million, was canceled, and the authorities were said to be investigating Star for selling illegal decoders to Chinese viewers.

Murdoch's patience finally cracked. All the years of appeasement went for nothing, when in September 2005, he publicly complained that News Corp. had "hit a brick wall in China" and accused the authorities of being "paranoid" about the foreign media. For good measure, he also criticized the US Internet portal Yahoo! for supplying the Chinese authorities with information that enabled them to uncover the identity of a local dissident journalist who was later sentenced to 10 years in jail. In November, 2005, Star announced that it was unlikely to make any "significant" money in its loss-making Chinese business for up to two years. The story seemed over when in June 2006, News Corp. announced it was selling a 20 percent stake in Phoenix to China Mobile, the leading state-controlled wireless operator. But Murdoch watchers have learned never to write him off. Soon after there were rumors that News Corp. might be joining forces with the Macquarie Group to buy out the telecoms and media assets – including the highly regarded NOW broadband TV business – of Richard Li's Hong Kong-based PCCW. Could this signal a new attempt on China for Murdoch? Don't miss Part III!

Moral: In China, the only certainty is that politics will always triumph over business. No *guanxi* will ever be strong enough to counter the government's determination to hold onto power – especially when it comes to the media.

A Learning Process

Many multinationals admit to having made mistakes in their approach to their Asian joint ventures and acquisitions, but did they learn from them? And, if not, how can they avoid falling into the same traps the next time?

These are good questions that usually remain unanswered. Few companies have the time or the processes to capture vital information about the evolution of their relationships with the companies they have acquired, or their partners, and describe what happened and what changes were made. Although successes may be celebrated by graphs showing production outputs and profit rises, failure and the reasons for it are usually quickly forgotten. Yet documenting this failure could help to build up valuable expertise at the center, which could then be transmitted to those about to be sent out to take over and continue the work in progress, or run new investments. Unfortunately, the present habit of rotating expatriate managers every three years, which has become the norm, militates against any long-term database of local knowledge and experience. The maxim that managers feel lost for the first year of their posting, come to grips with it during the second and only truly perform in the third holds for many. It is a pity then that after that one good year, they are sent back home or on a cross-posting. The experience they carry in their heads is often lost.

However, if this knowledge was recorded, it could be used to brief those just setting out, or to give presentations within the company. Inchcape of the UK, for example, developed a series of case studies that gave a picture of the company's operations, and these were given to new managers to read and learn from.[8] Cemex, the Mexican cement group, keeps an archive of documents on the PMI process for different acquisitions, which is used as a reference for new acquisitions.

Unfortunately, such forethought is rare. If, instead of burying mistakes, companies were able to analyze what went wrong and why, it might prevent heavy, unnecessary losses in the future, or enable companies to work faster in turning around a new acquisition. It might even prevent a second disaster.

Notes

1   *EIU Business China*, "Back from the brink," 15 February, 1999, pp1–2.
2   Taken from "Hindustan Lever Limited: levers for change," a case study by Charlotte Butler and Professor Sumantra Ghoshal, LBS-INSEAD-EAC.
3   Taken from "Ferodo (Thailand) Ltd." (A) and (B), case studies by Charlotte Butler, Anne-Marie Cagna and Professor Henri-Claude de Bettignies, 2001, INSEAD-EAC.
4   Taken from "Bull Run," case study by Ted Chan and Professor Gordon Redding, INSEAD-EAC and *Asiamoney*, "The Fair Weather Friend," by Fiona Haddock, December 2001–January 2002, 12(10).
5   *Far Eastern Economic Review*, "Star crossed," 27 July, 2000, pp30–2.
6   *Financial Times*, "China opens advertising to Murdoch's Star," 6 July, 2004, p15.
7   *The Economist*, "The end of the affair," 24 September, 2005, p74.
8   See "Managers & Mantras: One Company's Search for Simplicity," Charlotte Butler and John Keary, Wiley & Sons (Asia), 2000.

Acknowledgements

WHO DO WE THANK?

This book would not have been written if Robyn Flemming, who edited several of our previous books, had not detected the fact that we had a similar approach to writing and so should at least meet. Meet we did and over a long lunch opposite the Paris Bourse, the outline for this book evolved. As Robyn herself remarked, most "good" ideas developed over a long lunch evaporate as soon as the bonhomie induced by the wine wears off. But that was not the case for us. We ended up with a contract with Palgrave Macmillan.

And so it is the folks at Palgrave Macmillan who must also receive our thanks. Their enthusiasm and hard work in producing the book, especially Stephen Rutt who was our first contact with the company and has been the positive and encouraging *éminence gris* behind every edition, has been greatly appreciated.

Separately, Michael Backman would like to thank businessman and gourmet Jeffrey Tan of Melbourne for his many valuable insights on the practicalities of doing business across Asia, and also the many readers of his columns who have written to him with first-hand accounts of their own experiences.

Charlotte Butler would like to put on record her thanks to the Euro-Asia Centre and its directors, Arnoud De Meyer, Ben Bensaou and Gordon Redding, all of whom encouraged the writing of this book and gave her the time to work on it. She would also like to thank the Euro-Asia Centre faculty with whom she has worked over the last 15 years to produce the case studies that provide vivid illustrations for many of the book's chapters. Such a varied (in terms of nationalities, characters and expertise) team of colleagues has made for a rewarding, enjoyable and certainly never dull experience. Mary Boldrini was a tremendous help in tracking down sources and finally, a big thank you to my two great supports, Keeley Wilson and Joan Lewis.

London and Fontainebleau

Every effort has been made to trace all the copyright holders but if any have been inadvertently overlooked the publishers will be pleased to make the necessary arrangements at the first opportunity.

 # Abbreviations

AFTA	ASEAN Free Trade Association
AIDS	acquired immune deficiency syndrome
APEC	Asia-Pacific Economic Cooperation
ASEAN	Association of South East Asian Nations
BP	business processing
BPO	business process outsourcing
EIU	Economist Intelligence Unit
FDI	foreign direct investment
FIE	foreign-invested enterprise
FMCG	fast-moving consumer goods
GAPP	generally accepted accounts practices
HR	human resource
HRM	human resource management
IBRA	Indonesian Bank Restructuring Agency
ILO	International Labour Organization
IMF	International Monetary Fund
IPO	initial public offering
IPR	intellectual property rights

KPO	knowledge process outsourcing
LVMH	Louis Vuitton Moet Hennessy
M&A	merger and acquisition
NGO	non-governmental organization
NPL	non-performing loan
OECD	Organization for Economic Cooperation and Development
OEM	original equipment manufacturer
OPEs	out of pocket expenses
PMI	post-merger integration
PPP	purchasing power parity
R&D	research and development
RHQ	regional headquarters
SARS	severe acute respiratory syndrome
SEC	Securities and Exchange Commission (US)
SME	small and medium-size enterprise
SOE	state-owned enterprise
SRI	socially responsible investment
WFOE	wholly foreign-owned enterprise
WHO	World Health Organization
WTO	World Trade Organization

Index

A

Abbey bank 234
abbreviations 413–14
ABN Amro 101, 164, 200
  business processing operations in India
    53
accounting
  accuracy of financial information 2
  monitoring 397
  non-simultaneous closure of companies'
    books 307
accounting firms
  in China 73
  local partners 75
  mergers of 75
  see also auditing; auditors
accounting standards
  differences in 73
  in family firms 16
  worldwide harmonization of 73
acquired immune deficiency syndrome
  (AIDS) 6, 146
acquisitions, *see* mergers and acquisitions

adaptation to local conditions 265–78
  brands 267, 275, 288–9
  cultural habits 268–9
  distribution 266, 271
  fast-moving consumer goods (FMCG)
    sector 268–9
  key lessons 277–8
  marketing 266
  non-adaptation 275
  overadaptation 270
  packaging 267
  products 265–6, 269–73
  regional adaptation 272
Aditya Birla Group 65
administrative heritage 180
advertising 273–5, 282–5
  on the Internet 287–8
  restrictions on, in China 273–4
Africanization campaigns 56–7
AFTA (ASEAN Free Trade Association)
  tariffs 8–9
Aga Khan 57
Agilent Technologies, business processing
  operations in India 53

Agreement on Trade-Related Aspects of
Intellectual Property Rights (TRIPS)
353, 358
agricultural products 9
Ahold 252
aid programs 378–9
obstruction of 379
AIDS (acquired immune deficiency
syndrome) 6, 146
AIG (American International Group) 96,
261–2
Albany Molecular Research Inc. 236
Alcatel 11, 200, 317, 324
All-China Women's Federation 36
Allianz 321
alumni associations/loyalty 49–50, 214–15
American Express 321
business processing operations in India
53
American Home Products Corp. 127
American International Group (AIG) 96,
231, 261–2
America Online (AOL) 231
Amstrad 323
analysts' reports 16
Andersen-SGV 74
Anheuser-Busch 257
animal testing, outsourcing 236–7
annual general meetings, company directors
not attending 244
anonymous letters 189
Anqing TP Goetze Piston Ring Co. Ltd.
(ATG) 326
Ansett 267
AOL (America Online) 231
APEC (Asia-Pacific Economic Cooperation)
352
Apple Computer Inc. 127
arbitration 341, 345
international centers for 345
Arcelor 65
AriaWest 345
Arthur Andersen 73–4
ASB 317
Ascott serviced apartment group 57
ASEAN (Association of South East Asian
Nations) free trade zone 8–9
Asia Cement 45
Asian Delight ice cream 273
Asian economic crisis 1997-98 3, 94
banks 294–5, 301
effect on multinationals 176
opportunities provided by 251, 252–3
Asian Monitor Resource Center, China 371
Asia-Pacific Economic Cooperation (APEC)
352

Asia Pacific Indian Chambers of Commerce
and Industry (APICCI) 67
Asia-Pacific Industrial Property Center 352
Asia Pulp & Paper (APP) 73–4
Asiaweek 273
Asimco 208, 397–8
Asria (Association for Sustainable and
Responsible Investment in Asia) 374
assets, valuation 95
Association for Sustainable and
Responsible Investment in Asia (Asria)
374
Astra International 31–2, 96, 116
AstraZeneca 127
AT&T 318, 344, 345
audit committees, in listed companies 311
auditing 72–6
listed companies' accounts 74–5
auditors
professionalism of 72, 76
questions to ask 77
shortcomings of 73–4
see also accounting firms; auditing
Australia
anti-corruption legislation 385
corruption x
developed legal system 47
GDP per capita (disposable income) x
literacy (adult) x
population x
autonomy
of managers 183
of subsidiaries 398–9
avian flu 6
Aviva 235

B

B&Q 284, 329
Babas 44
bad news, reporting/non-reporting of 70,
188–9, 370
Baidu 287, 287–8
Bajaj Auto 145
Baker Hughes 74
Ballarpur Industries 66
Bangalore 150, 228
Bangkok Bank (Thailand) 296
Bangladesh
corruption x
GDP per capita (disposable income) x
literacy (adult) x
population x
Bank Negara (Malaysia) 294–5, 301
Bank of America 321
Bank of Asia (Thailand) 101, 164

Bank of Central Asia (Indonesia) 9, 263
Bank of China 9, 321, 322
Bank of Japan 300
Bank of Southeast Asia (Philippines) 301
bankruptcy 155, 341–3
banks 293–302
  in Asia 294
  Asian 1997–98 economic crisis 294–5,
    301
  autonomy vs. accountability 300
  borrowing from, strategy checklist 302
  central banks 300–1
  in China 321–2
  conflicts of interest 297–8
  deposits, prudent to diversify 301
  family connections among staff 300
  family control 296–8
  information leakages from 298–9
  in Japan 123–4, 294, 295–6, 300
  as lenders 299
  lending to themselves 296
  little interest in buying into 9
  mergers 301
  Western investment banks 76–7
  willingness to negotiate 301
  see also individual banks and under
    specific countries
BAT (British American Tobacco) 319, 357,
  374
Bayer 200
beer, in China 257
behavior
  changing patterns of 223
  during negotiations 90
Beijing International Switching Corp. 323
Berjaya Group 281, 282
Bhatia, Sabeer 64
BHP-Billiton 386
Bhumipol Adulyadej 44
Bhutan
  GDP per capita (disposable income) x
  literacy (adult) x
  population x
Big C 260
biomedical science, outsourcing 236
bird flu 6
Birla family 65
Birla Group 145
Bloomsbury (publishers) 225–6
Blue Circle 4
BMW 288–9
BMW Korea 138
BMW Tokyo 29
bodyguards, Hong Kong 71
Boeing 235

Bombay, see Mumbai
Bombay Dyeing and Manufacturing
  Company 61
Bonstar 282
Bonvests Holdings 281, 282
books
  about Asia 12
  copying 351–2, 360
Boots 126, 270
borrowing
  by Asian companies 304
  from banks, strategy checklist 302
  and property rights 340–1
Bose Corporation 64
brands 255–7, 279–80
  adapting to local conditions 267, 275,
    288–9
  brand names, mimicry 352
  consumers and 285–7
  different messages according to culture
    290–1
  indigenous to Asia 279–80
  journalists, and brand placing 288
  post-acquisition rebranding 164
  quality 256–7
  reverse-engineered from Asia to the
    West 289
  spending on development 280
  value for money 285
Brazil, outsourcing to 232
bribery 154
  response when asked for bribe 386–7
  see also corruption
Bridge Pharmaceuticals 236
British Airways, business processing
  operations in India 53
British American Tobacco (BAT) 319, 357,
  374
Brunei
  Chinese Chamber of Commerce 50
  ethnic Chinese in 41
  GDP per capita (disposable income) x
  literacy (adult) x
  Muslims in 192
  population x
Buddhism 125
bugging devices 361
Burger King 280
Burma, see Myanmar
business consultants
  faked data 71
  family and equity connections 72
  local 71–2
  out-of-pocket expenses (OPEs) 78
  questions to ask 77

size of firms 71–2
staff calibre 71, 72
subcontracting 72
see also consulting services; information gathering
business culture 109, 214–17
Japan 124–5
South Korea 135–8
see also culture
business intelligence gathering 70–1
business leaders, women 29–30
business process outsourcing (BPO) 53, 237
China 229
India 226–7
Malaysia 232
business schools 200–1
Businesswoman's Roundtable 32

C

Cable & Wireless 344
CAC Brake Ltd 397–8
Caijing 35, 38
Calcutta, *see* Kolkata
California Public Employees' Retirement System (CalPERS) 303–4, 374
call centers
Africa 232
China 229
inconvenience to customers 234
India 226, 231, 234
Malaysia 232
Philippines 231
Cambodia
corruption x
ethnic Chinese in 41
GDP per capita (disposable income) x
literacy (adult) x
population x
Cantonese 42, 42–3
Cap Gemini, business processing operations in India 53
Carlsberg 137, 374
Carlyle Group (US) 318, 319, 327
Carrefour 137, 252–3, 255, 335
adapting to local conditions in Taiwan and Indonesia 269
in China 258
Chinese accusations against 258
in India 148
IT capabilities 269
overadaptation in Japan 270
own *guanxi* 258
in Thailand 252, 260

withdrawal from Korea and Hong Kong 263
Carrian Group 74
carried interests 379, 387
cars
in China 328
piracy 329–30
Cartier 127, 283
case studies as source of information 12–13
Caterpillar Corp. 327
celebrity endorsement 285
cement manufacturers 103
see also Lafarge
Cemex 97, 98
PMI archives 410
censorship 273–4
centralization 180, 182
chaebol 95, 122, 132–5
and banks 295
gearing 134
chambers of commerce 82
Hong Kong 61
overseas Chinese 49, 50–1
overseas Indian 67
Chan, Ronnie 43
change
aspects of 211–12
behavior patterns 223
communication, internal 166, 221
cultural 163, 164–6
difficulties in making 216–17
effects of 221–3
in finance function 221
human resource systems 219
leadership in making 222–3
measuring 223–4
obstacles to 169–70
patience needed for 218–19
peer pressure for 223–4
prioritizing change areas 223
processes and systems 169–70
procrastination in avoidance of 222
rebranding 164
resistance to 212–13
strategies for 218–21
type and depth of 161–2
see also mergers and acquisitions
change management 211–24
principles of 224
Chao, Frank 45
Chaozhou, *see* Chiu Chow
Charoen Pokphand (CP) Group 114, 116, 252
Chearavanont family (Thailand) 43, 114

chemical/gas leaks 370
Chengdu 328
Chennai 228
Chew Choo Keng 22
chief executive officers (CEOs) in India 53
child labor 371, 372
China
    accounting firms, local 73
    advertising in 273–4, 282–3
    airports 151
    animal testing 236
    arbitration 341
    Asian Monitor Resource Center 371
    assembly lines 34
    attrition rate of Western companies 6
    bankruptcy in 155
    bankruptcy proceedings/enforcement in
        342
    banks 294, 295, 300, 321–2
    business process outsourcing (BPO)
        229
    call centers 229
    cars 328, 329–30
    cautious approach to 322–3, 335–6
    challenges facing 145–6
    changing rules and regulations 9, 318,
        319, 330
    Communism in 201
    consumers 285–6, 332–3
    contract approval 7
    controlling shares in state companies
        318
    corruption, *see* corruption in China
    counterfeiting 327–8, 330, 352
    diamonds 291–2
    directory assistance 229
    discrimination and non-enforcement of
        laws 36–7
    education 201, 327–8
    engineering focus in higher education
        229
    English language teaching 229, 327–8
    entering the Chinese market 315–16
    entry barriers to key sectors 318
    expanding economy 331
    expatriate managers in 176, 178
    female literacy and education 34
    female migrants in 26
    finance sector 327
    foreign companies in 320–1
    foreign direct investment (FDI) in 145,
        320
    foreign-invested enterprises (FIEs) 317
    franchising 330
    the future 336–7

future investment prospects 326–31
GDP per capita (disposable income) x,
    144, 331
government 146–7
government interference 330
government statistics 331–2
Great Western Development Policy 328
India compared with 143–59
information technology services in 229
infrastructure 148, 151–2
insurance 261–2, 327
intellectual property abuse 353–4
investment in 10–11
joint ventures 6, 317, 323–4
judiciary 156
key lessons 337
labor laws 166
labor shortages 373
lack of raw materials 146
legal services 318
leisurewear 327
light manufacturing exports 146
linguistic skills 229
listed companies' shares 318
literacy x, 34, 144
localization 7
luxury goods 328
management in 201–2
manufacturing 157–8
market assessment hints 333–5
market for consulting services 245
market returns, potential/actual 331
merger and acquisition failures 97–8
Ministry of Foreign Trade and Economic
    Cooperation (MOFTEC) 317
mobile phones 150
most influential women 36
movement of R&D operations to 11
Muslims in 192
names, meanings of 288–9
negotiating in 322–3
New Economic Zones 151
"Open Door" policy 315–16
outsourcing to 229–30
partnership struggles 316–31
piracy 316, 324, 329–30, 351
political risks 8, 9
population x, 144, 201
privatization 7, 147
R&D centers 324
recent development 145
relationship with Japan 256, 320
research and development 145, 158
sexual harassment 37
software piracy 351

State Economic and Trade Commission
    258
state-owned enterprises (SOEs) 316,
    324, 325–6
strengths and weaknesses 145
successful women, categories 35–6
surnames, spelling and pronunciation
    45–6
sweated labor 372, 372–3
telecommunications 318, 319
telecommunications infrastructure 229
television in 282–3, 283–4
Three Gorges project 364
tobacco products 352
trade with India 145
transport 149, 151, 152, 329
universities forming partnerships 200
US firms in 320
western companies as donors to Chinese
    schools 200
wholly foreign-owned enterprises
    (WFOEs) 317
women in 26, 26–7, 33–7
World Trade Organization membership
    251, 318, 326
youth market 332–3
China Construction Bank 321, 342
China Europe International business school
    (CEIBS) 200
China International Economic and Trade
    Arbitration Commission (CIETAC) 341
China Mobile 409
China Pacific Life Insurance Co. 327
Chinese family firms 110–14
    autocratic leadership 111
    centralization of power 110–11
    cronyism 113, 114
    lack of ostentation 111–12
    nepotism in 113
    new generation 113–14
    patriarchal influence 113–14
    reforms impeded 114
    secrecy culture 112
Chinese languages and dialects 42–4
    occupations and 48
Chinese (Lunar) New Year 194
Chinese overseas 40–51
    associations, clubs, societies 48–50
    business successes 46–7
    chambers of commerce 46, 50–1
    changing importance relative to overseas
        Indians 52, 68
    cross-border connections 83–4
    dialects and occupations 48
    economic crisis 41

home provinces of 42
legal contract enforcement mechanisms
    46
occupations and dialects 48
operating where legal protection is poor
    46–7
population in Southeast Asian countries
    41
self-help organizations 48
Chinese-owned firms, negotiating with 89
Chiu Chow (Teochiu) 42, 43, 48
Christian Dior 156
Chugai 128–9
Chung Eui-sun 135
cigarettes, see tobacco
Cisco 158
Cisco Systems 197
Citibank 231, 234
Citigroup 64, 200, 321
Citizen Ombudsman System, South Korea
    383
civil servants 391
classmate associations/loyalty 49–50,
    214–15
Coca-Cola 127, 137, 266, 288
Cogentrix 365
commission payments 379
commitment, in partnerships 119–20
Common Effective Preferential Tariff 9
communication
    with head office 179–80
    improving 166, 221
    in Japan 125
    with labor force 208
    regular meetings 221
    see also information
Communism 201
    women and 26–7, 33–4
community projects 259
companies
    non-simultaneous closure of companies'
        books 307
    see also listed companies;
        multinationals; unlisted companies
company culture, new staff and 206–7
company directors, and annual general
    meetings 244
competence profiling 205
competition 9–12
    becoming keener 263
    information collection about 10
    key lessons 263–4
    laws 341
    need for awareness of 398–400
    success breeding more obstacles 257–8

competitive prices 253
Computer Associates 64
confidence building, by consultants 248
confidentiality
    breaches of, and outsourcing 234
    consulting services and 248
    of information 72, 90, 360–1
    no observance of 214
    staff confidentiality 360–1
Confucianism 125, 135, 377–8
conglomerates, complex family structures
    242
connections
    cross-border 83–4
    developing 85–6
    network of 82
    political, see politically connected
        partners
    see also relationships
consulting services 238–49
    attitude of Asian firms toward 241
    clients' expectations of 246
    confidence building 248
    confidentiality agreements 248
    considerations in targeting Asian market
        247–9
    emphasis on goods before services
        238–9, 239
    fees 238, 240, 245, 247, 248
    low demand for 238–9
    market for 245
    need for vs. desire for 247
    outsourcing 240–1
    prior specification of work 246
    public relations (PR) consultants 246
    selling services 245–9
    subcontracting 240–1
    as targets for blame 245, 246
    working with client's staff 248, 248–9
    see also business consultants;
        management consultants
consumer market research 243
consumer protection laws 341
consumers
    as allies 260
    brand consciousness 285–7
    Chinese 285–6, 332–3
    Indian 286–7
    in Japan 125–6
contracts 343–5
    Asian perspectives on 344
    legal contract enforcement mechanisms
        46
    penalty clauses, effect on early
        relationships 343
    repudiation 344

signing 343–5
simplicity of 343
when law is poor 343–5, 347
written confirmation 343
Convention on Combating Bribery of
    Foreign Public Officials in International
    Business Transactions (OECD) 384–5,
    385
Coopers & Lybrand 75
coping strategies 194–5
copyright 350
    circumvention of 352
cornering, of stocks 309–10
corruption 8, 376–89
    in Asian countries x
    in China, see corruption in China
    cost of 380
    forms of 378–80
    in India 144, 153–4
    levels of 380
    moves against, in Asia 382–4
    moves against, internationally 384–5
    petty 378–9, 384
    purchasing and supply 388
    response when asked for bribe 386–7
    serious 379–80
    in South Korea 135
    strategies for dealing with 385–8
    women and 37–8
corruption in China x, 144, 153, 154–5,
    322, 329
    punishments for 382
    recorded increase in 377
    sanctions against 382
counterfeiting 275
    in China 327–8, 330
country managers 170, 171
credit ratings 304
criticism
    attitude to 76
    see also face
cronyism
    in Chinese family firms 113, 114
    in South Korea 135
cross-shareholding
    in family firms 17, 19
    Japan 124
cultural habits, adapting to 268–9
cultural knowledge and sensitivity 102
cultural sensitivity, post-merger 163
culture 84–5
    affecting consulting services 239–40
    company culture, new staff and 206–7
    influence on workplace 186–95
    manufacturing culture 171
    see also business culture

customer service 253–4
Cycle and Carriage Ltd (Singapore) 117

D

Dabhol Power 344
Daewoo 101, 133, 134, 136–7
Daft, Douglas 125, 177
Dah Sing Financial Holdings 44
Dairy Farm International 281
Danaharta 294
Dao Heng Bank Group (Hong Kong) 301
data mining 226
DBS Bank (Singapore) 244, 298, 301
De Beers 290–2
Debenhams 280
decentralization 180–1
Deepavali 193–4
defamation 345–6
defense forces, involvement in business
     391–2, 394
Defensor-Santiago, Miriam 91
Deloitte Touche Tohmatsu 73
Delta Airlines 231
Deming 125
deregulation, move toward 6
detergents 399–400
Deutsche Bank 136
Dharmala Group 41
diamond trade 59–60, 290–2
directors, independent 311–12
directory assistance 229
direct selling 260, 266–7
Disneyland 290
disposable income x
distribution, adapting to local conditions
     266, 271
divorce rates 28
Diwali 193–4
documentation and analysis, as aid to
     building on experience 409–10
Dongguan 26
Dongsuh Industrial Company Ltd 139–41
     division of responsibility 139
     growth of 140
     relationships 140–1
     technology transfer 140
Donorgate 86
Dorys Herlambang 31
dot-com services 240–1
Dow Corning 136
downsizing, post-acquisition 166–7
dowries 28
drugs
     clinical studies 236

drugs trade 12
     manufacturing 158
due diligence 82, 87–8, 168, 169, 321, 360
     cultural 101–2
     family firms 16, 24
     inadequate 100–1
     reports 69–70
     team membership 102

E

East Timor 47
     GDP per capita (disposable income) x
     literacy (adult) x
     population x
economic crisis, *see* Asian economic crisis
economic data 6
economic growth, women and 26
Economist Intelligence Unit (EIU) 3, 6
education
     China 327–8
     elementary and secondary 201
     engineering focus 227–8, 229
     see also business schools
Eka Tjandranegara 43
Ek-Chai Distribution System 252
Electronics City 228
electronics industry, R&D outsourcing 233
Eli Lilly 233
Elle 289
emergency plans 6
empowerment of managers 183–4
engineering focus in higher education
     227–8, 229
engineering graduates 199
engineers
     with management experience 202
     turnover 197
English, as world business language 52, 85
English language capability 226, 228, 229,
     230
     India 144, 146, 201, 226, 228
English language newspapers 12
English language teaching, China 229,
     327–8
Enoki, Keiichi 33
Enron Corporation 344
entertainment 386
entrepreneurialism 182
entrepreneurs
     distrustful of media 244
     ethnic Chinese emphasis on trade 239
     style of 242
environmental issues 363–4, 364–7
     downstream emissions 366

external environment 6–7
forest management 366–7
increasing Western and local lobbying 364
Ericsson 128, 324
Escort Group 58
Estrada, Joseph 38
ethical issues 363–75
Evalueserve 226–7
excise stamps and labels 380
expatriate managers, *see* managers, expatriate
expatriates working for Asian firms 189–92
coping strategies 194
ExxonMobil 6, 97, 259, 319, 374

F

face
concept of 76
loss of 91, 101, 105, 125, 188
Fair Labor Association 372
family connections 91–2
family control of listed companies 304
family firms 15–24
accounting standards in 16
assets 17
borrowing vs. new share issues 18
cash flow vs. profits 16
Chinese, *see* Chinese family firms
cross-shareholding 17, 19
effect of polygamy on 22–3
gearing ratios 18
guidelines on partnering 24
infighting 20–2, 55
influence of families 16
information needed in dealing with 23–4
maintaining family control 16–17, 18
Philippines seminar for business families 21–2
prestige 19
problems arising from structure of 18–19, 21
proportion of 16
pyramid structures 17, 19–20
reasons for existence 18
related-party transactions 17
voting rights 17, 20
women and 26
Far Eastern Department Stores 45
Far Eastern Economic Review 61, 244
Far Eastern Group 45
Far Eastern International Bank 45
Far Eastern Textiles 45

fasting, impact on productivity 193
fast-moving consumer goods (FMCG) sector, adaptation in 268–9
FDI, *see* foreign direct investment
Fengshun 43
Ferodo Ltd 401–4
Ferodo Thailand Ltd (FTL) 401–4
films, *see* movies
finance
monitoring 397
see also accounting; auditing; banks; borrowing
finance function, changes in 221
finance sector, China 327
financial information, accuracy of 2
financial transparency 168–9
fish sauce 272
Flexitronics 157
Flour Daniel 231
Focus Media Holdings 283
foot binding 33
Ford 4, 101, 136, 320
Foreign Corrupt Practices Act (FCPA) (US) 71, 74, 88, 384
foreign direct investment (FDI) 145
China 320
foreign-invested enterprises (FIEs), China 317
forest management 366–7
Forest Stewardship Council 366
Forever Living Products 260
franchising, in China 330
Freeport-McMoRan Copper & Gold 6, 365–6, 380
free trade zone 8–9
French language competency 233
friendships 85
Fujian conventions 49
Fumiko Hayashi 29
Fuzhou 42, 43, 49

G

Gadjah Tunggal Group 41, 44, 48, 246, 281
gambling 367
Gandhi Seva Loka 67
Gap 372
Gardenia Bakeries 277
gas leaks 370
Gazprom 319
GDP (Gross Domestic Product) x, 144
GE (General Electric) 53, 229, 324
gearing
gearing ratios in family firms 18
South Korea 134

GE Capital 137
Gecis 226
Gembel Group 60
General Electric (GE) 53, 229, 324
General Motors (GM) 101, 136, 320
Genpact 203
Gent, SR 63
geographical aspects, transport/political
   11–12
Ghana, call centers/outsourcing to 232
gift-giving 386
Giordano International 327
GlaxoSmithKline 233
Global Alliance for Workers and
   Communities 372
globalization 265–7
   "glocal" approach 267, 272
   South Korea 133
GM (General Motors) 101, 136, 320
Godrej Group 61
Goldman Sachs 118, 321
Gondokusumo family 41
goods before services 238–9, 239
goodwill
   attached to owners of firms 82
   generated by staying power 4
Google 137, 287–8
government, China/India 146–7
government partnerships 115
government projects 115
government spending plans 6
   establishing basis of 6–7
government statistics 70
graduates, in India/China 198, 199–201
   standard of 199–200
Graha Sindhu (Sindhi House) 67
Greenberg, Harold 261–2
Gross Domestic Product (GDP) x, 144
groups, non-simultaneous closure of
   companies' books 307
Guangdong Development Bank (GDB) 321
Guangdong Province 229
Guangnan (Holdings) Ltd 73
guanxi 81, 83, 109, 110
Gucci 328
Gujarati Hindus 56
Gunawan family connections 92
Gurgaon 228

H

Hadi, Susanto & Co 75
Haier CCT 323
Haier Group 29, 37, 145
Hainanese (Kheng Chew) 42, 43, 49

Hakka (Keh) 42, 43, 48, 49
Hanaro Telecom 96
Hang Lung 43
Harilela family (Hong Kong) 58–9, 66
   hotel holdings 58, 66
Hari Raya 193
HCL Technologies 233
health insurance claims 226
Heineken 374
Henghua 42, 43–4, 48
Hill & Associates 70–1
Hindalco 145
Hind Development Group 66
Hinduja family 58
Hindustan Lever (HLL) 398–400
hiring practices, Indians overseas 53
Hitachi 361
Ho Ching 29
Ho, Stanley 23
Hokchia 42, 43
Hokkien 42, 48
holograms 361
Honda 207, 316
Hong Kong
   banks in 294, 301
   Chinese General Chamber of Commerce
     in Hong Kong 50
   corruption x, 382–3
   GDP per capita (disposable income) x
   Hong Kong General Chamber of
     Commerce 61
   Independent Commission Against
     Corruption (ICAC) 382
   Indian Chamber of Commerce Hong
     Kong 67
   Indians in 55, 61
   Law on Bribery Prohibition 383
   literacy (adult) x
   Monetary Authority 301
   population x
   shipping 45
   textile industry 44–5
Hong Leong 42
Horlicks 280
hotels 58, 59, 62–3, 66, 297
Hotmail 64
HSBC 136, 228, 229, 235
Hsu family (Taiwan) 45
Huawei 145
Hubei Lihua 73
Huizhou 43
human resource issues, in mergers and
   acquisitions 166–8
human resource management (HRM) staff
   208

Hung Fung Group Holdings 311
Hu Shuli 35, 38
Hutchison Whampoa 113
Hyderabad 228
Hynix Semiconductor 96
hypermarkets 252–3, 253, 269, 270
Hyundai Group 133, 134, 135
Hyundai Securities 96

I

IBM 11, 127, 226, 228
IBRA (Indonesian Bank Restructuring
    Agency) 32, 75, 96–7
Icahn, Carl 98
ice cream 272–3
ideograms, translating 267
Idul Fitri 193
ignorance 3, 13
    changing balance of power 3–4
    closing options 4–5
    costs of 3–5
    vicious cycle of 3–4
    see also information
IKEA 129, 371
ILO (International Labour Organization)
    conventions 203
IMF, *see* International Monetary Fund
i-mode Internet access 33
Inchcape 119, 365
    case studies 410
India
    airlines 149–50
    bankruptcy in 155
    banks in 294
    business process outsourcing (BPO)
        226–7
    business school graduates 228
    call centers 226, 231, 234
    challenges facing 145–6
    China compared with 143–59
    class-conscious society 89
    consumers in 286–7
    corruption x, 144, 153–4
    drugs manufacturing 158
    education 201
    engineering focus in higher education
        227–8
    English language capability 144, 146,
        201, 226, 228
    female literacy 34
    foreign direct investment in 145
    GDP per capita (disposable income) x,
        144
    government 146–7

importance in world economy 53
information technology services in 226
infrastructure 148–51, 152
intellectual property abuse 354–5
IT industry shortage of professionals
    197
judiciary 155
knowledge process outsourcing (KPO)
    226–7
labor laws 147, 166
lack of raw materials 146
literacy x, 144
manufacturing in 157–8
as a market 156–7
mobile phones 150, 157
outsourcing to 226–9
population x, 144
power sector 148
privatization 7, 147, 150, 151–2
recent development 145
research and development 145, 158
retail industry 148
service exports 146
software exports 226
strengths and weaknesses 145
surnames 53, 58, 59, 61, 62, 64
telecommunications 150
textile industry 147–8
trade unions' resistance to privatization
    9
trade with China 145
transport in 149–50, 153
universities, private 199
Indian family businesses, infighting 55
Indian firms, negotiations with 89
Indian Institute of Management (IIM) 199
Indians overseas 52–68
    chambers of commerce 67
    changing importance relative to overseas
        Chinese 52, 68
    clan networks 53–4
    cross-border joint ventures 66–7
    cultural, language and religious
        differences among 53
    heads of multinational corporations 65
    hiring practices 53
    populations 55
    relationships among 54
    resentment toward 54
    in the West 64–5
Indonesia
    bankruptcy proceedings in 342
    banks in 294, 299, 301
    corruption x, 381–2
    Department of Manpower 189
    ethnic Chinese in 41

GDP per capita (disposable income) x
Indians in 55
intellectual property abuse 355
labor laws 166, 189
literacy (adult) x
local partners required by law 86
ministries and police powers 81
money lending 47
political risks 8
population x
privatization plans 7
resentment against Chinese 44
Sindhi chamber of commerce and
    cultural center 67
software piracy 351
state control 16
technical advisers 81
women in 30, 31
Indonesian Bank Restructuring Agency
    (IBRA) 32, 75, 96–7
Indorama Group 66
IndUS Entrepreneurs 67
Industrial and Commercial Bank of China
    321
industrial market research 243
information
    advantages resulting from 14
    ambiguity and inadequacies of 69–79
    blocking 216
    collecting, *see* information gathering
    in companies 70
    confidential 72, 90, 360–1
    economizing on 78–9, 89
    financial 2
    importance of local knowledge 2, 3–4,
        5
    on joint ventures 10
    local business cycles 3
    about political risks 8
    poor disclosure of 310
    as power 1–13
    on prospective partners 115–16
    reporting/non-reporting of bad news 70,
        188–9, 370
    in risk reduction 1–2
    sources of 12–13
    see also communication; ignorance
information gathering
    American approach 78–9
    Australian approach 79
    business intelligence 70–1
    about competitors 10
    failure to gather 2
    heeding of information gathered 5–6
    Japanese approach 71, 79
    local offices collecting 13

via networks of friends and colleagues
    81
ongoing 14
personally collecting 13
UK approach 79
see also business consultants
information technology services
    China 229
    India 226
    systems/skills 254–5, 269
Infosys 145, 150, 197, 228, 230, 233
infrastructure 11–12
    China 148, 151–2
    India 148–51, 152
    see also telecommunications
        infrastructure
ING, business processing operations in
    India 53
inhibitors, structural 268
insider trading 310
insurance, in China 261–2, 327
Integrity Pacts for Transparency in Public
    Procurement Procedures 387–8
Intel 158, 197, 328
intellectual property abuse 348–62
    combatting 357–61
    considerations before setting up in Asia
        361
    enforcement agencies underresourced
        359
    incentive gap reduction 359–60
    individual countries 353–7
    investigations 359
    "Leaders' Meeting" 357
    legal remedies 358
    lobbying 358
    mimicry 352
    quality of pirated goods vs. licensed
        products 350, 351, 355, 360
    technical solutions 361
    widespread practice 349–52
intellectual property protection 71
International Labour Organization (ILO)
    conventions 203
International Monetary Fund (IMF) 7, 251
    rescue package for South Korea 134,
        136
Internet
    i-mode 33
    profile building 287–8
    use by overseas Indians 55
    women and 27
investment banks 137
    Western 76–7
investment flows, local 47
iPods 127

Irama Unggal Group 66
Islam 192–4
  divorce rates 28
  women and 27, 30–3
Ismaili Khojas 56–7
ISO 9000 registration 170
IT United Corporation 229–30
Izumi Kobayashi 29

J

Jains 59–60
Japan
  administrative guidance 123
  banks 123–4, 294, 295–6, 300
  business culture 124–5
  communication in 125
  consumers 125–6
  corruption x
  cross-shareholding 124
  GDP per capita (disposable income) x, 130
  Indian Chamber of Commerce 67
  Indians in 55
  investment in Southeast Asia/China 10–11
  joint ventures 123, 126–32, 141
  keiretsu 122, 123–4
  Large-Scale Retail Store Location Law 130
  lawyers in 341, 342
  legal system 341
  lifetime employment 125
  literacy (adult) x
  market research 243
  Ministry of Economy, Trade and Industry (METI) 124
  Ministry of International Trade and Industry (MITI) 123–4
  numbers of directors 311
  partnerships with Japanese firms 122–32, 141
  Patents Office 352
  political risks 8
  population x
  relationship with China 256, 320
  restrictions on foreign participation 124
  shareholders' access to AGMs 309
  software piracy 351
  women in 26, 32, 33
Japan Brake International (JBI) 401
Japes family 47
jewelry 290–2
Jhunjhnuwala family (Singapore) 66
Jiang Peizen 36

Jiang Shia 35
Jin Mao Tower 152
Jirapat Sirijit 30
job descriptions 218
joint ventures
  break-up 396–7
  in China 6, 317, 323–4
  choosing local partner 86–8
  cross-border 66–7
  with family firms 17, 18, 21, 24
  importance of investigation time 88
  with Japanese firms 123, 126–32, 141
  learning process in 409–10
  relationship difficulties 401–4
  in South Korea 133, 136–41, 142
  see also partnerships
Jolibee Foods 42
journalists 69–70
  payments for brand placing 288
J.P. Morgan Chase 197
J.P. Morgan Chase Japan 29
judiciary
  China 156
  India 155
Jumabhoy family (Singapore) 55, 57, 66
  holdings 57
J. Walter Thomson 282

K

Kamunting Corp. 19
Kapuria family 66
Karachi, Greater Karachi Water Supply Scheme 388
Karaha Bodas 345
Kartini Day 31
Katoen Natie (KTN) 167–8, 181–2, 204, 206–7
Kazuyo Katsuma 29
KDDI 127
Keh (Hakka) 42, 43, 48, 49
keiretsu 122, 123–4
  cross-shareholding 124
Kentucky Fried Chicken (KFC) 256, 280
Kenya, call centers/outsourcing to 232
KFC *see* Kentucky Fried Chicken
Kheng Chew (Hainanese) 42, 43
Khosla, Vinod 64
kickbacks 379, 388
Kim Sung Joo 29
Kim Woo-choong 134
Kingsway Group 375
Klynveld Main Goerdeler 75
knowledge process outsourcing (KPO) 226–7

Kolkata (formerly Calcutta) 228
  leather industries 47
Konka Group 286
Kookmin Bank 134
Korea
  Indian Merchants Association 67
  Indians in 55
  intellectual property abuse 355
  state control 16
  women in 32
  see also South Korea
Korea First Bank 95, 98
Korean Exchange Bank (KEB) 135
KPMG 75
Kraft 320
Krishnan, T. Ananda 63
Kroll Worldwide 70
KT&G 98
Kuala Lumpur, Petronas Towers 63
Kumar, Sanjay 64
Kumar family (Singapore) 59
Kuok, Robert 43, 114
Kutch 56
Kwek Leng Beng, family connections 91
Kwek family (Singapore) 42
Kwok family (Hong Kong) 44–5

L

labor conditions
  Asian Monitor Resource Center 371
  child labor 371, 372
  sweated labor 363, 364, 371–3
labor force
  communications with 208
  effects of shortages 202–3
  lack of skilled workers and managers
    197–8, 198–9
  localizing 196–210
  poaching 202–3
  quality of 199
  recruitment 203–5
  retention 207–8
  returnees 204
  salaries 203
  training 205–7
  Western retirees 204
labor laws 9, 166, 189
  in India 147
Laem Thong Bank 62, 66
Lafarge 13, 184
Lafarge, acquisition case study 103–7
  approaches 105–6
  information gathering 104
  preparation 103

profitability 106–7
Lambert, Ken 402–4
Lamsam family (Thailand) 43
language competencies
  English, *see* English language capability
  French 233
  in India 144, 146, 201, 226, 228
  in Malaysia 232
Laos
  corruption x
  ethnic Chinese in 41
  GDP per capita (disposable income) x
  literacy (adult) x
  population x
Larsen & Toubro 203, 208
law(s)
  competition laws 341
  consumer protection laws 341
  enforcement problems 342–3
  precautions when law is poor 347
  rule of law 339–40
  vagueness in drafting 341
  see also entries beginning with legal
lawyers
  choice of 344
  drawing up contract 344
  in Japan 341, 342
leadership, in making change 222–3
Leading Women Entrepreneurs of the World
  awards 30
learning process in joint ventures 409–10
leather industries, Kolkata (Calcutta) 47
Lee, Dennis, family connections 91–2
legal codes 340
legal contract enforcement mechanisms 46
legal protection, poor 81
legal services, China 318
legal systems, developed 46
legislation 8–9
leisurewear 327
Lenovo 37, 145, 257, 289
letters, anonymous 189
Levi 372
LG Group 96, 133, 134
Li & Fung 19
libel, *see* defamation
Liem Sioe Liong 43
Lien Ying Chow 298
life sciences, outsourcing 236–7
lifetime employment, in Japan 125
Li Ka-Shing 43, 114
Lim Thian Kiat (T.K. Lim) 19–20
Lippo Bank 97
Lippo Group 44
listed companies 304

audit committees 311
auditors' reports 74–5
board size 311
buying into 312–14
changing auditors 75
China 318
excess funds 308
family control 304
independent directors 311–12
insider trading 310
listing as a form of dumping 306
morphing 308
ownership spread too thinly 306
payments for services to 307
poor disclosure of information 310
receivables 307
related-party transactions 307–8
rights issues 306–7
shareholder access to AGMs 308–9
share placings 306–7
stock price manipulation 309–10
see also groups
literacy
of Asian countries x
see also under individual countries
loans from banks 299
"circular" loans 300
localization of labor force 196–210
ABC (strategy guide) 209
China 7
logistics providers 329
Lohia family 66–7
Lone Star 135
L'Oréal 198, 332
loss of face 76, 91, 101, 105, 125, 188
loyalty vs. productivity 240, 242
Lum, Olivia 32
luxury goods 275
China 328
LVMH 127

M

M&A, *see* mergers and acquisitions
Ma, Fred 113
Ma, Mary 37
Macau, intellectual property abuse 355
McDonald's 137, 266, 276
McKinsey 226, 239, 245
Madras, *see* Chennai
Maglev trains 152
Makro 253
Malaysia
advertising in 274

Associated Chinese Chambers of
Commerce and Industry of Malaysia
50–1
banks 294, 294–5
business process outsourcing (BPO)
232
call centers 232
corruption x, 380–1
defamation action 346
ethnic Chinese in 41
GDP per capita (disposable income) x
Indians in 55
intellectual property abuse 349–50, 355
language competencies 232
literacy (adult) x
Malaysian Associated Indian Chamber
of Commerce and Industry 67
Malaysian Indian Congress 54
money lending 47
multicultural workforce 232
multimedia super corridor (MSC)
231–2
Muslims in 192
Optical Disc Act 2000 359
outsourcing to 231–2
political risks 8
population x
staff costs 232
state control 16
women in 30–1
Malaysian Multimedia Development
Corporation (MDC) 231
malpractice 215–16
Mamak people 192
management
in China 201–2
development programs 208
monitoring of local management 397
see also change management; media
management
management consultants
cultural problems faced by 242
see also consulting services
managers
international/regional cadre of 184
teamwork training 207
managers, expatriate 173–85
calibre of 177
in China 176, 178
communications with head office
179–80
coping strategies 194–5
different standards 178
empowerment and autonomy of 183–4

establishment of manager's own team
  218–19
families, drawbacks for 175
head office attitude toward 177–8
head office targets 179
importance of 176–7
insider vs. outsider stance 217
negotiating skills 178–9
postings to Asia 177, 183
preparedness for post 174–5, 183, 184
qualities and skills required in 178–9
relationship with multinational head
  office 175
support systems for 180–2
working alongside local staff 170
Mandarin (Putonghua) 42
manufacturing
  China/India 157–8
  labor turnover rates in China 198
manufacturing culture 171
Mao-Tse-tung 33
Marcos family (Philippines) 391
Marimutu family 63–4
marketing
  Asian vs. Western 11–12
  labor turnover in China 198
marketing adaptation 266
marketing services 245–6
marketing skills, strengths in 253–5
market niches 47
market research 243, 277
markets, fragmented, consolidation of 257
market segmentation 270
Marlboro 273
Marwaris 65
matrilineal groups 28–9
Matsunaga, Mari 33
Mattel 371
Mauritius, outsourcing to 233
Maxim's 281, 282
Maxwell, Robert 18
media
  advertising 273–5, 282–3
  English language newspapers 12
  relationship with 370
  selective reporting 69–70, 82
media management 243–4
media training 243–4
medical transcription 231
Megawati Sukarnoputri 31
Mehta, Kirtilal Manilal 60
Mei Da Coffee Co. 281
Meixian 43
Melwani family (Singapore) 59
Menzes, Victor 64

Merck 127
mergers and acquisitions (M&A) 94–107,
  257
  acquisition failures 396–7
  among Asian companies 103
  business plans 162, 163
  case study, Lafarge 103–7
  changes 161–2
  coordination mechanisms 170–1
  country managers 170, 171
  cultural change 163, 164–6
  downsizing 166–7
  enthusiasm and disillusion 95–8
  failures 97–8
  financial transparency 168–9
  human resource issues 166–8
  integration committee membership 162
  key lessons 107, 172
  opportunity for 94–6
  pitfalls 100–3
  post-acquisition trauma 160–72
  post-merger integration (PMI) 100, 102,
    162–3
  processes and systems 169–70
  quality improvement/control 170
  rebranding 164
  regional headquarters (RHQs) 171
  skilled workforce 167–8
  South African managers 165
  training programs 163, 164–5, 170
  valuation differences 101
  weighing the risks 99–100
  Western operational teams 162–3
Merrill Lynch 226
Merrill Lynch International 405–6
Merrill Lynch Japan Securities 29, 405
METI (Ministry of Economy, Trade and
  Industry, Japan) 124
Metro Manila 253
M Group (Thailand) 43
Micron Technology 96
Microsoft 11, 197, 226, 324, 351
migrant workers 198
military-backed companies 391–2, 394
mimicry, in circumventing copyright laws
  352
Min, Simon 139
Minangkabau 28–9
Minitel 324
minority shareholders 303–14
  sins against 305–12
  see also listed companies
Mirror Group Newspapers 18
MITI (Ministry of International Trade and
  Industry, Japan) 123–4

Mitsubishi 124, 126
Mittal, Lakshmi 65
Mittal Steel 65
mobile phones 286–7
    China 150
    India 150, 157
moneylending, Malaysia and Indonesia 47
Mongolia
    GDP per capita (disposable income) x
    literacy x, 27
    population x
    women in 26
morale, effects of change 222
Motorola 158, 287, 324
movies, pirated 348–50
    government censorship and 349
MphasiS 234
mu-chips 361
Mulia Group 43
multinationals
    administrative heritage 180
    attitude toward expatriate managers
        177–8
    communications with expatriate
        managers 179–80
    effect of 1997–98 economic crisis 176
    Indian heads of 65
    key lessons 183–4
    readiness to send staff to Asia 185
    relationship with expatriate managers
        175
    Western-centric outlook of 183
Multi-Purpose Holdings Bhd (MPHB)
    19–20
Mumbai 153
    flooding in 153
Murdoch, Rupert 318, 406–7
music, pirated 348–9
Muslims 192–4
    in Asia 276–7
    boycott of US products 276
Myanmar
    boycott of products from 374–5
    corruption x
    ethical issues 364, 374
    ethnic Chinese in 41
    GDP per capita (disposable income) x
    Indians in 55
    investment in 47
    literacy (adult) x
    Muslims in 192
    Myanmar Chinese Chamber of
        Commerce & Industry 50
    Myanmar India Business Club 67
    population x

N

Nakornthon Bank (Thailand) 301
names
    Chinese, meanings of 288–9
    Chinese surnames 45–6
    Indian surnames 53, 58, 59, 61, 62, 64
Nanda, Rajan 58
nationalist sentiment 256
NEC 257
negotiating skills, of expatriate managers
    178–9
negotiations 89–90
    basic principles 89–90
    with Chinese-owned firms 89
    impolite behavior 90
    with Indian firms 89
    often protracted 89–90
nemawashi 125
Nepal
    corruption x
    GDP per capita (disposable income) x
    literacy (adult) x
    population x
    women in 27
nepotism, in Chinese family firms 113
Nestlé 333
networked investment, Indians overseas
    66–7
Newbridge Capital Ltd 95, 98
News Corp. 407, 408–9
newspapers, English language 12
Ng, Cheryl 27
Nike 372
Nikko Asset Management 128
Nik Zainiah Nik Abd Rahman 30
Nirma 399–400
Nissan Motor Company 311
Nissan Motor India 29
Nizaris 57
Noida 228
Nokia 137, 229, 270, 286–7
North Korea
    GDP per capita (disposable income) x
    literacy x, 27
    population x
Novartis 127
NT Controller 255
NTT 344
NTT DoCoMo 33, 127
Nursalim family 41, 44, 48

O

Ocampo, Clarissa 38

occupations of overseas Chinese, linked to
    dialects 48
OECD, Convention on Combating Bribery
    of Foreign Public Officials in
    International Business Transactions
    384–5, 385
Office Tiger 227
Ogilvy & Mather 282
Olympic Games 284, 327
Optical Disc Act 2000 (Malaysia) 359
options 4–5
Oracle 11, 226
Oradee Sahavacharin 30
Orange (mobile phones) 118
Orient Overseas 45
outsourcing 225–37
    biomedical science 236
    breaches of confidentiality 234
    to China 229–30
    cost savings 225–6
    disposal of records 234
    to India 226–9
    key considerations 237
    life sciences 236–7
    to Malaysia 231–2
    to the Philippines 230–1
    political considerations 235
    reasons for 225–6
    security issues 233–4
Overseas-Chinese Banking Corporation
    (OCBC) (Singapore) 298
Overseas Union Bank (OUB) (Singapore)
    297–8

P

P&O Nedland, business processing
    operations in India 53
Pacific Century Cyberworks 73
packaging, adapting to local conditions 267
Pakistan
    corruption x
    GDP per capita (disposable income) x
    intellectual property abuse 356
    literacy (adult) x
    population x
    software piracy 351
Pao, Y.K. 45
Park Chung Hee 132–3
Parsis 60–1
    in Hong Kong 61
partners
    politically connected, *see* politically
        connected partners
    research on prospective partners 392–3
    types of 390–1

partnerships
    with Chinese firms 316–31
    choosing a local partner 86–8
    with family firms, guidelines 24
    government partnerships 115
    with Japanese firms, *see* partnerships
        with Japanese firms
    local partners required by law 86
    with Southeast Asian firms, *see*
        partnerships with Southeast Asian
        firms
    with South Korean firms, *see*
        partnerships with South Korean firms
    see also joint ventures
partnerships with Japanese firms 122–32,
    141
    key lessons 141
partnerships with Southeast Asian firms
    108–21
    control 118–19
    control vs. legal power 118–19
    failures 109–10
    information on prospective partners
        115–16
    key principles 120
    leveraging power 119
    objectives, cleared/shared 117–18
    partners to avoid 115
    reasons for 109
    trust and commitment in 119–20
    understanding business culture 109
    withdrawal strategy 120
    see also Chinese family firms
partnerships with South Korean firms 122,
    132–41
    key lessons 142
Patel, Karsanbhai 399–400
patents 350, 354
    royalty payments 352
patronage, Indians in Malaysia 54–5
Pearl River Delta 151
Peat Marwick 75
peer pressure, for change 223–4
Penang 47
People's Bank of China 29
People's Insurance Company of China
    (PICC) 261, 262
Pepsi-Cola 286, 289, 374
Peranakan 44
personalities in business community 82,
    82–3
Pertamina 97, 345
PetroChina 319
Petronas Towers 63
Pfizer 127
pharmaceutical industry 127, 233

Philip Morris 103
Philippines
    back-office work 231
    bankruptcy proceedings in 342
    banks 294, 301
    call centers 231
    corruption x
    English language abilities 228, 230
    ethnic Chinese in 41
    Federation of Filipino Chinese
        Chambers of Commerce and Industry
        51
    Filipino-India Chamber of Commerce
        67
    GDP per capita (disposable income) x
    Indians in 55
    intellectual property abuse 356
    literacy (adult) x
    medical transcription 231
    Muslims in 192
    outsourcing to 230–1
    population x
    telecommunications infrastructure 230
    wage costs 230
    women in 32
Philips 200
Phoenix (Qinghai) Satellite TV 407–8,
    408–9
Phoenix Pulp & Paper 66
PICC (People's Insurance Company of
    China) 261, 262
piracy
    China 316, 324, 329–30, 351
    software 349, 351
    see also cars; movies; music; and under
        individual countries
Pirelli 337
Pizza Hut 256
PLN 344
poison-pen letters 189
politically connected partners 390–5
    benefiting from office 392
    considerations in linking up with 395
    information about 394
    potential problems with 394–5
    uncertainty of political careers 391,
        392, 393, 394
    unwanted 393–4
political risks 8
political sensitivity, need for 407
politician-businessmen 391–2
polygamy, and family ownership 22–3
pooling, of stocks 309
Popo 43
population, of Asian countries x
Posco 134

power
    balance of 3–4
    from information 1–13
power plants 344–5
power sector, India/China 148
Prachai Leophairatana 114
Precious Shipping 66
Premier Oil 374
Premjee Group 66
President Enterprises 281
prices, competitive 253, 254
Price Waterhouse 75
princelings 392
privatization 7
    China 147
    India 147, 150, 151–2
    move toward 7
    state's problems with land title 340–1
    trade unions' resistance to 9
Procter & Gamble (P&G) 231, 233, 333
product adaptation 265–6, 269–73
productivity, vs. loyalty 240, 242
professionals, types of 189
property rights 340–1
protected sectors 263
protective barriers 250–1
Proton 256
Prudential 235
PSA Peugeot Citroen 316
PT Astra 207
publicity, countering negative 259
public relations (PR) consultants 246
Pudong 152
    International Airport 152
Pune 228
purchasing, corruption and 388
Putonghua (Mandarin) 42
Putrajaya 231
pyramid structures, in family firms 17,
    19–20

Q

quality, post-merger quality
    improvement/control 170
Quek Leng Chan, family connections 91
Quek family (Malaysia) 42

R

Rachmadi, Bambang 276
Rafidah Aziz 31
Ramadan 193
ramping, of stocks 309
Ranbaxy 145
rebranding, post-acquisition 164

receivables 307
Red Bull 289
red tape 340
Reebok 372
regional headquarters (RHQs) 171
related-party transactions 307–8
 family firms 17
relationships
 Asian–Western 4
 China–Japan 256, 320
 in Chinese business dealings 54
 company linkages 92
 developing 85–6
 difficulties with 401–4
 family connections 91–2
 importance of 80–3
 in Indian business dealings 54
 among Indians overseas 54
 with local people 258–9
 with local staff 88
Renault–Nissan partnership 128
research and development (R&D)
 centers in China 324
 faked results 324
 hubs 145
 move to China 11
 outsourcing 233
retail sector
 India 148
 labor turnover 197
retention of labor force 207–8
Reuters 227
Revision of US Trade Act 252
Riady, James 86
Riady, Mochtar 44
rice trade 66
rights issues 306–7
Rini Soewandi 31–2, 38
risk reduction, information role 1–2
Roche 128–9
Rockport Shoes 280
Rotary clubs 49, 82
Royal Sporting House 62
rumors, malicious 277
Russia, outsourcing services 232
Rustan Coffee Corp. 281
Ruttonjee family 61
Ryu, Hong Woo 139

S

safety standards 367–9
 teaching of safety habits 368, 369
salaries 203
 basis of 219

Salim family 9, 41
Salim Group 43, 97
Sampoerna 103
Samsung 133, 135, 252
Samsung Electronics 134
Sanan Kajornprasart 383
Sarbanes-Oxley Act (US) 228–9
SARS (Severe Acute Respiratory Syndrome)
 6
Sazaby Inc. 281
Schlumberger 335
Scotts Holdings 21, 55, 57
secrecy culture, in Chinese family firms 112
security issues, in outsourcing 233–4
segyewha 133
Seiyu 129, 130, 131–2
self-help organizations, Chinese overseas 48
Senna Li 35
service exports, India 146
Severe Acute Respiratory Syndrome (SARS)
 6
sexual harassment, in China 37
SGV 74
Shalimar Paints 66
Shanghai 152–3
Shanghai Automotive Industry (SAIC) 324
Shanghai Baosteel 29, 37
Shanghai Bell 317
Shanghainese 44
Shanghai stock market 318
shareholders, single controlling shareholder
 16
share placings 306–7
Shell 205, 319
Shenzen 373
Shiites 57
Shin Corp., share price 310
Shinsege Group 281
Shintoism 125
shipping, Hong Kong 45
Shisheido 256–7
shopping malls, India 157
Shroff family 61
Shroff offices 61
Siam Cement 3
Siam Polyester 67
Sidharta & Sidharta 75
Sidharta, Sidharta & Harsono 74
Siemens 161, 183, 229, 323
Sikhs 62
 in Thailand 62
Silicon Valley, California 64
Silicon Valley Technology Group 66
Silver Kim 32
Sinar Mas Group 41, 74
Sindhis 58–9

chamber of commerce and cultural
center 67
Sindoh Ricoh 137
Singapore
banks in 294, 296, 297–8, 301
biomedical science outsourcing 236
Chinese relocation to 41
corruption x
corruption free 377–8
Corrupt Practices Investigation Bureau
(CPIB) 382
developed legal system 47
ethnic Chinese in 41
GDP per capita (disposable income) x
Indians in 55
International Arbitration Center 345
literacy (adult) x
Monetary Authority 301
Muslims in 192
political risks 8
population x
Prevention of Corruption Act 383
Singapore Chinese Chamber of
Commerce and Industry 51
Singapore Indian Chamber of
Commerce and Industry 67
software piracy 351
state control 16
Tamils in 63
women in 26, 32
Singapore Airlines 244
Singapore Hong Kong Properties
Investment (SHKPI) 310
Singapore Land 297
SK Group 134, 135
skills gap 188
SK Telecom 29
Skyworth 284
SMGR (Semen Gresik) 97
smuggling 12, 354
Social Accountability International (SAI)
371–2
social etiquette 84
social events 82
socially responsible investment (SRI)
373–5
social responsibilities 259
Soeharto family 9, 392, 393–4
Soeryadjaya, Edward, family connections
92
Soeryadjaya family (Indonesia) 26
Soeryadjaya, William 44
SOEs, see state owned enterprises (SOEs)
software
in China 230
exports from India 226, 230

piracy 349, 351
Sondhi Limthongal 43
Sony 128, 332
Sophonpanich family (Thailand) 40, 43,
296
South Africa, call centers in 232
South African managers, mergers and
acquisitions 165
Southeast Asian firms, see partnerships with
Southeast Asian firms
South Korea
banks in 294, 295
Board of Audit and Inspection 383
business culture 135–8
business environment 137–8
chaebol 95, 122, 132–5
Citizen Ombudsman System 383
corruption x, 135
cronyism 135
firms expanding into China 10
foreign investors' influence 138
GDP per capita (disposable income) x
gearing 134
IMF rescue package 134, 136
joint ventures in 133, 136–41, 142
literacy (adult) x
mergers and acquisitions 95, 98
move to more flexible labor market 138
political risks 8
population x
privatization plans 7
tobacco in 252
trade unions 133, 136, 137
trade unions' resistance to privatization
9
see also Korea; partnerships with South
Korean firms
sponsorship 283–5
celebrity endorsement 285
sports businesses 62
sportswear manufacturers 371
Srifeungfung family (Thailand) 43
Sri Lanka
banks in 294
corruption x
GDP per capita (disposable income) x
literacy (adult) x
population x
Srisakdi Charmonman 22
staff
Asian vs. Western expatriates 186–8
local 7
promotion 188
running private businesses 214–15
salary 188
staff appraisal 219–20

Standard Chartered Bank 98, 213, 301
Starbucks 280–2
   local partners 281–2
Star TV 406–9
state control of companies 16
state owned enterprises (SOEs), in China
   316, 324, 325–6
status symbols 275
staying power 119
   generating goodwill 4
stock price manipulation 309–10
Stringer, Sir Howard 128
structural inhibitors 268
Style Surfers 27
Subhawat, Veeravej 401–3
subsidiaries, autonomy of 398–9
Sungjoo Group 29
Sunkyong 133
Sun Microsystems 64
Sunnis 57
supply, corruption and 388
supply chain management 254
Sura Chansrichawla 62, 66
surnames
   Chinese, spelling and pronunciation
      45–6
   Indian 53, 58, 59, 61, 62, 64
Susilo Bambang Yudhoyono 97
sweated labor 363, 364, 371–3
SWOT analysis 5–6, 9
Sykes Enterprises 231, 234

T

T&N, joint venture strategy 139, 140, 402
Taco Bell 256
tailoring 62
Taipu 43
Taiwan 47
   banks in 294
   corruption x
   firms expanding in China 10, 11
   GDP per capita (disposable income) x
   intellectual property abuse 356
   literacy (adult) x
   population x
Taiwan Semiconductor Manufacturing Co.
   (TSMC) 197, 204
taizi 392
Talwar, Rana 213
Tamils 63–4
Tan Chong Group 21
Tan family (Philippines) 42
Tan, Vincent 346
Tang, Henry 45
Target Media Holdings 283

Tata Consultancy Services (TCS) 145, 197,
   230
Tata family connections 92
Tata Group 61
Tata Motors 145
Tata Steel 145
taxation revenue 380
tax stamps and labels 380
TCL 145, 257, 286
teamwork training, for middle managers
   207
technical advisers, in Indonesia 81
Tejaphaibul family (Thailand) 43
telecommunications
   in China 318, 319
   in India 150
telecommunications infrastructure
   China 229
   Philippines 230
Telekomunikasi Indonesia (Telkom) 344,
   345
television
   in China 282–3, 283–4
   program sponsorship 284
Telstra 344
Temasek Holdings 29, 298
Teochiu (Chiu Chow) 42, 43, 48
terrorist threats 6
Tesco
   adapting to local conditions 270
   in India 148
   IT capabilities 255
   in South Korea 252
   in Thailand 116, 252, 255, 259, 260
Tesco-Lotus 252, 255
Texmaco Group 63
textile industry, Hong Kong 44–5
textile trade, global 147–8
Thai Boonpong Group 401–4
Thai Farmers Bank 43
Thailand
   bankruptcy proceedings in 342
   banks in 294, 301
   corruption x
   corruption website 383–4
   ethnic Chinese in 41
   foreign firms in 252
   foreign investment in 7
   GDP per capita (disposable income) x
   Indians in 55
   intellectual property abuse 356
   literacy (adult) x
   local partners required by law 86
   Muslims in 192
   National Counter Corruption
      Commission 383

political risks 8
population x
privatization in 7
Sikhs in 62
software piracy 351
state control 16
Thai Chinese Chamber of Commerce
    51
trade unions' resistance to privatization
    9
women in 26, 30
Thai Petrochemical Industries (TPI) 114
Thai Prasit Insurance Co. 62
Thakral, Kartar Singh 62–3
Thaksin Shinawatra 7
Thames Water 319
Thaworn Phornpapha 22
Three Gorges project, China 364
Tiang Chirathivat 22
title
    and privatization 340–1
    proof of 340
tobacco 251–2, 273, 284, 319
    counterfeit products 352, 357
Total 374
Toyota 124, 207
trademarks 350
trade unions
    resistance to privatization 9
    South Korea 133, 136, 137
training
    to close skills gap 188
    labor force 205–7
    media training 243–4
    training programs, post-merger 163,
        164–5, 170
Transparency International 8, 387–8
    corruption index 382
transport
    China 149, 151, 152, 329
    India 149–50, 153
TRIPS (Agreement on Trade-Related
    Aspects of Intellectual Property Rights)
    353, 358
Triumph (lingerie) 374
trust 4, 141, 191
    in Chinese business dealings 54
    in Indian business dealings 54
    in partnerships 111, 119
Tsinghua University 324
tsunami 6
Tung, C.Y. 45
Tung Chee Hwa 45

U

Ugandan Indians 56–7
U-Marine Shipping 45
Unilever 180–1, 184, 205, 274–5, 286, 323
    local adaptation 270–3, 274
    see also Hindustan Lever (HLL)
United Industrial Corporation 297
United Kingdom
    corruption x
    GDP per capita (disposable income) x
    literacy (adult) x
    population x
United Overseas Bank (UOB) (Singapore)
    296, 297–8
United Overseas Land 297
United States of America (US)
    corruption x
    Foreign Corrupt Practices Act (FCPA)
        71, 74, 88, 384
    GDP per capita (disposable income) x
    IndUS Entrepreneurs 67
    literacy (adult) x
    population x
    states considering restrictions on
        outsourcing 235
    US firms in China 320
universities
    China, plagiarism/faked research 324
    private, in India 199
unlisted companies
    buying assets only 305
    buying into 304–5
    related-party transactions 307–8
Unocal Corp. 374
US-China Business Council 261
US Trade Representative (USTR) 251, 252

V

Vellu, Samy 54–5
Vendôme Group 275
Victorias Milling Co. 74
Vietnam
    corruption x
    ethnic Chinese in 41
    GDP per capita (disposable income) x
    intellectual property abuse 357
    literacy (adult) x
    mergers and acquisitions 98
    population x
    software piracy 351
Vietnam Professional and Businesswoman's
    Network 27
Vijaykumar, B., & Co. 60
Vijay Shah 60

Virgin Group 120
Vital Bridge Khongguancun Drug
    Development Laboratory 236
Vodafone 126–7
Volkswagen (VW) 324
voting rights, in family firms 17, 20

W

Wadia family 61
Wah Kwong Shipping 21, 45
Wall's ice cream 272–3
Wal-Mart 372
    in China 320
    in India 148
    in Japan 129, 130–2
    in South Korea 137
Walt Disney Co. 290
Wan Azizah Wan Ismail 44
Wang-Lee family (Thailand) 43
watermarks 361
Webgirls International 27
websites
    foreign language versions 289
    information from 12
    for reporting corruption 383–4
    use by overseas Indians 55
Wee Cho Yaw 296, 297
Wharf/Wheelock group 44
Whirlpool 320, 328
wholly foreign-owned enterprises
    (WFOEs), in China 317
Widjaja, Eka Tjipta 22
Widjaja family 41
Wing On Group 45
Winsor Textile Group 45
Wipro 145, 150, 197, 228, 230, 233
women
    in Asia 25–39
    business leaders 29–30
    in China 26, 26–7, 33–7
    and corruption 37–8
    factors in raising profile of 26–7
    in government 31
    historical context 27–9
    Leading Women Entrepreneurs of the
        World awards 30
    Muslim 27, 30–3
    organizations 27
    outside view of 25–6

property-owning 28
setting up own business 34–5
successful, categories 35–6
see also under individual countries
Wong, David 44
Woo, Peter 44
workplace factions 187–8
World Bank
    business processing operations in India
        53
    study of publicly traded companies 16
World Chinese Entrepreneurs' Convention
    49
World Expo 327
World Trade Organization (WTO) 7, 99,
    251, 353, 358
    China's membership 251, 318, 326
World-Wide Shipping 45
WTO, see World Trade Organization
Wu Xiaoling 29, 37
WuXi PharmaTech 236–7

X

Xiang Fei 36
Xie Qihua 29, 37
Xinran 36, 37
Xugong Group Construction Machinery Co.
    318

Y

Yahoo! 287
Yamaichi Securities Co. 405
Yang Li 34
Yang Mianmian 29, 37
Yao Ming 285
Yeo Hip Seng Holdings 21
Yongding 43
Yoon Song Yee 29
Yoo Sung Enterprise Co. Ltd 139
Yoshie Motohiro 29
Yum! 256

Z

Zara 327
Zeti Akhtar Aziz 30–1
Zhu Rongji 261

82 184 BR 8034
05/07 FM
04-172-00 Ohio
3MGroup